Poverty Orientated Agricultural and Rural Development

Over the last twenty years the proportion of development cooperation resources earmarked for agricultural development has dwindled to between 6 and 7 per cent of total bi- and multilateral Official Development Assistance. This is despite the fact that 80 per cent of the world's poor live in rural agricultural areas, and that the poor are disproportionately affected when political, military and natural events lead to regional or global food shortages.

Hartmut Brandt and Uwe Otzen's key book undertakes a wide-ranging conceptual reorientation of development cooperation, criticizing the current orthodoxy and its bias towards urban areas, and argues that in order to effectively alleviate poverty across the world, agricultural and rural development measures need to be implemented by central and subnational governments, aid agencies and the private sector. The authors investigate the world food question, the current pressures it is under and its link to rural poverty, and set out the policies that need to be undertaken to reduce global poverty.

Hartmut Brandt began his professional education with three years of farming practice (1960–62) and continued with eight years of academic study and research in agricultural sciences and economics at Kiel University, Technical University of Berlin and Makerere University College, Kampala. Thereafter, followed 32 years of applied research, consulting work and postgraduate training based at the Deutsche Institut für Entwicklungspolitik (DIE). Dr Brandt retired in 2002 but continues his consultative activities.

Uwe Otzen is senior research fellow at the Deutsche Institut für Entwicklungspolitik (DIE). He studied international agricultural science at the Technical University of Berlin, where he obtained his PhD in 1973. He worked four years in Malawi as agricultural consultant and project manager for a regional development project of the GTZ, the German Agency for Technical Cooperation, before he joined the Deutsche Institut für Entwicklungspolitik in 1977, where he worked as a research fellow in the Africa Department. Between 1982 and 1986 he spent four years in Zimbabwe as an agricultural and rural development advisor to the Ministry of Lands, Resettlement and Rural Development in Harare.

Routledge Studies in Development and Society

Poverty Orientated Agricultural and Rural Development

Hartmut Brandt and Uwe Otzen

Routledge
Taylor & Francis Group

LONDON AND NEW YORK

First published in German (2004) by Nomos Verlagsgesellschaft

English-language translation first published 2007
by Routledge
2 Park Square, Milton Park, Abingdon, Oxon OX14 4RN

Simultaneously published in the USA and Canada
by Routledge
270 Madison Ave, New York, NY 10016

Routledge is an imprint of the Taylor & Francis Group, *an informa business*

© 2007 Hartmut Brandt and Uwe Otzen

Printed and bound in Great Britain by
TJI Digital, Padstow, Cornwall

British Library Cataloguing in Publication Data
A catalogue record for this book is available from the British Library

Library of Congress Cataloging in Publication Data
A catalog record for this book has been requested

ISBN10: 0–415–36853–7 (hbk)
ISBN10: 0–203–02875–9 (ebk)

ISBN13: 978–0–415–36853–7 (hbk)
ISBN13: 978–0–203–02875–9 (ebk)

67346344

Contents

Part B
Institutional and organizational ways for rural communities of sub-Saharan Africa to reduce poverty

Illustrations

Part A
Approaches to poverty reduction through agricultural development

Boxes in the text

Diagrams in the text

Figures in the text

Tables in the text

Tables in the appendix

Part B
Institutional and organizational ways for rural communities of sub-Saharan Africa to reduce poverty

Boxes in the text

Figures in the text

Figures in the appendix

Tables in the appendix

Preface

The background to this study is formed by the major changes in the global agrarian structure that have been clearly emerging since the beginning of this century. Two factors in particular – demographic changes and a virtually fixed global cultivated area – are resulting in a decline in the amount of cultivated land per capita and a need for crop yields to be increased. They are joined by the rapid commercialization of agricultural production in the wake of global urbanization. Through trade, the agriculturally strong countries of the world will increasingly help to supply the countries that are marginal in terms of natural resources.

The growth of the world population has fallen sharply in recent decades. The global growth rate in the next two decades is expected to be no more than about 1 per cent p.a. At the same time, urbanization is accelerating in the developing countries, and in twenty years more than half the world's population will be living in towns and cities. As a global average, rural population figures are already stagnant. Only in sub-Saharan Africa is the rural population still rising. Here too, however, the agricultural workforce is likely to be already in decline because AIDS is taking a heavy toll and because most of those migrating to the urban areas are young people of working age. In the next two decades at least, the world's agricultural population and the rural workforce will shrink significantly – replicating the situation that occurred in the German Reich, for example, in the late nineteenth and early twentieth century. There is little chance, on the other hand, of increasing the global cultivated area from its present level, mainly because of high investment and production costs during or after land development. Yet old arable land is being lost to degradation, desertification, expanding urban areas and the use of land for transport and other infrastructure. Natural soil fertility is at risk, particularly in the tropics.

The conclusion to be drawn from all this is, firstly, that the increase in agricultural production made necessary by the growth of demand will have to be achieved primarily by means of capital intensification using technical advances. Secondly, the transformation of primary products to meet urban final demand will gain in importance very rapidly as urbanization continues. Both the intensification of capital investment and the transformation of primary products will, however, lead to an exponential increase in energy costs as a proportion of consumer prices. Security of energy supply will thus become a key aspect of global food security in the future.

The world food question will not be a problem of primary resource availability for the next decade, but it does depend primarily on the global organization of the agricultural markets and the stability of energy supply. In the final analysis, then, the most important requirements for future food security and poverty reduction in the world will be political stability both globally and in individual countries and the freedom of markets from disruption. It is above all the poor who are affected when political, military and natural circumstances and events lead to regional or global food shortages. Given the scarcity of land and the very high level of rural poverty, what is mainly needed if poverty is to be reduced is increased agricultural productivity. To neglect the development of agriculture and rural areas in this situation would be to treat poverty as a secondary issue.

For the next generation poverty reduction will be achieved primarily through agricultural and rural development, since some 80 per cent of the world's poor live in rural areas, and shortages of foreign exchange and financial, human and social capital will for the time being prevent urbanization and industrialization from attaining anything more than inadequate rates of poverty reduction. However, agriculture and rural areas will be able to develop satisfactorily only if the contributions made by central and subnational government and the private sector are so designed as to be institutionally and organizationally effective, the agricultural policy framework ensures that the poor have access to resources and there is sufficient incentive to be productive and innovative within a positive and reliable framework of world agricultural markets and international agricultural policy.

The authors derive this view from the experience of centrally administered rural development programmes (1975–85), structural adjustment policy (1985–95) and Sector Investment Programmes (since 1996) gained during the GDI's postgraduate training courses abroad and the policy advice it provides. They have not sought to conceal this opinion in reports, statements and essays; but even when it comes to political conceptions, "there is a time and a place for everything." Although analyses before their time, if well done, may grip a group of experts, they have little practical impact on the conception debate.

In the winter of 2001–02 it became apparent from discussions among German development cooperation practitioners and within the Federal Ministry for Economic Cooperation and Development (BMZ) that there is again growing recognition and awareness in both German and international development cooperation of the pivotal role that agricultural and rural development have to play in poverty reduction. The international debate embracing the World Bank, the regional development banks, the OECD countries' DAC and the major bilateral donors also shows that the time is ripe for a fresh attempt at agricultural and rural development and for conceptual reorientation. The authors have seized the opportunity and undertaken a wide-ranging conceptual analysis of the issue in this study. The examination of conceptual experience in the past few decades and the findings of recent quantitative cross-section analyses make it clear that poverty reduction requires both agricultural and rural development measures by central and subnational government and the private sector and an appropriate agricultural policy environment. Despite this, donors' material efforts and recipients' policies have largely ignored agriculture and rural areas since about 1980. To correct the resulting constraints, not to mention the misallocation of resources, it will be necessary not only to switch funds and alter the national and international agricultural policy environment but also to adopt a more efficient organizational and institutional approach, for the inefficiency of centrally guided agricultural and rural development measures in earlier conceptual phases has been very sobering. In view of the experience of past development policy, and especially the constraints and weaknesses of Integrated Rural Development (1975–85), a proposal for the organizational and institutional decentralization of government measures is outlined in the second part of the study; it calls both for the strengthening of subnational authorities and for the activation of the private sector and the rural population's capacity for self-help.

Not all the problems associated with agricultural and rural development are addressed, of course: the discussion does not turn to the coherence of the industrialized countries' agricultural policies, the problems of donor coordination, the recipients' capacity for conception and implementation or, in particular, sociopolitical change in the recipient countries, which has its own dynamic, which will, in turn, eventually determine the success or failure of a decentralized approach to promotion. This is in itself a reference to areas in which development cooperation practitioners should make serious efforts and gain experience in the future. What is fairly certain is that the socio-political developments and requirements for the success of a decentralized approach will pose their own problems.

The authors are convinced that the complexity of socio-political development necessarily requires a process of trial and error in development cooperation, since planning and achieving social and economic development is not an exact science. Nonetheless, the attempt must not be a gamble: it requires a conception based on best available knowledge and skill. An admission that planning capacity is limited is thus in no way a plea for development cooperation on the off-chance. It goes without saying, however, that willingness to learn and flexibility during implementation are then, as it were, the better parts of a conception.

The two main parts of this study, that concerning agricultural development and that devoted to institutions and organization, are preceded by brief summaries, which also refer to the most important substantive links between the two parts. Any attempt at theory-oriented coordination of the two parts would have been artificial and of little benefit in view of the complexity of the subject matter. What therefore binds the two parts together is the attempt to present the case for the urgently needed conceptual reorientation towards more effective poverty reduction. The first part examines a wide range of experience of agricultural development and defines a set of core instruments; the second outlines an institutionally and organizationally decentralized approach.

The design of this study was widely discussed in professional circles, where it aroused considerable interest. The authors wish to thank fellow professionals in the BMZ, BMVEL, KfW, GTZ, Welthungerhilfe and other NGOs and their colleagues at the German Development Institute for their contributions to the discussion. These helped to clarify some contentious issues and to eliminate some of the inadequacies in the argument; despite this, differences of opinion emerged in certain respects. It is therefore more than a cliché for the authors to state that they are solely responsible for the analyses, conclusions and recommendations contained in this study – not least because they express specific criticisms of practical implementation and the orthodoxy of current sectoral priorities in bi- and multilateral development cooperation.

Abbreviations

ACF	Agricultural Consultative Forum
ACP	African-Caribbean-Pacific
AfDB	African Development Bank
ASIP	Agricultural Sector Investment Programme
BMZ	Bundesministerium für wirtschaftliche Zusammenarbeit und Entwicklung (Federal Ministry for Economic Cooperation and Development)
BMVEL	Bundesministerium für Verbraucherschutz, Ernährung und Landwirtschaft (Federal Ministry for Consumer-protection, Nutrition and Agriculture)
CARD	Co-ordinated Agricultural and Rural Development Programme
CAS	Country Assistance Strategy
CBO	Community Based Organization
CCD	United Nations Convention to Combat Desertification
CCD	Cabinet Committee on Development
CD	Community Development
CDF	Comprehensive Development Framework
CDO	Community Development Officer
CFA	Communanté Financière d'Afrique
CGIAR	Consultative Group on International Agricultural Research
CIF	Community Investment Fund
CIM	Centre for International Migration
CIS	Commonwealth of Independent States
CLA	Community Livestock Auxiliary
CLDP	Communal Lands Development Programme
CME	Coordinated Market Economy

COD	Conference on Desertification
CPI	Consumer Price Index
CSD	Commission for Sustainable Development
CSO	Civil Society Organization
DAC	District Agricultural Committee
DAO	District Agricultural Office
DDC	District Development Committee
DDCC	District Development Coordination Committee
DDF	District Development Fund
DFID	Department for International Development
DIE	Deutsches Institut für Entwicklungspolitik
ECA	Economic Commission for Africa
ECDPM	European Centre for Development Policy Management
ENDA	Environment and Development Activities
ESAF	Enhanced Structural Adjustment Facility
EU	European Union
FAO	Food and Agriculture Organization of the United Nations
FDT	Farmers Development Trust
FES	Friedrich-Ebert-Stiftung
FINNIDA	Finnish International Development Agency
FMS	Financial Management System
FOB	Free on Board Ship
GDP	Gross Domestic Product
GEAR	Macro-Economic Strategy for Growth, Employment and Redistribution
GNP	Gross National Product
GOPP	Goal-Oriented Project Planning
GPEA	Gender-specific Participatory Extension Approach
GTZ	Deutsche Gesellschaft für Technische Zusammenarbeit
HIPC	Heavily Indebted Poor Countries
HYV	High-Yielding Variety
IDA	International Development Agency
IDP	Integrated Development Planning
IFAD	International Fund for Agricultural Development

IFC	International Finance Corporation
IFPRI	International Food Policy Research Institute
IGT	Intergovernmental Transfers
IMF	International Monetary Fund
IRD	Integrated Rural Development
IRI	International Republican Institute
JICA	Japanese International Co-operation Agency
KAS	Konrad-Adenauer-Stiftung
KfW	Kreditanstalt für Wiederaufbau
LDC	Least Developed Country
LED	Local Economic Development
LME	Liberal Market Economy
LP	Linear Programming
M&E	Monitoring and Evaluation
MAFF	Ministry of Agriculture, Food and Fisheries
MCDSS	Ministry of Community Development and Social Services
MCT	Ministry of Communication and Transport
MDGs	Millennium Development Goals
MENR	Ministry of Environment and Natural Resources
MFA	Ministry of Food and Agriculture of Ghana
MFED	Ministry of Finance and Economic Development
MFEPD	Ministry of Finance, Economic Planning and Development
MINMEC	Ministerial Members of Executive Council
MLGH	Ministry of Local Government and Housing
MLGPA	Ministry of Local Government and Provincial Affairs
MLGTP	Ministry of Local Government and Town Planning
MLRRD	Ministry of Lands, Resettlement and Rural Development
MOL	Ministry of Lands
MPACD	Ministry of Provincial Affairs and Cooperation Development, Pretoria
MTEF	Medium Term Expenditure Framework
MTIEF	Medium Term Income and Expenditure Framework
MUV	Manufacturing Unit Value
NBI	National Business Initiative for Growth, Development & Democracy

NCOP	National Council of Provinces
NCP	National Council of Provinces
NDCC	National Development Coordination Committee
NEAP	National Environmental Action Plan
NEDA	Netherlands Development Agency
NEPAD	New Partnership for African Development
NERICA	New Rice for Africa
NGO	Non-Governmental Organization
NORAD	Norwegian Agency for Development Co-operation
ODA	Official Development Assistance
OECD	Organization for Economic Cooperation and Development
PA	Project Appraisal
PDC	Provincial Development Committee
PDCC	Provincial Development Coordination Committees
PER	Public Expenditure Review
PPP	Purchasing Power Parity
PRS	Poverty Reduction Strategy
PRSC	Poverty Reduction Support Credit
PRSP	Poverty Reduction Strategy Paper
PSE	Producer Subsidy Equivalent
RDP	Reconstruction and Development Programme
RMA	Road Maintenance Authority
RRA	Rapid Rural Appraisal
RSA	Republic of South Africa
SADC	Southern African Development Community
SAF	Structural Adjustment Facility
SALGA	South African Local Government Association
SAP	Structural Adjustment Programme
SARD	Sustainable Agricultural and Rural Development
SIDA	Swedish International Development Co-operation Agency
SIP	Sector Investment Programme
SME	small and medium-sized enterprises
SNRD	Sector Network Rural Development
SWAP	Sector Wide Approach

TOT	Terms of Trade
UAA	Utilized Agricultural Area
UN	United Nations
UNCED	United Nations Conference on Environment and Development
UNCOD	United Nations Conference on Desertification
UNDP	United Nation's Development Programme
USAID	United States Agency for International Development
USDA	US Department of Agriculture
VIDCO	Village Development Committee
WADCO	Ward Development Committee
WARDA	West African Rice Development Association
WCARRD	World Conference on Agrarian Reform and Rural Development
WTO	World Trade Organization
ZANU(PF)	Zimbabwean African National Union (Patriotic Front)
ZIMCORD	Zimbabwe Conference on Reconstruction and Development

Part A

Approaches to poverty reduction through agricultural development

Hartmut Brandt

Fine words about a Doha development round ring hollow and appear cynical in the face of foot-dragging on reform of the EU's Common Agricultural Policy; and the US farm bill, which further entrenches protectionism. The consequences for Africa are literally a matter of life and death.

Niall FitzGerald (*Financial Times*, 12 June 2002)

Introduction

Over the past 20 years the proportion of development cooperation resources earmarked for agricultural development has dwindled to between 6 and 7 per cent of total bi- and multilateral ODA. Although the proportion devoted to rural areas is two to three times higher, it is still completely inadequate in view of the spatial distribution of poverty. This increasingly raises doubts about how well targeted the allocation of resources is, for the overriding objective of bi- and multilateral development cooperation is poverty reduction and 75 to 85 per cent of the poor live in rural areas of the recipient countries. Recent empirical literature clearly shows, moreover, that agricultural and rural development is the only way to come close to the goal of halving poverty by 2015. The resources that can realistically be expected will not suffice for the poor to be productively accommodated in urban areas.

This study adopts a wide-ranging approach to the problem, taking account of the serious threat to the developing countries' agricultural sectors posed by distorted food prices in the world markets. For where are the poor to find work if food dumped at low world market prices and the neglect of agricultural innovation policies mean that domestic agriculture is no longer competitive even in internal food markets, or competitive only in market niches protected by transport costs, and domestic industry is similarly unable to ensure enough employment because of the lack of internal purchasing power and inadequate access to export markets – not to mention the problem of financing the investments required for these purposes or the necessary industrial competitiveness.

The study proceeds in four stages, beginning with a description of the world grain market's prospects, an indicator of the world food situation and the developing countries' role in the world food economy. The second step is to consider the new, donor-induced urban bias in development cooperation, which focuses poverty reduction measures on the towns and cities. The distorted world agricultural markets are seen as one of the main causes in this context. Thirdly, the conceptual experience of agricultural development policy is described and discussed in terms of its poverty-reducing effect. As the fourth step, the recent literature on poverty regressions at a macroeconomic level and in the agricultural sector is reviewed, the basic conclusions on the issue of poverty reduction being summarized. The final section recalls the main instruments used in poverty-reducing agricultural development policy – price, market and trade policy, innovation policy and land reform – which must complement the measures taken to reduce poverty. If those instruments are neglected, structural reforms and institutional and organizational capacity-building will remain largely ineffectual.

It is hoped that this study will help to initiate the changes that need to be made to the sectoral priorities of development cooperation, since agriculturally based economies and societies can afford to neglect agriculture only at the expense of stagnation and continuing poverty.

Bonn, November 2002

Summary

Conclusion

Experience in the past four decades clearly indicates that rapid poverty reduction in pre- and early-industrial economies can be achieved only through a combination of agricultural and rural development. It could not yet be accomplished through urban and industrial development if only because of shortages of foreign exchange and constraints in the financing of the necessary investments, not to mention the problem of delays in adapting social institutions and attitudes. In an early phase urban and industrial development depend on the agricultural sector's social transformation function and on its market and factor contributions and are thus closely linked to agricultural growth. An increase in total agricultural productivity (through technical progress and investment) is the key to poverty reduction. It leads to rising wages and ground rents in real terms and – depending on the price policy and/or transformation costs – to declining food prices. Poverty is also reduced by multiplier effects in the rural economic circuit. Empirical evidence shows that training, agricultural research and road-building are the most important levers available to government and development cooperation for reducing poverty. However, they operate satisfactorily only where the agricultural policy environment meets three requirements: first, distribution of land ownership that shares the ground rent structurally and provides security for small-scale farming; second, an agricultural price and trade policy that offers sufficient incentives to be innovative and to invest; third, an innovation policy that introduces the findings of applied agricultural research effectively into general rural practice. Failure to meet these requirements largely obstructs the means of reducing poverty through agricultural and rural development.

Where seriously distorted world market prices of food freely imported are passed on to internal markets, urban demand for food largely ignores domestic agriculture. If, at the same time, the production and marketing of agricultural raw materials are denied government promotion through research, extension, infrastructure and trade, they have little chance of competing in the world markets, which are also likely to be suffering from serious indirect distortion. Where liberal price and trade policies of this kind are pursued, however, experience shows that government innovation policy measures are consistently neglected. Even when priority is given to the promotion of social and physical infrastructure in rural areas, for example, far-reaching poverty reduction is impossible in these circumstances because the regional economic circuit lacks a purchasing power base and because imports of textiles and processed agricultural products at distorted prices neutralize multiplier effects and growth potential. At best, there is rapid migration to the urban areas, where poverty then concentrates owing to the poor competitiveness of industry and constraints in the national budget. At the present extremely distorted world market prices of primary and processed foodstuffs, liberal agricultural policies by developing countries are thus almost bound to prevent rapid poverty reduction. This is especially true of smaller developing countries dominated by agriculture. Most larger developing countries, on the other hand, have made greater efforts to alleviate the paralysing effects of distorted world markets on their own agricultural sectors by granting direct and/or indirect subsidies – as evidenced by the agricultural policies of India, China, Indonesia and Vietnam – but the defence is crumbling. In China, for example, concealed rural unemployment is rising sharply, and there has been increased migration to the urban areas since the agricultural price and trade policies were liberalized following China's accession to the WTO, so far without any compensatory subsidies for agriculture. An adjustment of this policy through the application of trade policy safeguard measures seems quite possible under the internal pressure of growing unemployment and poverty.

Development cooperation too has taken the increasingly unfavourable or dysfunctional agricultural policy framework as a datum for 20 years and largely withdrawn from the promotion of agriculture. Recent examples of Poverty Reduction Strategy Papers, however, seem to be again placing greater emphasis on the role of agriculture and rural development in poverty reduction. The countries concerned are the Gambia, Malawi, Rwanda, Yemen, Zambia and especially Ethiopia, probably because transport costs give them extensive natural protection against commercial grain imports.

Fundamental incoherence can be detected between industrialized countries' agricultural policies and their development cooperation or, more precisely, development cooperation policies have adapted their priorities over the years to the distorted price ratios and neglected agricultural policies of LDCs accordingly by largely forgoing the promotion of agriculture. In view of the USA's and EU's recent decisions on the direction to be taken by their agricultural policies, the prospects for less distorted world agricultural markets are not good, unless a further reduction in subsidies is agreed at the WTO's Doha Round. The physical and non-physical infrastructure of rural areas has also been badly neglected. However, this is hardly the way for development cooperation to achieve far-reaching poverty reduction in agriculturally based pre- and early-industrial economies. Not without reason and to the considerable benefit of poverty reduction, the large Asian developing countries have hitherto, or until recently, maintained a minimum level of tariff protection for agricultural products and an effective agricultural innovation policy.

Global Poverty Distribution and World Agricultural Markets

The number of poor people in the world with a daily per capita income of <US$ 1 (PPP) is estimated at about 1.3 billion. Poverty is centred on the countries of sub-Saharan Africa and South Asia. In South Asia about 75 per cent of the poor live in rural areas, in sub-Saharan Africa about 85 per cent. The main problem for the survival of the poor is nutrition. Qualitative malnutrition and calorific undernourishment are the consequences and indicators of poverty. Where poverty is prevalent, undernourishment is also prevalent. The FAO estimates that there were 777 million undernourished people in the world in 1997/99. Trends in calorific undernourishment in the various regions of the world have differed over the past 20 years. In East Asia the number of undernourished people fell by 72 per cent, which can be ascribed to China's successful economic and agricultural development. Its agricultural development has, however, been at serious risk since the liberalization of its agricultural price and trade policies. In South-East Asia undernourishment fell by 29 per cent, in South Asia by 11 per cent. Given the population growth rate, these are astonishing improvements, which are due primarily to successful agricultural development policies and the technical advances of the Green Revolution. In sub-Saharan Africa, on the other hand, the number of undernourished people rose by 47 per cent. This reflects the generally desperate politico-economic situation, inappropriate agricultural policies, or agricultural policy chaos, and rapid population growth.

In urban and rural areas the poor spend 75 to 85 per cent of their income on food. The ratio of food prices to disposable income largely determines the nutritional situation of the poor. Food price increases of, say, 30 per cent would already reduce the quantitative demand for food among the urban poor to a level of general calorific undersupply. In rural areas the effects of market forces on undernourishment are, as a rule, partly cushioned by subsistence niches of the poor and the fact that the market causes farm workers' wages to rise with grain prices, though not at the same rate.

The world market in foodstuffs influences the agricultural policy environment, particularly of small and medium-sized countries, directly through the level and movement of prices and indirectly through debilitating repercussions for the innovation and structural policy components of agricultural policy. The distortions in food prices are likely to have major effects of the same nature on the world market prices of agricultural raw materials as a result of product substitution by producers. A quantitative study would show that the industrialized countries even manage to an (albeit relatively limited) extent to make good the losses to their economies caused by their agricultural policies in the case of imports of agricultural raw materials. Over the past 40 years technical progress and agricultural subsidies have meant that the global food supply trend has always outstripped the demand trend, and prices have fallen by about 70 per cent in real terms. In global terms, natural resource availability will not pose any nutrition problems for the next decade either. There are sufficient land and productivity reserves for market equilibrium to be maintained at virtually stable real prices – provided that no major destabilizing, market-disturbing upsets occur in the global political situation, especially with regard to crude oil supply, since energy is the key input for general scientific and technical progress in agriculture and for the transformation activities of the food-processing and marketing sectors.

In some regions of the world, however, serious poverty and nutrition problems are becoming apparent. In sub-Saharan Africa a tendency for per capita production to decline is emerging. Urbanization rates of 4 to 5 per cent p.a. and declining foreign exchange revenue make food supplies increasingly dependent on continuing external allocations. The weaknesses of the agricultural policies of the sub-Saharan African countries as regards infrastructure and organization required lead times under innovation policies of up to 20 years and have created a problem of global political importance for poverty reduction and food security. In South and South-East Asia the productivity reserves of the Green Revolution are quickly running out. In some countries or areas intensive rice and wheat production is already posing serious agronomic problems. Further development here very much depends on the future financial endowment of the national agricultural policies, the environment created by price and trade policies and, in many places, the policy on land tenure. From China to India, the question that arises for each country is whether the current inward-oriented agricultural policies and the moderate protection they afford against imports should be retained or whether the food markets should be generally liberalized with or without compensatory payments to producers.

A crucial determinant of the prospects for poverty reduction in the sub-Saharan African and the Asian, and especially South Asian, countries is the direction which agricultural policies take in the future, since poverty is largely a rural phenomenon and its reduction very much depends on the implementation of appropriate agricultural and rural development policies. This is particularly true of the sub-Saharan African countries, where, owing to the stagnation of industry and medium-sized businesses, rural–urban migration is generally equivalent to a change of location for the poor from the rural areas to the towns and cities and their atmosphere, without their real standard of living improving to any significant extent. In the Asian countries this is less pronounced because their manufacturing industry and service sector are more dynamic and their urbanization rates are far lower. Sub-Saharan Africa and South Asia will continue to be the focal points in the fight against undernourishment and poverty. What is certain is that, owing to the omissions of their agricultural development policies and their neglect of physical and non-physical rural infrastructure, the food import requirements of the sub-Saharan African countries will rise sharply and will need financing. It will be for the agricultural surplus countries to address this situation for a fairly long transitional period with distribution-oriented food aid that disturbs markets as little as possible, but they must avoid abusing the plight of the sub-Saharan African countries by neglecting development cooperation in the agricultural sector and dumping their heavily subsidized food surpluses on them. Sustained poverty reduction in sub-Saharan Africa is not to be had without successful agricultural and rural development. All empirical data of recent years on development policy since 1955 support this conclusion. The natural production potential, the peasant human capital and the tried and tested production methods are there: it is the undistorted world markets and the efficient national agricultural policies that are missing.

More and more voices have recently been heard warning of the consequences of placing excessive emphasis on urban development in pre- or early-industrial economies. This is especially true of the sub-Saharan African countries, where young people of working age are migrating to the towns and cities – because of the lack of economic prospects in the rural areas – leaving mothers and children, the elderly and infirm behind in the villages. At urbanization rates of 4 to 5 per cent, which greatly exceed urban economic growth rates, there will soon come a time when it is no longer possible to stabilize the resulting socio-political and economic imbalances in the usual makeshift way by having development co-operation subsidize the urban areas – and, in many cases, by siphoning off proceeds from the raw material exports and economy of the rural areas.

New urban bias in development cooperation

Nonetheless, aid has bypassed agricultural and rural areas for about 20 years. It could well be said that the donors are to blame for a new urban bias, especially in the sub-Saharan African countries. In 1998–99 agriculture accounted for only 6.3 per cent of the DAC donors' and 6.8 per cent of the multilateral donors' gross ODA. Of this, only what is not spent on administration, coordination and overheads gets through to the villages. The decline in the real volume of assistance received by agriculture from the developing countries' own resources has paralleled the reduction of development cooperation resources. It probably averages under 5 per cent of government spending in the LDCs. Total expenditure on rural areas is higher, though also totally inadequate. Development ideas and aid allocations among both recipients and donors are overly focused on physical and non-physical urban infrastructure. This is true of financial cooperation and of technical cooperation. Where are qualified agriculturalists still to be found in development cooperation?

This approach has so far been maintained even though – as stated above – 75 to 85 per cent of the poor live in rural areas and the empirical data of recent years clearly show that without agricultural and rural development there will be no rapid poverty reduction. The possible causes of this inconsistency have hardly been discussed. The most plausible of a number of explanatory hypotheses are, firstly, the comparatively high risk attached to the implementation of agricultural projects in the given circumstances and, secondly, a general blocking of development cooperation in the agricultural sector as a result of a relaxed global agricultural market situation, in which it is tempting to suppress thoughts of the poverty problems in the rural areas of the developing countries and so to overlook them. The two hypotheses could also be combined and lead to the assumption that the donor countries have not been prepared to reform their agricultural policies thoroughly so as to give agriculture in the Third World a chance to develop, uncertain though the outcome would be.

The OECD countries' agricultural subsidies amount to about US$ 327 billion p.a. With the implementation of the USA's new Agriculture Act and the EU's eastward enlargement, they could again rise to US$ 350 billion p.a. or more without the present agricultural policy system being abandoned. In view of the unfavourable environment this would create for the partner countries' agricultural sectors, forgoing development cooperation in the agricultural sector seems reasonable. If this were true, it would be a case of inverse coherence (within the meaning of the Treaty establishing the EU) of the donors' agricultural and development policies: the development policies, not the agricultural policies, would have adjusted.

Seriously distorted world market prices of food, the neglect of agriculture and rural areas in development cooperation and similar neglect of agricultural policy, especially in the sub-Saharan African countries, are among the principal causes of continuing poverty and stagnation. Most of the large Asian countries, on the other hand, have hitherto, or until recently, continued to protect their agricultural sectors by moderate tariffs from the distorted world market prices. But, following its accession to the WTO, China has liberalized its trade and prices, and others may follow its example. It remains to be seen whether the agricultural research and innovation policies pursued by the large Asian countries can maintain the present momentum of productivity growth for the next generation and whether the resources needed for this will be available. The sub-Saharan African countries will be the main problem area for poverty reduction. After the initial successes achieved by the structural adjustment policies (1983–95) sizeable levies are again being charged on certain foodstuffs in the sub-Saharan African countries at PSEs of –20 to –30 per cent, in the face of the give-away prices in the world food markets. Domestic food production is no longer keeping pace with population growth, the rural population of working age is migrating to the urban areas, the industrial sector is stagnating and is hardly competitive in the world market, and the towns and cities are surviving primarily on informal small businesses, ODA and funds siphoned off from the proceeds of raw material exports. The political elites of the sub-Saharan African countries have come to terms with the situation – for the time being. The donors are making great efforts to reduce poverty – but not in rural areas and not by means of agricultural development policy.

Poverty reduction under changing agricultural development policy conceptions

A comparison of the experience gained under the ten-year concepts of agricultural development policy since 1955 already gives some insight into the requirements for and approaches to successful poverty reduction. Community Development (1955–65) sought to stimulate rural development by activating peasant self-help. The donors collaborated with the rural elites, and agricultural production and the question of land ownership and income distribution were neglected. The importance of price and trade policies, land tenure and innovation policies and policies on services and cooperatives were overlooked. As a result, agricultural production and productivity stagnated, food prices rose because of stagnating supply, demand grew, and urban and rural poverty continued to spread.

The Green Revolution (1965–75), which operated with a package of innovation policy instruments, led to rapid growth of production and productivity and far-reaching poverty reduction in urban and rural areas. It was essentially confined to Asia. This policy was supported by moderate input subsidies and negligible tariff protection. Hasty criticism addressed to the donors ran down this concept before it could be propagated in the sub-Saharan African countries. The top-heavy African administrative systems would probably have been completely incapable of implementing such a policy. The exceptions were the introduction of hybrid maize in Kenya's peasant farming sector and the growing of cotton in the West African savannah.

Integrated Rural Development (1975–85) was a centrally planned and implemented multi-sectoral approach. It failed because of inefficient allocation of resources, coordination problems, disputes over regional priorities, the distribution of resources and follow-up costs that could not be financed. Agricultural innovation policy was no more than a side issue. Sustained effects on production by and the incomes of the target groups did not occur, and the poverty-reducing effect fell flat despite explicit orientation towards the target groups and poverty.

Structural Adjustment Programmes (1985–95), which were largely confined to the sub-Saharan African countries, corrected the distortions in agricultural price ratios for a number of years. What they gave to the peasants through more favourable producer prices they took away by winding up government or parastatal extension services, which the private sector was never able to replace with more efficient services.

Sector Investment Programmes (1995–?), the latest concept, are based on the sectoral concentration of donor resources, but have yet to be adopted by the recipients because of interdepartmental conflicts of interest in the recipient countries and conflicts and friction among the donor countries. In fact, they have not yet emerged from the experimental stage. The Poverty Reduction Strategy Papers, which are drawn up by the recipients as part of the donors' HIPC II debt relief initiative, have so far largely neglected agricultural development or taken far from adequate account of it. They are therefore unable to provide any concepts likely to succeed in reducing rural poverty.

Experience of agricultural development policy conceptions since 1955 thus shows that the reduction of rural poverty cannot be had without effective government innovation policy (advances in production technology, extension, adult education, agricultural credit, expansion of rural infrastructure). Although central government must develop the broad lines of this policy, provide for as compatible price, market and trade policies as possible and make the necessary budgetary resources and central organizations available, implementation should be decentralized in accordance with the subsidiarity principle, since the required coordination can be assured only on the spot by the district administrations, local authorities and peasant cooperatives as well as the local offices of the line ministries. Human capital, institutions and organizations at this level are, in the final analysis, crucial for successful agricultural development and poverty reduction. Decentralization calls for a regionally graduated system of politico-organizational, administrative and fiscal powers, based on clear legal precepts. It can evolve only as the outcome of long-term political processes (see Part B). The aim, then, is not to replicate the old IRD with its mistakes, but to arrive at a decentralized approach that has the support of society.

Recent empirical data on poverty-oriented development policy

The Integrated Rural Development decade was, of course, triggered by the assumption that the trickle-down effect of economic growth had failed as a means of improving the incomes of the poor. Extensive international cross-section analyses using aggregated country data now prove the opposite with considerable statistical safety: "growth is good for the poor." The poorest 20 per cent derive roughly proportional benefit from economic growth. If, besides economic growth, the distribution of land ownership and training levels are included as independent variables, it is evident that percentage improvements in the distribution of ownership and human capital have two to three times more impact on the incomes of the poorest quintile than percentage improvements in per capita incomes in the economy as a whole.

Besides growth and the distribution of resources, sectoral contributions to poverty reduction in India were examined. It was found that growth in the agricultural and tertiary sectors had a pronounced poverty-reducing effect in both rural and urban areas, while industrial growth increased poverty – even in urban areas. The latter effect was caused by capital-intensive industrialization in a comparatively closed economy. The positive effects of the growth of the agricultural and service sectors stem from the high labour intensities in these sectors and from the strong multiplier effect of agricultural growth. This relationship between causes and effects is typical of countries with a peasant agrarian structure in the early-industrial phase of development, but not of countries with a quasi-feudal agrarian structure – as will be shown.

It is clear from Indian and Chinese cross-section analyses that for countries with a peasant agrarian structure increasing agricultural productivity is the key to poverty reduction. This has its effect through rising wages for farm workers, declining food prices, rising physical productivity of the land and the peasants' share of the growth of ground rents. These factors are joined by the employment-creating multiplier effects of agricultural growth (in local business) of typically 1.4 to 1.8. The most effective agricultural policy approaches to increasing total agricultural factor productivity are agricultural research and extension, education and road-building. In China's case rural electrification must be added to the list. What should not be overlooked, however, is that this effect chain from the promotion of the infrastructure variables just mentioned through productivity to incomes and income distribution presupposes the conditions created by agricultural policy in India and China – namely the given price, market and trade policies and agrarian structures. Where the agrarian structure is feudalistic and/or the agricultural sector is subject to heavy indirect taxation and/or distorted world market prices of primary and processed foodstuffs are passed on in full to internal markets, the infrastructure–productivity–poverty reduction effect chain does not produce anything like the favourable results referred to above, because it is above all price incentives and the distribution of land ownership that bring about wide-ranging peasant initiative and the favourable secondary effects it has in the regional economic circuit.

In the western region of China, which is marginal in terms of its level of development and natural conditions, the cost-efficiency of these poverty reduction instruments is 10 to 20 times higher than in the already comparatively well–developed coastal region. Similar experience is reported from India. There would thus appear to be a kind of law of diminishing returns governing the poverty-reducing effect of government agricultural and rural development measures. In both India and China investments in irrigation equipment proved unprofitable and relatively cost-inefficient in reducing rural poverty. This confirms the global experience with irrigation projects in development cooperation, which is, however, largely due to uneconomic, central production prescriptions.

The situation in Latin America is fundamentally different. Here poverty reduction does not parallel the growth of overall per capita income. In contrast to the Indian and Chinese experience, agricultural growth does not have any significant effects on the proportion of the population living below the poverty line, whether rural or urban. With the current distribution of land ownership and the social structure in the Latin American countries, there is little chance of reducing rural and urban poverty by means of agricultural development policy and rural development – apart from agricultural reforms, which have, however, failed in the past or come to a halt half-way, or succeeded only in specific local cases.

Here the poverty-reproducing effect of quasi-feudal land tenure systems and large-scale agrarian structures is evident. It is not only that the poor have hardly any share of ground rents: the multiplier effect of agricultural growth is also negligible, because the demand from the large farms is for comparatively foreign-exchange-intensive industrial capital goods and inputs, and the demand from large landowners is for industrial consumer goods and urban services. Furthermore, large farms are always organized along comparatively capital-intensive and highly labour-extensive lines. Far-reaching poverty reduction in this case would call, first and foremost, for determined land reform, backed by services provided by cooperatives and appropriate national framework legislation.

Where the sub-Saharan African countries are concerned, the data are such that no more than inadequate empirical studies are available. It can be assumed that the empirical data on Latin America provide some initial indications of the situation in sub-Saharan African countries with a large-scale agrarian structure. Countries with a peasant agrarian structure should not ignore India's and China's experience. The same can be said of the conception of agricultural price, market and trade policies. The wide range of experience of project, programme and agricultural policy in Africa indicates that this assessment is correct. Initial quantitative cross-section comparisons and empirical case studies have produced four basic statements:

- Economic policy reform measures and political stability have the effect of reducing poverty.
- Poor transport links and major obstacles due to transport costs preserve poverty.
- Education and access to land reduce poverty.
- Erratic events, such as drought and disease, are decisive causes of poverty.

The donors should bear in mind that poverty-reducing development cooperation with sub-Saharan African countries requires at least some protection against distorted world agricultural markets and far greater promotion of agriculture and rural areas, and especially of training, road-building and cost-efficient food security policy. But before these findings become relevant to practical agricultural policy, political systems must be democratized. The rule of law and civil security are undoubtedly the basic requirements for success in the fight against poverty.

Recommendations

This part of the study concludes with the following principal recommendations (broken down in Chapter 15):

1   The coherence (within the meaning of the Maastricht Treaty) between the EU's agricultural policy and the development cooperation policies of both the Member States and the Commission should be further improved.
2   To this end, the process of liberalizing the industrialized countries' agricultural policies during the forthcoming round of world trade negotiations should be resolutely continued.
3   It should be considered whether, given the distorted world food markets, the agriculturally based LDC economies can forgo a minimum of tariff protection for both primary and processed foodstuffs without seriously impeding their growth and employment prospects.
4   Development cooperation partners should think about the incompatibility of their present allocation priorities (physical and non-physical infrastructure and social services in urban areas) with the overriding objective of efficient poverty reduction. It should be remembered in this context that some 80 per cent of the world's poor live in rural areas and that agricultural and rural development have been proved to be by far the most efficient means of reducing poverty. They should ask themselves whether the present policy of supporting unbalanced urbanization rates – especially in the sub-Saharan African countries – can be sustained financially and politically in the longer term.
5   Rural infrastructure, agricultural research and extension, adult education, health care and primary schools in rural areas should be permanent priorities for development cooperation in the sub-Saharan African and South Asian countries with a view to reducing poverty. This task cannot be performed

with a centrally planned economy – along the lines of the old IRD, for example: what is needed is a decentralized, subsidiarity-based approach, in which district administrations and peasant cooperatives have a fundamental role to play. The capacity-building needed for this and the necessary institutional and organizational reforms will, however, take at least a decade (see Part B).

6   Attaching greater importance to agricultural and rural development will entail appropriate switching of funds in the budgets of the development cooperation partners, and this should be undertaken gradually.

7   Where land reforms have led to the successful redistribution of land titles, they should be backed by infrastructure development and the promotion of support services. The refinancing of land reform banks should be considered in the light of the general situation in each case.

In view of the prospects offered by the industrialized countries' agricultural policies (and especially by the new US agriculture legislation and the EU's eastward enlargement) a further reduction in global agricultural subsidies and in the corresponding distortions of competition in the world agricultural markets is unlikely in the near future. It is extremely doubtful that in these global circumstances the environment for agricultural and rural development in the Third World can be radically improved – this being especially true of the sub-Saharan African countries, which opened themselves to the world agricultural markets under the policy of structural adjustment – or that the current allocation of resources under development cooperation policies can be revised. An attempt should nevertheless be made. It should certainly include advocacy of moderate tariff protection in the developing countries for primary and processed foodstuffs – roughly equivalent to the price distortions in the world market. But, above all, development cooperation should continue the struggle against the industrialized countries' world-market-distorting agricultural policies with determination and stamina, just as the Treaty establishing the EU calls for coherence between European agricultural and development policy – and this not as inverse coherence to the detriment of the effectiveness of development cooperation. The long lead times in both the coherence debate and decentralized agricultural and rural development should not deter the development cooperation administrations. Both can give the short-term tasks of ensuring peace and providing food aid and disaster relief the prospect of a more effective development phase to follow.

Part I   Background to the problem: world food question

1   Overview

Long-range forecasts of the world food situation usually cover a period of 20 or 30 years. They are confined to the cereals (wheat, rice, feed grains) for which basic global statistics (crop areas, physical yields, trade, prices) are available. The data on other foodstuffs are inadequate by comparison.

The cereals do at least account for some 70 per cent of global calorie consumption and for 50 per cent of cultivated arable land. Substitution processes naturally occur on the supply and demand sides in the event of price movements, especially at times when the market situation is extreme, but they remain within comparatively tight limits, and from a long-term perspective the amount of arable land, physical yields and the contributions made by the various cereals to calorie consumption are the most informative of the available indicators of the global food situation on the supply side.

Studies of the prospects of the world grain sector come to widely differing, even conflicting conclusions. Some authors forecast an essentially trouble-free supply situation for 2020 and beyond (Johnson 1999; Paarlberg 2000; Runge and Senauer 2000), others see a situation of global food insecurity looming (Brown 1996), yet others refer to the central role that international agricultural development policy must play (Pinstrup-Andersen and Babinard 2000), if the next generation is not to face structural world food crises. There is general agreement on the extent to which global demand will increase, but opinions differ widely as regards supply-side expectations.

It goes without saying that not only do the authors' assessments reflect different technical views, but that value premises and ideas on agricultural policy – perhaps even internalized interests – also play a part. This study proceeds from the basic assumption, backed by many years of observing agricultural development in numerous Third World countries, that even if natural resources are protected, the field-tested options for improving output through technical advances and increases in intensity will easily suffice for at least the next generation to satisfy aggregate demand at constant to slightly rising real prices – as long as political conditions permit energy-intensive agriculture characterized by an international division of labour and if the agricultural development measures needed on the supply side are taken in good time, i.e. with a lead time of 15 to

20 years. But there is room for serious doubt as to whether a forward-looking agricultural policy of this kind can be achieved.

However, perpetuating the development of production and supply, especially in the sub-Saharan African and South and South-East Asian countries, is one thing. Providing for global ad hoc measures to ensure food security when regional natural disasters and political disturbances occur is another matter.

The main aim of food security policy must always be orientation towards poverty, for there are some 1.3 billion poor people[1] and 780 million undernourished in the world today. Shortages of supply due to structural conditions and disasters threaten the lives of the poorest quarter of mankind, whether at national, regional or global level. As a rule, the other three-quarters are still able to obtain the bare essentials for their sustenance even when food prices rise by using assets, borrowing or forgoing other forms of consumption.

2   Demand

The following equation is used to estimate the growth of demand for cereals:

$$N = P + I_c \bullet E$$

where: N = annual growth of quantitative demand (percentage)

P = population growth (percentage)

I_c = annual growth of real per capita income (percentage)

E = income elasticity of quantitative demand (change in demand in per cent per real change in income in per cent)

In long-range forecasts account is taken of an empirically measured decline in income elasticity as per capita income rises. In this way the trend in quantitative demand starting from a base level is estimated. Real price movements, which ensure quantitative balance between demand and supply in the markets, are not taken into account. In other words, constancy of price ratios is assumed.

In the following the three determinants of the trend in demand are first presented globally and by regions of the world in their orders of magnitude.

2.1   Population growth

The global rates in the growth of the world's population have fallen rapidly in the past 30 years, and, according to World Bank and United Nations assessments, this trend is likely to continue in the 21st century (UN 2000; World Bank 2000a). Taking a broad view, a decline in the global growth rate from 2.1 per cent p.a. in the period 1965–70 to 0.85 per cent p.a. in the period 2020–25 is becoming apparent:

Period	Population growth
1965–70	2.10 % p.a.
1995–00	1.43 % p.a.
2000–05	1.24 % p.a.
2020–25	0.85 % p.a.

According to these most recent data, the annual growth rates in the period 2000–20 will average about 1.05 per cent p.a. Consequently, the world population will rise from about 6.0 billion in 2000 to about 7.7 billion in 2020.

Declining population growth rates are accompanied by rapid urbanization (see Tables 1 and 7). The link between these two variables is complex and society-specific. In 1970 some 700 million people (18 per cent of the world population) lived in towns and cities; by 2020 the figure will have risen to about 4.0 billion (52 per cent of the world population). As, on a global average, the growth of urban areas is already absorbing population growth, the rural population has been almost stagnant since about 2000 and will have declined significantly in absolute terms in one to two decades. Only in Africa will there be any appreciable growth in the rural population until 2030. Urbanization and the numerical stagnation of the rural population will have a profound influence on the world food economy. Commercialization and linkages between agriculture and the economy as a whole will grow rapidly, and nowhere will it be possible to continue increasing the numbers of workers in order to raise agricultural output – with the possible exception of sub-Saharan Africa. But even here young people of working age are fleeing from the villages to the towns because development policy has neglected agriculture and rural areas and life in rural areas is therefore an unattractive prospect. Mothers and children, the old and infirm are left behind. The AIDS pandemic in particular is reducing the growth rate of agricultural workers. Seen as a whole, however, the labour capacity of the sub-Saharan African agricultural sectors is already shrinking – despite the growing rural population. The ratio of consumers to available labour is also becoming steadily less favourable.

Table 1 Rural population growth rates, 1960 to 2030, in per cent p.a.

Region	Rural population (in m)	Growth rates	
	2000	1960–2000	2000–2030
Africa	487	1.93	0.91
Asia	2331	1.37	−0.90
Europe	184	−0.81	−1.42
Latin America	128	0.37	−0.18
North America	71	0.35	−0.65
Oceania	9	1.35	0.51
World	3210	1.18	0.01

Source: UN (2001), p. 28.

2.2   Per capita income

In the period 1965–98 global per capita income rose by 1.4 per cent p.a. in real terms. In East Asia the growth was 5.7 per cent p.a., in sub-Saharan Africa 0.3 per cent p.a.. The forecast of demand at the end of the chapter is based on historical figures since the weight carried by income growth is relatively insignificant because of the low income elasticities in the above estimating equation. Although speculation with assumption spreads would be possible in view of the considerable uncertainties as regards the trend in incomes in Eastern Europe and the CIS countries, well-founded average assumptions cannot be made.

2.3   Income elasticity of demand

According to an IFPRI survey of experts, the global income elasticity of demand for cereals was about 0.15 in the reference year, 1997 (IFPRI 2001). In 2020 it will probably be no more than about 0.07.

2.4   Forecast of demand

Assuming for the period 2000–2020 average annual population growth of 1.05 per cent, growth of 1.5 per cent in real per capita income and an income elasticity of demand for cereals of 0.12, average annual growth of demand will be 1.05 + 1.5 per cent • 0.12 = 1.23 per cent. According to the compound interest formula, world grain production would thus have to rise by 27.5 per cent by

2020 to satisfy world demand at the real price level of the 1990s. At a trend value of world grain consumption of 2050 million tonnes in 2000, this is equivalent to a rise in production or supply of 560 million tonnes. IFPRI expects world demand for cereals to be 2500 million tonnes in 2020.

3   Supply

Will the global supply of cereals be increased by 1.2 to 1.3 per cent p.a., or from 2000 to 2600 million tonnes, from current production in the period 2000–20 in line with the probable trend in demand? The expansion of cultivated arable land, the cultivation of fallow arable land and an increase in yields are the three main options. If producer prices of cereals were to rise in relative terms, increasing the amount of land under cereals by substituting them for other crops would also be conceivable, but this fourth option is relevant only in the context of short supply and sharply rising grain prices compared to the prices of other agricultural products. Moreover, it would produce no more than a relatively insignificant increase in total calorie yield.

3.1   Available arable land

Some 1.5 billion ha of arable land is in cultivation throughout the world. A further 1.7 to 1.9 billion ha of potential arable land is under pasture, forest and bush (Scherr 1999; Feder and Keck 2001). The amount of cultivated arable land rose by a mere 2 per cent from 1979–81 to 1989–91, while world agricultural output increased by about 14 per cent in the same period (WRI 1994). This trend continued in the past decade. Little of the rise in world agricultural production today is due to an increase in arable land. This is confirmed by a basic finding of project practice in the past 20 years: at current price ratios and resource availability, increasing output by intensifying arable land already in cultivation is, as a rule, far more cost-efficient than bringing new arable land into cultivation, the investment costs of which are very high by comparison.

3.2   Soil fertility in the tropics

Bringing new land into cultivation is therefore a very limited option. Of the still unused reserves of arable land, >90 per cent is tropical land whose natural soil fertility is fragile. Conventional use would lead to soil degradation after a mere two to three years, meaning a loss of productivity due to erosion and to chemical and physical changes to the soil. Exceptional cases of unused tropical land with more stable natural soil fertility – e.g. alluvial soil – usually require very high development investment. Losses of arable land due to erosion, urbanization and infrastructure development similarly indicate that the global area of arable land will not be increased appreciably from the current 1.5 billion ha.

From the angle of the soil fertility problem, tropical production locations can be categorized as follows:

- zonal locations
  - arid and semi-arid climates (<800 mm annual precipitation)
  - subhumid and humid climates (>800 mm annual precipitation)

- azonal locations
  - highlands
  - alluvial soils.

Whatever soil fertility problems they may have, tropical locations enjoy one major advantage: they receive about 100 per cent more solar energy per unit area than locations in the more temperate parts of the world (Holliday 1976). Provided that soil fertility is preserved and adequate services and water and appropriate production technology are available, correspondingly high energy yields from the cultivated land are possible.

Zonal *soils of the humid and subhumid climates*, however, lack almost all the main constituents that give rise to natural soil fertility: clay minerals, lime and humus, apart from special forms of humus (Finck 1963). The cation exchange capacity is, as a rule, <10 per cent of average brown earth in temperate climates. The pH values are usually <5.0 in the top soil. They fall with depth of soil, and this is matched by a rise in the concentration of aluminium in the soil solution to toxic levels. This restricts the root space and soil water available to plants. The reserves of plant nutrients are largely to be found in the living and dead vegetation and the humus. The assimilative efficiency of plants is therefore based on continuous organic nutrient circulation, with termites taking care of the mineralization of the dead organic matter (Sanchez 1979).

To protect organic soil matter, farmers must above all ensure that land is shaded as much as possible. At a tropical location in Uganda, for example, the soil lost some 20 tonnes of organic carbon and 2.8 tonnes of exchangeable cations per hectare (in the root zone down to a depth of 45 cm) over three years of arable farming; left fallow under elephant grass for three years, the soil recovered 16 tonnes of organic carbon and 1.9 tonnes of exchangeable cations. The pH value and reserves of phosphorus and nitrogen changed in much the same way (see Table A25). Permanent cropping with lost mineral nutrients replaced and organic material used as a mulch is best able to maintain the balance between the decline and supply of organic matter. The permanent growing of annual crops, however, makes it imperative not only to replace minerals but also to leave the land fallow or to intercrop fallow plants (e.g. varieties of leucaena in alternate rows).

At *semi-arid locations* unregulated ley farming systems dominate, with 30 to 60 per cent of arable land left fallow. The production systems feature cereals (primarily varieties of millet), grain legumes and transhumant livestock. The soils usually have a higher nutrient status and exchange capacity than in areas with more rainfall. Unfavourable soil hydrology, erosion susceptibility and, in many cases, extreme phosphate deficiency form the natural barriers to soil fertility. Lasting improvement in soil fertility and crop yields can be achieved by changing to regulated ley farming and adding rock phosphate and stable manure to the soil (Pieri 1989). To improve soil hydrology, the main options are tie ridging with an ox team and small dams along contour lines (Ohm and Nagy 1986). The cumulative effect on yields of the application of mineral and organic fertilizers is a key finding in tropical arable farming (Pieri 1989). The same is true, moreover, of the farming of low-sorption sandy soils in Europe (Schultz-Lupitz 1885).

At <400 mm annual precipitation, only *extensive ranching* is possible without irrigation. Traditional forms are notorious for ruining natural pastureland by overstocking. Production techniques used in ranching offer the possibility of grazing that does less damage to the land at such locations. They work on the principle of rotational grazing: fencing and subdivision of the area, a supply of drinking water, regulated grazing and stalk fodder reserves in ungrazed 'reserve camps' are the most important measures (Andreae 1972). Supplementary fodder-growing occurs only when price ratios are extremely favourable. The fall in real prices in the world meat markets has led to a distinct extensification of ranching systems everywhere in the last two decades. The minimum capital intensity of regulated rotational grazing is no longer economically sustainable at many locations at present global price ratios (without subsidies).

Soils and climates in tropical highlands permit very intensive land use systems to be employed sustainably. Examples here are terraced rice-growing in the Malayan culture area, tea-growing in Sri Lanka and East Africa, the growing of Arabica coffee in Central America and regulated ley farming combined with milk production in East Africa and the Caribbean. The labour intensity of these systems is typically 3000 to 5000 hours/ha. Given adequate rainfall and a favourable agricultural policy environment, tropical highlands permit very high production intensities. Their advantages lie in a richer mineral soil component, a more stable organic soil component and, not least, the better health and, therefore, greater working capacity of the people. Where, however, semi-arid climatic conditions and a high altitude coincide, erosion can quickly assume catastrophic proportions, since intensification without irrigation at such locations is possible to only a very limited degree. Significantly, the Incas always combined their highly intensive terrace cropping with technically sophisticated slope irrigation (Donkin 1979; Masson Meiss 1984).

Owing to their high clay and silt content, *alluvial soils* are characterized by a relatively high sorption capacity and favourable nutrient status. Level ground also permits gravity irrigation, as in the riverine areas of the Nile. The main problems are the danger of salination, human health hazards caused by waterborne diseases and considerable dependence on trouble-free organization and input availability. Where there is an efficient agricultural policy and appropriate production technology, however, very high yields can be achieved sustainably on tropical riverines. It is undoubtedly no coincidence that the first advanced civilizations in the history of mankind evolved in the fluvial plains of the outer tropics.

The *soil fertility issue* cannot be reduced to a technical partial problem; it always arises in the longer term as an aspect of the development of an agricultural production system in line with the dynamism of its political and socio-economic location. Seen in economic terms, soil fertility problems are investment problems. High real interest rates, which prevail in the LDCs owing to the shortage of capital and the undeveloped money and credit markets, obstruct or prevent investment in soil fertility. Imports at distorted world food prices, excessive taxes on agricultural raw material exports and overvalued domestic currencies have the same effect. In many cases, not even spending on commercial fertilizers, let alone long-term investment in the soil, pays off in such circumstances. *Land law issues* often form a further structural obstacle to the maintenance of soil fertility: where land ownership is collective and non-exclusive, no farmer will resort to long-term investment in soil fertility. Consequently, soil degradation throughout the world is very largely due to distorted world markets and to inefficient or structurally passive agricultural policies.

3.3   Soil erosion

The effect of wind and water on land with no vegetation on it, the state it is in after being ploughed or grazed bare, for example, erodes the surface. Permanent plant growth is the most effective means of containing erosion. On average, soil erosion, the most serious form of soil degradation, causes the annual loss of 30–40 tonnes of soil matter per hectare from agricultural land in the tropics (Pimentel *et al.* 1987 and Pimentel 1998; Scherr 1999, pp. 17–19); natural soil formation, however, replaces only 1–2 tonnes per hectare each year. Annual erosion losses in Europe and North America average 10–20 tonnes per hectare.

Soil erosion in the tropics is facilitated by inadequate fallowing of arable land and overstocking with cattle. At a cautious estimate, some 0.5 per cent of the world's 1.5 billion ha of arable land is irretrievably lost to erosion every year. The natural yield potential of the cultivated area is reduced by about 1 per cent each year by losses of humus and nutrients. Except in the sub-Saharan (Drechsel *et al.* 2001) and some Central American countries, this effect has hitherto been overcompensated for or concealed by increases in expenditure on commercial fertilizers and the growing of higher-yield varieties. The erosion process therefore continues latently over many years. Excessive intensification without regard for the environment, on the one hand, and poverty, a shortage of land for the poor and ill-conceived agricultural policies, on the other, are the societal causes. As a rule, there is no more than a vague idea of the 'need for action' under agricultural policies. In practice, it then usually amounts to 'coordination Platonism', with no agricultural policy countermeasures of any substance being taken.

It cannot be denied that there are voices which, working from an historical longitudinal comparison of available soil analyses at two locations, declare all estimates of degradation to be untenable on methodological grounds. In reality, they argue, global soil degradation is insignificant and of no relevance to the global food supply (Lindert 1996; Johnson 1999). While the criticism of the methodology is naturally accepted as a spur to progress and the improvement of the methodology, a much broader empirical base is needed before the results of decades of research into degradation throughout the world can be declared obsolete. It would appear that bias led by personal interest has had a part to play in this. Leaving aside the Lindertian case studies referred to above, global soil research shows that soil degradation, and especially erosion, will be a threat to the global food supply for future generations and is one of the main causes of poverty. Although European experience indicates that, after intensification of producer price ratios and changes to land tenure systems, periods of extensive farming during which the land is overexploited are followed by periods of soil conservation and improvements to soil fertility – German agricultural economics of the nineteenth century was essentially economics of soil fertility (Otzen 1992; Brandt 1994, 1995b). However, the argument by analogy with present-day tropical agricultural sectors is misleading, mainly because the fertility of tropical soils is far more fragile than that of soils in temperate climates owing to the special conditions prevailing in the tropics as regards soil chemistry, soil physics and climate. When the final stages of soil degradation are reached, a return to the original level of soil fertility is seldom possible, even with heavy investment. Skeletal soils, laterite concretions or 'green deserts' of *Imperata cylindrica* (spear grass) very often form the last, virtually irreversible stage of inappropriate use.

The lateritic soils of the inner tropics cannot be used sustainably or profitably for permanent arable farming or grazing. One day in the distant future it may be possible to replace the natural forest sustainably with mixed stands of timber or crop sequences that do little damage to the soil. For the time being, however, mankind depends on the aforementioned 1.5 billion ha of cultivated arable land for its food and fibre.

3.4   Land development on balance

What land reserves are reclaimed for use are more than offset by the growth of urban areas, the development of infrastructure and soil erosion. The amount of land given over to urbanization and industrialization is, at most, about 0.05 ha per urban dweller (Crossen and Anderson 1992, p. 24). By 2020 between 50 and 100 million ha of today's arable land is likely to be lost in this way, since most of Asia's urban growth centres are situated in fertile arable regions. Some 38 per cent of cultivated arable land is so used that it is being degraded by erosion and changes to soil chemistry and physics (see Table 2). After evaluating 16 studies, Scherr comes to the conclusion that degradation is insignificant for about 75 per cent of agricultural land, but that in Africa and Central America five to eight millions hectares of arable, pasture and forest land are being lost to degradation each year (Scherr 1999). In a global perspective the rising demand for food will have to be satisfied through the intensification of already cultivated arable land. As the number of agricultural workers is already stagnant, this will have to be achieved with technical, yield-increasing advances by means of capital intensification and intensification of energy inputs.

Table 2 Degradation of global arable land

Region	Arable land (m ha)	Thereof degraded	
		m ha	%
Africa	187	121	65
Asia	536	206	38
Latin America	180	92	51
North America	236	63	26
Europe	287	72	25
Oceania	49	8	16
World	1475	562	38

Source: Scherr, S.J. (1999), p. 18.

3.5   Increase in yields and production forecast

Supply can be sustainably increased through the use of fallow arable land only in the temperate zones because of the problem of fundamentally different soil fertility. Fertile arable land – e.g. in fluvial plains – can normally be redeveloped and farmed profitably by the private sector only if the very high development costs are heavily subsidized and/or real producer prices rise well above the average level of the past decade. The FAO's global land and yield statistics since 1985 reveal the following range of possible production in 2020 (see Table 3). Expected yields are pitched rather low in view of the scope that exists for intensification. Even the pessimistic variant is a mere 150 million tonnes less than the aforementioned demand forecast of 2600 million tonnes. The optimistic variant, which abides by historical maximum areas and quietly optimistic yield expectations, already indicates a 340 million tonne production or supply surplus. The greatest uncertainties in this rough calculation are, on the supply side, the development of the sown area in North America and the CIS and the trend in yields in Africa, Asia and the CIS. But losses of arable land to urbanization, infrastructure expansion and soil degradation must also be borne in mind. If it is assumed that only 80 million ha of arable land – i.e. about 30 per cent of the above global figures for losses to erosion and urbanization – are lost by 2020 and the yield from the land lost is imputed at 3.0 tonnes per ha, the optimistic variant is already reduced to 2700 million tonnes in 2020, which is slightly above forecast demand. The approaching productivity crisis in Asian rice-growing, which accounts for 25 per cent of world grain production, should also be considered (see Box 1). China is not internationally competitive in the case of wheat, maize, soya beans or rapeseed because of production and transport costs associated with the main growing areas (see Table A24). The future development of the world

Table 3 Estimates of world grain production in 2020

Region	Area (m ha)		Yield (tonnes/ha)		Production (m tonnes)	
	optimistic	pessimistic	optimistic	pessimistic	optimistic	pessimistic
Asia	310	305	4.5	4.3	1395	1312
Africa	130	95	1.6	1.5	208	143
South America	55	50	3.2	2.8	176	140
North America	95	78	4.8	4.4	456	343
Europe	75	70	5.0	4.6	375	322
CIS	110	92	3.0	2.1	330	193
World	775	690	3.8	3.6	2940	2453

Source: FAO data, etc.

market very largely depends on how China's agricultural policy reacts to this situation under the WTO agreements. Can China afford accelerated change to its social and economic structure, or will it resort to delaying matters by indirectly subsidizing agriculture?

If China liberalizes its price and trade policies without compensating its producers, it will give strong support to the price trend in the world markets; if it compensates its producers (following the EU's example, by paying subsidies related to area or even by taking trade policy safeguard measures), the distortion of the world food markets will continue as before (Wencong 2001). In late 2001 it was still possible to assume that real prices in the world market might rise to about 120 to 130 per cent of the 1999–2000 average by 2010–20 (von Witzke 1999).[2] The untapped yield potential in the world would be enough in itself to permit this (Schug 1996). The present low prices in the world market are due to surplus stocks, which are in turn due to a cyclical decline in demand in the late 1990s. The USDA estimates that prices will rise by 25 to 30 per cent by 2010 (USDA 2001). It is apparent, then, that moderate increases in real prices are probable. In the context of a poverty-oriented agricultural development policy there would thus be an urgent need to solve the core problem facing world food security: the eradication of poverty, hunger and undernourishment. However, sweeping changes to the US agricultural policy were made in March 2002. Direct farm subsidies were increased by US$ 19 billion p.a., i.e. by 70 per cent.

Box 1 **Soil degradation due to permanent intensive rice-growing – end of the Asian countries' self-sufficiency in rice?**

In 2020 3.7 billion people, about half of mankind, will be living in Asia. Their staple food is rice, which accounts for 40–60 per cent of calorie consumption. No more than a minor increase in the area under rice, 133 million ha (multiple cropping included), is possible. The transition to regulated irrigation requires investment of US$ 3000–5000/ha (Pingali *et al.* 1997, p. 194 ff.). Higher output must be achieved by raising yields, especially as land is being lost to urbanization and infrastructure development. The growth in yields in Asian rice-growing, however, is stagnant:

Period	Increase in yield	Increase in area	Increase in output
1975–85	2.9 % p.a.	0.4 % p.a.	3.3 % p.a.
1985–90	1.3 % p.a.	0.0 % p.a.	1.3 % p.a.
1991–2000	1.3 % p.a.	0.0 % p.a.	1.3 % p.a.

Even where per capita income is comparatively high, dietary habits are such that there is virtually no substitute for rice in Asia (Pingali *et al.* 1997, p. 126 ff.). Assuming an income elasticity of only 0 and population growth of 1.05 per cent p.a. for the period 2000–20 (World Bank 2000a), yields and rice output will also have to rise by about 1.05 per cent p.a. if self-sufficiency in rice – the principal article of faith of Asian rice policies – is to be maintained. Rice production will have to rise from 540 million tonnes today to 660 million tonnes in 2020.

Is this realistic, given the aforementioned limits to the area available and trend in yields? In 1970 experts still agreed that permanent intensive rice-growing with two or three harvests a year was possible without any fall in yields: "In a wet-rice region the habitat remains unchanged" (Ruthenberg 1980, p. 213). In 1997, however, Pingali *et al.* refuted this expectation in a comprehensive analysis and proved that intensive wet rice-growing in Asia faced agro-ecological crisis (Pingali *et al.* 1997).

In a controlled experiment it was found that yields fall by 70–100 kg/ha p.a. in all major Asian regions where rice is grown intensively and permanently and harvested twice or three times a year (Pingali *et al.* 1997, p. 62 ff.). This trend is already apparent in countries where rice is grown intensively (see Table A1). In contrast, yields are still rising at locations where growing is more extensive owing to natural or social conditions or infrastructure and where modern intensive growing is only just being (or has only just been) introduced. Much the same is said of wheat-growing in Punjab: "… the trends in Punjab might be an early warning that the types of input-intensive technologies fostered by the green revolution might slow down or preclude growth possibilities in the long run. Research and development might have to be redirected toward work designed to maintain the yield gains from past research" (Murgai 1999).

> The technology of the first Green Revolution (hybrid seed, irrigation, high input intensity, permanent wet rice-growing with two or three harvests a year) has proved not to be sustainable. The decline in yields is primarily due to physical and chemical soil degradation and an accumulation of plant pests and diseases – an absolutely classic syndrome of biased land use. The cure will require, in particular, the alternation of wet rice-growing and dryland farming and substitute mineral and organic fertilizers.
>
> Very high-yielding varieties, which have a yield potential 25–30 per cent higher than the hybrids of the first Green Revolution, will not be ready for general use for another 10 to 15 years. They too will require crop rotation and the application of appropriate organic and intensive mineral fertilizers and sprays.
>
> If the rate of increase in output lags significantly and persistently behind the rate of increase in demand in Asia, tension will rise in the world rice market. Rising prices would exacerbate the situation of the poor and hungry, particularly in South Asia.

The implications for agricultural policy of the EU's eastward enlargement from 2004 should also be borne in mind. The two factors will probably ensure the long-term depression of world market prices unless the forthcoming round of world trade negotiations leads to a further reduction in the industrialized countries' agricultural protection and direct subsidies (*Handelsblatt* 13 March 2002, p. 8). However, there is as yet no sign of this happening.

4   Main development problem of the world food issue: poverty, hunger, undernourishment and malnutrition

The minimum daily food energy requirement for a healthy body and an active life averages 2300 kcal per head of the population. Inadequate food intake over a lengthy period leads to malnutrition and undernourishment. The consequences of undernourishment are: "Emaciation of the body, apathy, susceptibility to diseases, premature death" (Deutsche Welthungerhilfe 2001). This means human suffering on a horrifying scale and economic losses. Undernourishment and malnutrition are caused by poverty in a highly complex relationship of causes and effects (von Braun *et al.* 1998; Wiesmann *et al.* 2000). They have a very adverse and long-term effect on the productivity of labour, the incomes of the poor and macroeconomic growth: hunger among children diminishes their prospects, and this for the rest of their lives.

4.1   Incidence of undernourishment

In the period 1997–99 about 777 million people were suffering from undernourishment throughout the world, some 39 million fewer than seven years before (FAO 2001a). The main areas of undernourishment in the world are South and South-East Asia and sub-Saharan Africa (see Table 4). In the last of these re-

Table 4 Numbers of undernourished people, by regions of the world, 1979–99 (in millions)

Region	1979–81		1990–92		1997–99	
	absolute	% of pop.	absolute	% of pop.	absolute	% of pop.
Sub-Saharan Africa	132	38	166	35	194	34
South Asia	339	38	307	27	303	24
East Asia	455	29	291	16	127	10
South-East Asia	93	26	81	18	66	13
Latin America	47	13	58	13	54	11
Middle East, North Africa	22	9	26	8	32	9
Transformation countries	26	6	26	6	27	6

Source: Deutsche Welthungerhilfe (2001); FAO (2001b).

gions undernourishment is on the increase because of war, inadequate agricultural policy, economic stagnation and poor income distribution. Some 75 per cent of the undernourished form part of the rural population of Africa and Asia. Families in developing countries who live primarily by selling their unskilled labour are always at risk of hunger and undernourishment – where they are not already affected – because they have few assets to which they can resort to ensure a minimum of nutrition at times of hardship. This is especially true where a worker has many children to feed and/or diseases reduce working capacity.

4.2 Disposable income, food consumption, undernourishment

More than 98 per cent of the incidence of undernourishment can be statistically attributed in an international cross-section comparison to inadequate calorie intake (von Braun *et al.* 2001). Von Braun *et al.* also show in an international cross-section that 74 per cent of nutritional status can be ascribed solely to the distribution of GNP per capita (ibid.).

Because of its importance for their very existence, the food problem is, alongside health hazards, housing and personal safety, the main concern of poor people. Currently, about 1.3 billion people in the world (28 per cent of the population of the developing countries) have to get by on a daily income of less than US$ 1 (PPP). In sub-Saharan Africa 48 per cent fall into this category, in South Asia 40 per cent (IBRD 2002, p. 58). They spend 75 to 85 per cent of their income on food (von Rümker 1972; King *et al.* 1997; Peter *et al.* 1983; Brandt 1991; Teklu 1996), while middle-income groups in the industrialized countries typically spend only 15 to 20 per cent of per capita income on food and semi-luxuries.

The same tendency as in the international cross-section can, of course, be seen within developing countries, whether in rural or urban areas: the lowest quarter in income terms spend 85 per cent of their income on food, the highest quarter only 30 per cent (see Tables A2, A3, A6, A8 to A11, A22 and A23) (Teklu 1996; Akindes 1999; Savadogo and Kazianga 1999). The empirically measured income elasticities reflect the same circumstances in both national and international cross-section analyses (see Table A4) (Rosegrant *et al.* 2001a, b).

The link between per capita income and food consumption (and nutritional status) to which reference has just been made corresponds, of course, to Engel's Law, one of the oldest basic findings on nutrition and economics, according to which the proportion of expenditure on food falls as disposable per capita income rises. It will be consulted here again in some empirical breadth because it suggests a central point in the following line of argument: poverty-oriented agricultural development policy should not only address itself to producers, but also consider its target groups in terms of both the spending of income and its origin.

5   Relevance of food prices to poverty

This introductory chapter concludes with a brief explanation of why the food and grain markets are so very important for the real livelihoods and nutritional situation of the poor. The links in the chain of this argument are taken up again and discussed in greater depth later in this study (see Chapter 6.2).

5.1   Reference level: domestic market

The ratio of food prices to disposable income is of decisive importance for food consumption by and the nutritional situation of the poor in urban areas, as is immediately evident from the large proportions, 75 to 85 per cent, of budgets devoted to expenditure on food. Even moderate rises in consumer prices of 20 to 30 per cent threaten the physical existence of the lowest urban income quartile, primarily because there is usually some considerable delay in urban areas before disproportionately low wage increases follow a price rise caused by economic or weather conditions (see Chapter 12.2). In economies which are remote from world markets and where climatic conditions are unstable, subsidized government storage of cereals is therefore essential if social and economic conditions in the towns and cities are to remain stable (Brandt 1985), since at times of drought real grain prices may rise by 400 to 500 per cent in the free markets of these countries, as the example of Sudan shows (see Diagram 1). Similar fluctuations occurred in the Sahel countries in the 1980s.

The rural poor, on the other hand, are affected in three capacities: as consumers and/or as wage-earners and/or as producers or recipients of rent income. The real net effect of changes in food prices in relation to real income, food consumption and nutritional situation depends on the socio-economic situation or functional sources of income of the poor. In general, fluctuations in food prices

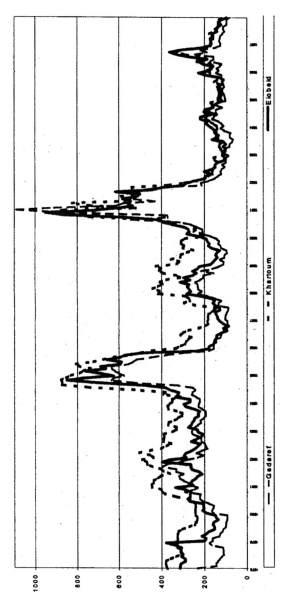

Diagram 1 Real wholesale prices of sorghum in Sudan, monthly averages, 1978–97 (£/sack)[a]

[a] CPI-deflated, January 1990 = 100.

Source: Hassan (1993); Hussein (2002).

and the income situation of the poor rural population change in the same direction, the proportion depending, however, on the individual's socio-economic situation (see Chapter 13.1). Generally speaking, however, the trend in their income in real terms is less dependent on the trend in food prices than is that of the urban poor. An exception here are transhumant livestock farmers and nomads, since livestock prices are at their lowest when grain prices rise sharply at times of drought.

5.2   Reference level: world market

As has been pointed out above, there may be moderate increases in world market prices towards the end of the current decade (see p. 12), principally because

- reserves of fertile land can be brought into cultivation today only at very high investment costs, which will not be worthwhile without government subsidies;
- over 90 per cent of the land reserves is characterized by very fragile soil fertility and is not therefore suitable for sustainable arable farming;
- government agricultural innovation policy as the driving force behind advances in agro-technical productivity has been increasingly neglected in many developing countries in the past two decades (see Chapter 6). This is true of the majority of developing countries, but more so of sub-Saharan Africa.

The last of these factors might spur future agricultural innovation policy – as soon as real producer prices rise sustainably – since agro-technical progress is largely induced by prices under free-market conditions (Hayami and Ruttan 1971). However, time lags of 10 to 20 years between the price incentive and successful innovation must be remembered in this context. The supply trend is accordingly inclined towards imbalance, which tends to cause a price–innovation cycle. The introduction of clover into German agriculture in the early 19th century prompted similar observations by A.D. Thaer (Brandt 1991). The rise in productivity in Central Europe and England's import barriers then resulted in depressed grain prices for a generation. More recent examples are the rise in productivity in the industrialized countries after the Second World War, the Green Revolution in South and South-East Asia from 1970 to 1990 and the effects on prices of improved durum wheat varieties in the American Midwest in the 1920s (Benn 1992).

Price fluctuations in world grain markets have a surprisingly strong impact on the developing countries' domestic markets – directly through trade and smuggling and indirectly through food aid (Koester and von Braun *et al.* 1995; Mundlak and Larson 1992). They are therefore extremely important for rural incomes, the urban cost of living and rates of urbanization and demographic transformation in the LDCs, for agro-technical progress and economic development and for food consumption and the nutritional situation of the poor in urban and rural areas.

The importance of world grain markets for the nutritional status and real live-lihoods of the poor is growing with rapid worldwide urbanization. It should be remembered that in 1970 about 18 per cent of the world's population lived in towns and cities; by 2020 the figure will have risen to about 52 per cent. World supplies of food in 1970 did not, on average, have far to travel from the producer and were energy-extensive. The scarcity of land and urbanization will lead to a far more energy-intensive world food economy by 2020, since increases in yields, transport, processing and marketing require increasing rates of energy consumption for the marginal quantum of supply. The danger of future market disruptions – due to future political conflicts or world energy crises, for exam-ple[3] – resulting in food price rises and so in disastrous famine in the poorest countries of the Third World grows accordingly.

Increasing urbanization requires not only rapidly growing food sector link-ages in the economy as a whole: it is also bound to lead to the greater politiciza-tion of the poverty problem – just as rural poverty becomes urban poverty as a result of migration. For the rural poor are, as a rule, barely organized politically, whereas the urban poor are where the political action is taken, and they are also organized politically in parties and workers' associations (Bates 1998). It can already be seen how erratic price rises in the world grain market will impact on the developing countries' domestic markets and, owing to internal pressure, lead to a fundamental reappraisal of the importance of their agricultural and food security policies. The only question is when. The focus will then be on the fol-lowing policy measures:

- increases in production and productivity through technical advances;
- (state-subsidized) development of new arable land;
- poverty-oriented market and trade policy measures;
- initiatives to strengthen international measures to insure against domes-tic losses of production.

The general neglect of agriculture and rural areas in development cooperation will then no longer be sustainable since, as food prices rise throughout the world, agricultural development policy is bound to become a component of global security policy.

Sub-Saharan Africa and South Asia will remain the focus of attention in the fight against undernourishment and poverty. "... Sub-Saharan Africa is the only region in which the number and percentage of children who are malnourished is expected to rise, rather than fall, over the next 20 years" (Rosegrant *et al.* 2001a, b). What is fairly certain is that the problems of the sub-Saharan African coun-tries, structurally rigid as they are, will not be overcome in the short to medium term. The need for food imports will continue to rise sharply. It will be for the world's agricultural surplus countries to take account of this situation by provid-ing generous distribution-oriented food aid (food-for-work and other similar programmes) that disturbs the market as little as possible, but they must not neglect the promotion of agricultural development or misuse the plight of the sub-Saharan countries to dump heavily subsidized bulk food supplies.

In the South Asian countries, on the other hand, the main aim must be to safeguard and continue the advances made in production technology in the past 30 years, but their ruling classes are unlikely to evade the question – raised externally and/or internally – of radical land reform.

Part II Motive for the study: new urban bias in development cooperation

The first development decade (1955–65) was overly focused on industry in theory, the conception of development policy and the allocation both of development cooperation resources and of the recipients' national budgets. Since then development policy has completed, in theory and practice, the full cycle of initial agricultural pessimism and industrial fundamentalism through concentration on agricultural and rural development and back to priority for the promotion of industry, the urban social sectors and central government, with agriculture very largely neglected (see Chapter 9). In view of the social and economic imbalances that occur in the course of rapid or premature and accelerated urbanization – such as poverty, undernourishment, social alienation and crime, and the problem of a national budget chronically in deficit – voices are heard warning of the imbalances due to the excessive emphasis placed on the industrial and urban development of pre- or early-industrial economies (Mellor 1998a,b; IFAD 2001). This is especially true of the sub-Saharan African countries, where the young people of working age migrate to the towns and cities, leaving mothers and children, the elderly and infirm behind in the villages. Whole classes of school-leavers in sub-Saharan African villages between Khartoum and Johannesburg today sit on packed suitcases because there are no economically attractive prospects in the rural areas and hope of a job in the formal sector or just casual labour is still preferable to the wretchedness of village life. Happiness is to be found in the towns and cities, even if you have to sleep in a shack made of plastic and cardboard and your stomach is rarely full, because hope is the more important part of happiness.

But there will soon come a time when it is no longer possible to stabilize the resulting socio-political and economic imbalances in the usual makeshift way by having development cooperation subsidize the urban areas – and siphoning off resources from the economy of the rural areas.

6 Neglect of the agricultural sector in development cooperation

Even during the IRD decade the promotion of the agricultural sector began to take a back seat (see Chapter 9.3). The ensuing SAPs and SIPs sought to correct the distortion of agricultural price ratios, but rural infrastructure, technical innovations and extension services continued to be ignored. Parastatal extension services, and especially the parastatal marketing organizations in the sub-Saharan African countries, were simply liquidated.

Since the mid-1980s agriculture's share of total ODA has been dwindling. IFAD's summary of the present development financing situation is accurate and by no means exaggerated:

> The real value of aid fell sharply between 1987–88 and 1997–98. The share of aid going to low-income or least-developed countries, which contain over 85 per cent of the poor, stayed around 68 per cent and agricultural aid collapsed. ... most treatments of urban poverty are welfare-oriented, often mainly depending on upgraded housing.
>
> (IFAD 2001, p. 1 ff.)

Available data on the sectoral allocation of ODA endorse this assessment. In 1998–99 only 6.3 per cent of the DAC donors' and 6.8 per cent of the multilateral donors' gross ODA went to agriculture (OECD 2001a). Since 1980 agriculture's share of total ODA has been reduced from 12.4 per cent to its present level. Australia, Belgium, the United Kingdom and the latecomers to development cooperation Greece, Ireland, Spain and Portugal have increased the proportion of their ODA that goes to agriculture, but as their contributions are comparatively modest, the effect on the overall situation is slight. In 1999 a mere four donors accounted for 72 per cent of global agricultural aid:

Japan	41 %
UK	12 %
USA	11 %
Germany	7 %
Other DAC members	28 %

After the success of the Green Revolution the agricultural component of the bilateral donors' ODA was reduced by 51 per cent from 1986 to 1994, but since 1995 it has been raised again by about 10 per cent in real terms. The only data so far available for 2000 and 2001 concern the World Bank and regional development banks (IBRD 2002). The decline after 1986 particularly affected the components of agricultural aid that had a direct impact on production (FAO 1996). The rise since 1996 has been geared primarily to such new areas of concern to development policy as environmental protection, resource stabilization and sectoral capacity- and organization-building. In the World Bank's case the proportion of the total financial volume devoted to agriculture fell from 32 per cent (1977–79) to 9 per cent (1999–2001). However, contributions to rural areas accounted for 25 per cent of the total financial volume in 1999–2001. The proportion of World Bank loans allocated to agriculture fell by a third from 1993–95 to 1998–2001. The proportion of contributions pledged for agriculture and rural areas in the case of the EU's development cooperation was (ECDPM 2002, p. 5):

1986–90:   24.0 %
1991–95:   6.2 %
1996–98:   2.2 %

The decline in the real volume of assistance received by agriculture from the developing countries' own resources paralleled the reduction of development cooperation resources. In many cases it now stands at less than 5 per cent. Although rural areas as a whole account for a significantly larger share of national budgets, it too has fallen to clearly inadequate levels over the years. Development ideas and fund allocations among both recipients and donors are now, as a rule, overly focused on physical and non-physical urban infrastructure. This is true of financial cooperation and of technical cooperation. Where are agriculturalists still to be found in development cooperation?

Mellor rightly points out that the agricultural and economic development of sub-Saharan African countries in particular have suffered under this change:

> Asian countries, in general, did not lose in this shift of donor priorities away from agriculture, because they already had the basic institutions of agricultural development and lobbies of farmers who could protect those institutions. But Africa has suffered by the shift of foreign aid away from agriculture over the past decade.
>
> (Mellor 1995a, p. 59)

The renewed siphoning off of resources from African agriculture at the end of the century in contrast to the subsidization of Asian agricultural sectors underlines this statement. Most of the sub-Saharan African countries have highly negative PSEs for foodstuffs (see Table A5). As a rule, agriculture's share of governments' current and investment spending in these countries remains well below 10 per cent, and in the majority even below 5 per cent – a completely inadequate level.

6.1   The causes

The immediate budgetary causes of this situation were general constraints and the requirements arising from the designation of new focal areas (such as policy-oriented programmes, promotion of administrative capacities and of social sectors, environmental protection and resource stabilization). The literature and professional colleagues refer to a wide range of ideas and motives possibly behind this (Totter and Gordon 2000), although no attempt has yet been made at a quantitative review. In an attempt to derive some explicatory hypotheses, these driving forces can be summarized in the following four groups:

1   The theoretical and conceptual image that the technocratic and political elites in both recipient and donor countries have of the development process is

influenced by a mental urban bias, which leads to the neglect of agriculture and rural areas.

2   The self-interest of political elites in recipient countries leads to dysfunctional agricultural policies, if not to the obstruction of agricultural development.

3   A difficult technical, organizational, institutional and price policy environment means that there is a relatively high risk of failure and that, on average, the cost–performance ratios of agricultural and rural development projects are less favourable than those of measures taken to assist urban infrastructure and social services. Difficult to implement and comparatively risky, they seem unattractive in assessments by donor administrations in particular.

4   The industrialized countries, and especially the net agricultural exporters among them, see the world food problem as having been essentially solved since the successes of the Green Revolution, which also had appreciable effects on the world agricultural markets, and in view of the long-term decline in real world market prices (see Diagram 2). The importance of agricultural development for the developing countries' domestic economies and poverty situation is easily overlooked in this optimistic view.

These four hypotheses are examined more closely in the following, with the last, on which there is as yet no literature, singled out as probably in greatest need of explanation. However, it also becomes apparent that an attempt at a comprehensive explanation would certainly have to include the second and third hypotheses as well.

Hypothesis 1, referring to the *mental urban bias* of agricultural development policy elites, has recently been discussed by John Mellor with an eye to the change of paradigm and shifts of conceptual and practical emphasis that have taken place at USAID since 1985. His proposition reads:

> Foreign aid has a natural tendency to encourage urban elites and urban-oriented processes because it comes from countries that are largely urbanized.
>
> (Mellor 1998a, p. 60 ff.)

> An urban-based intelligentsia (including development economists) ... and urban-based political systems all combine to provide an intellectual basis and political pressure for directing resources to the urban sector.
>
> (Mellor 1998b, p. 137)

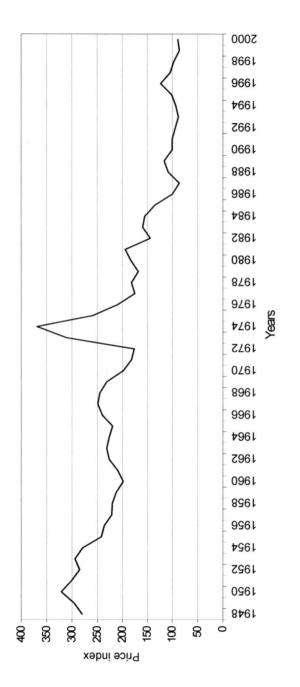

Diagram 2 MUV-deflated world market prices of grains (1990 index = 100)

Source: IBRD (2002): Global Commodity Markets, Washington, DC.
        IBRD (1994): Market Outlook for Major Primary Commodities, Washington, DC.

This bias, with its socio-psychological causes, is now so dominant, Mellor continues, that it refuses to accept either the global empirical data on agricultural income and employment multipliers or the positive real wage effects of agricultural growth on the poor:

> All this evidence about agriculture's role in promoting growth and reducing poverty has meant nothing to urban-oriented governments and urban-dominated foreign assistance agencies.
>
> (Mellor 1998a, p. 62 ff.)

The criticism directed explicitly at USAID is that in a 'non-technical atmosphere' the central positive role played by agricultural growth in the LDCs in the fight against poverty, the position of women, resource stabilization and small business is not only overlooked but, implicitly at least, based on opposing hypotheses or convictions (Mellor 1998a, p. 61).

What should we think of this explanation for mental urban bias? Frankly, the argument does not seem particularly sound. Firstly, it was, of course, USAID, the Ford Foundation and the World Bank which, in the latter half of the 1960s, launched the Green Revolution, which had such unprecedented success. Such a success is not forgotten in an organization's tradition in ten years. Secondly, the drastic cut in agro-scientific staff in these three organizations and almost all donor countries in the mid-1980s was an organizational measure and no coincidence. That the disciplines that have since dominated (the soft social sciences) have held their place at the trough in the well-known academic infighting is another story. The hypothesis of mental urban bias does not, at least, provide a convincing explanation for the decline in agricultural aid. It seems more like a fairy tale.

Hypothesis 2, that of the *dominant self-interest of political elites*, claims that ruling political elites – especially those that lack democratic legitimacy – act in accordance with the overriding maxim of retaining power and gaining material advantages, but not with any defined idea of public welfare.[1] In view of the enormous importance of agricultural policy for distribution in LDCs, this is one of the main levers used by political elites to gain and retain power – and to make a great deal of money in the process. The mechanics of the procedure have been generally known since the 1980s debate on and policy of structural adjustment, especially with regard to sub-Saharan African economies (Bates 1981; Brandt *et al.* 1986, Vol. I, p. 157 ff.). The main starting point is the import of food at heavily depressed world market prices, which are still, as a rule, the subject of regionally targeted foreign subsidization. Particularly in coastal towns and cities, along the main infrastructure axes and in the capitals, the less there is left of import rents or import taxes for the power network comprising the political elite and the import trade, the more these world market prices undercut the prices of domestic products. Interests in industrialized countries appear in many cases not to be neutral:

Evidence suggests, however, that private agents are capturing these transfers in some cases. Companies such as flour mills that process imported grain are obvious candidates. ... If the EU's bonus export subsidy expenditure is being 'repatriated', ... this would be the cause for a completely different set of concerns regarding CAP spending.

(Wehrheim and von Cramon-Taubadel 1997, p. 55)

The author will not deny that questions outside his terms of reference have occasionally occurred to him during his advisory activities (Brandt 1994). The more the political class needs the political support of urban consumers, the less it resorts to siphoning off the proceeds from imports. Despite all the successes of structural adjustment, this 'spin' has so far always reproduced itself under the real politico-economic conditions of the world agricultural markets and sub-Saharan African countries. The distortions in the sub-Saharan African food markets are due to three factors: general dumping by the industrialized countries in the world markets plus regionally selective export subsidies, negative PSEs and overvalued currencies (the last of these applying to about 30 per cent of all sub-Saharan African countries).

The political goodwill of the farming population – if needed at all to safeguard power – is ensured by means of input subsidies and, by way of exception, regionally targeted agricultural and rural development projects. Democratization is, however, strengthening the position of the rural population:

Where Third World governments are subject to competitive elections, for example, the evidence suggests they are more sensitive to rural interests, for farmers constitute a political majority in many developing countries.

(Bates 1998, p. 237).

On balance, the peasants of the sub-Saharan African countries are again heavily burdened today by agricultural policy as a result of food imports and inefficient export marketing (and a wide productivity gap in rural areas), much as they were when the Structural Adjustment Programmes were first launched in 1982–83. The productivity gap has widened steadily with the constant stream of technical advances made in other areas of the world, while stagnation has occurred in the sub-Saharan African countries. It signifies a serious locational and competitive disadvantage, which can be overcome only with temporary subsidization, efficient innovation policy and sustained labour cost advantages. Country analyses, agricultural policy studies and a wide range of anecdotal reports underline the considerable explanatory strength of Hypothesis 2, especially as regards the agricultural policies of the LDCs (Verheye 2001).

But who wants to know anything about this in practical development cooperation today? PRSPs, for example, have until recently neglected the agricultural sector and ignored the fact that, despite high urbanization rates, poverty in the LDCs is still mostly to be found in rural areas. The PRSP for Ethiopia in particular places some emphasis on agricultural and rural development, probably because of the strong natural protection against grain imports afforded by transport costs. And there is surely no denying that the concentration of development cooperation measures on urban areas is grist to the political elites' mill, for what, besides cheap food, would be more tangible and visible to the urban electorate than schools, hospitals, roads, water supply, sanitation and refuse disposal – and, what is more, these physical advances go a long way to determining not least the real quality of life of the rulers and the rich themselves.

Hypothesis 3, concerning the *specific difficulties encountered in implementing measures to promote agriculture*, feeds above all on the negative experience gained from the multisectoral integrated rural development programmes of the third development decade (see Chapter 9.3), which featured coordination chaos and structural dependence on subsidies. An added factor is the high implementation risk arising from the vicissitudes of the weather and overall agricultural policy where projects continue for a comparatively long time. The interplay of heavily dumped world market prices and the LDCs' consumer-oriented price, market and trade policies is particularly detrimental to the financial profitability of agricultural projects and makes them crisis-prone. The BMZ says, for example:

> ... viewed in the short term, investments turn out relatively often to be less profitable than in the urban sector. Positive effects of measures often become apparent only after some time has elapsed.
>
> (BMZ 2001, p. 13)

Not inconsiderable importance should undoubtedly be attached to Hypothesis 3 at the level of aid management, for why should the administrator of a country aid package go against donor and recipient preferences and choose the stony and risky path of promoting agriculture when higher professional plaudits are to be earnt on the smooth paths of urban infrastructure and social sector development?

Hypothesis 4, that of the *price-induced neglect of the agricultural sector in development cooperation*, has so far received very little attention in the literature. This does not in any way mean that it is implausible. In informal discussions with experts it is not infrequently pointed out that the long trends in the real world market prices of food and agricultural raw materials (see Diagram 2) indicate not increasing scarcity but, on the contrary, that supply is rising faster than demand for imports. It is also asserted with an eye to the future world food situation that the production reserves of the northern industrialized and transformation countries and of the traditional southern food exporters are easily enough to satisfy world demand for imports for at least the next generation. It is also pointed out that the problem of rural poverty cannot be solved simply by promoting agriculture: industrial development in the urban areas and additional non-agricultural jobs in the rural areas will also be needed.

While all this is undisputed, it is also true to say that industry, services and agriculture and the urban and rural areas must develop in a division of labour – with relative growth rates one to the other, which will depend, among other things, on the level of national productivity and per capita income and on available foreign exchange and investable resources. As historical examples and experience in the past 45 years have shown, however, pre- and early-industrial starting positions, with their weak capital base, agriculture accounting for a large proportion of value added, a completely inadequate fund of human capital and considerable incremental demand for agricultural products, now call for priority to be given to the development of agriculture and rural areas (see Chapter 8.2) – if, that is, poverty reduction is the objective. Or are we to let it come to the horror scenario of the urban areas in the sub-Saharan African countries, subsidized by development cooperation transfers and domestic trade, attracting the young members of the population who are capable of work, without gaining any appreciable comparative advantages in industrial competition, while agricultural productivity stagnates at best and the villages become the forgotten permanent sanctuary of mothers and children, the elderly and the infirm?

All in all, the lack of debate does not indicate that Hypothesis 4 is implausible, but rather that it is a sign of 'selective amnesia', the suppression of the subject by means of undiscriminating optimism about the world food situation, which overlooks the internal social and economic conditions in the developing countries. In this view it is enough simply to be aware of the unfavourable conditions for infrastructure and agriculture to capitulate from the outset and not even to launch agricultural projects (see Hypothesis 3). There are undoubtedly circles, too, who are shocked by the fact that Vietnam, for example, despite its shortage of land, is already producing exportable rice surpluses after a few years of modern agricultural development.

6.2   Agricultural policy distortions: industrialized countries, world markets, developing countries

As will be shown in the following pages, distorted world market prices of food, the neglect of agricultural and rural areas in development cooperation and similar neglect of agricultural policy in developing countries where agriculture is dominant, especially in sub-Saharan Africa, are largely to blame for continuing poverty and economic stagnation. All the large Asian countries, on the other hand, have so far maintained at least some protection of their domestic agricultural sectors against distorted world market prices (see Table A5). It remains to be seen whether their agricultural research and innovation policies can build on the successes of the past 30 years in Asia and maintain the present momentum of productivity growth for the next generation (see Box 1).

The agricultural products traded in the world markets are usually divided into two groups: first, such foodstuffs as grain and meat, and second, such agricultural raw materials as coffee and cotton. Since 1952–54 the trend in real market prices, i.e. prices deflated by the MUV index, has been constantly downward (see Diagram 2), with the price of the staple grain falling to about 30 per cent of its initial level and the prices of the beverages coffee, tea and cocoa falling to about 25 per cent. This long-term decline in real prices has had an adverse effect on the terms of trade of the net agricultural exporters among the developing countries. Continuously rising quantities of agricultural products have been needed to pay for imports of industrial inputs and capital goods. In addition, producer price ratios in industrialized and developing countries have developed in line with the trends in the world markets, unless the vicissitudes of national agricultural policies have caused deviations. The forces behind the decline in real prices are, firstly, the 'treadmill effect' and, secondly, agricultural policies that depress prices and distort competition, especially those pursued by industrialized countries. Conditions have not improved significantly, despite all the efforts to liberalize in the past decade (Windfuhr 2002). The EU's grain production, for example, rose from 179 million tonnes in 1992 to 211 million tonnes in 1999 even though the grain market has been largely liberalized. The compensatory payments made for land under cereals still provide ample incentives to produce, since in the long term, after input intensities have been adjusted, the overall cost/output comparison matters for investment and production decisions. In the industrialized countries grain, oilseed and sugar yields have risen by about 2.5 per cent p.a. in the past 30 years. The annual increase in milk yield per cow has been of a similar order of magnitude.

The reasons for the treadmill effect are to be found on the supply side and the demand side. On the supply side yield-increasing technical advances have continually led to rises in factor productivity or corresponding cost reductions, which means expansion of supply. In the case of the agricultural raw materials there have been absolutely revolutionary increases in the yields of all products owing to successes in plant breeding and more efficient production methods. As this group comprises – with the exception of cotton – perennial tree and shrub crops, it has been possible to use cuttings to propagate the selected parent plants asexually, thus avoiding the problem of subsequent genetic segregation and corresponding yield depression. As advances have been made in cultivation methods, yields have risen three- to fivefold in many countries since 1960/65, be it in the growing of coffee, tea, cocoa or palm oil. Where the cereals wheat, maize and rice are concerned, there have been similar advances in productivity in the Asian and many Latin American countries. In the case of rice in particular, hybrid seed, improved fertilizer application, irrigation, mechanization in the shape of the two-wheeled tractor and two or three harvests a year from the same land have led to yield increases of up to six times the usual starting level (see Box 1). However, the higher the cultivation intensity and, therefore, yields are driven, the less sustainability can be regarded as a static concept. It requires, in fact, a continuous struggle for what has been accomplished or an adjustment or response to natural challenges.

Demand for agricultural raw materials backed by purchasing power, on the other hand, has lagged well behind the supply trend. In the industrialized countries it rose by 1.40 per cent p.a. compared to 0.9 per cent population growth, an income elasticity of 0.20 to 0.30 and a per capita income growth rate of 2.0 per cent. The rise in demand for foodstuffs in the industrialized countries was even somewhat lower. In view of high population and income growth rates and income elasticities of around 0.50, the growth of demand in many developing countries amounted at times to 3 to 3.5 per cent p.a. Here too, however, Engel's Law applies in full upwards of a per capita income of about US$ 1500. The supply trend always outstripped demand in the world markets for both agricultural raw materials and foodstuffs. Market equilibrium was achieved by means of falling real prices.

This treadmill effect was hampered by national agricultural policies in some cases, exacerbated by them in others. The sub-Saharan African countries, for example, abandoned their shares of the agricultural raw material markets voluntarily, as it were, by pursuing agricultural and food policies marked by urban bias. Until 1983–85 producer prices were depressed to absurdly low levels by overvalued currencies and export taxes, and innovation policy and rural infrastructure were neglected. This led to a decline in productivity and output. The result was similar in the case of foodstuffs, boosted by imports and sometimes by food aid. The industrialized countries, on the other hand, subsidized their food production and disposed of their mounting surpluses in the world markets. In contrast, the Asian countries have pursued a policy of moderate price support and input subsidization since the 1970s.

After some initial successes achieved with the structural adjustment policies during the structural adjustment decade (1983–95) the old distortions of food prices at producer level have returned to the sub-Saharan African countries – probably not least because of export subsidies granted by some industrialized countries, which are deliberately depressing import parity prices for some regions of the world even below the already distorted world market prices (see Table A5). Domestic food production is scarcely keeping pace with population growth, the rural population of working age is fleeing to the urban areas, the industrial sector has hardly any comparative advantages, and the towns and cities are surviving primarily on the value added in the 'informal sector', ODA contributions and funds siphoned off from the agricultural sector and exports of mineral raw materials. The political elites of the sub-Saharan African countries have come to an arrangement, and the donors are endeavouring to reduce poverty – but not in rural areas and not by means of agricultural development policy.

The treadmill effect has been increasingly exacerbated since the 1970s by the price-distorting effects of the industrialized countries' agricultural and trade policies. According to model-assisted assessments by the now extensive literature, stagnating domestic demand, rising productivity and supply-promoting agricultural policies (support price regime entailing minimum producer prices, tariff protection against imports and export refunds as well as a wide range of instruments for direct income transfers to producers) are depressing the world market prices of all agricultural products well below the level of the undistorted equilibrium prices which would occur if agricultural policies were liberal and did not grant subsidies and if the world market were not distorted. The range of price distortions varied in the past decade depending not only on the product but also on the general situation created by national agricultural and trade policies in line with the state of implementation of the WTO's Uruguay Round (see Table 5). Unlike the above estimates, a more recent study reaches the conclusion that, although complete liberalization of the OECD countries' agricultural policies would lead to a shift in global shares of production and trade flows, it

Table 5 Global effects of current agricultural policies on prices
(undistorted prices = 100 per cent)

Authors	Goldin/Knudsen[a]	Tyers/Anderson[b]	USDA[c]
Reference year	2002	1990	2001
Milk products	−34 %	−51 %	⎫ −22 %
Beef	−21 %	−33 %	⎭
Sugar	−37 %	−18 %	−16 %
Wheat	−23 %	−11 %	−15 %

Sources: [a] I. Goldin and D. Knudsen (1993), p. 91.
         [b] R. Tyers and K. Anderson (1992), p. 217.
         [c] USDA and ERS (2001), p. 8.

would cause no more than minor changes to world market prices, except in the case of milk products. However, the high value of the dollar in the base year used for the estimate results in the effects of liberalization on prices being underrated. The authors point out in this connection:

> The high dollar exchange rate reduces some of the starting levels of price policy distortions considerably ....
>
> (Britz and Schmidhuber 2002, p. 103)

The distortions centre on milk, sugar, beef, wheat and rice of the foodstuffs and on cotton of the agricultural raw materials. The developing countries' domestic markets are affected to differing degrees, depending on their production and trade structures and their price and trade policies. To examine this, a brief calculation will be presented. The value of the world production of cereals, oilseed, sugar, milk, beef, sheep and goat meat, pork, cotton, eggs and poultry at CIF or FOB prices is about US$ 850 billion. This compares to some US$ 330 billion in agricultural subsidies paid by the OECD countries. If demand were completely price-inelastic and, taking the average over the years, marketed output and subsidies covered costs, the price distortion would be −330/(850 +330) = −28 per cent of an undistorted world market price level. For a price elasticity of aggregate supply of 0.30 in the short term and 0.60 in the long term and a price elasticity of demand of −0.20 corrected distortion rates of −18.9 per cent and −23.7 per cent, respectively, are calculated.[2] At farm gate prices the distortion rates would be far higher because the trade margin between ex farm prices and CIF or FOB prices is relatively larger than the proportion of the appropriate transformation chain attributable to subsidies.

The example of sugar, probably the most highly subsidized product, relatively speaking, apart from milk products, will be taken to illustrate the distortions with somewhat more recent data (Borrell and Pearce 1999). In 1997 the world market price of raw sugar was US$ 254/tonne. The producer price was about US$ 600/tonne in the EU, US$ 1000/tonne in Japan and US$ 450/tonne in the USA. The prices of 40 per cent of the sugar produced in the world were >150 per cent of the world market price. Only Australia, Brazil and Cuba (together accounting for some 20 per cent of world production) produced at world market prices without subsidies. Depending on what supply reactions are assumed, experiments with models of the world sugar market show prices rising to US$ 320 or 350/tonne in the event of complete liberalization. This is equivalent to the distortion of the current world market price by –26 per cent or –38 per cent of a genuine equilibrium price. The global welfare gain if sugar policies were completely liberalized has been estimated at US$ 4.7 or 6.3 billion. About three dozen developing countries would, however, lose a total of US$ 0.86 billion in export subsidies, which the EU and USA currently pay them each year under import quotas. The EU pays about US$ 400/tonne in producer subsidies and US$ 400/tonne in export subsidies to get rid of its surpluses in the world market – economic madness!

The political administration continues to harbour the prejudiced view that world market prices are irrelevant to the developing countries' domestic prices. This view has been refuted empirically (Mundlak and Larson 1992; FAO 1997). Domestic and world market prices of wheat correlate with an R^2 value of typically 0.80. If the exchange rate is added as an explanatory variable, the coefficient of determination rises to well over 0.90. Grain prices are, in turn, very closely correlated in the developing countries' domestic markets (Wehrheim and von Cramon-Taubadel, 1997). The push towards the liberalization of trade policies during the WTO's Uruguay Round further increased the integration of the national food markets into the world market – at least in the large coastal urban areas and the inland centres connected to them by modern infrastructure and in the catchment areas of the transport axes.

The world market prices of foodstuffs probably have a major impact on the prices of agricultural raw materials, primarily through product substitution at producer level. The cross-price elasticities between food prices and the supply of raw materials appear to be considerable. In an example for cocoa from Ghana they amounted to –0.39 related to the price of rice and –0.27 related to the price of maize (see Table A28). In aggregate form, the relation between food and agricultural raw material prices is as follows:

$$E_K \cdot V_{PN} \cdot A \cdot \frac{1}{E_N} = V_{PR}$$

where: E_K = cross-price elasticity of raw material supply in relation to food prices

E_N = price elasticity of demand for raw materials

V_{PN} = price distortion in the food market

V_{PR} = derived price distortion in the raw material market

A = area influenced by world market prices

A rough calculation using plausible elasticity assumptions underlines the relevance of the supposition.

Where E_K = –0.20

V_{PN} = –20 %

E_N = –0.25 and

A = 0.50

V_{PR} is –8 %. Given sufficient empirical data and an accurate analysis, it might very well be found that the price distortions in the world food markets cause major distortions in the agricultural raw material markets. In view of the importance of this relation for agricultural development, scientific studies of this aspect are needed to estimate as undistorted supply elasticities as possible for the main countries exporting agricultural raw materials, with account taken of cross-price effects. The development of food production against the background of producer price trends in sub-Saharan African countries clearly shows at least that there may be strong supplier-side substitution relations between food products and exported raw materials. It is evident, for one thing, that the producer prices of raw materials usually improved relative to food prices following structural adjustment and liberalization (Kherallah *et al.* 2000, p. 15). The real consumer and producer prices of foodstuffs fell, mainly because declining world market prices now had a greater impact on internal markets and more food aid was imported (Jayne *et al.* 1996). As a rule, raw material production then developed more favourably than food production (Seppälä 1996, p. 3 ff.).

The agricultural policies of the OECD countries thus also have a decisive influence on agricultural price ratios in the developing countries through the world markets, and this in respect of both food products and exported raw materials. In the past decade this led to serious market disturbance in importing developing countries where a number of products was concerned. One particular cause of this was the EU's producer and export subsidies. In a number of cases there was a significant lack of coherence between the EU's development cooperation measures and its agricultural export policy: grain and beef in West Africa, beef and canned vegetables in the RSA, sugar confectionary in Swaziland, milk powder in Jamaica, Tanzania and Brazil, tomato concentrate in West Africa (see Box 2).

Box 2 **Lack of coherence between the EU's agricultural and development policies**

The EU price and trade policy system that applied to the main agricultural products until 1992 comprised: support for domestic prices well above the world market price level, achieved by means of administered minimum prices, storage, export subsidies and import levies equivalent to the difference between world market prices and domestic prices. Sugar beet and milk were also subject to production quotas. Anticipating the forthcoming Uruguay Round of the WTO, the EU took the first steps towards the liberalization of its agricultural trade. From 1993 to 2000 the internal markets in cereals, oilseed and grain legumes were largely liberalized in price and trade policy terms, a first step also being taken in the case of beef and lamb. Among other things, this meant shifting the financing of subsidies from the consumer to the public purse. The EU's annual spending on agriculture rose from € 11 bn in the early 1980s to € 46 bn in 2002. Producers were not compensated entirely in keeping with the status quo; PSEs fell except in the case of beef and poultry meat:

	1986–88	2000
Wheat (%)	52	43
Oilseed (%)	59	30
Sugar (%)	60	49
Milk (%)	57	43
Beef (%)	59	75
Poultry meat (%)	14	57
All agricultural products (%)	44	38

The decision taken by the Council of Ministers in March 1999, known as 'Agenda 2000', continues the liberalization with partial compensation from the EU budget:

- beef: intervention prices –20 per cent in three stages from 2000, direct subsidies > +100 per cent;
- cereals and oilseed: intervention prices –15 per cent in three stages from 2000 to 2002, compensation in the form of non-crop-specific area subsidies, 10 per cent set-aside of grain area;
- milk: intervention prices –15 per cent in three stages from 2005/6, milk quotas +1.5 per cent, from 2005 direct subsidies per milk cow;

World market models show that the current world market prices of the most important foodstuffs are, depending on the product, 10 to 40 per cent below the equilibrium prices in liberalized world agricultural markets. The EU's agricultural policy is likely to be responsible for about a third of this. The EU's Agenda 2000 and steps taken by other industrialized countries toward liberalization during the current WTO Round may be a further step in correcting the distortion of the world markets, the scale and effects of which cannot, however, yet be foreseen. With its contribution to the effect of dumping on world market prices, the EU is failing to comply with the coherence requirement of its Maastricht Treaty on a global scale (Koester *et al.* 1995), since dumping by the industrialized countries is largely ruining the developing countries' prospects of becoming competitive in agricultural products. The result is a general and profound lack of coherence.

There are also product-specific cases of regionally discriminating export subsidies, each of which has resulted in serious disturbances in developing countries' domestic markets and threatened or prevented the success of development cooperation projects launched by the EU or its Member States. In the 1990s the following cases of this specific lack of coherence became known (Brandt 1995a; Eurostep 1999a, 1999b; OXFAM 2001a, 2001b):

- beef: West Africa, RSA, Namibia

- cereals: West Africa

- milk: Jamaica, Tanzania, Brazil, India

- tomato puree: West Africa

- chickens: Gambia

Despite the aforementioned steps taken by the EU towards liberalization, the pressure its agricultural policy exerts on world market prices is likely to continue by and large, since it can be seen that the 'product-linked' subsidies will by no means remain neutral in their effect on production but uphold major intensity incentives. Where total supply is price-inelastic, the removal of any such short-term incentives will be quickly made good by autonomous technical progress. Furthermore, the compensatory payments will make it possible to effect investments that have an impact on production and supply in the medium to long term, since all factor inputs are eventually variable and so have an effect on supply. The EU's grain production, for example, has grown by 4 m tonnes p.a. since 1992. The EU accounts for about 33 per cent of the agricultural subsidies paid out by the OECD countries. There is an added effect: the EU focuses what room for manoeuvre it still has to subsidize exports on the raw material component of its exports of processed agricultural products. The removal of import barriers in a number of developing countries in the context of the Uruguay Round or regional free trade agreements with developing countries enables EU processors to take advantage of the subsidies and their relative cost-efficiency (due to technology). Confectionery, bread, cakes, pastries, pasta goods and canned fruit and vegetables are the first examples of goods disturbing the markets of the RSA and other SADC member countries. The DFID quotes a description of the situation in Kenya: 'Just about all processed food ingredients used in Kenya are imported. This is because one can get quality goods for a lower price by importing subsidised products in bulk. There is no market for local people. They cannot compete with international subsidies. It's the subsidies that are keeping them poor.'[a]

On balance, it should be emphasized that the pressure on the world market prices of foodstuffs will continue. If the EU's agricultural policy system is transferred to the new, eastern European Member States after the adjustment of subsidy levels, the price distortions in the world food markets are bound to be further exacerbated because of increases in supply caused by the subsidies. With its latest Agriculture Act, the US Administration intends to increase direct subsidies to agriculture to about US$ 190 bn, or by about 70 per cent, over the next ten years. This step would similarly exacerbate the price distortions in the world cotton and food markets and have other adverse implications for the global agricultural system and the developing countries' agricultural policies.

Though perhaps not intended as such, this will have the effect of subsidy-assisted predatory competition, which the larger developing countries will not allow to pass without fighting back (tariff protection, direct subsidies, complaints to the WTO). There is also likely to be increasing competitive pressure on the processing of agricultural products in developing countries, since the USA too is pursuing the goal of expanding the export-oriented processing of agricultural raw materials.[b] This competitive pressure is unfair if the raw material inputs of processors in the industrialized countries correspond (as a result of direct subsidies) to the distorted level of world market prices.

Notes: [a] Association for Better Land Husbandry, Kenya, quoted in: DFID (2002), p. 19
[b] Congress of the US (1995)

In the wake of the Uruguay Round there has now been a partial removal of price support and related measures (tariff protection against imports and export subsidies). However, the resulting abolition of indirect producer subsidies, which the consumer paid, was largely offset by direct subsidies from the public purse (Tangermann 1999; Anderson *et al.* 2001; OXFAM 2001a). The EU in particular chose this course of direct subsidization in the form of land and livestock premiums combined with set-aside, production quotas and other dirigistic measures designed to limit production. However, viewed as a whole, these have been no more than first steps (see Table 6). As a weighted average of the OECD countries, the net protection coefficient has fallen from 1.61 to 1.43 since 1986–87, and the indirect or consumer-side share of total producer subsidies has fallen from 84 to 71 per cent, but total producer subsidies have fallen only from 39 to 34 per cent of gross producer output (including subsidies).

Table 6 OECD agricultural indicators

Indicator	1986–87	1998–2000	1998	1999	2000
Production (US$ bn)	559	651	668	653	637
PSE[a] (US$)	236	258	254	274	245
PSE[b] (%)	39	35	34	37	34
NPC[c]	1.61	1.46	1.44	1.51	1.43
TSE[d] (US$ bn)	298	341	339	356	327
TSE[e] (%)	53	52	51	55	52
Consumer share[f] (%)	67 (84)	55 (73)	55 (74)	57 (74)	53 (71)
Taxpayer share (%)	33 (16)	45 (27)	45 (26)	43 (26)	47 (29)

[a]   PSE (producer subsidy equivalent) = direct + indirect producer subsidies;
[b]   PSE (%) = PSE•100/(financial producer contribution + direct subsidies);
[c]   NPC (net protection coefficient) = (financial producer contribution + output-related subsidies) / world market parity producer contribution;
[d]   TSE (total support equivalent) = PSE + government contribution towards physical and non-physical infrastructure of agriculture + training;
[e]   TSE•100 / (financial producer contribution + direct subsidies);
[f]   Consumer share of TSE or PSE (%).

Source: OECD (2001b).

Although initial model calculations have found that the Uruguay Round liberalization measures have slightly increased prices in the world agricultural markets, the findings of available studies diverge considerably (Valdes and Zietz 1995). Only the actual production response in the next few years will tell. In the EU's case, for example, it must be assumed that product-related direct subsidies will have a major impact on production in the shape of the amount of land cultivated and the size of the dairy herd, since they reduce the financial risk and increase producers' time liquidity; furthermore, the payments can be attributed to the area of land that farmers devote to the growing of each crop. Both might offer an incentive to undertake cost-reducing investments and to bring input intensity closer to the theoretical optimum. With the given area-related compensatory payments it is, moreover, possible to arrange crop rotation so that it partly compensates for the declining use of nitrogenous fertilizers.

In March 2002 it became known that under its latest Agriculture Act the USA would raise direct subsidies in the coming decade to US$ 190 billion, i.e. by 70 per cent. The effects on development policy, the industrialized countries' agricultural policies, the global agricultural situation and the WTO process cannot yet be predicted in any detail, but they will be far-reaching. And already the call is going out in the old EU for higher compensatory payments for oilseed and durum wheat. There is no telling yet what the implications of the forthcoming eastward enlargement will be for the distortion syndrome in the world agricultural markets.

Initial experience indicates that, with the removal of the tariff protection for processed agricultural products introduced by the developing countries, competition from industrialized countries is breaking into the developing countries' markets and may threaten the initial successes they have achieved with industrialization (see Box 2).

It must be remembered in all this

> ... that the WTO member countries are free to set higher food safety standards than those included in the Codex Alimentarius, which was negotiated at international level.
>
> (Hauser 2001)

Here the industrialized countries in particular have an emergency brake, which they are already busy applying (von Braun *et al.* 2001).

The developing countries are preparing themselves differently for world markets and financial competition in their agricultural policies. The large Latin American and Asian countries have been able (at least until the late 1990s) to maintain moderate tariff protection for agricultural products and/or comparatively moderate subsidies, as the available PSE figures show (see Table A5). Some sub-Saharan African countries, on the other hand, have highly negative PSE figures for wheat, rice, soya, edible oil and milk.

The widely differing PSE figures for these groups of countries are an indication of fundamentally different general national agricultural policy designs in the world's major regions. The industrialized countries pursue their heavily subsidized agricultural policies, promote services, physical infrastructure and human capital for the agricultural sector and increase land productivity and livestock performance by 2 to 3 per cent p.a. The South American and Asian countries have moderately positive PSE figures, which at least partly offset the industrialized countries' dumping and the distortion of the world agricultural market prices. The agricultural policies of India, China, Indonesia and Vietnam support their agricultural sectors with tariff barriers and/or input subsidies. These countries are making serious efforts to organize and promote their agrotechnical progress and their services and human capital independently. Taking a subregional average, the sub-Saharan African countries have negative PSE figures for some foodstuffs. The domestic producer prices of foodstuffs are typically 20 per cent below the world market parity level.[3] This does not, however, take account of the effects of some countries' overvalued domestic currencies on price ratios. The neglect of agriculture and rural areas in development cooperation and the dominance of anti-agricultural price policies determine the overall agricultural policy situation in the sub-Saharan African countries: neglect of services, poor human capital formation, decaying rural infrastructure and stagnating productivity at a low level. And this has its own logic: where production for the market becomes unprofitable because of distorted producer price ratios and neglected productivity, the cost of promoting innovation and infrastructure can likewise be saved for the time being.

Distortions are also to be found in processing – in this case, among the developing countries. Some Asian textile exports are heavily subsidized. This begins as early as the stage at which cotton is produced domestically and continues in the subsidization of processing. Without regional tariff protection, therefore, it will hardly be possible to develop a cotton-processing industry in sub-Saharan Africa (Guttenberg-Jacobi 1993).

An objection to the call for the liberalization of the industrialized countries' agricultural policies that is frequently heard in the public debate is that those who actually stand to gain from such liberalization would not be the LDCs but a few efficient agricultural exporting countries in the South (Argentina, Uruguay, Brazil, Chile, Australia, New Zealand, RSA), since typical LDCs will derive little benefit from real rises in world market prices owing to a number of structural obstacles (centralized administrative system, undeveloped physical and non-physical infrastructure, inadequate level of agricultural production technology, management problems, inadequate capital endowment of rural activities, inefficient marketing systems). This argument cannot, of course, be dismissed where the short and medium term are concerned. But the incentives to the LDCs to improve their infrastructure and agricultural policy environment that will eventually emanate from improved price ratios should not be underestimated – especially if development cooperation becomes involved by placing the emphasis appropriately. In this respect it must, of course, be remembered that the world market models referred to above are based on supply and demand elasticities, i.e. on historical figures. Beyond the medium term of three to five years they do not permit a reliable forecast, especially if sweeping changes are made to agricultural policy on the supply side. Thus if the distortion margins of world market prices and the industrialized countries' additional export subsidies, which are discriminatory in terms of import regions, were siphoned off in the LDCs, import prices could be raised to a level at which the domestic food products in local markets again had a chance to compete and develop. In addition, innovation-assisted production policies are urgently needed for agricultural raw materials to enable foreign exchange to be earnt. On the one hand, as world demand is very price-inelastic, this would be to the detriment of world market prices; on the other hand, shares of the world market, especially those of the sub-Saharan African countries, have become so small that the economic advantage of such a policy is obvious – especially if the opportunities presented by modern yield-increasing production methods are seized.[4] The international community cannot expect the sub-Saharan African countries to continue forgoing the opportunities offered by an active policy on agricultural raw materials.

7   Neglect of agriculture in the sub-Saharan African countries

Owing to a policy of excessive siphoning off of resources from the agricultural sector, of indirect and direct subsidization of industry and of hypertrophic public consumption, the growth processes of sub-Saharan African economies first came to a halt in the 1970s – while public and foreign debts rose sharply (Lipton 1977; World Bank 1982; Brandt *et al.* 1986). After the World Bank's Structural Adjustment Programmes (1983–95) had initiated the abolition of subsidies, the correction of distorted domestic price ratios, the deregulation of markets, the reduction of public consumption, debt rescheduling and/or the cancellation of public foreign currency debts, the recipient–donor community took, as new concepts (SIPs and PRSPs) were introduced, to promoting the towns and cities and the urban sector in a more biased way than could ever have been envisaged. The new urban bias is essentially donor-induced. Donor contributions in the context of development cooperation, the import of foodstuffs at unrivalled low prices and the siphoning off of proceeds from exports of raw materials, if not by means of export taxes, then through inefficient marketing systems now organized by the private sector, are, with difficulty, keeping the heads of the urban population above water, while the rural population has been plunged into a deep economic and social crisis in which its very existence is at stake. Added factors are – and this is a crucial difference from the 1970s – legal uncertainty, an escalation of crimes of violence and a multitude of violent conflicts: as recently as 1980 Nairobi, Johannesburg, Accra, Abidjan and Dakar were still functioning cities; living in them today is like living in limbo, especially for the poor slum-dwellers.

Nor, conceptually, does the new urban bias have a viable future. The population growth rates of the sub-Saharan African urban areas are, at four to five per cent, well above comparable figures for other regions of the world (see Table 7). The financial resources needed for housing and infrastructure are not available, and the slums are spreading. The processing industry can, as a rule, survive only in domestic market niches and is developing at totally inadequate growth rates. Industrial value added as a proportion of the GNPs of sub-Saharan African economies fell from 38.2 per cent in 1980 to 29.2 per cent in 1999. Where are the jobs to come from? The result is mass poverty and a struggle for survival in the informal sectors of the towns and cities (Amis and Rakodi 1994; De Haan 1997).

Table 7 Annual urban population growth rates, 1985–90 to 2005–2010 (per cent)

Period	Region					
	East Africa	Central Africa	Southern Africa	West Africa	Asia	South America
1985–90	5.66	4.10	2.90	5.25	3.60	2.74
1990–95	5.55	4.60	2.87	5.08	3.22	2.38
1995–00	5.15	4.12	2.92	4.80	3.03	2.06
2000–05	4.92	4.36	2.91	4.48	2.80	1.83

Source: UN (1998), p. 120 ff.

In the medium term, development policy and development cooperation will not avoid the classical realization that in pre- and early-industrial economies growth of productivity, production and incomes in agriculture form the irreplaceable basis of industrialization and poverty reduction (see Chapter 12.2). And this is all the truer as long as infant industries are not yet internationally competitive (Mellor 1995a,b; Priebe and Hankel 1980). For the time being, then, it can be said:

> The absence of a clear development strategy for peasant farmers is one of the main causes of Africa's decline. The governments are almost entirely composed of city-dwellers who are interested in the welfare of the capital and the army, in which they invest state monies.
>
> (von Lucius 2001)

Of course, through the chain of effects consisting of resource degradation, declining incomes and underemployment at such natural marginal locations as the northern parts of the Sahel countries, population growth also exerts considerable rural–urban migration pressure, which has an impact just as (but also because) economic and agricultural policy does (see Box 3).

Box 3 Carrying capacity estimates for the Sahel

The ecological carrying capacity was calculated at 21m people for firewood requirements and estimated at 36 m people for arable and livestock farming. In 1997, 50 m people were living in the Sahel. 36 m of them in rural areas. In 2010 the total population will be about 73 m, the rural population about 46 m. The carrying capacity for firewood will then be exceeded by 250 per cent, that for arable and livestock farming by 28 per cent. However, these average figures fail to reveal widely differing regional situations as regards primary resource overuse. In the subhumid zone (more than 800 mm annual rainfall) the effects of overuse are still reasonably tolerable, while in the semi-arid zone (600 to 800 mm annual rainfall) they are already serious:

Country	Rainfall (mm p.a.)	Agric. & livestock (m people)	Firewood (m people)	Population (m people) 1981 Rural	1981 Total	1997 Rural	1997 Total	2010 Rural	2010 Total
Saharan	<200	1.0	0.1	0.8	0.8				
Sahelo-Saharan				1.0	1.0				
Sahelian	200–400	3.9	0.3	3.9	4.0				
Sahelo-Sudan	400–600	8.7	6.0	11.1	13.1				
Sudanian	600–800	8.9	7.4	6.6	8.1				
Sudano-Guinean	800	13.8	7.1	3.6	4.0				
Total	–	36.3	20.9	27.0	31.0	36.4	50.3	46.2	73.3

It should be remembered, however, that much of what is considered constant in carrying capacity estimates like those above is not in fact, or need not remain, constant: per capita consumption, production methods and intensities. population distribution in the geographical area, level of economic differentiation and division of labour, social standards and institutions and practical economic behaviour.

Source: World Bank (2000b); Brandt and Neubert (2000).

Part III Poverty reduction in the conceptual experience of agricultural development

8 Role of agriculture in the early-industrial phase of economic development

8.1 Excursus – towards an understanding of the subject matter

The theoretical and conceptual ideas of the first development decade (1955–65) placed the emphasis on the government promotion of industry, while neglecting and exploiting agriculture. What was overlooked with this inference by analogy from Soviet experience was, firstly, that the USSR was able to build on the considerable success achieved in industrializing Tsarist Russia to a level which had not been reached in 1955 by any developing country apart from two or three in South America; secondly, developing countries with traditional peasant structures had nothing like the state power or an urban elite so well educated in the humanities and the sciences as the Soviets had employed to cope with capital formation, technical progress and their model of societal organization; thirdly, the inertia of the developing countries' pre-industrial social and economic structure was underestimated.

For the researchers and concept designers of the 1950s the development problem was essentially a matter of calculating how to form capital, using three or four variables, because they thought they knew what was in principle necessary: government-controlled investment of agricultural and foreign savings in the industrial sector and socio-economic structural change induced by industrial growth. The leading minds among them were something like chief ideologists, for they had very little idea backed by experience of traditional societies or the specific features of production methods in tropical agriculture. Their fundamentalist view of industry was, of course, as admissible as other designs produced by the social sciences, as long as they remained deductions, but – and this leap occurred in a trice – when it became the prescription for the socio-economic development of whole countries and areas of the world and was, moreover, put into practice, results were bound to be disappointing (Dumont 1962; Brandt 1965).

In some cases considerable time was to elapse before the industrial fundamentalism of the first few years was adjusted or abandoned in practical development work: it was a process that did not begin in India and Indonesia, for example, until 1965–66, in China until 1978 and in the sub-Saharan African countries until 1983. Except in the Asian countries, which have long pursued a successful agricultural development policy to offset the adverse social and economic effects of the excessive industrialization and urbanization of old, the neglect of agriculture, the processing industry and services in rural areas persists to this day – especially in the sub-Saharan African countries. To the detriment of the development of many economies, the anti-agrarian ideology was supported by a highly disruptive factor, the effects of which favoured the tendency towards urban bias in development policy for many years and continues to do so in sub-Saharan Africa today: since the early 1970s the generous subsidies granted under the agricultural policies of certain industrialized countries have had a profound retarding effect on the agricultural and economic development of many of today's LDCs through distorted world market prices, plentiful food aid and the subsequent neglect of developing countries' agricultural policies.

Despite all this, both academic and practical development policy has learnt a great deal over the past four decades about a wide range of instrumental issues and, no doubt, the theoretical and conceptual aspects. It is largely agreed today – in theory and from more recent empirical experience at least – that agricultural development forms the basis of economic and societal progress at the development stage of initial industrialization. The relationship between the agricultural and industrial sectors is recognized as being distinctly complementary in the process of social and economic growth: 'They must be nurtured by the state with the same care and maintained side by side at the same level and with the same strength. To raise one and want to depress the other is to paralyse one foot so that the other may stride ahead. ... It is a frivolous dispute over what should have preference for the good of the state, the factories or the fields, but one in which practical and theoretical statesmen have so often engaged in recent times' (Thaer 1809–12, p. 161 ff.). By the mid-1980s this had also been appreciated by contemporary researchers: "... the functions which the agricultural and industrial sectors must perform in order for growth to occur are totally interdependent" (Hayami and Ruttan 1985, p. 40). It was not, however, so widely appreciated as to have been able to prevent extreme bias in the allocation of development cooperation and domestic resources to industry and the service sectors in the urban areas of many LDCs during the past decade. Seen from the angle of what is known now, the extreme urban bias in the deployment of development cooperation resources is particularly hard to understand – at first glance at least.

There is no viable theory capable of providing a reasonably sound explanation for the causes and effects of the socio-economic development process and so enabling the development policy practitioner to guide this process safely and purposefully. Development policy, understood as an analytical task, has a similar cognitive subject and thus similar cognitive problems to the writing of history. The historian's appreciation of the limits to his ability to understand the causes and effects of the development process is also true of development policy once it looks beyond narrow aspects of the problem as a whole:

We are all reluctant philosophers of history, whether we like it or not. The only decision we are entitled to take is on whether we make our view of history as explicit as possible, expound it in context and bring it into line with the known facts or whether we intend to assert it more or less unconsciously and unsystematically. If we do the latter, we run the risk of passing off certain ideas as 'truisms' and then using them untested and uncritically.

(Gellner 1995, p. 1)

If 'view of history' is replaced by 'ideas on the development process', for example, this statement is also entirely true of development policy. The development process cannot be accurately explained with a few variables. Its prophets, however, are still resorting to the old trick of reducing the problem to two or three 'causes' and suggesting that the available resources and policy instruments are having a profound effect. The theoretical constructs then become in a trice prescriptions for the socio-economic development of whole countries and areas of the world. Implementation usually produces unexpected and sometimes disappointing results.[1]

Although it would be taking scepticism about the transparency and feasibility of the development process too far to forgo explanatory, and thus reductive, auxiliary arrangements (because working hypotheses or conceptions must be accounted for), it should still be emphasized that development policy is, in a very distinctive way, an art doctrine, a patchwork, so to speak, of theorems, experience of specific issues and working hypotheses. Given a limited understanding of the causes and effects of the development process and in view of the vicissitudes of the political environment (in both recipient and donor countries), it can show the actors no more than the approximate direction they should take – for the time being in each case. There is, realistically, no other way of proceeding: goal-oriented action to the best of one's albeit limited knowledge and with limited resources – empirical process – then reappraisal, etc.

It goes without saying that it is not only the ways in which a socio-economic system responds during this sequence of events that can change but also the political priorities set and assessments made by development cooperation actors. There is ample practical evidence of this. Consequently, deciding where the emphasis should lie in development policy, as in the development cooperation administration's sectoral or country concepts, amounts to little more than stock-taking in its prescriptive range beyond the budget allocation. Thus one of the main determinants of the changes to the list of German development cooperation measures in recent years has been the cutbacks in other donors' measures and the learning and opinion-forming processes taking place in recipient countries. It is, in any case, going too far to think that the partner countries' policies can be influenced substantially and in the long term, since the bilateral donors use relatively modest resources and play no more than a supportive or cautiously corrective role in the solution of individual problems, but they do not exercise power of any consequence. On the whole, development cooperation is part of the development process – often having a favourable catalytic effect – but it is not its master.

The practical importance of these statements can hardly be emphasized enough. The laborious process of gaining experience, the conceptual vicissitudes in development cooperation in the past 40 years (see Figure 1) and the present search for theories and concepts for the sub-Saharan problem should be recalled in this context. It ranges from the price and incentive fundamentalism that was apparent in the World Bank's structural adjustment policy to propositions derived from the philosophy of history on the peasantry's social self-isolation and refusal to yield to the ruling domestic elites (Hyden 1983; Kabou 1991). A change of conception is not, therefore, proof of previous incompetence, but the necessary consequence of changed circumstances and newly gained insights.

8.2   Agricultural contributions to economic development

Since towns, the state, trade, manufacturing industry and a money economy have existed, it has not escaped the notice of people engaged in economic activity, and especially the political thinkers among them, that agricultural market conditions interact closely with the other sectors or sources of income in the economy as a whole. According to an old German saying, if farmers have money, the whole world has money. This vulgar-physiocratic conclusion, whether originating in the sixteenth or the nineteenth century, verifies it. And how movements in grain prices relate to crop yields (weather, production methods), war, peace and foreign trade has served people of all ranks as a topic of conversation – right after the weather. The classical agricultural economist Albrecht D. Thaer at least had very clear ideas on the determinants of prices and on the supply of and demand for cereals and labour (Thaer 1809–12). In Friedrich Aereboe's work the systematics of economic interactions between agriculture, the rest of the national economy and the world economy is already largely developed (Aereboe 1928), and he knew how to use it in a dynamic context. Following in the tradition of this thinking is an essay by his pupil Karl Brandt, who as early as 1965 was beginning to recognize the erroneous courses being taken by many developing countries, the consequences of which are still having an impact today (Brandt 1965). Aereboe was already focusing on such aspects of agricultural multifunctionality as public health, demographic role, employment and domestic demand.

Concepts for agriculture and rural areas[a]	Model	Measures	Weaknesses	Core findings
Community Development (1955–65)	Agriculture and traditional rural society are obstacles to modernization for a dynamic industrial sector.	• Activation of peasant self-help • Breakdown of traditions • Young people employed as 'change agents'	• Importance of land ownership system, income distribution and price, trade, land tenure and innovation policies were overlooked	Efficient agricultural policy, know-how, legitimacy and physical resources are needed.
Green Revolution (1965–75)	Increase in productivity through technical progress and support services are the key to growth in agriculture.	• Economic incentives through price, market and trade policies • Promotion of technical progress and innovations • Agricultural extension and credit, moderate import substitution and training	• Concept successful only in Asia • No direct account taken of inequality • Adverse ecological effects (salinization and exhaustion of soil)	Instruments used to increase production can be guided and are effective, but this does not mean ecological and social issues are automatically considered.
Integrated Rural Development (1975–85)	Rural development is impeded by constraints in (non-) physical infrastructure. Centrally planned and implemented multisectoral approach in rural areas is intended to take account of this.	• Allocation of more resources to social sectors (health, education) • Distribution-oriented project policy at district level	• Adverse environment (land tenure system, price policy) was not changed • Multisectoral approach too complex for centralized implementation • Excessive coordination and organization effort required	Coordination at local level is imperative for successful development strategy; sustainability of financing must be taken into account.
Structural Adjustment Programmes (1985–95)	Distorted economic environment disturbs economic balance and thus rural development.	• Correction of distorted exchange rates • Deregulation of markets • Privatization of agricultural extension services • Liberalization of price, market and trade policies	• Distorted world market prices persisted and affected domestic markets • Private services were not an efficient substitute for public services • Multinational transformation chains	Free market is precondition for development, but scarcity situation must not be distorted from outside; efficient substitutes for public services are not easy to find.
Sector Investment Programmes (since 1995)	Concentration on one sector, developing countries responsible for programme conception, donors bow to recipient's conception in coordinated manner.	• Comprehensive, clear strategy for agricultural sector, infrastructure, education and agricultural innovation, capacity-building • Donor coordination • Employment of domestic experts	• Possible overtaxing of existing agricultural administrations • Danger of donor dominance and of emergence of parallel administrative structures • Multinationals firmly installed	Wide range of Sector Investment Programmes cannot be implemented without functional decentralization and professionally adequate financial planning. Agricultural sector hitherto neglected by donors and recipients.

Figure 1 Concepts of agricultural development policy, 1955–2002

[a] The various phases overlap by about three years in each case.

Source: Gennes and Schwethelm (2002; unpublished and unfiled seminary laboration): group work forming part of the GDI's post-graduate programme.

The post-war debate brought further clarification. The starting point was provided by the empirically proven idea that sectoral shares of aggregate value added change in a characteristic way as per capita income rises. The relative decline of the agricultural sector in terms of its value added and its labour and capital resources was recognized as being, in accordance with Engel's Law, a necessary consequence of rising real incomes. Labour migrated from agriculture in pursuit of the productivity-induced higher wages in the non-agricultural sectors. Relatively favourable interest on capital in the urban areas acted as an incentive to transfer some net agricultural savings. In agriculture too, an increase in productivity due to technical advances and capital intensification was the result of and precondition for the transfer of factors and a balanced transformation process throughout the economy. Johnstonian systematics (Johnston and Kilby 1975), which can already be called 'classical', cites the following economic contributions by the agricultural sector to economic growth:

- Resource contributions

  - The agricultural sector releases labour for the enlargement of labour capacity in the secondary and tertiary sectors.
  - In the long term it tends to contribute savings to the initial formation of capital in the non-agricultural sectors.
  - It finances its own net investments from its own financial savings and through labour accumulation.
  - Through its net exports and savings it contributes to the availability of foreign exchange for industry and services. This enables capital goods and inputs that cannot yet be manufactured economically by domestic industry to be procured.

- Market contributions

  - The agricultural sector demands services and manufactured products.
  - It supplies foodstuffs and agricultural raw materials.

Each of the two sectors, of course, represents a submarket for the other's sales. Industrialization and macroeconomic growth, which is still vital to the developing countries today in view of their population growth rates, are, if only for this reason, scarcely possible without agricultural growth.[2] The interdependence of the two sectors naturally becomes the closer the more the conditions of a closed economy prevail in a given case and thus the less opportunities are (or can be) seized to secure the purchases and sales of one or other sector and some of the required foreign exchange and capital through foreign trade or foreign debt. A shortage of foreign exchange as a result of poor industrial competitiveness links agricultural and industrial growth – an argument against unrestricted trade liberalization at a time of badly distorted world agricultural markets that should be taken seriously. The continuing deterioration of their barter terms of trade during the past 40 years has indeed been one of the factors that have made agriculturally dominated LDCs, or their economies, dependent on transfers of finance and manpower, credit raised abroad, food aid and subsidized food imports. The decline in net capital imports in the past decade has, however, constantly reduced their import capacity. In this situation intersectorally balanced agricultural and economic development is likely to gain in importance again in these countries in the next few years.

As regards the European countries' experience of development in the 19th century, Bairoch shows that the conditions of quasi-closed economies were prevalent, and this because of the major obstacles encountered by the grain trade owing to transport costs, the lack of industrial competitiveness with British industry, which was far superior in quality and costs, and a serious shortage of foreign exchange. Industrialization was at first inward-oriented and was preceded by an initial increase in agricultural productivity lasting 30 to 50 years (Bairoch 1976, p. 466 ff.; especially p. 472 ff.). However, there are factors that tend to loosen the sectoral interdependence in today's developing countries, namely rising coastal urbanization leading to cities with over a million inhabitants, accompanied by real increases in transformation and especially transport costs for domestic agricultural products and by the superior financial competitiveness of food imports that are heavily subsidized (by industrialized countries). Although the social sciences, which are at present conceptually dominant, like to theorize on the basis of transport ideally costing nothing, agriculture linked to markets is heavily influenced by the transport cost factor – at least under conditions of pre- and early-industrial infrastructure (see Chapter 13.1.2). The studies of Heinrich von Thünen, the father of agricultural economics, might be recalled in this context. The aforementioned factors cause a strong tendency to separate urban demand for food from domestic supply. They weaken the contributions to the market made by domestic agriculture in general (Brandt 1994, p. 43 ff.).

8.3   Factor proportions theorem of agricultural development

The driving forces behind the intersectoral movement of factors thus include price differences. Real wage differences and the hope of a job attract young people to the city (Todaro 1981), and urban investment opportunities have much the same effect on domestic savings. Factor prices in rural areas tend to follow. The changes in price ratios now have a profound influence on the development of agriculture, and especially on its factor combination, production methods and organization of production. This has been repeatedly shown and proved in theory and empirical practice since the early nineteenth century.

Albrecht D. Thaer and Heinrich von Thünen had already pointed to the influence of factor price ratios on the intensity of agriculture (Thaer 1809–12, p. 104; von Thünen 1990, p. 545 ff.). In his theory of management and agricultural policy Friedrich Aereboe described the factor proportions theorem of agricultural development in great detail in the 1920s (Brandt 1994, p. 116 ff.). His understanding of the means of increasing intensity and achieving scientific and technical progress in agriculture led Aereboe to take an anti-Malthusian, optimistic view of productivity. He referred to the following ways of increasing agricultural production and productivity (Aereboe 1919, p. 262 ff.):

- substitution of arable land for forest and pastureland;
- restriction of fallow land;
- use of stable manure and intercropping;
- deeper cultivation of arable land;
- introduction of new fertilization, sowing, maintenance and harvesting techniques;
- expansion of intensive crops;
- making the earth's surface free for the growing of foodstuffs by using the resources of the earth's interior.

Speaking as an agricultural economist with links to practical farming, Aereboe concludes: 'It is not the land question that primarily determines man's and the nation's diet: it is the means of exploiting the land and man's knowledge which do this' (Aereboe 1925, p. 11 ff.). Even today this will continue to be true of the next two or three decades, provided that secondary energy prices do not rise much above their present level in real terms.

After the Second World War Herlemann took up the subject again with his theory of the stages of agro-technical progress (Herlemann 1954; Herlemann / Stamer 1958). His neo-classical design is based on three conclusions:

The organization of agricultural production in individual economies seeks equilibrium within the meaning of the neo-classical theory of production, which exists as a result of the least-cost combination of the factors of production land, labour and capital at optimum production intensity (see Chapter 10.1).

Factor price ratios depend on agriculture's land and labour resources and on the stage reached in the economy's development; however, they are modified by agricultural price and trade policy: net exports raise the relative level of producer prices, the intensity of production and, of the factor prices, primarily ground rent.

In the development of the economy the agricultural sectors typically pass through stages of factor combination and production technology corresponding to their initial land and labour resources.

In the course of industrialization densely populated countries (e.g. Germany and Japan) proceed from a pre-industrial 'compression stage' of labour-intensive agriculture to an 'intensification stage', in which yields increase as a result of biological and technical advances and rising capital and labour intensity. This is followed by the 'mechanization stage', in which manual labour is replaced by capital. This development sets in as soon as wages begin to rise appreciably in relation to the prices of capital goods and interest rates. Finally, there is the 'enlargement stage', in which the increase in areas farmed, full mechanization and the migration of labour are the determining factors. Besides the rise in the relative cost of labour, the relative stagnation of demand, as explained in Engel's Law, now has a retarding effect on real product prices. The 'treadmill effect' asserts itself.

In thinly populated countries (e.g. the USA and New Zealand) the 'enlargement stage', or acquisition of land, comes first. Owing to the relative scarcity of labour, initial industrialization rapidly leads to a rise in the relative cost of labour. The export of agricultural products and the import of capital reinforce this trend, and the agricultural sector enters the 'mechanization stage'. Finally, rising domestic demand for and the export of agricultural products and the exhaustion of free land reserves lead to price ratios that give rise to the 'intensification stage'. This is again followed by the treadmill effect.

What the two patterns of development have in common are population growth, rising demand for agricultural products, a relative decline in the cost of capital, and agricultural research and industry that produce innovations to overcome shortages, e.g. the farm machinery industry in the USA and the chemical industry in the German Reich. Eventually factor combinations and production methods become more similar: the densely populated country substitutes capital for labour by means of mechanization, while the thinly populated country increases yields, i.e. substitutes capital for land. In the 1970s Hayami and Ruttan finally reformulated the factor proportions theorem of agricultural development in a broadly based cross-section analysis (Hayami and Ruttan 1971, 1985) and showed that even agricultural research tends to focus on shortages and so produces cost-efficient production methods.

It should also be pointed out that in the practice of agricultural development complementary effects between biological and mechanical/technical advances have been exploited at all times. Although price ratios determine the main technological tendency, land- and labour-substituting innovation patterns are in principle by no means mutually exclusive. Thus the work involved in the 'intensive farming" of the German Reich from 1865 to 1950 could not have been performed without the achievements of mechanization using draught animals (see Table A15). A parallel, recent example is the mechanization of Asian rice-growing with the two-wheel tractor, accompanied by a rapid increase in yields.

Fundamentally speaking, energy is, as it were, the common medium of modern agricultural development: in one case energy primarily replaced the production factor land through the use of capital; in the other it replaced labour. Thus Central European agriculture currently consumes >700 kg oil equivalents of secondary energy per hectare and year; US agriculture consumes >1000 kg/ha. A future of energy-substituting technical progress is not yet visible from the price ratios – but it may one day become a dire necessity for political reasons (Pimentel, undated).

The pattern of the interdependence of agriculture and non-agriculture and the factor proportions theorem of agricultural development largely determine the view taken in this study. Nonetheless, the full significance of conditions with respect to social institutions and of the main aspects of the accumulation of social and human capital is taken into account: otherwise it is impossible to deduce approaches to poverty-oriented agricultural development that are relevant in practice.

9   Agricultural policy conceptions 1955–2000

From the beginning of the Korean War the democratic industrialized countries and the Communist dictatorships faced each other, full of distrust and armed to the teeth. As the West's supreme power, the USA pursued (under the Truman Doctrine of March 1947) an effective policy of containing the Communist dictatorships of the Eurasian continent. The decisive theoretical and practical impulses for development cooperation between the western democracies and what later came to be known as the 'Third World' also came from the USA as a complement to the containment policy.

Development cooperation was meant to promote socio-economic development in the countries of the 'Third World' so that they would not try their luck with a Communist dictatorship. The recent history of the People's Republic of China, North Vietnam, Cuba and other countries had shown, after all, that peasant societies – especially those with experience of a feudalistic agricultural structure – could quickly embrace Communism.

9.1   Community development (1955–65)

The first development decade was characterized by the idea that industrialization was not only the goal of economic development but also the way to achieve it. The paradigmatic influence of the Soviet model dominated the scene. The slogan ran: "Industrialization is the best policy for agricultural development." The agricultural sector was thus seen less as a market for the products of domestic industry and a supplier of agricultural products, labour and capital than as a stronghold of societal resistance to modernization, which urbanization and industrialization would overcome in due course.

Three myths and one empirical fact in particular accounted for the agricultural pessimism that went with the dominant industrial fundamentalism. Firstly, traditional agriculture was perceived with the prejudice of inverse supply behaviour, dating as far back as the age of colonial plantation agriculture (Boeke 1953). The corresponding theory of the traditional small farmer rooted in subsistence, trying to avoid seeing his holding integrated into the market and so reacting to real producer price or wage increases with reduced labour or product supply, justified both the indirect taxation of the agricultural sector that consisted in the siphoning off of producer prices and the neglect of agricultural innovation and structural policy. The parallel idea of labour in agriculture having a marginal product of zero and of a corresponding reservoir of surplus labour or a completely elastic supply of labour as against industry's demand for labour went a step further (Lewis 1954; Fei and Ranis 1964). Another popular idea was that the capital coefficients of agricultural production are comparatively very limited: despite high taxation, investment in expansion in agriculture could still be effected without difficulty through the investment of labour. It was not until the early 1980s that this erroneous assessment was finally corrected.[3]

The Prebisch thesis of the long-term decline in the real prices of agricultural and mineral raw materials endorsed the industrial fundamentalism of the first development decade (Prebisch 1959; Leibenstein 1957). The Nobel Prize winner A.W. Lewis included labour-intensive industrial products:

> The terms of trade are bad only for tropical products, whether agricultural or industrial, and are bad because the market pays tropical unskilled labour, whatever it may be producing, a wage that is based on an unlimited reservoir of low-productivity food producers.
>
> (Lewis 1955, p. 281)

This assessment has in effect proved true of both raw materials and labour-intensive industrial products until the present day.

This view and the agricultural pessimism mentioned above gave rise to the import-substituting industrial fundamentalism of the first development decade. Its theoreticians regarded the agricultural sector and rural population as a source of capital, labour and food for the industrial sector (see, in particular, Hirschmann 1958). The expected contribution of capital to industrialization was to be achieved indirectly through depressed producer prices in the agricultural sector and excessively high consumer prices of industrial products. However, the dependence of expanding agricultural supply on prices, innovation and investment and the roles of the agricultural sector and rural population as buyers of industrial products and a source of employment for a rapidly growing population were overlooked. In the end the agricultural and industrial sectors blocked each other. The agricultural sector stagnated because it was neglected by innovation policy, and the industrial sector stagnated because of the wage-increasing effect of the ensuing rise in food prices and/or the lack of foreign exchange due to food imports, which caused corresponding production bottlenecks in the industrial sector. The concept of community development adapted in every way to the priority of industrial development, and the myths referred to above justified this: large economically untapped reserves of labour in the agricultural sector, inverse agricultural supply and low capital/output ratios in the agricultural sector obviated the need for special efforts that would have meant competing with the industrial sector for resources. It was enough from this standpoint for the resistance to innovation of a rural population bogged down in traditional standards and institutions to be broken and the physical and non-physical infrastructure of the villages to be developed through self-help.

The chosen means were visual and verbal propaganda and the organization and guidance of self-help groups in the villages. It was thought that 'pep talks' on modernization and guidance by committed young people would be enough to break the 'ice of tradition' and initiate a process of self-help from the bottom up. The importance of policy on prices and trade, policy on land tenure and innovation and policy on services and cooperatives was overlooked in the meantime.

The results were disappointing – especially in terms of poverty reduction, whether among the peasants or the consumers.

Economically, CD displayed a double weakness. First, it enlarged social services more rapidly than the production of rural incomes. Secondly, it could not significantly improve the condition of the distressed poor, the sharecroppers and laborers. Both aspects of rural poverty, low production and unjust distribution, were not significantly changed by CD.

(Holdcroft 1978, p. 27)

Although self-help generated some apparent prosperity before it collapsed, the social standards, institutions and structures did not change, agricultural workers, tenants and smallholders refused to cooperate, and the absence of agro-technical innovations led to stagnant or even declining food supply and enormous food problems in the urban areas. This was particularly true of the Indian subcontinent, where land is relatively scarce and where only extensive food aid prevented famine on a disastrous scale in the 1960s (Kumar 1987)

... after its first decade of operations the CD Programme had not significantly altered the basic conditions of rural life in India. Abject poverty, malnutrition and ill health and above all India's worsening food crisis had but one remedy – a larger production from the land.

(Coombs and Ahmed 1974)

In Latin America – with the exception of a few countries – the feudalistic land tenure systems changed not one iota. In Africa rural poverty continued to be fairly tolerable for a further decade thanks to the traditional land tenure systems, plentiful land, parastatal marketing organizations that were still efficient for the moment and reasonably 'fair' producer price policies.

The inward-oriented industrial development of the first decade failed primarily because of intersectoral imbalances: indiscriminate, excessively high tariff protection for the industrial sector, the resulting unfavourable terms of trade for agriculture and the rural economy and the neglect of innovation and structural policy for agriculture. Vietnam today demonstrates that a model of industrialization which enjoys selective tariff protection and is inward-oriented and reasonably balanced macroeconomically and intersectorally can be highly successful. However, the collapse of the world market prices of raw coffee due to 'oversupply' from Vietnamese growers must be seen as collateral damage. This underlines how important it is for the industrialized countries at last to liberalize their agricultural policies, so that the developing countries may earn more foreign exchange by their own efforts.

9.2 Green revolution (1965–75)

Against a background of stagnating production and chronically rising grain prices in South Asia, agricultural development policy was reoriented in theory and practice. T.W. Schultz, who was later to win the Nobel Prize, was the leading reformer (Schultz 1964). He put forward a concept of agricultural development policy that assigns to agriculture a key role in a growth concept based on innovations in production technology and on economic incentives (see also Krishna 1967, p. 497 ff.). His main propositions read as follows:

- Owing to agriculture's market contributions, economic development needs agricultural growth that avoids rising food prices and generates domestic demand for industrial products.
- Agriculture can make its essential factor and market contributions to economic growth only if price incentives, technical advances and investment permit sufficient growth of production and productivity for this.
- Traditional peasant farmers are economically efficient but poor. They optimize their resource use to ensure a balance between profits and risks. Relative producer prices thus have 'correct' effects on the organization of production, agricultural supply and agricultural development (investment, innovations, productivity, incomes), which are decisive in the long term where there is a complementary innovation policy.
- The readiness of traditional peasant farmers to adopt innovations is determined by their calculation of risks and profits. They react 'correctly' to economic incentives (changes to prices and productivity).
- The marginal product of their labour is clearly positive.
- A price, market and trade policy that offers sufficient economic incentives is the initiator of and basic requirement for economically compatible agricultural development.
- Scientific and technical advances in agricultural production that offset shortages, plus extension and training for the rural population, are, together with price incentives, the lever for agricultural development that will be crucial in the long term.
- The ideology and practice of centrally managed large farms lead to highly inefficient agricultural production.

The explanatory strength of Schultz's ideas on traditional peasant farming and the correctness of his systemic concept of agricultural development policy, which relies on the exploitation of instrumental complementary effects or interactions, has since been repeatedly confirmed.[4]

Moreover, the traditional lines of this thinking date back to the debate on agricultural policy in the 1920s. There are, in particular, many affinities with the work of Friedrich Aereboe, to which subsequent literature has scarcely referred (Aereboe 1925, 1928). In Boserup's theory of population-induced agricultural development seen from a historical angle, in which a distinction is made between periods of scientific and technical progress and periods of pre-scientific and pre-technical progress (see Box 4), Schultz's approach is extended to include interactions with social change.

Schultz's incentive-, training- and innovation-oriented theory of agricultural development, known in the literature as the 'high pay-off model', laid the foundations for the concept of the Green Revolution, which dominated the agricultural policies mainly of the Indian subcontinent and East and South-East Asia during the second development decade (1965–75) and beyond and continues to influence the development of general rural production to this day. The aim here is to increase yields through the intensification of capital and labour using biological and technical advances (seed, commercial fertilizers).

Small-scale irrigation and appropriate mechanization usually complemented this package. It was implemented with agricultural extension and short-term loans. Success depended on agricultural price ratios and attainable advances in productivity that gave farmers strong economic incentives to adopt the seed-and-commercial-fertilizer technology. Although producer prices usually fell after the successful adoption of the innovations, sufficiently strong profit incentives to retain and further improve the new production methods persisted because of import substitution, rising demand for cereals and the reductions in production costs due to the innovations, since peasant supply is ultimately guided (notwithstanding socio-institutional influences) by gross margins and their risk spreads, which depend, of course, on a wide range of prices and on physical productivity.

The World Bank's project policy in this field was known for short as the 'minimum package deal', not only in Asia but also in Latin America and Africa. The brilliant success of production in Asia and Latin America contrasted with failure in Africa in all but a few exceptional cases. Here the Green Revolution was restricted to enclaves of large commercial farms in the East and South of the continent. The semi-commercialized small farms were not promoted but neglected. The causes of the failure lay partly in the increasingly unfavourable agricultural policy environment (anti-agricultural price, trade and exchange rate policies, the administration's efficiency problems, the absence of ready-to-use and profitable innovations, the inefficiency of or capacity gaps in agricultural services, undeveloped infrastructure), partly in the extensive factor proportions and corresponding social conditions. Where, however, something like a 'reasonable' policy on prices and extension services was pursued and the shortage of land had already been reflected in the peasant economy, impressive results were achieved in Africa too. In Kenya, for example, small farmers adopted hybrid maize in the 1960s and 1970s more quickly than farmers of the USA's Midwest had done 30 years before (Gerhart 1975). Hybrid maize enjoyed similar success only in Zimbabwe's commercial farm sector (Eicher 1995). Small-scale tea-growing in East Africa and cotton-growing in West Africa by the *système filière* are other examples of successful innovation policy in sub-Saharan Africa. In West Africa new rice varieties are an innovation with the potential to achieve economic import substitution in the rice market, given undistorted international competition and efficient agricultural policies (see Chapter 13.2).

***Box 4* Agro-historical view: population growth, factor proportions and technical progress, standards and institutions**

W.A. Lewis always bore in mind that a traditional agricultural population has labour reserves. These reserves could be activated by compulsion or economic incentives to increase agriculture's contribution to the market and accumulation of capital and to effect the necessary agricultural investments through the accumulation of labour. Karl Marx had already asked in his analysis of capitalist accumulation: 'What is a working day? ... By how much can the working day be extended beyond the time needed for the reproduction of labour?' (Marx 1962, p. 625). Accumulating capital by increasing the individual's workload to the physical limits at a reproductive hourly wage was, of course, a feature of early industrialization in the northern industrial countries. This was true both of countries with a capitalist structure and of those with a Communist social and economic structure. The Stalinist period in the former USSR after 1928, for example, clearly demonstrates this: 'The purpose of collectivization was to subject agriculture to the conditions of state accumulation, and this purpose was initially achieved without an absolute increase in the productivity of peasant labour by extensifying the peasant's working day, reducing his remuneration, etc.' (Hofmann 1956, p. 26). In the China of the 1970s 50 million agricultural working years were invested directly each year in land improvement and infrastructure (Ullerich 1979). In northern German agriculture a wage-earner's working year was 4000 hours and more before the First World War (Rehbein 1911). There is evidence of southern German farming families still having similar workloads in the 1920s (Münzinger 1929). Real wages in pre- and early-industrial European agriculture were correspondingly abysmal (see Table A7) (Abel 1978); ground rents accounted for about 50 per cent of value added (Clark 1960). In the one case prevailing social norms and institutions made the accumulation of capital possible, in the other it was ensured by ruthless, coercive means. In the Asian developing countries similar real agricultural wages of about 0.3 kg GE/hr were still common in the 1970s.

The Malthusian agricultural condition or movement of real wages and population density in opposite directions and the plight of workers in pre- and early-industrial 'pauperism' are well documented in the history of European agriculture (Abel 1978; Brandt 1994, p. 2 ff.). Only the burgeoning advances in science and technology eliminated them. The Asian developing countries have had the same experience, rural wages tripling in real terms in the 1980s and 1990s.

Boserup draws historical experience and a wide range of empirical data on Third World peasant farming together to form a theory of population-induced agricultural development. In this theory she assumes exogenous population growth and shows that increasing population density leads to changes in social institutions, attitudes to work, investment and agricultural production methods. Where labour or capital intensity of production rises, for example, food production per capita of the population can be kept at roughly the same level for much of the population increase even under pre-scientific conditions. However, this path eventually leads to peasant pauperism with extreme labour intensity of production, subsistence wages and an extremely high annual workload per worker until scientific and technical advances are introduced. Densely populated agricultural economies find it far easier than their thinly populated counterparts to introduce scientific and technical production processes:

... primitive communities with sustained population growth have a better chance to get into a process of genuine economic development than primitive communities with stagnant or declining populations, provided of course the necessary investments are undertaken.

(Boserup 1965, p. 118)

The industrialization of western Europe, Japan, Taiwan, South Korea and the People's Republic of China began with a long-term situation of extreme relative land shortages and very low real wages in both absolute and relative terms. After generations of adjusting their economic attitudes (to work, saving, investment, innovation and the market) the rural population (peasants, artisans, service providers) were receptive to the requirements of industrialization from the outset, and social organization and institutions favoured markets, competition in efficiency, accumulation of capital and progressiveness. This is known from Taiwan and Japan, for example (Smith 1959, p. 212; Park and Johnston 1997, p. 202).

Of the period of scientific and technical progress in the industrialized countries of Europe and Asia, each of which evolved industrially from a situation of pre-industrial pauperism lasting several generations, it can thus be said:

Population growth is the great driving force of all progress. ... Wherever we look, it is not the area of land or the fertility of the soil that determines the leeway for food sufficiency but the means available for exploiting the land and man's intelligence, vigour and thrift. ... However, it is man's will and understanding which must ensure healthy social development and the speculative human mind that must ensure technical progress.

(Aereboe 1925, p. 14 ff.)

In contrast, the successes achieved in development from a labour-extensive starting position were financed not from ground rents but from wages. The land settlement economies of the British Crown (USA, Canada, Australia, New Zealand) opened up agricultural land and natural resources without difficulty, as it were, at the first capital- and labour-extensive attempt. The settlers had brought with them in their minds social norms, institutions and forms of organization of the market economy and scientific and technical knowledge. The indigenous population, still at the hunter-gatherer stage of civilization, was not able, willing or allowed to adjust and was de facto dispossessed. The industrial capital followed as soon as lucrative export opportunities emerged in the world market.

Even today large parts of Latin America are dominated by post-colonial, feudalistic land tenure systems, which stand in the way of independent family farms, thus cutting the ground from under the feet of a rural economy featuring a division of labour, or depriving it of demand, acting as a strong incentive to leave the land and encouraging the growth of the city slums. In sub-Saharan Africa the agricultural population is now growing at only about 1.5 per cent p.a. because of rapid rural–urban migration, and agriculture's labour capacity is probably already dwindling because it is above all young workers who are moving to the cities and above all young people who are being carried off by the AIDS pandemic. The intensity and technology of production are stagnating because, with few exceptions, agricultural development policies have been seriously neglected or badly designed. In this situation rural society can hardly undergo a process of spontaneously generating social norms and institutions centred on gainful pursuits or produce human capital of an appropriate quality – along the lines, say, of the period during which the old industrialized countries were engaged in labour-intensive development. Intensive peasant agriculture is not yet the nation's business school in this case. In the urban centres, for example, the mentality of 'making a kill' predominates, while institutions of social solidarity continue to be largely confined to the extended family and the tribe and rooted in the home village. The traditional requirement that the members of extended families share with and help each other impedes the accumulation of capital. Import-substituting industrialization in sub-Saharan Africa in the 1970s therefore failed principally because of the incompatibility of the labour, organizational and management requirements of large industrial enterprises with the norms and institutions of traditional societies. If greater emphasis had been placed on crafts and small-scale industry and a selective regime of tariff protection had been ensured, the outcome would probably have been far more favourable. The social institutions are, however, changing under the pressure of urbanization and the influence of western culture (Tiffen *et al.* 1995; Wiggins 1995). The socio-cultural adjustments may soon reach the stage where self-perpetuating development processes occur, similar to those of the latest Asian examples.

There are some historical examples of traditional, extremely labour-intensive agriculture in sub-Saharan Africa (Ludwig 1967; Netting 1968; Savaget 1981) and many recent examples of African farmers reacting economically to changed scarcities and becoming innovative (Tiffen *et al.* 1995; Sanders *et al.* 1996).

How should the effects of the Green Revolution be judged? It should be remembered that it led to an historically unprecedented increase in production, without which there would have been a serious food crisis in Asia since the 1970s. It also created the agricultural production base for the industrial growth of the 1980s and 1990s (FAO 1995b, p. 5 ff.). Without the previous successes of the Green Revolution, shortages of savings and, above all, foreign exchange would have prevented industrial growth in Taiwan, South Korea, India, China, Thailand, Malaysia and Indonesia on the scale that was in fact achieved.

A first wave of criticism in the 1970s, however, focused on an unfavourable distribution effect of the Green Revolution, which was assumed rather than empirically proved (Griffith 1979)[5]:

- Large farmers and landowners were given precedence over peasant farmers and farm workers in absolute and relative terms through rising ground rents.
- They derived other advantages from the better access they had to complementary means of production and services (water, pumps, electricity, extension, formal agricultural credit).
- It was also expected that the landowners would drive out their tenants and farm the land themselves because of the higher profits they could make. It was also thought that there was a tendency for land ownership to become more concentrated because of the rising concentration of incomes.
- Rising incomes would lead to the partial mechanization of farms operated by wage labour, thus making wage labour redundant. It was even thought that a tendency for wages to fall could be detected.

In a review of twenty years of the Green Revolution backed by figures, later criticism came to a more balanced and even distinctly positive verdict, at least as regards the socio-economic effects (Hayami and Ruttan 1984; Mellor and Desai 1985; Singh 1990; Hazell and Ramasamy 1991):

- It had become apparent that neither the distribution of farmland nor the status of farmers in land law represented a serious obstacle to adoption – apart from the slow initial speed of adoption by the smaller farms, which soon caught up with the larger farms as time passed. Although the smaller farmers participated with a time lag, they quickly took full advantage of the productivity potential offered by the innovations.
- The productivity- and cost-reducing effects of the biological and technical innovations proved to be largely the same for farms of all sizes.
- The wages or incomes of workers in rural areas rose in real terms as a result of:
  - rising real wages for farm work,
  - a declining cost of living as a result of declining food prices in real terms,
  - increasing employment in and outside agriculture.
- Although mechanization led to some redundancies, they were primarily due to distorted prices of capital goods (overvalued domestic currency, interest rate subsidies).
- The incomes of the urban and rural poor rose in real terms owing to the relative decline in food prices.
- Rising agricultural value added and the increased demand for consumer goods[6] gave rise to considerable additional value added in the up- and downstream sectors of agricultural production and in manufacturing industry, which primarily benefited the wage-dependent population through rising real wages.

In the literature it is always emphasized (indeed, it has almost become an agricultural self-evident truth) that the effect of the Green Revolution on income distribution depends on the distribution of ownership, and especially that of land[7]. Not everything became worse, therefore. Referring to southern India, for example, Hazell and Ramasamy write:

> ... there were sizable across the board-gains in income, employment, and the quality of diet for the rural households, and these were not accompanied by any worsening of the interhousehold distribution of income. Nor is there any evidence that the distribution of land deteriorated, ...
>
> (Hazell and Ramasamy 1991, p. 251)

All in all, then, the Green Revolution made a major contribution to economic growth and poverty reduction in rural and urban areas. The critical evaluation of the experience gained from it has increased awareness of the opportunities for and limits to reducing poverty through agricultural development:

... without HYVs [high-yielding varieties], the difficulties facing the poor would have been far worse. There is little hope for redressing poverty without an even more widespread and rapid adoption of HYVs. They cannot alleviate poverty by themselves, however, ... they are absolutely necessary but by no means sufficient for the reduction of poverty. The gains of the worse-off would have been even more widespread if they had been preceded or accompanied by a really effective program to redistribute rural assets. Without new technologies, such a program would merely have redistributed poverty; without reforms the widespread adoption of new technologies has greatly helped but cannot solve the problems of poverty.

(Singh 1990, p. 200)

The data on the development of the Indian agricultural sector are impressive evidence of this (see Table 8).

Under conditions of rapid population growth, agricultural innovation policy can indeed make a substantial contribution to poverty reduction through its effects on wages and product prices, but solving the poverty problem requires a great deal more, namely an agricultural reform where the distribution of land ownership is quasi-feudal, plus economic growth in the urban areas, non-agricultural jobs, human capital formation and, finally, social policy. Seen as a whole, poverty reduction is a task for two or three generations.

The weakness of the Green Revolution, with hindsight, lies in the harmful effects it had on the environment, which raised doubts about its sustainability in many places. The accelerated introduction of pump irrigation using ground water in Punjabi wheat-growing, for example, is resulting in salinization of the soil at many locations today, 15 to 20 years on. At the same time, the ground water level is sinking. A strong lobby of large farmers is not exactly facilitating a policy of resource stabilization. In the intensive wet-rice areas of Asia soil exhaustion is becoming apparent, its actual causes still unclear (see Box 1). In general, the tendency in Asian rice-growing since the late 1980s has been for yields to rise at a slower rate in some cases, to stagnate in others and gradually to decline

Table 8 Development of the Indian agricultural sector, in per cent p.a.

	1958–75	1976–94
Proportion of population below poverty line	1.18	−1.91
Real wages	0.33	2.84
Real consumption per capita	−0.93	1.76
Agricultural output/ha (sown area)	1.51	2.91
Agricultural output/capita (of agricultural population)	−0.01	1.15

Source: Datt and Ravallion (1998).

in yet others, depending on the ecological burden. The environment is suffering a wide range of consequential damage, and the real prices or cost of using the factors labour, land and water are rising appreciably to the detriment of the competitiveness of domestic rice production. Accordingly, what is primarily called for there these days is the 'sustainability' of land and water use.

It is an unanswered question today whether the successes of the Green Revolution could be maintained and then continued at a higher level of productivity if a fresh boost was given to agro-technological innovation.[8] Agrawal arrives at an assessment of the prospects that is likely to be true not only of India but also of China and South-East Asia:

> Without the Green Revolution, it would have been almost impossible in the past to obviate the occurrence of famines in India and other developing countries. Without Sustainable Development it may be difficult to save most of the rural poor of the South from hunger in the future.
>
> (Agrawal 1991, p. 357)

9.3   Integrated rural development (1975–85)

By the mid-1970s the disappointment in the authoritative circles of international development cooperation with the supposed and actual cases of the Green Revolution having an adverse effect on distribution had led to a change of paradigm. What now became decisive was the goal of satisfying basic human needs better by adopting the direct project or programme approach. An influential role in this reorientation was also played by the supposed absence of the trickle down effect which it had been hoped import-substituting industrialization would have.

Particularly influential in this context was a study by Chenery (Chenery *et al.* 1974). The strategy of redistribution with growth propagated in this study led to a far greater allocation of development cooperation resources to the 'social sectors', without a hand being laid on import-substituting industrialization. The integration goal of the multisectoral conception passed through a number of intermediate stages to basic-needs- and target-group-oriented integrated rural development. In rural areas this amounted to development cooperation approaches to distribution-oriented, multisectoral project policy at regional or subregional level (in the districts). After the great drought of 1972–75 food security programmes were added (see Box 5). Account was taken primarily of social services and occasionally of crafts and regional physical infrastructure (World Bank 1988). In sub-Saharan Africa and a number of small Central American countries policy on agricultural innovation and services was increasingly neglected or replaced with food-for-work programmes. The latter provided specific, but short-term, employment among the poor they reached. In addition to or uninfluenced by IRD, however, the larger Asian countries – having a better understanding and to their own benefit – continued with the policy of agricultural innovation that the Green Revolution had initiated.

Box 5 **Food security programmes in the Sudano-Sahel**

After the great Sahel drought of 1972–75 the German development cooperation community implemented, in addition to IRD, food security programmes from Dakar to Mogadishu, which cost at least DM 1 bn in donor resources from 1975 to 1995. The programmes focused on the establishment of extensive parastatal reserve stocks (including stored grain) and on grain market statistics and a system of early warnings of drought and food shortages. It was found that, while traditional peasant storage was technically far more efficient and far less expensive than large-scale government storage, the middle and lower income groups could not then afford the price rises of up to 400 per cent when drought occurred. Only subsidized parastatal storage and rapid imports could prevent this. But how far, depending on intervention price policy, the volume taken into intervention and the origin of the grain stored, government storage is a substitute for peasant storage and what form a cost-efficient national storage policy involving peasant storage should take are questions which have never been posed with any force. There are reports from various sources that the quantities stored by peasants have fallen sharply over the past 20 years. One key question remains unanswered: did government storage policy in the Sahel countries in the end shift food insecurity from the urban population to rural marginal groups? At least where there are shortages, Heinrich von Thünen's theory has in some ways been turned upside down in the Sahel countries: the consumer prices of cereals are lowest in the urban centres and highest in the peripheral agricultural regions, where poverty reigns (Brandt 1984).

During the IRD decade development cooperation increasingly neglected agricultural innovation policy measures. In the mid-1980s the following conclusions were drawn: first, the problem of administrative coordination and organization (with government departments among themselves and with the donors) proved to be, as a rule, extremely expensive and, at worst, insoluble. Second, the recipients (whether the government or the target groups) were eventually unable to afford the follow-up costs of the multisectoral measures. Third, IRD similarly failed to bring about any appreciable change to the general aspects of land tenure systems relevant to distribution or poverty. By the mid-1980s this concept, with its roots in practice, had essentially collapsed. The World Bank summarized its wide experience as follows:

The warning – that these area projects might suffer from a design that is too ambitious and complex, require exceptional leadership, and cannot always be supported on a sustainable basis – has proved all too true in many cases. It recommends "… that planners and implementers should in most cases resist the temptation to assume that the integrated implementation, preferable as it is in ideal situations, is likely to be feasible in practice".

(IBRD 1988)

Looking back, there is something quite bewildering and tautological about this approach: development is the direct elimination of the most obvious features of underdevelopment, the differences between the given and the target (developed) state of a rural region were to be eliminated quite simply with a comprehensive package solution by means of integrated multisectoral measures of the donors' and recipients' coordinated development administrations and so, in a way, by hybrid centrally planned means. This was bound to raise insurmountable organizational and allocational problems and problems associated with the financing of the follow-up costs and with the interregional distribution of resources. In particular, the approach was consistently pursued along the lines of a centrally controlled economy (top down) and/or by means of parallel, project-specific administrative structures, without the options of decentralization and the coordination of measures at the level of local and district administrations having been seriously examined. Furthermore, it was able to do precious little to overcome the inertia of socio-political conditions, and especially the inadequate agricultural policy environment (above all, in the sub-Saharan African countries). In many cases the failure of the parts of the programmes devoted to the agricultural sector was due not least to impatience and the absence of a proper review of the advice given from a domestic economy and farm economic standpoint (see Chapter 11.2): all in all, it had become very clear that, despite its explicit orientation towards target groups and poverty, IRD had not, for the reasons given above, had the effect of sustainably reducing poverty. In general, resources had clearly been used inefficiently and unsustainably.

9.4   Structural adjustment programmes (1985–95)

The SAPs were economic policy concepts for strengthening or reviving growth initially of the Latin American economies, but then of the sub-Saharan African economies too. The gradual liberalization of trade and exchange rate policy, the reduction of government consumption and the elimination of government economic dirigisme were the principal measures taken under the World Bank's guidance to regain economic equilibrium. Debt rescheduling and cancellation operations and new loans linked to the implementation of these macropolicy measures were the steps taken by the donors to ensure acceptance of the SAPs within the framework of development cooperation. Despite widespread praise (Picciotto and Wearing 1997), there is no evidence that the Structural Adjustment Programme for the sub-Saharan African countries had had any lasting success (Engberg-Pedersen and Udsholt 1997). The economic recovery that occurred after 1993/94 was largely due to a raw materials boom in the world market. It could not be maintained during the slump of the late 1990s. However, there is no denying that things might have been even less favourable had there been no structural adjustment.

The adverse effects on growth and distribution of a price and exchange rate policy that siphons off resources had been revealed by Ghana's agricultural sector as early as the mid-1970s (Brandt 1994). In an international cross-section analysis Lipton painted an impressive picture of misconceived agricultural and economic policies (Lipton 1977). The World Bank took responsibility for the implementation of the SAPs in 1982. The main aim of the agricultural policy component was to correct the distortions of agricultural price ratios and to privatize parastatal agricultural services.

During the SAP decade the importance attached to the promotion of agriculture in development cooperation continued to wane (see Chapter 6). Hardly any projects aimed at the direct promotion of agricultural production were now implemented. The reduced resources were used primarily to promote self-help and develop organization. Government (or parastatal) agricultural services were badly neglected (Duncan and Howell 1992) and, in the case of the marketing organizations, largely abandoned.

> Particularly doing away with the statal and parastatal agricultural marketing enterprises did not produce those efficiency gains hoped for. Today resulting privatised marketing systems are hampered by local extortion, lack of knowledge as to quality grading, export marketing and coping with price risk. Inefficiencies and a high overall transformation risk inflate trade margins. Farmers are deterred by a big price risk.
>
> (Brandt 1997, p. 17 ff.)

Increasing the rural population's capacity for self-help was one of the main project policy topics of the debate on the conception of agricultural development policy during the SAP decade (Gsänger 1994). On the practical side, projects also increasingly emphasized measures to develop organization. What projects were still implemented in the villages primarily consisted of measures to stabilize resources. The conceptual debate was dominated by aspects of the sociology of organization in conjunction with environmental objectives. What was overlooked in an approach featuring communications fundamentalism was the fact that agricultural production formed the income base of 70 per cent of the population. Agricultural production and innovation policy were simply forgotten and continue to be so to this day.

The three large Asian countries (India, China and Indonesia) did not, however, allow their agricultural development policies to be run down: they persisted with the innovation policies of the Green Revolution, maintained moderate tariff protection for agricultural products (roughly equivalent to the price distortions in the world markets) and in no way forswore further price, market and trade policy measures. In sub-Saharan Africa, on the other hand, the agricultural development policies continued to deteriorate. The increase in agricultural production and supply it was hoped liberalization would bring failed to materialize. Aggregate agricultural supply obviously reacts reasonably price-elastically only where there is an appropriate innovation policy and efficient services (Bond 1983; Binswanger 1990). However, it should also be remembered in this context that a real decline in world market prices had become the long-term trend as a result of the 'treadmill effect' and the industrialized countries' dumping practices (see Chapter 6.2).

In turning away from production and constructive agricultural policy, rural development policy and practical development cooperation again resembled the basic image of community development in the First Decade:

> The development expert's task has changed; it is not primarily technical advice that is wanted but the monitoring and guiding of social processes and advice on organization.
>
> (Körner 1996, p. 114)

But so far this has filled hardly anyone's stomach, experts and counterparts aside!

The SAPs failed to have a poverty-reducing effect in agriculture and rural areas because of the omissions and shortcomings described above and the generally passive attitude towards agricultural development policy. Moreover, fundamental methodological problems have meant that no one has yet been able to provide convincing evidence that the promotion of self-help has an impact on development (Steinich 1997).

9.5   Sector investment programmes and capacity-building (1995–present)

Since 1990 an intensive debate on the politico-economic environment in the 'recipient countries' (Waller and Lingnau 1995) has reflected an essential conclusion drawn from the SAP decade:

> … that the internal political environment in the partner countries is the main determinant of the success or failure of development.
>
> (BMZ 1996)

Whether it is primarily important or as important as the international environment (see Chapter 6.2) or whether there may be interaction between the two causes is a moot point, but it is generally agreed today that it is an essential requirement for the success of development cooperation measures. From this, Germany's development cooperation, like that of other donors, has deduced the following requirements for successful cooperation, each of which is subdivided further and operationalized as a qualitative assessment of the tendency (BMZ 1996):

- respect for human rights;
- participation of the people in political decisions;
- rule of law and a guarantee of legal certainty;
- introduction of a social market economy;
- orientation of government action towards development.

A positive general tendency and the fulfilment of not less than a 'minimum of these internal conditions' help to determine whether or not aid is granted and if so, how much. These are among the requirements considered when Agricultural Sector Investment Programmes (ASIPs) are designed. They are intended to help further improve the political and economic environment (by increasing participation and shaping the sectoral development conception). Seen from this angle, the ASIPs are the conceptual sectoral expression of this new policy.

In the mid-1990s the World Bank identified the following weaknesses of its project policy in sub-Saharan Africa:

> Insufficient local ownership and commitment; the lack of any noticeable 'trickle down' effect from some individual projects; projects not sustained or maintained after initial implementation; confusion and dissipation of effort caused by different approaches pushed by different donors; excessive numbers of expatriate technical assistance personnel and weakening of government capacity by the creation of donor-financed project units; and finally, a lack of satisfactory results from some adjustment operations, especially with regard to the allocation of public expenditure.
>
> (Harrold 1995, p. 11)

SIPs are meant to take account of these weaknesses or to eliminate them. After extensive discussions between the partners concerned, the World Bank finds itself playing the part of leading donor without any great enthusiasm and subject to future experience. A number of SIPs have been implemented since 1996, all in sub-Saharan African countries (Foster *et al.* 2001). Initial conceptual designs of Sector Investment Programmes are characterized by the following measures or requirements:

- one body responsible for the planning, management and monitoring of all the sector's public expenditure (including financial ODA);
- clear sectoral strategy and policy as a fundamental requirement;
- definition of all powers and responsibilities;
- adoption of the approach by the donors involved;
- approximation of the donors' processing arrangements and monitoring and evaluation procedures;
- widest possible use of local advisory and implementing capacities.

It remains to be seen whether this fresh attempt culminates in a viable conception (Wolff 1997).

The success of the Sector Investment Programmes will depend in particular on the willingness and ability of the sub-Saharan African managerial elite. There are still major constraints in this respect, since the dominance of foreign experts has prevented domestic experts in many countries from assuming the role of responsible planners and managers for four decades, and in other cases dictatorships and/or clientelism have disoriented or dysfunctionalized the public and private functional elites (Jaycox 1993). Resorting to polemical exaggeration, Bierschenk *et al.* assume that the development cooperation community today is far more traditionalist and reluctant to accept change than the societies it is at-

tempting to make more dynamic (Bierschenk *et al.* 1991). Berg considers it possible to reform technical cooperation so as to force domestic expertise to play a
far stronger part in the planning and implementation of projects (Berg 1993).
The World Bank believes the lack of capacity, meaning the ability to analyse
problems, design solutions and implement appropriate measures, to be the dominant constraint in the implementation of SIPs. It is making appropriate capacity-
building efforts. Integrated, intersectoral approaches are excluded as unpromis-
ing after the IRD experience (1975–85).

A survey of 30 programmes in various sectors (SIPs) of 18 countries reveals
the general problems associated with the approach, which also occur in agricultural sectoral programmes: implementation and budget management prove to be
very difficult in the given staffing, institutional and organizational circumstances, and this from central to local government level. In practice, the road to
viable decentralization is long and strewn with obstacles (KfW 2000). Beyond
this, a consolidated account of the impact of the ASIPs is not yet available. Problem areas are already emerging, however. During the SAP decade the sub-
Saharan African governments largely withdrew from services for the agricultural
sector, if not totally, then certainly from funding. Land tenure issues do not normally fall within the agriculture minister's terms of reference. As a rule, they
are, moreover, a highly potential source of domestic conflict. Questions relating
to infrastructure, agricultural market structure, agricultural price, market and
trade policy and exchange rate, monetary and credit policy are settled by other
government departments – often not as befits thriving agricultural development.
Thus agricultural price incentives created by the SAPs in many countries were
swallowed up by inflation and excessively high exchange rates. Inefficient private marketing systems also played their part.

The ASIPs thus have, on the one hand, clearly insufficient control over the
decisive levers of growth in the agricultural sector and influence over the distribution of incomes. As long as the biased concentration of development cooperation on the urban sectors continues and price ratios in the world markets are as
they are (see Chapter 6.2), the political quarters there will, on the other hand,
have little incentive to concern themselves with domestic agriculture. The scope
for action left to the agriculture ministers and so to the ASIPs in the case of agricultural services does not, as a rule, appear to be sufficient to launch a successful
agricultural policy (Foster *et al.* 2001). Besides the distorted price ratios in the
world markets in processed and unprocessed agricultural products and the blocking of agricultural development policies by interministerial conflicts of interest,
it has been not least the conflicts and quarrelling which, as everyone knows full
well, occur in the 'donor community' over interests and agricultural policy and
administrative procedures that make ASIP processes seem not very likely to
succeed.

What was needed in Africa was every conceivable concerted effort to with-
stand the comparative advantages which the old industrialized countries have
acquired in the markets in the areas of technology, infrastructure and organization and the subsidization and dumping practices to which they resort. This
should have included the well-organized production of agricultural raw materials

and semi-luxuries for export (by the *système filière*, for instance), defence against distortions of food prices and appropriate tariff protection for food processing and the textile industry; but the political elites of the sub-Saharan African countries have hitherto lacked both the understanding of the need for and the class interest in a separate agricultural development policy, which the Asian governments have to a high, or sufficiently high, degree because in the countries of Asia the rural population carries considerable weight in domestic politics. In this overall situation the ASIPs can hardly contribute to poverty reduction. Ake outlines the dilemma in sub-Saharan Africa with the socio-political insight of the domestic expert:

> There is no indication yet that we understand the need to develop ourselves, or care enough about development. ... In Nigeria as in most African countries the commitment of leadership to development is non existent or too weak and undisciplined to matter.
>
> (Ake 1996, p. 1 ff.)

Other African authors claim that development cooperation is stabilizing this situation (Kabou 1993).

9.6   A brief review of socio-political problems in decentralized rural development

The attempts at agricultural sectoral development programmes that have been made since 1995 once again confirm the conclusion drawn long ago that the planning and implementation task involved cannot be successfully performed at the level of central government (see Part B). The aim should be the organizational and functional decentralization of the recipients' administrations.

Decentralization is primarily a question of changing social institutions and political organization, which is, as a rule, strongly resisted. There are two main problems in this context. Central government has difficulty in relinquishing power (authority and budget resources) to subordinate units and to democratic representative bodies at district and local level. In addition, considerable tension often occurs between the administration, the formal organizations representing the people and the formal legal system on the one hand and the traditional, informal holders of power, organizations and institutions on the other. The lines dividing the two sides are often difficult to recognize and hardly open to outside influence (by development cooperation). A new conception, 'decentralized rural development', should therefore emerge or operate with the patience and open time horizon for which the call so often goes out; for it is certain that the main conflicts referred to above can be resolved neither to order nor overnight.

As a statement based on experience, there is no doubt after four decades of development cooperation that intercultural communication and joint learning by development cooperation partners can greatly accelerate the resolution of such conflicts. It is therefore inappropriate to reach into the poison cabinet of the philosophy of history out of frustration or, as it were, as a substitutive activity, but it cannot be denied that serious frictions can also occur in development cooperation.[9] OECD experts say, for example:

> The results of aid are often unsustainable, a point on which all parties involved are in agreement, and which bears a feeling of impotence, even of failure. ... it is seen as something to be endured rather than desired. ... As a general rule, dialogue between donors and recipients is strained and difficult ... Donors often appear to be getting recipient countries to accept their aid projects rather than actually providing the aid. As a result, the 'sale' of a project is accompanied by a variety of benefits to the receiving institutions, such as the supply of equipment, subsidies and in many cases wages. ... Aid to the Sahel is currently perceived as a free good ... So there should be no surprise if this service is used too liberally and without regard to the consequences.

An attempt at a 'home-made' analysis of the situation produces something like the following explanatory model: the ruling classes and urban civil society in the LDCs naturally want to come closer to material standards like those applying in industrialized countries. This is almost bound to result in their neglecting the economic interests of the large majority, and especially those of the rural population, when it comes to the allocation of government resources and the distribution of the tax burden (direct and indirect). This does not, of course, happen without feelings of guilt and self-doubt. It also sets the rural population against the urban elites. The latter are in turn sometimes pushed around by material upstarts of donor officials, with this or that conviction. This causes strong resentment. Both the projected feeling of guilt and the resentment on the part of one section of the recipient elites and, on the other hand, the donors' unrealistic ideas of time and budgets eventually dysfunctionalize dialogue and cooperation.

This highly problematical triangular relationship between the target groups of development cooperation and recipients' and donors' administrations will not be considered further here. It is bound to become one of the main problems for future sectoral programme financing (because it can be instrumentalized domestically by recipients), the conception of which is currently the subject of intense debate. What is certain is that the slogan 'recipients in the driver's seat' must be taken seriously if the recipient–donor relationship is to improve. This also means, however, that the recipients must assume responsibility for the sectoral programmes.

Part IV Economic growth, agricultural development, poverty reduction

The complex interactions between economic growth, agricultural development[1] and poverty reduction are described here in four stages in an analysis reduced to essential references, with economic growth assumed in this context to be an exogenous datum:

- links between economic and agricultural development (see Chapter 10);
- driving forces behind agricultural development (see Chapter 11);
- economic growth and poverty reduction (see Chapter 12.1);
- agricultural development and poverty reduction (see Chapter 12.2).

As everything is linked to everything else in the cross-section theme of poverty reduction, this approach entails a number of arbitrary definitions. The chapter merely shows how economic growth and agricultural policy can increase agricultural production and value added and how they can reduce poverty (see Figure 2). Policies concerning the installation and maintenance of physical infrastructure and state government social services are not discussed. They are beyond the scope of this study.

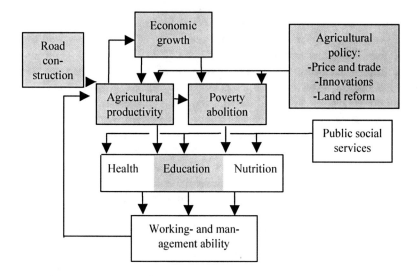

Figure 2 Line followed in Part IV[a]

[a]   Hatched areas indicate subjects considered in this study; arrows show
     postulated directions of influence.

Source: Author's own design.

10   Economic and agricultural growth

10.1   Linkage through mutual demand

From experience in the old industrialized countries it is known that the agricultural and non-agricultural sectors grow side by side, as Clark was first to demonstrate in great detail (Clark 1957). For the period 1955–80 a wide range of studies confirm this finding in a global context.[2] Both past and more recent experience shows that the agricultural growth rate at the early-industrial stage of development is typically two-thirds of the non-agricultural rate. After 1980 this
link becomes less rigid. Referring to a dozen Asian countries, Mellor points to
the 'classical' close correlation between the two sectors in contrast to the absence of any link in groups of African and Latin American countries (Mellor
1995a). This new trend is probably due not least to liberalization and the influences of development cooperation.

In Asia and Europe each sector's demand for the other's products and factors
of production has linked the sectoral growth rates. Above all, the effect of
Engel's Law ensures a relative decline in the agricultural sector's sales in the
internal market compared to value added in the non-agricultural sector as real
per capita incomes rise (Goreux 1959; Stevens 1965; Lluch *et al.* 1977; Ingco
1990). The less significant agricultural exports become, relative to production or

domestic demand, the more closely agricultural growth is linked to macroeconomic growth. Conversely, agriculture's demand for means of production and farming households' demand for consumer goods have a major impact on the growth of the non-agricultural sectors (see Chapter 12.2).

As the developing countries (with the exception of those in sub-Saharan Africa) have shown, a factor of overriding importance for the growth of agricultural productivity and incomes and for agro-technical progress has been the real increase in wages since about 1970. Agriculture has reacted with labour migration, capital intensification and technical progress, unless prevented from so doing by dysfunctional agricultural policies. The agricultural sector's marginal value products adjust to the changed factor prices (see Chapter 8.3). Where full use is made of agricultural land, the land use price is formed in accordance with its marginal value product in the neo-classical production equilibrium:

$$\frac{dY}{dA} \cdot \frac{P_y}{P_A} = \frac{dY}{dK} \cdot \frac{P_y}{P_K} = \frac{dY}{dB} \cdot \frac{P_y}{P_B} \geq 1$$

where: $\underline{dY}$ = physical marginal products; $dA_{etc.}$ = (labour, capital, land); Py = product price level; $P_{A\ etc.}$ = factor prices (labour, capital, land)

In the neo-classical production equilibrium any change in price ratios must be followed by an adjustment of the physical marginal products in the shape of a change to the factor inputs and/or to the level of the production function. In the normal case of rising agricultural production the latter is equivalent to technical progress and capital intensification – a commonplace no doubt, but an elucidatory one.

Since the end of the Second World War such adjustment reactions to changes in factor price ratios have occurred throughout the world, country for country, accompanied by falling product prices in real terms. Combinations of land- and labour-substituting technical advances, labour migration and capital intensification which are appropriate to scarcities – in accordance with the prevailing agricultural policy environment – have both helped to cause the long-term decline in prices on the supply side and ensured economic adjustment to this decline, since agro-technical progress is both a cause and a consequence of changes in price ratios.

Linked to the commonplace arising from a standard farm budget namely, that farmers gear their allocation decisions, among other things, to probable gross margins and investment costs, are two more interesting observations, which are discussed below in greater depth:

- What is easily overlooked in the debate on the causes of growth in the agricultural sector is that not only changes in price ratios but also changes in physical marginal factor products have an impact on profitability and intensity. When real prices fall, technical progress is the driving force behind the increase in intensity. However, productivity rises far more slowly in the process than the profit risk. This reduces the incentive to be innovative and to invest – an entirely rational reaction.

• In contrast to the global post-war experience of agricultural growth while the agricultural sector's terms of trade fell and productivity rose sharply, there were instances in the nineteenth century of economic and agricultural development while agriculture's terms of trade rose and physical productivity increased at least five times more slowly, as the example of the former German Reich, its agricultural development geared to the internal market and protected against imports, shows (see Box 6).

Box 6 **A case of agricultural development accompanied by rising sectoral terms of trade, Germany 1825–1914**

After the Napoleonic Wars the peasants of the German states were freed from their old feudal burdens and from the compulsory cultivation of the old three-field rotation system. Agriculture thereafter adjusted itself economically to price ratios. The agricultural sector's terms of trade rose between 1825 and 1875 by about 100 per cent (see Table A12) because supply followed demand. Agriculture increased output by adopting more intensive production systems, which meant, above all, raising the intensity of labour and capital goods rather than inputs, since scientific advances were only just beginning to put in an appearance. Scientific and technical advances that consumed secondary energy were not introduced until after the First World War. Aggregate productivity rose mainly as advantage was taken of complementary effects in crop sequences and between vegetable and animal production. The restriction of natural grassland through its conversion to arable use, the restriction of fallow, the expansion of field forage and root crop cultivation and the doubling of livestock between 1820 and 1870 made it possible to increase production profitably. From 1800 to 1885 rye yields and milk yields per cow rose by about 50 per cent (see Table A12) without secondary energy being used. In other European countries similar growth rates were achieved in pre- and early-industrial agriculture (Bairoch 1976, p. 484). By comparison, the Asian countries have increased yields by a five- to tenfold annual rate since 1970, while real producer prices have fallen. In their case it has been rising aggregate factor productivity that has provided sufficient intensification incentives despite declining producer price ratios. In Germany, on the other hand, the agricultural sector was protected against the real decline in world market prices from the 1870s. From 1885 the number of workers stagnated as the demand for industrial labour grew. Real wages began to rise. Although animal power was now being used to mechanize farm work, the labour this released was used to cope with the further increases in root crop and field forage cultivation and to meet the demand from the growing animal production activity. The purchasing power of agricultural product prices for means of production continued to rise until the First World War. During that war the number of agricultural workers began to decline; it was not until about 1955 that animal power gave way to motor power.

Rising labour and capital intensity, and especially land- and labour-substituting technical advances and the expansion of specifically intensive farm activities, were the means used to increase supply. Scientific and technical advances did not begin to play a part until after 1870 – first with the introduction of potash and phosphate fertilizers, the selective breeding of useful plants and animal power. Artificial nitrogenous fertilizers were used in small quantities after the First World War. Even during the period of initial industrialization, 1825–1875, the German states were (despite the free trade policy of the German Customs Union of 1834) advocates of largely inward-oriented agricultural development, since transport costs afforded extensive natural protection. Scientific and technical advances that consumed secondary energy had yet to be introduced. With the agricultural sector's terms of trade rising, structural change was comparatively slow. With the emergence of overseas competition in the late 1870s, agricultural free trade was then abandoned. The highest per capita output at the lowest wage resulted in ground rents accounting for a very large proportion of agricultural value added, from which agricultural capital intensification and substantial contributions to net industrial investment were financed (Brandt 1994, p. 10 ff.). This contrasts with what the Asian developing countries experienced after 1955: product prices falling in relative terms and yet intensity increasing through the introduction of scientific and technical advances that consumed secondary energy and provided sufficient economic incentives by increasing aggregate factor productivity.

Where the sub-Saharan African countries are concerned, the question is how pre- and early-industrial economies are to develop if their domestic markets are flooded with dumped food and textile imports, while their exports of raw materials fall into the trap of price-inelastic demand for imports. On the other hand, Vietnam's current model of inward-oriented industrialization protected by tariffs is producing appreciable growth rates.

10.2   Urbanization

Towns and cities form the living and working space of the non-agricultural population, whose visits to villages in the countryside are as a rule confined to occasional weekends or holidays. Where economic development is just beginning, 10 to 20 per cent of the population live in urban areas, compared to 80 to 90 per cent in fully developed economies. According to Engel's Law, agricultural products are bound to account for a decreasing proportion of total final goods in the economy as per capita income rises. As, on the other hand, the labour market ensures the approximation of agricultural wages *mutatis mutandis* to the trend in urban wages, agriculture too must increase its productivity through technical progress and (labour- and land-substituting) capital intensification. The agricultural labour force and population as a proportion of the total population therefore decline as soon as the growth process begins, although labour force numbers continue to rise in absolute terms during a period of initial industrialization.

Viewed globally, the agricultural population is now increasing in absolute terms only in the sub-Saharan African countries. However, the urbanization rates in these countries easily exceed those in the Asian developing countries (see Table 9). As growth rates in the urban sectors of the Asian countries are well above their urbanization rates, there are instances of per capita incomes in the towns and cities rising in real terms.

In the sub-Saharan African countries, on the other hand, urbanization rates greatly exceed economic growth in the urban areas. In 1990–95 the urbanization rate was 4–5 per cent, the urban economic growth rate at most 1.5 per cent (see Table 10). This finding appears to be even more critical in view of the large development cooperation share of the financing of government services and urban infrastructure, which is likely to amount today, depending on the country, to US$ 80–100 per capita of the urban population. Typically, 60–70 per cent of national budgets are financed by aid, as far as aid can be seen to be properly budgeted.

This discrepancy shows that a large majority of those migrating to urban areas in the sub-Saharan African countries end up in poverty. It must be asked, however, just how realistic the economic statistics are. It is likely that insufficient

Table 9 Growth rates in selected sectors, by regions of the world, 1990–95, in per cent p.a.

Region	Agriculture	Industry	Services
Sub-Saharan Africa	1.5	0.2	1.5
East Asia	3.9	15.0	8.4
South Asia	3.0	5.3	6.0

Source: World Bank (1997).

Table 10 Demographic data on selected regions, 2000

Region	Population growth in %	Urban population growth in %	Rural population growth in %	Proportion of urban population in %
West Africa	2.77	4.64	1.51	40
East Africa	2.81	5.04	2.05	25
South-East Asia	1.75	3.33	0.45	37

Source: UN (1998).

account has been taken of the whole informal sector in towns and cities. On the other hand, this discrepancy is also a strong indication of oppressive poverty, the relative undersupply of social services and a general lack of prospects in rural areas of which people are today very aware.

One of the main causes of this imbalance is the neglect of agricultural policy. This can be attributed to the price trend in the world agricultural markets and its causes, the policy of cheap bread in the urban areas and the siphoning off of resources from the agricultural sector through the taxation of its exports, the excessive trade margins of inefficient marketing systems and (in about 30 per cent of sub-Saharan African countries) overvalued exchange rates. Added factors are the neglect of the agricultural sector in development cooperation and the general isolation of the domestic agricultural market from the coastal urban agglomeration centres because of dilapidated infrastructure and uncertainty and the resulting comparatively very high transformation costs. Another very important factor is, however, the movement of people fleeing war and civil war in a number of countries.

All in all, there are thus clear signs that rural–urban migration in the sub-Saharan African countries, unlike the Asian developing countries, is occurring on a relative scale which exceeds by far the proportions of urban–rural development that is reasonably balanced in economic terms. This should also be a particular cause of concern because of the absence of employment prospects due, for example, to the sharp increase in industrial production for export. Mainly to blame for the flight from the land are, then, first, the lack of prospects in agriculture, second, a policy of cheap bread in the urban areas supported by imports and, third, the concentration of development cooperation on the towns and cities.

11   Driving forces behind agricultural growth

11.1   Empirical evidence at sectoral level

Successful agricultural development presupposes coordinated innovation and structural, price and trade policies. Price policy is, however, a key element of agricultural development policy. Experience shows that the more favourable the price ratios, the more easily innovations are adopted in rural areas. It is only in the light of experience of innovations that the effects they have on profitability become relevant to further decisions. Protection against distorted world market prices and renunciation of export taxes are therefore, in practice, preconditions for increases in productivity everywhere. The domestic price elasticities of the supply of individual agricultural products are no lower in developing countries than in industrialized countries (Askari / Cummings 1976; Bond 1983; Cleaver 1985; Chibber 1988). The magnitude of the cross-price elasticities of the supply of export and food crops similarly indicates major price-oriented substitution reactions by the agricultural sectors. Relative prices thus play an important part in sectoral factor allocation and in the development and adoption in rural areas of innovations that increase productivity. This does not in any way mean that peasants are profit maximizers, simply that agricultural policy analysts and practitioners would be well advised to take due account of price and productivity trends and their effects on rural allocation decisions.

It is only since the early 1980s that a number of empirical studies have been made of the determinants of the aggregate supply reaction at sectoral level.[3] Until then it had been generally assumed that aggregate supply in the agricultural sector in relation to the sectoral terms of trade amounted to similar orders of magnitude as that of individual products. This argument by analogy proved to be erroneous.

A number of analyses of aggregate supply have corrected the picture. The short-term[4] elasticities of aggregate supply are usually around <<0.20. This is not really surprising since in the short term capacity endowment, management skills, production methods, social institutions and administrative structures are capable of no more than minor changes – capacities can be enlarged only within tight limits in the short term. Only in the longer term can production conditions be arranged more flexibly. Accordingly, an increasing time lag in the response of production to the sectoral terms of trade gives rise to higher elasticities of sectoral supply of up to 1.0 (see Table 11). The full supply response requires a reaction period of up to 20 years because of the lengthy interactions of price ratios, the adjustment and adoption of technical advances and the necessary investment (Mundlak *et al.* 1989). The long-term sectoral elasticity of supply in particular seems to increase with the level of agricultural and economic development: the more advanced it is, the more adaptable it becomes.

Regression analyses assign a far greater influence (measured as elasticities) on sectoral production performance to three groups of structural variables – human capital, level of production technology and infrastructure – than to the sectoral terms of trade (Antle 1983).

Ignoring the problems of statistical methodology for the moment, the following conclusions have been drawn from the estimates of sectoral supply (Mundlak *et al.* 1997):

Table 11 Aggregate elasticities of production in the agricultural sectors of India, Africa and Argentina

Country/region	Short-term	Long-term
Africa[a]	0.10–0.22	0.11–0.34
India[b]	0.20–0.30[b]	0.40–0.50
Argentina[b]	0.21–0.35	0.42–0.78

[a] Spread from nine country studies, omitting the two extremes;
[b] Fluctuation margins due to different modelling and/or estimate.

Source: Chibber (1988); Binswanger (1989).

- The aggregate price elasticity of supply is, as a rule, <<0.20 in the short term and up to 1.0 in the long term.
- The elasticities of production related to the mobile factors of production, labour and capital are far higher in the long term than in the short term.
- The elasticities of production related to the structural variables human capital, level of production technology and infrastructure are highest as a cross-section or in the long term.

In view of these findings those who determine development policy tend to promote the structural variables and to neglect the price and innovation policy side, where, that is, agriculture and rural areas are even mentioned by the donors in their discussions. What is, of course, overlooked in this context is that the sectoral terms of trade have a major indirect influence in the long term on progress to a higher level of production technology and, together with this, on the intensity of the mobile factors capital and labour, as Hayami and Ruttan have painstakingly proved (Hayami and Ruttan 1971). Binswanger gets right to the heart of the matter:

> Agricultural growth is the outcome of a process in which farmers respond to improved farm profits. Changes in profits, in turn, derive from the interplay of prices, improved infrastructure and better services, and enhanced technology. ... The aggregate long run response of agriculture to price changes is large, and ultimately comes from private decisions to migrate and invest.
>
> (Binswanger 1990, p. 243)[5]

Government could, of course, pursue a consumer-friendly price policy while attempting to promote the agricultural sector with the second incentive, increased productivity (through technical progress, infrastructure expansion and human capital formation) – and, seen ex post, this, of course, accounts for the treadmill effect: relatively falling product prices due to technical progress, which increases supply more quickly than demand can follow (see Chapter 6.2). But *ex ante* an anti-agricultural price and trade policy destroys essential incentives to discover and shape technical advances and to adopt them in agriculture, since even farmers in the industrialized countries have learnt only in the past 20 years to look ahead and prepare for the treadmill effect in their investment and migration decisions in line with the *ex ante* slogan 'grow or go'.[6] This is joined by another phenomenon: countries which burden their agricultural sectors with export taxes, externally subsidized imports and overvalued exchange rates usually let the innovation and structural policy instruments of agricultural policy go to waste. We need only compare the agricultural policies of the sub-Saharan African countries with those of the Asian countries (India, Thailand, Malaysia, Vietnam, China, Indonesia). An agricultural sector that forgoes government promotion of structural development and technical progress, as is largely the case today in sub-Saharan Africa, is lost in international competition and also renounces the most important means of reducing poverty.

11.2   Micro-economic analysis and innovations

Without innovations in production technology there is no lasting increase in agricultural supply. They do not happen by chance, but require, under pre- and early-industrial conditions, the interaction of government-promoted agricultural research and experimental and extension work organized along cooperative lines. The research priorities and extension services provided can address rural problems only if they are identified by domestic economy and farm economic analysis that is well understood in social and production technology terms. There are plenty of examples of inappropriate extension messages that were propagated hastily before a domestic economy and farm economic review had been undertaken. Nor is delegating the innovation problem to the target groups an adequate solution, since peasants do not, of course, have any experience of impending innovations or innovations yet to be developed. Unfortunately, with the exception of a few countries, agricultural policy and development cooperation have in practice lost sight of production. The peasants are left to themselves with their problems and yet are expected to hold their own in the market against highly productive and, moreover, heavily subsidized foreign competitors.

In the name of ownership it is often asserted in this context that development cooperation can no longer take care of everything. What is, of course, overlooked is that what is at stake here is not some small-scale project but a socio-economic appreciation of the livelihoods of 70 per cent of the population and 75 to 85 per cent of the poor. It is also true to say, of course, that this may bring to light some inconvenient data on the agricultural policy environment and its effects on agricultural and rural poverty.

In the late 1970s empirical data on farm economics in the Third World were still well enough advanced for it to be possible to submit agro-technical innovations to a microeconomic examination to determine their advantages and disadvantages for the most important farming systems – and this in a socially and technically well-understood manner. This is possible today, at best, in India and the main South-East Asian rice-growing areas. Where in sub-Saharan Africa does anyone still ask about soil fertility, price ratios, production methods, productivity, gross margins, means of production, value added or non-agricultural sources of income and household needs?

Basically, most of what needed to be said about the analysis of peasant family farming systems had already been said in the European theory of management in the 1920s, which followed an inductive line of argument, starting from comparative bookkeeping data and operating statistics (Aereboe 1923; Tschajanow 1923; Laur 1927). For tropical and subtropical locations the best overview so far is that compiled by Hans Ruthenberg (Ruthenberg 1980). In its economic activities and lifestyle the peasant family first endeavours to maintain the physical basis of its livelihood and its social status. Once these are secure, an increase in capital and an improvement in status are added to differing degrees, depending on the societal context. This guarantees an 'adequate' gain within the limits of available resources, social norms and institutions and subjectively acceptable economic risks.

Production risks are far greater in the tropics than in the more temperate regions because of the serious fluctuation in precipitation, as an example from Zambia's dry savannah shows (see Diagram 3). This is a series of preliminary calculations that make for an exemplary description of the highly dramatic spread of total gross margins calculated with actual data within the capacity framework of land, labour and tractive power in line with weather patterns. In the practice of innovation policy, model estimates relating to types of family farm, risk limitation, capital situation and credit restrictions need, of course, to be made more comprehensive. Such considerations should be essential from the angle of feasibility and success where the aim is to introduce innovations in production technology into rural practice. Let it be stated clearly once and for all: rapid rural appraisal – *veni, vidi, vici* in the village, as it were – may give an initial overall impression of conditions at the location concerned, but it cannot replace the well-understood domestic economy and farm economic analysis when it comes to changing family farm systems and investment in rural practice and where agricultural policy should be thinking in microeconomic terms on the supply side with respect to a country's most important farming systems.

The farmer weighs up risks and profit opportunities one against the other when, learning by doing, he sorts out the organization of his farm. In this, the exploitation of complementary and supplementary relations among the products plays an important role (humus, labour, liquidity, risk balance, etc.). The globally decisive locational factors, which also assert themselves in their respective situations, are:

- natural conditions;
- price fluctuations;
- average price ratios (dependent on price and trade policy, market and transport infrastructure and market situation of production);
- social conditions;
- state of and practicable options offered by production technology;
- endowment with factors of production; and
- skills of the farm operator, male or female (and of the farming family), as manager(s) and worker(s).

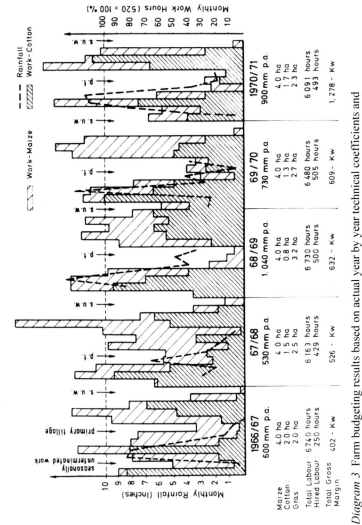

Diagram 3 Farm budgeting results based on actual year by year technical coefficients and gross margins, basic ox-plough technique and resource set unchanged

Source: Technical Coefficients and Gross margins from Hailey 1971.

s.u.w. = seasonally
unterminated work;
p.t. = primary tillage

Thus price ratios with a long time lag in some cases bear much of the responsibility for investment, labour migration, technical progress and organizational intensity[7] of production. On the other side are the instruments which affect structures and have a bearing on improvements in infrastructure, human capital and production technology. Mistakes on either side can largely block the effectiveness of agricultural policy.

This is not meant to portray farmers as notorious profit maximizers. The social influences on factor allocation may be considerable, especially where there is a quasi-feudalistic land tenure system or semi-commercialized agriculture. This is evident from an example in Togo, where ethnicity has an unmistakable influence in small-scale farming (see Table 12).

Table 12 Selected productivity and income parameters of the four farming systems[a] in the central region of Togo, 1989–90

Parameter/farming system	Kotokoli	Kabyé	Koussountou	Peulh	Weighted average
Persons/farm	8.2	8.4	10.1	9.4	8.7
Full-time workers/ farm	1.9	2.2	2.3	2.7	2.2
Area (ha)[b]	1.89	2.89	3.07	2.34	2.63
Area/full-time worker (ha)	1.02	1.33	1.31	0.86	1.20
Shares of total area given over to most important crops (in %)[c]					
– yams	19.4	16.6	1.6	14.3	17.1
– manioc	30.1	1.9	8.0	13.5	10.5
– sorghum	27.8	58.8	33.5	47.8	46.8
– maize	10.1	8.3	22.3	18.8	11.7
– cotton	4.5	10.9	7.1	2.7	7.6
– other	8.1	4.4	12.5	2.9	6.3
Share of animal production in value of production	4.0	8.2	2.7	33.9	8.8
Working hours/year/ha[d]	1535	1373	1192	1694	1415
Working hours/year/full-time worker[d]	1375	1829	1825	1060	1610

Table 12 (cont.)

Parameter/farming system	Kotokoli	Kabyé	Koussountou	Peulh	Weighted average
Agricultural income/farm (FCFA)	268700	238400	299700	401700	269600
Cash income per household (FCFA)	182100	104300	145300	233000	140600
Agricultural income/ha (FCFA)[e]	142200	82500	97600	171700	107100
Agricultural income/hour (FCFA)[f]	101	82	105	83	90
Share of non-agricultural income in total income	1.6 %	7.0 %	5.3 %	4.6 %	8.8 %

[a] Based on empirical farm surveys and a static-descriptive farm model.
[b] Annually cultivated area. Excluding fallow and extensive pastureland.
[c] As single crops or as dominant crop in mixed cultivation.
[d] Arable farming only.
[e] Area needed for pasture not included since it is, as a rule, freely available.
[f] Working hours of working family members.

Source: Schadek (1992), p. 120.

12   Growth and poverty reduction

The closely linked causes and effects of economic and agricultural growth have already been discussed (see Chapter 8.2). On the one hand, it was emphasized in this context that agriculture and non-agriculture are linked by contributing markets and factors to each other; on the other hand, reference was made to the tendency for the two sectors to become delinked owing to the liberalization of foreign trade. It was also stressed that price policy, innovation policy, infrastructure development and the promotion of human capital formation are the main levers of agricultural development policy. On the basis of the now copious empirical literature, this chapter first describes the effects on the poverty situation of economic growth and of support measures taken under development policies, and especially infrastructure development and human capital formation, and then emphasizes the major importance for poverty reduction of agricultural development, technical progress and increased productivity in agriculture.

The recent empirical literature applies regression analysis to both aspects. Aggregated country statistics are taken as the basis for cross-section analyses of groups of countries or districts and/or time series analyses. The second step is to interpret the causes of significant links between 'explanatory' factors and dependent variables. The literature thus essentially adopts a heuristic-inductive method; deductive arguments are added in the discussion of the findings. A critical examination thus needs to be made both of the statistical approach adopted in each case and of the theoretical interpretation of the conclusions drawn.

12.1   Economic growth and poverty reduction

The economic history of the industrialized countries shows that after an early-industrial phase the real incomes even of the poorest 10 or 20 per cent of the population rise with GNP in the long term. This finding influenced expectations for Third World development until the early 1970s. Economic growth was the overriding objective; the trickle-down effect would ensure that poverty was reduced. What was overlooked was that a long-term trend is not always bound to be smooth from the outset. Kuznets' analysis, which demonstrated with the aid of historical data on the American, British and German economies that the real incomes of poor groups may fall during the period of initial industrial development (Kuznets 1955), was at first overlooked. The reappraisal of current experience led to conceptual reorientation at the World Bank from 1974/75 (Chenery *et al.* 1974). The trickle-down effect was considered inadequate, and the growth-oriented concept gave way to redistribution-oriented measures controlled by government – primarily in the form of the increased promotion of social services. Only recently, however, have growth regressions provided empirical clarification as to whether or not economic growth in the developing countries had the effect of reducing poverty in the first three or four development decades and which of the structural starting conditions have a disruptive or favourable influence.[8]

'Growth is good for the poor,' Dollar and Kraay (2001) conclude from a cross-section analysis covering 137 countries in the past four decades. In a single regression they calculate an elasticity of per capita income in the lower quintile in relation to macroeconomic per capita income of 1.07. The model 'explains' 86 per cent of the statistical variation of the target variables. The approximately proportional share of economic growth enjoyed by the poorest 20 per cent proves to be statistically stable even when the regression takes account of other independent variables. Although such growth-promoting factors as the rule of law, the development of the financial sector and liberal foreign trade have an effect on the per capita income of the poor through higher macroeconomic growth, they do not increase the share of the poorest 20 per cent in national income. Formal democratic institutions and state social services similarly have no influence on the per capita incomes of the poor in the empirical analysis. The proportional share of the poor in growth also remains practically unchanged over time. Only anti-inflationary macropolicy and a reduction in government consumption slightly increase the share of the poor in national income.

According to global empirical data on recent decades, then, there would seem to be a kind of 'iron rule' that the poorest 20 per cent benefit proportionally from economic growth and that income distribution is, to some extent, societally predetermined and separate from the process of economic growth. But then what explains the differences in national income distribution, which are substantial even when the world's regions are compared (see Table A16)?

The only possible explanations left are really the lack of factors of production producing a rent that are available to the poor, the declining status of their personal human capital, their lack of integration into structures of relationships and power in society that are relevant to incomes and also different patterns of sectoral priorities in development policy. The relevance to distribution of the availability of means of production, personal human capital (Birdsall and Londono 1997; Deininger and Squire 1998) and the sectors in which growth is concentrated (Ravallion and Datt 1996) is indeed empirically proven, but there appear to be no studies on the influence of the access of the poor to the power structure.

Birdsall and Londono considered 43 countries using two sets of data at least five years apart in each case and calculated that, besides capital accumulation and the rate of investment, the variables with a significant influence ($R^2 = 0.70$) on economic growth were land distribution and the distribution of human capital (measured as a training index). As regards the growth of the incomes of the poorest quintile, the influence of the inequality of land ownership and levels of training, estimated as an elasticity, was found to be two to three times greater than that of macroeconomic growth. The higher the investment and the more equally distributed land ownership and levels of education, the greater the economic growth – especially of the poorest 20 per cent of the population (Birdsall and Londono 1997). With regard to the effects of land distribution and investment on growth, Deininger and Squire achieved a similar statistical result a little later and drew similar conclusions (Deininger and Squire 1998).

As a result of these studies it can be regarded as confirmed that the distribution of resource (and especially land) ownership and human capital are factors which partly explain the differences in income distribution (Gini index) among economies and have a major influence on the effect of growth on distribution; but a more balanced distribution of human capital can be achieved by development policy means only in the very long term and, to judge from all practical experience, a balanced distribution of land ownership – or the elimination of feudalistic conditions – within a reasonable period is possible only in revolutionary situations (see Chapter 13.3). Even under these conditions land reforms usually fail in the end unless the instruments of agricultural policy are employed to support the land-use reforms that are needed at the same time.

Another way, more open to influence by development policy, of improving the income situation of the poor while national income inequality is reduced is the sectoral targeting of economic growth – or at least so India's experience indicates. Using an impressive database of 33 country-wide Indian household surveys undertaken from 1951 to 1991, Ravallion and Datt (1996) astonishingly show that the growth of the industrial sector increases poverty both in rural areas and in the towns and cities, i.e. throughout the economy (see Table 13). Growth of the primary and tertiary sectors, on the other hand, has the effect of reducing poverty. The authors comment on their findings as follows:

- Agricultural growth and growth of the tertiary sector greatly reduce poverty in urban and rural areas, whereas industrial growth increases poverty sharply, even in urban areas.
- This is primarily due to capital-intensive industrialization in a largely closed economy.
- 'Fostering the conditions for growth in the rural economy – in both primary and tertiary sectors – must thus be considered central to an effective strategy for poverty reduction in India. ... This result underlines the importance of making a successful transition to an alternative industrialization process; even then (we suspect), the tail will not wag the dog. But it could surely do a lot to help it move.'

(Ravallion and Datt 1996, p. 19)

Another finding is worth mentioning: rising agricultural prices in real terms increase rural poverty, probably because producer price rises are not followed by

Table 13 Elasticities of the percentage of the rural and urban population living below the poverty line in relation to the sectoral components of economic growth,[a] India, 1951–91

Independent variables	Dependent variables		
	Economy-wide poverty (% below poverty line)	Urban poverty (% below poverty line)	Rural poverty (% below poverty line)
Growth of primary sector	−1.16	−0.32	−0.86
Growth of secondary sector	3.41	0.61	2.53
Growth of tertiary sector	−3.42	−0.70	−2.37
Rural TOT[b]	0.94	—[d]	0.73
Urban TOT[c]	—[d]	0.25	—[d]
R^2	0.75	0.49	0.70

[a] double-logarithmic estimate;
[b] rural price index divided by national deflator;
[c] urban price index divided by national deflator;
[d] not considered because insignificant.

Source: Ravallion and Datt (1996), p. 23.

a proportional increase in the wages of the poor owing to the comparatively elastic supply of labour and inelastic demand for labour (see Chapter 13.3.1).

All in all, it can be said that:

- the incomes of the poor rise roughly in proportion to economic growth;
- more balanced distribution of land ownership and human capital have favoured a more balanced distribution of incomes as a result of the poor deriving proportionally higher benefit from the growth process;
- growth of the primary and tertiary sectors has a balancing effect on income distribution in rural and urban areas and nationally. Industrial growth has the opposite effect (in the case of inward-oriented industrialization).

These findings reflect the high labour intensity of growth in the agricultural and service sectors and a strong multiplier effect of agricultural growth (see Box 6). These are advantages for poverty-reducing economic development, which capital-intensive industrialization does not offer in its early phase.

With the discussion of the effect of sectoral growth priorities on distribution, the closing questions of this study are reached. How do agricultural development and poverty reduction go together causally? What effects do the core instruments of agricultural development policy (price and trade policy, innovation policy and land reform) have on the poverty situation?

12.2   Agricultural development and poverty reduction

The links between agricultural development and poverty reduction are best explored by considering India's experience, because it has been conducting surveys of households since 1951 – there are probably now more than 40 of them – and has exemplary agricultural statistics broken down by regions in accordance with the administrative hierarchy. In addition, covariances between poverty criteria and locational factors emerge clearly because of the major locational differences in regional social and economic structures and basic endowment with physical and non-physical infrastructure and human capital.

Measures to promote the primary and tertiary sectors are the development policy levers used to reduce poverty (see Table 13). Ravallion and Datt also show that economic growth in India's rural areas has been even more effective in reducing poverty than growth of the agricultural sector on its own (see Table 14) (Ravallion and Datt 1996). This effect primarily benefits the reduction of rural poverty, since the elasticity of urban poverty in relation to rural growth remains comparatively very limited. The elasticity of national poverty reduction in relation to rural growth is three times as high as the corresponding urban elasticity.

Table 14 Elasticities of the percentages of the rural and urban population living below the poverty line in relation to rural and urban growth,[a] India, 1951–91

Independent variables	Dependent variables		
	Nation-wide poverty (% below poverty line)	Urban poverty (% below poverty line)	Rural poverty (% below poverty line)
Growth of primary sector	−1.16	−0.32	−0.86
Urban growth	−0.55	−0.56	−0.169[b]
Rural growth	−1.46	−0.08	−1.14

[a]   double-logarithmic simultaneous estimates;
[b]   statistically insignificant.

Source: Ravallion and Datt (1996), p. 15, 23.

Estimates indicate that strong multiplier effects of growth having a considerable impact on employment occur between the sectors in the rural areas, while the growth of the formal (capital-intensive) industrial sector has no more than a slight multiplier effect and impact on employment. Put succinctly:

> Both the urban and rural poor gained from rural sector growth. By contrast, urban growth had adverse distributional effects within urban areas, which militated against the gains of the urban poor. And urban growth had no discernible impact on rural poverty.
>
> (ibid, p. 19)

The Indian case thus makes it clear that without agricultural and rural development there is no poverty reduction.

In a further study Ravallion and Datt differentiate these findings and show that in a cross-section comparison of the Indian states, non-agricultural growth had a stronger poverty-reducing effect the more favourable the environment or starting conditions: agricultural productivity, level of education and government spending on the development of rural areas (Ravallion and Datt 1999).

The increase in agricultural productivity, measured as crop yields, had the effect of reducing rural poverty primarily in three ways: through the direct effect of increasing yields (operating mainly through ground rent) and indirectly through rising wages and falling food prices. Almost half of the reduction in rural poverty was achieved in the long term through the effect of falling prices, 27 per cent through the effect of rising real wages and a further 27 per cent through the direct effect of yields. This shows that among India's rural poor the consumer's interest in low prices and the worker's interest in higher wages easily outweigh the producer's interest in higher ground rent (Datt and Ravallion 1998): very few of the Indian poor own even a small plot of land.

Using an estimation system of simultaneous equations, Shenggen Fan *et al.* examined the influence of the instruments of agricultural and rural development on rural poverty. They found that road-building and agricultural research and extension are by far the most efficient means of combating rural poverty in India, the next most efficient being education and other rural development measures (see Table A17). The intermediary factors were increases in total factor productivity, increases in real rural wages, reductions in real grain prices and increases in employment in the non-agricultural rural sectors (Fan *et al.* 1999).

Similar findings on China were obtained by the same statistical method (Fan *et al.* 2000). High analytical accuracy is achieved because of the contrasting phases of Chinese agricultural development since the Communist revolution (see Table A18) and through the breakdown of the analytical findings by main economic regions.

Chinese agricultural development from 1978 followed a course of simultaneous and mutually complementary increases in land and labour productivity. The production-increasing effect, first, of producer price ratios and, second, of the peasants' freedom to make their own arrangements is clear from the Chinese experience (see Table A18). The growth of agricultural production amounted to a mere 2.1 per cent p.a. when the economy was centrally planned, as compared to 6.6 per cent p.a. once compulsory levies were largely abandoned and tenant peasant farmers were able to operate freely (1978–84). After the liberalization of the price and trade policies and thus approximation to badly distorted world market prices in 2002, the Chinese agricultural policy again begins a fundamental learning process. It would not be surprising if China soon resorted to safeguard measures under its trade policy.

In China's case education, agricultural research and extension were the most cost-efficient means of reducing the proportion of the rural population living below the poverty line (see Table A19), followed by road-building and electrification. The cost efficiencies of poverty reduction were 10 to 20 times higher in the western region, which is marginal in terms of development and natural conditions, than in the already comparatively well-developed coastal region. Similar empirical findings are reported from India (Fan and Hazell 2000). There thus appears to be here a kind of declining rate of return in the case of the poverty-reducing effect of government agricultural and rural development measures, which, when viewed from the distribution angle, argues against the regional concentration of expenditure, particularly when it comes to favourable locations.

Investment in large-scale irrigation proved to be surprisingly unprofitable and inefficient as regards the reduction of rural poverty in both India and China (see Tables A17 and A19). This finding confirms experience gained from development cooperation projects some time ago. In practice, however, it is apparent in many cases that it is not errors of technical design or the intensity of capital spending on infrastructure (dams, canals, locks, earthworks) that cause the economic outcome to be negative but the centrally decreed misallocation of water and irrigated land when, for example, what is produced is not fruit, vegetables and milk for the local market, despite adequate demand backed by purchasing power, but, because of central crop planning, sugar or cotton.

A Pakistani study refers to the unfavourable rural income distribution which results from the extremely biased concentration of land ownership. As under early-industrial conditions in other economies of Europe and Asia where land is scarce, here, too, ground rents are likely to account for about 50 per cent of value added. The poor derive only 5 per cent of their income from rents. Their most important source of income consists of remittances from relatives who have found work in the towns or cities. In view of the distribution of land ownership, which is a socio-political datum, educating and training the poor are the basic options for reducing poverty here (Adams and He 1995). Hayami infers from a comparison of agricultural development in Indonesia, Thailand and the Philippines that the unequal distribution of land ownership in the Philippines has been one of the main causes of the comparatively low growth of agricultural production. He shows that the industrial and large-land-owning interests and families are closely linked here. They pursue an industrial policy protected by tariffs, with selective promotion of the plantation sector:

> In contrast, the rural countervailing power was comparatively high in Indonesia, Malaysia and Thailand, because the urban business elite were predominantly ethnic Chinese.
>
> (Hayami 2000, p. 30)

Hayami concludes his comparison with a wide-ranging assumption:

> … the agrarian structure of a nation … should have a far reaching influence on the value system in its society and the organization of its political economy and, hence, on policy choice.
>
> (ibid, p. 31)

Here we have an apt pointer to the problem of rural poverty under the Latin American conditions of feudalistic land tenure systems. Two of the main findings of a broad-based cross-section analysis of Latin American countries (De Janvry and Sadoulet 2000) are, firstly, that the elasticities of urban and rural poverty in relation to national per capita income are −0.95 and −0.75, respectively. Here again, then, 'growth is good for the poor'; yet growth of the national economy does not correct the inequality of income distribution, but exacerbates it. Secondly, it is evident, in contrast to the Indian and Chinese experience, that agricultural growth does not have any significant effects on the proportion of the population – whether rural or urban – living below the poverty line. With the present distribution of land ownership and social structure in the Latin American countries, a reduction of rural poverty by means of agricultural development is hardly possible, unless agricultural reforms are undertaken, and, with few exceptions, they have failed in the past, or come to a halt half-way.

The full relevance of the distribution of land ownership to poverty is apparent here. Not only do the poor have hardly any share of ground rents: there is virtually none of the demand for local non-agricultural goods and services that would create employment, since the large farms need industrial inputs and capital goods and the large landowner wants industrial consumer goods and city services. Furthermore, the large farms are organized along comparatively labour-extensive lines. The impact of the local agricultural growth multiplier is relatively limited for the reasons given. Only in the urban areas do the poor have a chance of increasing their real incomes appreciably – and that is where they migrate to. Thus De Janvry and Sadoulet summarize the main finding of their cross-section analysis of growth, poverty and inequality in Latin America as follows:

> ... growth was always ineffective in reducing inequality, ...Hence, while it cannot be said that growth is inequalizing, neither can reliance be placed on growth to reduce inequality. Other instruments need to be used for this purpose, basically focusing on enhancing control over assets of the poor and on equalizing opportunities in accessing the markets, institutions, and public goods that determine the income generation value of these assets.
>
> (ibid, p. 284 ff.)

To put it even more succinctly, under feudalistic land tenure conditions growth results in no reduction of inequality and only a disproportionately low reduction of poverty. Far-reaching poverty reduction in this case would require resolute land reform backed by decentralized implementation and services organized on a cooperative basis and an essential minimum of national framework legislation. Society's desire for this must, of course, grow in the democratic debate, and implementation calls for stable democratic majorities.

The irrelevance of agricultural growth to both rural and urban poverty reduction caused by the extremely unequal distribution of land ownership that is typical of Latin American economies is not, by and large, emphasized in global cross-section analyses. The conclusion is, then, that 'growth is good for the poor.' The other influences continue to be assigned to the 'unexplained' residual spread. Only Deininger and Squire have shown, in 1996, that the initial distribution of land ownership is of prime importance for the poverty-reducing effect of growth (see Chapter 12.1). Timmer considers this problem further in an international cross-section analysis. He defines an elasticity of connection, i.e. the elasticities of agricultural and non-agricultural growth related to national per capita income. The inclusion of a 'dummy variable', which assigns the value '1' to countries with unequal income distribution and the value '0' to the rest, reveals the relevance of the initial income distribution to the orders of magnitude of the elasticity of connection. In countries where the difference between the average per capita income of the highest quintile and the corresponding figure for the lowest quintile is more than twice the average for all quintiles,

> ... the poor are nearly left out of the growth process altogether, and agriculture is no more effective in reaching them than non-agriculture.
>
> (Timmer 1997, p. 23)

In countries where income distribution is particularly unequal, agricultural growth thus continues to have a very limited effect on the income situation of the lowest quintile (see Table 15). These are typically agricultural countries with a pre- or early-industrial economic structure and feudalistic distribution of land ownership. In such cases agricultural reforms are the precondition for effective poverty reduction in rural and urban areas. There are perhaps 25 countries of this kind in the world.

In these countries there is little chance of reducing rural poverty by means of agricultural policy and rural development until an agricultural reform has been undertaken to eliminate the feudalistic agrarian structure.

Initial studies of the conditions for poverty reduction in sub-Saharan Africa tend to produce findings similar to the statistically broad-based studies conducted in China and India (Christiaensen *et al.* 2002). Four main conclusions emerge. Firstly, political stabilization, economic stabilization and economic growth reduce poverty. Secondly, remoteness and high transport costs insulate large parts of the sub-Saharan African countries from positive, i.e. poverty-reducing, developments in their central areas. A marginal situation preserves poverty to some extent. Thirdly, it is found that training and access to land reduce rural poverty. Fourthly, it is confirmed that poverty is very much due to the erratic incidence of drought and disease and, specifically, the AIDS pandemic in the East and South of Africa, which is robbing families of their breadwinners, and the droughts in the semi-arid climate zones in the North and South of the continent.

Table 15 Elasticity of connection in countries with very unequal income distribution

Independent variables	Average per capita income				
	1st quintile	2nd quintile	3rd quintile	4th quintile	5th quintile
Productivity of agricultural labour	0.26	0.81	0.97	0.88	1.22
Productivity of non-agricultural labour	0.45	0.82	0.95	0.93	1.04

Source: Timmer (1997), p. 21a.

13   The problems posed by poverty-oriented agricultural policy

A review of empirical studies of the determinants of poverty confirms the existence of a complex relationship between causes and effects. The scale of rural poverty depends primarily on the total factor productivity of agriculture and the predominant land tenure system. The higher productivity rises and the more equally land ownership is distributed, the less rural poverty there is. On the other hand, a definite poverty-reducing effect cannot be ascribed to real producer prices, since price rises that benefit the land-owning producer reduce the real income of consumers who obtain their supplies from the food market. In the long term, however, real producer prices are major determinants of investment behaviour and thus of the trend in productivity. They too, then, have the effect of reducing poverty in the long run.

The level of factors of direct relevance to poverty is influenced by sectoral and macropolicies:

- macroeconomic growth policy
- infrastructure development
- policies of human and social capital formation
- components of agricultural development policy
  - price, market and trade policy
  - innovation policy
  - land reform policy.

The poverty regressions relating to India's and China's agricultural development that were discussed above naturally include those countries' agricultural policy environment as regards price ratios, technical progress and land tenure. In both cases these factors were classified in an international comparison as being favourable for the trend in production. In dysfunctional agricultural policy circumstances the poverty-reducing effects of training, infrastructure development and research would have been far less pronounced. The more efficient the national agricultural policy is in design, the more effective these measures are in relation to poverty reduction. Since China liberalized its agricultural price, market and trade policies following its accession to the WTO, without paying direct subsidies to compensate for the resulting losses of rural income, poverty has again been rising sharply. Today 150 to 200 million agricultural workers are unable to find work above subsistence level. They have thus joined the ranks of the hidden unemployed. Increased rural–urban migration is the result:

> … the great upheaval in agriculture has only just begun. 200 million redundant rural workers are a potential cause of unrest that will cause the party leadership some trouble yet.
>
> (Kolonko 2002)

Because of liberalization, then, Chinese agriculture is today threatened from the liberalized food markets by poverty-increasing developments in the price policy environment similar to those occurring in the sub-Saharan African countries.

Government agricultural policy may influence factor intensities, the production trend and productivity in agriculture in three ways: by changing producer price ratios, by improving production methods and by reforming conditions pertaining to social institutions. Improvements in physical productivity may lead to rising production despite declining producer prices in real terms, and that, of course, is what has happened throughout the world in the past 40 years: higher productivity, increased supply, demand lagging behind relatively, falling real prices (see Chapter 6.2). Where they do away with latifundia ownership and feudalistic land tenure systems, land reforms can not only significantly improve rural income distribution but also greatly increase the intensity of production and the efficiency of farm management and labour by changing motivation and economic objectives.

These three components of agricultural development policy are discussed in the following pages, since experience shows that they must supplement the structure-related measures (training, infrastructure development and research) so that the poor may derive full benefit from them by their own initiative. What use are a good road to the market and agricultural training if price ratios are distorted *ad absurdum*? This approach is not adopted with the intention of providing a comprehensive overview of the instruments of agricultural development policy, which would also have to consider a range of other services and the direct measures of agricultural environment policy (see Figure 3).

13.1   Price, market and trade policy

The distribution-oriented agricultural policies of the former Comecon countries were determined, from producer to consumer, by administered prices and quantitative controls. Much the same was true of developing countries with a socialist agricultural policy (China, Cuba, Ethiopia, Tanzania, etc.). Centrally planned agricultural policies, characterized by centrally decreed quotas and prices, compulsion and controls have gone out of fashion throughout the world in the past decade. The EU, however, maintains the old minimum-price/compensatory payment/quota system for a number of products.

Centrally planned price and quantity control led to the widespread misallocation of national resources everywhere and so to losses of growth, even in developing countries. An example of this is the inefficiency of government and parastatal grain marketing boards and the policy of pan-territorial pricing, the inferior utilization of foodstuffs as animal feed in cases of consumer-oriented low-price policies, the local black and grey markets in processed products and agricultural means of production and all the trappings of harassment, bribery and so on. The social costs of a centrally planned agricultural policy are exceedingly high everywhere. Developing countries are least able to afford them.

Problem area/policy	Regulatory requirement
I Distortion of price ratios	1 Price, market and trade policy – price levels, price fluctuations – market structure – quantitative interventions (interregional, intertemporal)

II Food security
a) increase in agricul-
   tural output,
   maintenance of sustainability
b) adequate distribution
   of foodstuffs
	– foreign trade regime
	– supplies for poor groups
	2 Innovation policy
	– training
	– research
	– extension

III Increased efficiency of
   agricultural services
	3 Other service policy
	– formalization and promotion of
	   rural financial sector
	   (saving, credit)
	– input supply
	– promotion of cooperatives

IV Employment-creating land tenure system	4 Agricultural reform policy – distribution of land ownership – water rights, grazing rights – tenancy law, law of succession – regulation of land market

V   Limitation of environ-
   mental damage
	5 Direct agricultural environment
	   policy measures
	– protection zones, use zones
	– erosion control
	– pollution due to synthetic means
	   of production
	– preservation of genetic resources

Problem: agricultural output and its distribution are linked systems. Each agricultural policy measure has an impact on all problem areas. Strong interactions occur among the various instruments. There is no off-the-peg agricultural development policy. Each country must develop its own agricultural policy empirically and inductively not only at normative but also at technical and instrumental level. However, there are well-documented global empirical data on the causes and effects linking agricultural policy instruments, which argue against biased instrumentation and refer to basic complementary effects. What is now an empirically broad-based theory of instruments is the real advance in knowledge that practical and academic agricultural development policy has made in the past 40 years.

Figure 3 Policy on the agricultural sector

Source: Author's own design.

Although a partial price and distribution policy geared to poor target groups is feasible under market economy conditions – one need only think, for example, of the subsidized distribution of food to the poor in return for food stamps and of the well-organized food-for-work programmes – even such limited approaches to distribution-oriented market policy require a great deal of monitoring and administration – not to mention the notorious inefficiencies involved.

The general raising or lowering of the food price level by means of trade, tax and subsidization policy is unsuitable for combating poverty because of the very wide variation in the effect it has on the heterogeneous groups of the poor. Raising prices makes the urban poor worse off in real terms. As a rule, the rural poor are not hit so hard because rural wages usually rise with producer prices, though not at the same rate. Price increases benefit the land owners and farmers who produce surpluses, provided they own the land they farm, as a result of the higher ground rent. Globally, consumer-oriented 'low-price policies' relating to foodstuffs are almost completely confined today to the sub-Saharan African countries. Depending on the country, they are made possible by overvalued exchange rates, bulk supplies of food aid and – given the price distortions in the world markets – relatively extensive imports of food that is directly subsidized by the exporting countries. The rural poor living inland derive little or no benefit where they live because of high transport and other transformation costs and, in some cases, trade oligopolies, and so they migrate to the towns and cities in search of cheap bread.

13.1.1 Agricultural prices and wages

In the short term agricultural wages follow producer prices, but usually at a lower rate: real wages thus fall as producer prices rise. As the neo-classical market model shows, the more elastic the supply of labour and the more inelastic the demand for labour, the more sharply wages in kind fall (see Diagram 4). It can thus be said of India, for example:

> Looking back over 40 years or so one finds that higher relative prices of food in India have typically been associated with higher poverty incidence and lower real agricultural wages.
>
> (Ravallion 2000, p. 351)

This has often been observed in the agricultural sectors of pre- and early-industrial economies. Albrecht Thaer found in nineteenth century German agriculture that wages followed grain prices, but at a lower rate of increase (Thaer 1809–12, Vol. I, p. 109 ff.). In lean years other factors enter the equation, depressing wages in kind to famine level. In 1973, a normal year, for example, the typical grain price and agricultural wage patterns in Bangladesh proved to have an elasticity of wages to grain prices of about 0.75 (see Diagram 5) (Sen 1981). In 1974, a year of drought, on the other hand, real wages fell very steeply (see Table A21) (ibid., p. 145).

GE, W

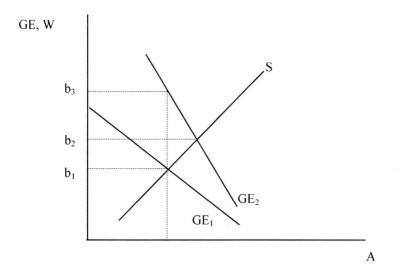

GE = P• y' = marginal monetary return on labour in grain production c.p.; P = grain price; y' = marginal yield of labour; S = labour supply; A = quantity of labour; b_3–b_1 = shift of function due to doubling grain price; b_2–b_1 = rise in wages by about 28%; W = wage rate

Diagram 4 Grain prices and agricultural wages in the neo-classical model

Source: Author's own design.

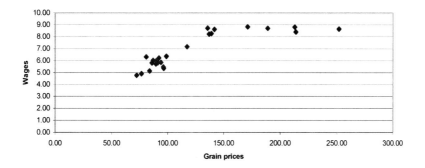

Diagram 5 Grain prices and wages, Bangladesh, 1973–74 (in Rps)

Source: Sen (1981), p. 145.

It goes without saying that wages do not rise at the same rate as marginal physical productivity either, since the marginal monetary return is the product of the grain price and the marginal physical return. In Asian countries falling agricultural output prices have even been accompanied by rising rural wages since the 1970s. Besides physical productivity growth, the extensification of labour enforced by rural outmigration – in turn induced by rising urban wages – has played a significant role here. Where there is a rapid rise in productivity accentuated by a shrinking agricultural labour force agricultural wages will rise as a rule despite falling output prices.

Continuing economic growth will be accompanied by falling agricultural output prices and despite that a sustained increase in rural wages due to labour migration from agriculture, capital intensification and technical progress (see Diagram 7). This is what has happened in India (see Table 8), and in both Bangladesh and Indonesia real rural wages have risen by some 250 per cent over the past 20 years up to about 6.5 to 7.0 kg of husked rice per working day. Aggregate economic growth and increases in physical agricultural productivity provide for rising real wages of the rural poor and thereby reduce mass poverty. What they do not achieve in wage growth the poor gain in consumers' surplus (see Diagram 6). In a word, agricultural productivity growth is the central lever for poverty eradication in industrializing economies.

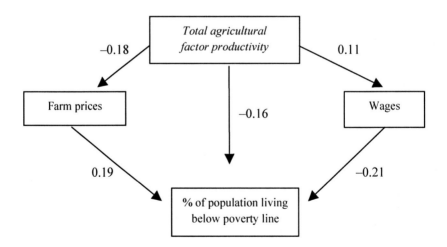

Diagram 6 Total factor productivity and reduction of rural poverty in India, 1960–93[a]

[a] Figures in the diagram represent elasticities.

Source: Fan *et al.* (1999), p. 38.

Wages and grain prices are among the core data on rural economics and poverty conditions, in which hardly anyone in development cooperation has unfortunately taken an interest for about 20 years. There is no provision for them in rapid rural appraisal. Long series of different locations are even far less frequently available.

13.1.2   Transport costs and market segmentation

Under the conditions of sub-Saharan African agricultural sectors in particular, high transport costs often result in the segmentation of internal grain markets because the rural transport infrastructure has been systematically neglected for about 25 years and is in a very poor state. As a rule, the large towns and cities are situated on the coast or are at least linked to the coast by the main communication routes. Away from the coast and the principal infrastructure axes freight rates and transport costs are likely to be very high because of the poor state of the roads (see Table A20). An example will serve to illustrate this. The cost of transporting cereals between a port and an inland village is as follows:

300 km by heavy lorry (300 x 0.15 €/tonne)	45.– €/tonne
20 km by pick-up (20 x 0.85 €/tonne)	17.– €/tonne
5 km by donkey-cart (5 x 0.60 €/tonne)	3.– €/tonne
Total	65.– €/tonne

At a wholesale price of 150 €/tonne at the port the import price at the village is 215 €/tonne and the export price 85 €/tonne. While the market price at the village remains within this price spread, its grain market is of no interest to traders in the coastal town. The farther inland the village is situated and the higher the freight rates, the greater the difference between import and export parity prices, with the result that world market prices are at first seasonally irrelevant and eventually irrelevant throughout the year to local pricing in remote parts of the country as the distance to the market increases. A group of high-ranking sub-Saharan African politicians and economists with an interest in agriculture thus remarked recently that

> ... transportation costs for food are so high that imports become prohibitively expensive on leaving the vicinity of coastal ports.
>
> (Badiane and Delgado 2002)

Consequently, Heinrich von Thünen's spatial concept of prices is, as it were, turned upside down in many sub-Saharan African countries when there is a poor harvest: grain market prices are then at their lowest in the central urban markets (where they are often reduced further by subsidies) and at their highest, because of high transport costs, on the rural periphery, which is partly supplied from the central markets.

Demand in the world market and the large coastal towns and cities creates a peri-urban ring in which vegetables, fruit, root crops, tubers and plantains are grown intensively. This is followed by a second ring, in which the classical raw materials for export are grown, and, on the periphery, by extensive ranching or the growing of spices, medicinal plants and, in some cases, narcotics, depending on the natural conditions (Alexander 2002). Cereals, oil seed and grain legumes are grown primarily to satisfy demand inland and to ensure the subsistence of peasant households, and this the more extensively in relative terms, the higher the cost of transport to the coastal town or the world market. They have little chance of competing in the coastal towns, in the central locations linked to the world market or in the world market itself.

This also shows, moreover, why export cash crops will continue to be essential for the development of the sub-Saharan African agricultural sectors for at least another generation, since they yield no less than cereals and their market price is higher – ten times higher in the case of cotton and coffee, for example. Percentage transport costs therefore burden these products with only one-tenth of the corresponding figure for cereals over the same distance. There is no doubt that the erratic nature of the grain markets, the general collapse of the production of raw materials for export in the sub-Saharan African hinterland (in brief: the absence of agricultural prospects) and the supply of the central urban markets with cheap and often regionally subsidized grain and other food imports from the world market are, in addition to the concentration of development cooperation on urban areas, among the main causes of the completely unbalanced urbanization rates in sub-Saharan African countries.[9]

The far-reaching positive effects of road-building on the integration of agriculture into the market and on value added, employment and material living standards, and the material social situation are evident, for example, from a World Bank and KfW project implemented in Guinea from 1991 to 1996:

- reduction of transport costs by a third
- increase in market activity by 500 per cent
- increase in cultivated area by 61 per cent
- increase in agricultural output for the market by one-third.

Equally dramatic improvements occurred in agricultural extension, health care, drinking water supply and housing. They were joined by pronounced (measured) multiplier effects in the up- and downstream rural economy (KfW 2002, p. 8). If efficient agricultural price, market and trade policies entailing the siphoning off of the margin of distortion in food imports and active promotion of the export marketing of agricultural raw materials could now be added – how well a country might at last develop economically and socially.

13.2   Innovation policy

At national level agricultural innovation policy usually has three priorities: adaptation research, extension and adult education.

Building on the findings of global pure research and cooperating closely with organized rural practitioners, practical adaptation research is meant to find appropriate solutions to current technical, economic and socio-organizational problems.

Proposed solutions are propagated in rural areas by means of extension. In this, experimentation organized along peasant cooperative lines, followed by group extension, has a central role to play. The substance of the extension should have been reviewed and adapted during a process of experience and discussion in research and rural practice before it is propagated over a wide area. It should be recommended to the peasants as 'if-then rules' that enable them to effect the adaptations specific to their holdings. If success is to be sustained, it is also essential that the conclusions drawn and questions raised during extension work are reported back to the regional or national agricultural research level as part of a well-organized reporting system.

Farm management skills are the most important means of production of all once an agricultural sector is reasonably well integrated into the market. This has repeatedly been shown by comparative farm statistics throughout the world. Adult education in domestic economy and farm economics is therefore a vital component of any sustainably efficient innovation policy. In view of the poor infrastructure and shortage of funds available to the agriculture ministries, peripatetic teachers who give courses in the villages are often the most appropriate means. To motivate staff, it is very important in this context to ensure that there is a career structure for social agronomists, beginning with work as peripatetic teachers.

All this is well documented from the European and American tradition and the developing countries' experience since 1955. It is not rebutted by the fact that mistakes have been made, as when unprofitable, excessively risky or oversized innovations have been propagated. As a rule, such mistakes are caused by analyses of problems that focus too heavily on the social or economic aspects or on production technology, as is almost bound to be the case when the services of a socio-institutionally well-understood analysis of family farming systems are eschewed.

Innovation policy naturally requires organization that can be sustainably financed. This includes the peasants' participation in the financing of experimentation and adult education.

Of greatest importance for any success is a balanced dialogue between researchers, teachers and extension workers on the one hand and rural practitioners on the other. Top-down decrees and also allowing the 'practical opinion' to apply in principle have an equally dysfunctional effect. Innovation policy simply cannot take advantage of the idea of 'ownership' to shirk the responsibility of fostering the process of discussion between researchers, extension workers and rural practitioners as the main component of the innovation process.

Innovation policy is the main driving force behind increases in production and productivity. It reduces urban poverty by increasing supply and, where appropriate, reducing food prices unless a development of this nature is blocked by trade policy interventions. The essential alleviating effects on rural poverty occur through rising ground rents of holdings at least partly integrated into the market and through rising remuneration in real terms. This is what has happened everywhere in Asia in the wake of the Green Revolution. In this, however, the trend in numbers of rural workers plays a fundamental role. If the number of workers increases more quickly than the demand for labour, real wages can hardly rise. Where the increase in productivity is persistently higher than the growth of the labour force or the latter even shrinks, real wages rise. This has been the case in the agricultural sectors of European countries since the early nineteenth century and of Asian countries since about 1970 (see Diagram 7).

As regards today's developing countries, there is no compelling reason to be pessimistic about productivity. Over the past four decades research has identified a wide range of technical ways of increasing agricultural productivity at tropical and subtropical locations. This is even true of cereal-growing locations in the Sahel, which are agronomically difficult and marginal in terms of climatic conditions (see Box 7). The FAO reports a new example of success (FAO 2002, p. 20 ff.): the WARDA has successfully crossed Asian high-yielding varieties of rice with the disease- and pest-resistant West African species. The new NERICA variety combines resistance and increased yields. The new rice increases yields per hectare by 25 per cent at a low-input intensity and by up to 250 per cent at a high-input intensity. Yields rose rapidly, the annual increases from 1994 to 2000 being:

Côte d'Ivoire	15.0 %
Togo	15.0 %
Zambia	9.3 %
Niger	6.6 %
Mali	3.1 %
World (for comparison)	0.8 %

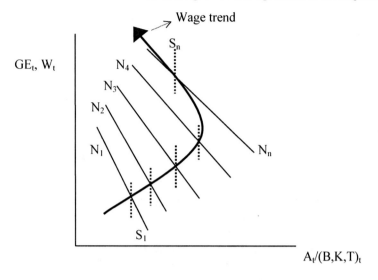

GE$_t$ = marginal monetary return; A$_t$ = labour over time; W$_t$ = wage rate;
(B,K,T)$_t$ = land, capital, technology over time; S$_1$ ... S$_n$ = time bound labour supply;
N$_1$ ... N$_n$ = time bound labour demand.

Diagram 7 Labour market pattern of the rural wage trend

Source: Author's own design.

***Box 7* Increase in grain yields in the Sahel**

A team from Purdue University spent several years experimenting before developing an innovative package for the millet-growing system in Upper Volta's Plateau Region, applying the farming systems research approach in a peasant environment. The package includes tie ridging and moderate application of mineral fertilizers (Nagy and Ohm 1985a). There are complementary interactions between the two innovations. Tie ridging using animal power saves labour and improves soil hydrology. The result is both higher yields and greater yield security. On this basis the application of mineral fertilizers then becomes possible at less risk to crops and, as the 'icing on the cake' as it were, may significantly improve the profitability of the overall package. In the whole-farm calculation (LP model) the household's grain production rises by up to 60 per cent and farm income by 38 per cent where these innovations are used on an optimum scale (ibid., 1985b).

Other major capacity limits of the farming system are the small proportion of organic soil matter and liquidity shortages. An added problem is posed by the relatively high prices of commercial fertilizers. The next step should therefore be to develop the appropriate application of rock phosphate (possibly combined with organic fertilizers), since the West African countries (Senegal, Mali, Niger, Togo, Benin, Nigeria, Burkina Faso) have large rock phosphate reserves, and some of the arable land in these countries is extremely low in phosphates.

From the development policy angle it should be remembered that agronomic research in the Sahel can look back on at least 30 years' experience and has made some fundamental discoveries in important areas (mineral fertilizers, organic fertilizers, crop sequences, soil management) (Pieri 1989). In the future, the main aim must be to integrate these partial findings into the socio-ecological combination of peasant farming systems. Development cooperation may have an important contribution to make in this respect in the future (Davies 1986).

If the whole of West Africa followed suit and the new variety is combined with favourable price, trade and input policies, increases in production of 250,000 to 750,000 tonnes p.a., depending on the scenario, would be possible. This would be quite an achievement for the world rice and grain markets (see Box 1). No great search would be needed to find enough success stories emerging from agricultural research to fill a whole book. Of course, knowledge at agricultural research stations does not in any way automatically mean introduction into rural practice. This requires at least some physical and non-physical infrastructure and an appropriate agricultural policy environment.

13.3   Land reform

Apart from the settlement economies of the British Crown, all successful cases of agricultural and economic development in modern times have begun with land reforms. They are the most enduring topic in the conceptual debate on agricultural development policy. They can take the credit for a number of successes, but also for many dashed hopes. It is hardly an exaggeration to claim that working through land reforms is like reinventing the wheel (Kirk 1998). Nonetheless, in some regions of the world great hopes are still pinned on future land reforms as the crucial means of achieving far-reaching poverty reduction in rural areas, examples being southern Africa, Latin America, the Philippines and, for sure, Pakistan if social and political conditions there permit the poor to express their will democratically.

By analogy with De Janvry, land reforms can be defined as follows: changes to the institutions of land use and land ownership made by government in order to resolve economic and political inconsistencies and conflicts, without altering the networks of dominant social relationships (De Janvry 1984). This definition contains, of course, a *contradictio in adjecto*, since in pre- and early industrial societies the system of land ownership is the pivot on which the social structure and the balance of political power turns – the literature is bursting with relevant statements of these basic facts. Successful, nationwide agricultural reforms that change land ownership radically therefore presuppose the elimination of this balance of power. However, this starting position is to be found only in exceptional situations in history, and sweeping agricultural reforms have occurred only after lost wars and successful revolutions. As a rule, evolutionary agricultural reforms 'from the top down' have therefore been agonizingly slow and, in the end, have remained a patchwork (BMZ 1999; Deininger and Binswanger 1999).

Land cannot be physically enlarged and is stationary. Its price in relation to the prices of the two factors of production labour and capital rises with population density and natural soil fertility – assuming for the moment that the state of economic development and other socio-economic factors that influence land prices are constant. Poor countries with very unequal distribution of land ownership and high population density are usually candidates for land reforms on economic and social grounds.

13.3.1 Social and economic incentives for land reform

The need for land reforms has been considered particularly urgent

> ... in semifeudal agriculture where problems of perpetual indebtedness for consumption tie the direct producer into a set of marketing, technology and production relations.
>
> (Atkins 1988)

Where the settlement of the land is fairly dense, the ground rent amounts to 40 to 50 per cent of the net value added in agriculture and, depending on the concentration of land ownership, flows into relatively few hands. Personal income distribution is accordingly very unbalanced.

In this situation it is possible in the event of successful land reform to combine an improvement in income distribution with higher economic efficiency, since large farms, and especially semi-feudal latifundia, usually operate at significantly lower total factor productivity than peasant farms (see Box 8). As a

---

Box 8 **Agricultural growth multiplier and the distribution of land ownership**

Demand from peasant households and farms in developing countries is almost entirely confined to agricultural products, craft products and services which are produced with local, untradable, or hardly tradable, resources and offered in the villages and small market towns. As a rule, rural non-farm craft and trade have fairly extensive free capacities. Rising peasant demand therefore has a significant multiplier effect on growth. Much the same can be said of downstream activities relating to the processing and marketing of the peasants' produce, as in the case of local food processing and marketing. The aggregate growth multiplier is typically 1.50 to 2.00 (World Bank 1986, p. 80; Haggblade and Hazell 1989; Haggblade *et al.* 1989; Delgado *et al.* 1998; Rosset 1999; Irz 2001). An agricultural value added of 1.00 thus induces additional non-agricultural economic growth of 0.50 to 1.00 of the original impulse. However, it should also be realized that the import of low-quality mass-produced manufactures and of processed agricultural products (the latter at distorted prices) increasingly curtails both the short- to medium-term multiplier effect and the long-term growth of non-agricultural trade.

This aggregate multiplier conceals what might be termed an intra-agrarian multiplier. For if peasant families attain an additional cash income, they often spend well over 50 per cent of it on the purchase of such higher-quality foodstuffs and semi-luxuries as coffee, tea, sugar, milk, meat, pastries, dried fruit and vegetables and home-brewed beverages and also on agricultural wage labour (see Tables A3, A22 and A23) (Brandt 1971; von Rümker 1972; King and Oamek 1983). Depending on the price elasticity of the agricultural factor supply, this may have considerable intrasectoral multiplier effects, and will certainly have such effects in the longer term after appropriate investments have been effected.

Confirmation of the pronounced multiplier effect of peasant demand on employment and growth is provided by the high elasticities of poverty reduction in relation to agricultural growth, as calculated in Asia (see Chapter 12.2); in Latin America, on the other hand, there is no evidence of them. Demand from small Asian farmers is largely confined to local goods, the production of which is labour-intensive. Hence the pronounced multiplier effects. Demand from the large land owner in Latin America, however, is largely confined to means of production and consumer goods, which are produced by capital-intensive means or imported. Furthermore, his mode of operation is comparatively very labour-extensive and capital-intensive. His demand does not matter much for the local rural economy. As his linkages with the regional rural economy are weak, growth of the agricultural sector has hardly any poverty-reducing effect where the agrarian structure is based on large farms.

Wherever radical land reforms were successfully carried out after the Second World War to bring about a peasant agrarian structure, the immediate consequence was not only economic growth but also rapid poverty reduction, as the examples of Japan, South Korea, Taiwan and the People's Republic of China show (Sobhan 1993). A European example is the Estonian agricultural reform of 1919–20 (Brandt *et al.* 1993).

Even the protracted and by no means radical agricultural reforms undertaken in 16 Indian states since 1958 have had a marked poverty-reducing effect (Besley and Burgess 1998). From Brazil there are reports of similar effects, both of spontaneous land occupation and of orderly reform: 'Land reform beneficiaries in Brazil have an annual income equivalent of 3.7 minimum wages, while still landless laborers average only 0.7 of the minimum. Infant mortality among families of beneficiaries has dropped to only half of the national average' (Rosset 1999, p. 112). Local mayors have recently begun to support the spontaneous occupation of land, having recognized the effects completed reform projects have had in reviving the economy of the administrative centres.

An argument frequently advanced against the break-up of large farms is that peasant farms are relatively cost-inefficient. Rosset demonstrates convincingly that peasant farms in both developing and industrialized countries operate not only more intensively and with higher yields than large farms but also more efficiently in terms of total factor productivity. Where land is scarce, the only argument against small peasant farms is that there are not enough plots of land capable of supporting a family – especially in the industrialized countries. The slogan 'grow or go', however, applies only to full-time farms. As soon as a peasant family has sufficient opportunity to earn a non-agricultural income within a reasonable distance of where they live, the argument based on farm size no longer applies. In terms of total factor productivity small farms are at least on a par with large farms even in the USA (Peterson 1997). The minimum amount of land needed to produce an adequate income very much depends on the location. In South-East Asian rice-growing it is <1.5 ha, on Namibia's and Australia's extensive ranches it is >10,000 ha.

Land reforms also have the effect of reducing poverty by making for the more equal distribution of ground rent. Ground rent increases as a proportion of value added by an agricultural sector as land becomes scarcer. As Colin Clark demonstrates in the case of English agriculture before 1870, ground rent accounted for about 40 per cent of net value added in agriculture while farm labourers were working for a pittance (Clark 1960 and 1968). In the former German Reich the proportion was probably slightly higher. In Asian rice economies the proportion of ground rent may be hardly smaller even today. Land reforms thus have their redistribution effect primarily through the more intensive operation of the beneficiaries, a more equal distribution of ground rents and the subsequent dynamism of the regional economic circuit.

rule, a large farm is run far more extensively than a small or medium-sized farm because it has higher daily wages to pay and incurs higher costs in supervising and monitoring the whole work process. In addition, a large farm is often used for the inflation-proof diversification of larger assets: although no real losses are made on the estate, maximum profit is not the aim either. Unlike a peasant farm, a large farm is not, as a rule, closely integrated into the regional economic circuit. Successful land reforms therefore have a pronounced multiplier effect on employment and incomes in up- and downstream sectors. Because they work harder, peasants have lower implicit hourly wages than workers on large farms, they work far more carefully, and they adapt their work flexibly to the vagaries of weather patterns. Land ownership gives them investment security and thus an incentive to save and invest. It is also required by the bank as security for formal production-financing loans. Furthermore, peasants spend some of their rising income on higher-quality agricultural products, which has a multiplier effect on growth in the agricultural sector itself.

13.3.2   Systematics of reform projects

By analogy with De Janvry, the following basic forms of land tenure system can be distinguished:

- semi-feudal large farm
- capitalist large farm
- capitalist-peasant full-time farm
- small subsistence farm
- small farm linked to the market
- capitalist association of producers
- socialist cooperative
- socialist state farm.

Radical or revolutionary land reforms can now be described as the transformation of one form of land ownership into another. The means used to this end are the redistribution of land ownership, the amendment of land ownership law, the amendment of land use law and settlement measures. There are also restrained or evolutionary land reforms, which are confined to the amendment of land use law. The wide range of options and the specific nature of the overall socio-political situation necessarily make of each land reform a special case.

Land reforms often proceed in several stages: in the Chinese example, from the feudal manorial system through the socialist cooperative farm to the peasant farm linked to the market on the basis of land owned by the state or the local authority. The land reforms in Mexico, Peru, Honduras and Chile – to name but a few – passed from the semi-feudal large farm through the socialist cooperative farm to the peasant farm linked to the market.

After numerous, highly disparate land reforms between 1950 and 1980 there are two regions left in the world where development cooperation will be called upon during the next two or three decades to promote land reforms: southern Africa, including the Republic of South Africa (RSA), Zimbabwe and Namibia, and Latin America (Garibay 1999). In the Philippines there is a danger of the agricultural reform coming to a halt half-way, as has regularly happened in Latin

America in the past. The southern African reforms are likely to be the most important for the EU and its Member States, given the regional priorities of their development cooperation. Serious socio-political, administrative and organizational, financial and farming problems will undoubtedly arise in this context, as is already becoming clear in Zimbabwe's case (Otzen 2000; Schwarz 2002).

13.3.3   Land reforms in the twentieth century

From 1947 to 1951, in response to American pressure, Japan, South Korea and Taiwan carried out land reforms that did not include settlement activities but simply turned the tenants of feudal manorial systems into land owners, with moderate compensation paid to the former owners (Binswanger and Elgin 1998). This step was the precondition for the unprecedented development of productivity in those countries' rice-growing systems. Similar examples are to be found in the German states after the Napoleonic Wars and in Estonia from 1920 to 1922 (Järvesoo 1939), where the former tenants were not, however, required to pay any compensation to the former landowners, since the land was expropriated. This land reform model (transfer of land to sitting tenants with or without compensatory payments) was, on the whole, extremely successful, because the former tenants were already equipped with the necessary stock, were familiar with the local economic system and had already proved themselves in their dual role of managers and workers, thus obviating the need for a whole panoply of special services and administrative and organizational facilities, with all the costs they entail. The political requirements for the success of these reforms should not, of course, be overlooked: the weakening of feudalism by the French Revolution of 1789 and the collapse of Tsarist Russia and the Japanese empire.

The land reforms in Latin America were less successful (Garibay 1999). Seven countries resorted to the redistribution of land involving a change of ownership (Mexico from 1920 to 1928, Bolivia in the 1950s, Cuba, Chile and Peru in the 1960s and Nicaragua and El Salvador in the 1980s), while minimal reforms of land use rights were undertaken in seven other countries (Brazil, Guatemala, Honduras, Ecuador, Colombia, Venezuela and the Dominican Republic). In the latter group there was no appreciable change in the distribution of land ownership (see Table A26).

The Latin American agricultural reforms, like the 1982 reform in the Philippines, have suffered from shortages of funds and constraints in administrative organization and agricultural technology but, above all, from political obstruction by the formal feudal landlords and their political clientele.

13.3.4   Implementation difficulties and preconditions for success

Even in purely agricultural areas land prices are usually well above the capital value of the land when used for agricultural purposes. Besides the possibility of land being in demand and kept as an asset that retains its value, Binswanger and Elgin cite a whole series of factors that frequently cause land prices to exceed the present value of net agricultural returns (Binswanger and Elgin 1998, p. 324). In view of the overvaluation of land compared to the options for using it for agricultural purposes, however well they may operate, farmers can afford the interest and repayments on unsubsidized loans after a land reform entailing the compensation of the former owners at market prices only if they forgo a great deal of consumption, and even heroic efforts to save would not be enough in 'free' land and capital markets. This very soon results in their having to resell the acquired land because of their additional debts, as has frequently happened in the wake of Latin American land reforms. Hence the need, where expropriation is not possible, for loans to purchase land or for the purchase price to be heavily subsidized, and the more overvalued the land compared to its agricultural capital value, the more generous the subsidization should be. One way of indirectly reducing land prices is to reduce the ground rent by imposing a land tax on large farms or latifundia. On the other hand, the massive increase in demand during a land reform programme would raise land prices sharply. Taking everything into account, the price of land (as an unavoidably 'political' price) should be based on a precisely calculated capital value with due regard for the land tax on large farms.

In a number of land reforms – in southern Africa, for example – the state reserves the right of first refusal in all sales of agricultural land. At the same time, it levies a relatively high land tax, which reduces ground rents and thus land prices. This approach has the advantage of ensuring that land is acquired more cheaply, but it also has major disadvantages, in that in this situation the large farms seek to withdraw as much capital as possible from their farms, thus contracting their balance sheets, and, in so doing, reduce the natural capital comprising soil fertility and timber stands. This leaves the beneficiaries of the land reform with bare land.

A cardinal error that repeatedly occurs in land reforms entailing the resettlement of farmers is that the people resettled are not up to the task either as managers or as workers. A settler who is unwilling or unable to play this dual role is unsuitable. Not even social arguments can refute this conclusion: land reforms cost the state too much for that. Land reforms should be poverty-oriented, but they are not welfare programmes.

Another mistake that is frequently made is to leave settlers with completely inadequate non-land capital stock. They are then able to farm at less than optimum intensity and have difficulty in obtaining a ground rent and so in servicing their land loans. If this is to be avoided, the design and equipment of settlers' holdings must be based on a sound preliminary calculation. The disdain for technical and economic detail so often encountered in development cooperation and measures to combat poverty is a particularly serious error in the case of land reforms.

Success is similarly threatened by constraints in up- and downstream services (extension, credit, purchasing and sales). In major reform projects cooperative solutions with government support are appropriate, for who would entrust these functions, so decisive for success, to the market blindly, as it were, in such unstable, politically controversial situations? The market, as everyone knows, has no conscience – and its actors have interests which may extend well beyond trading profits. It should also be pointed out that land reforms have often suffered serious delays because of administrative bottlenecks. In the resulting lack of clarity, from the land survey to the entry in the land register and the granting of the loan, the sabotaging of the project by politically powerful landowners then often begins. The Philippines and many Latin American countries provide examples of land reforms being obstructed or thwarted in this way (Garibay 1999, p. 31 ff.).

13.3.5 'Successes' without land ownership being changed

Since the early 1950s the states of the Indian Union have undertaken reforms of land use law that strengthen the position of tenants and share-croppers and eliminate the institution of intermediate landlord or rent collector. Even these moderated land reforms have had a significant poverty-reducing effect through rising wages. In an econometric analysis this effect is estimated to be equivalent to that of a 10 per cent increase in per capita income (Besley and Burgess 2000).

In 1978 China abandoned its cooperative-socialist land tenure system for the 'household production responsibility system', under which the former cooperative farmers became state tenants operating independently under long-term leases. From 1978 to 1984 agricultural production rose by 6.6 per cent p.a. In the 1990s the agricultural markets were 90 per cent liberalized. Output rose again, though this time with the help of subsidies.

The examples of the two largest Asian countries might one day be significant for the sub-Saharan African countries, if the aim is to enshrine in law long-term security of land use on a cooperative, but exclusive basis under general socio-political and administrative conditions that do not yet permit successful reforms of land ownership.

13.3.6 Land reforms in Southern Africa

The land reforms in southern Africa have reached different stages. In Swaziland some two-thirds of the land has so far been transferred from white settlers to indigenous black settlers. Malawi has just launched a poverty-oriented programme of land distribution. Large plantations are being redistributed to the landless poor. In Mozambique the large farms that were nationalized in 1975 have almost all been leased without being divided up. In Namibia and the RSA agricultural policy is groping its way towards viable reform concepts. Only 1 to 2 per cent of the land occupied by large farms has so far been redistributed or indigenized. In Zimbabwe the problem of the government occupation of the settlers' property has been largely 'solved' de facto through purchases (of about 25 per cent) or expropriation.

In none of these last three countries has the government made a clear political statement on the distribution of land ownership that is the goal, on the prospects for land ownership and land use law or on the importance attached to the fight against poverty in the land reforms. On independence the land law inherited from the former colonial power was enshrined in the constitutions of all three countries. This legalized

> ... more than a century of land grabbing by whites, an outcome strongly re-sented by Africans across the region.
>
> (Adams and Howell 2001, p. 1)

The political process of abolishing the distribution of farmland and the land law prescriptions of the first hour of colonialism is farthest advanced in Zimbabwe, chaotic though the process may be. It is completely impossible to make any reliable forecasts of the further course of the reform processes and the resulting agrarian structure and distribution of land ownership. Despite all the sympathy for the dispossessed settlers and the condemnation of the breaches of the law, future political action must also take account of the general political situation as it is and of the implications it has for the region as a whole.

As land reform is an extremely domestic issue, development cooperation would be well advised not to interfere in the political course of events. Neither the governments nor the black majority of the population want this. Understand-able though the impatience may be, when it comes to land reform processes, poverty-oriented development cooperation will have to wait and see whether or until structural objectives and procedures governed by the rule of law conducive to or at least compatible with poverty reduction emerge. In areas where the white large farmers or large landowners give way to indigenous blacks without any major changes in the average size of farms, the fight against poverty will initially gain little from indigenization. Where, on the other hand, a small-scale agrarian structure begins to emerge, fertile ground for poverty-oriented development cooperation will result – if that is what the partner countries want. In Zimbabwe this could very soon be the case, provided that the rule of law and democracy are restored, the departing land owners are appropriately compensated and the land-grabbing excesses of the ZANU functionaries and high-ranking military men are reversed. If land reforms resulting in small-scale farming structures are to succeed, it is important for the settlers to be up to the task of acting as workers and managers. A critical selection of poor settlers based on appropriate criteria thus seems advisable, since land reforms should not be confused with welfare programmes, for which there are more efficient instruments.

Part V Conclusions and recommendations

14   Conclusions

1   Poverty is primarily due to socio-structural conditions and to the level of
    social and economic development reached by agriculture and the rural areas.
    Of the world's poor, 80 per cent (about 1 billion people) live in rural areas –
    75 per cent in Asia, about 85 per cent in Africa.
2   Poverty reduction is the declared overriding objective of development co-
    operation pursued by bi- and multilateral donors, as analyses and conception
    papers show. Despite this, the agricultural sector accounts for only 6 to 7 per
    cent of donor resources, which are declining in real terms. After the cost of
    administration and coordination has been deducted, 4 to 5 per cent may
    reach the villages.
3   In the sub-Saharan African countries in particular this pattern of allocation
    by the donors is reinforced by a development policy which partly neglects
    and partly impedes the agricultural sector: negative PSEs for food products
    and, as a rule, significantly less than 5 per cent of current and investable
    budget resources allocated to agriculture.
4   Viewed as a whole, the world food situation does not – assuming world
    peace and functioning markets – pose any serious problems for the next
    generation. However, there are signs of a future structural supply gap of
    alarming proportions in the sub-Saharan African countries because of inade-
    quate increases in productivity in agriculture and – compared to economic
    growth in the towns and cities – excessive urbanization rates. If the finan-
    cing of the imports needed to fill this gap is ensured and if agricultural de-
    velopment policy is neglected, sub-Saharan Africa is in danger of becoming
    the dumping ground for the world's food surpluses, which are likely to con-
    tinue to occur in the future because of heavily subsidized agricultural pro-
    duction in the industrialized countries. In the Asian countries it is impossible
    to tell at present whether agricultural production faces a productivity crisis
    or whether, if a greater effort is made under agricultural policies, past rates
    of growth in total factor productivity can be repeated.
5   In the light of recent research on the links between the causes and effects of
    poverty and faced with the nutritional prospects for sub-Saharan African
    countries, all that can be said is that the donors' allocation of resources is in-
    appropriate to their objectives. Accordingly, a new urban bias has domi-

nated the budget allocations and agricultural policies of the sub-Saharan African countries for more than ten years.

6   As things stand, no more than working hypotheses on the causes can be formulated. Among the causes cited in this study are the donors' neglect of internal social and economic conditions in view of a structurally relaxed global market situation in the case of agricultural products and the relative ease with which urban development projects can be implemented.

7   Recent research on the pattern of causes of poverty leads to the following main conclusions:

   a   A simple cross-section analysis reveals that poverty (per capita income of the lowest quintile) decreases at least proportionally as national per capita income rises.

   b   Agricultural growth results in a disproportionately high reduction of poverty, far higher than macroeconomic growth is capable of.

   c   These findings are not true, or are true to a far lesser degree, of countries with a quasi-feudal society and large-scale agrarian structure, as are typically to be found in Latin America (some 25 countries throughout the world).

   d   Under the conditions of peasant land tenure systems, increasing agricultural productivity is the key to poverty reduction. This has its effect through rising physical productivity, demand for labour, rising wages, declining food prices and the peasants' share of the growth of ground rents. These factors are joined in the medium term by major multiplier effects in local business.

   e   The most important tools in a policy of poverty reduction are rural road-building, applied agricultural research and extension, the training of farmers and other components of human capital formation (health, nutrition, primary education).

   f   Of fundamental importance is the agricultural policy environment. Economic production incentives appropriate to the physical productivity and price situation must be sufficient, and the risk components of propagated innovations must remain within limits acceptable to farmers. All this calls for an effective innovation policy and appropriate price, market and trade policies for agricultural products. In countries with a quasi-feudal societal and large-scale agrarian structure a policy of agriculturally based growth continues to be ineffective in reducing poverty. It is thus true to say that there will be no poverty reduction without agricultural reform.

8   Successful land reforms after 1945 entailed the abolition of semi-feudal land tenure systems after lost wars or successful revolutions. In all these cases there was rapid poverty reduction and economic growth. Evolutionary approaches to land reform, which have been attempted in Latin America, have, as a general rule, lapsed into generation-long processes without any

clear success because of the obstructive activities of the large land-owning class and a number of economic, technical, organizational and legal errors, constraints or omissions. It is impossible to tell at present whether the pending/current land reforms in southern Africa will eventually fit more into the successful revolutionary pattern or into the more or less unsuccessful evolutionary pattern.

15   Recommendations

1   German development cooperation policy should continue to press for coherence (within the meaning of the Maastricht Treaty) between the EU's agricultural policy and the development cooperation policies.

2   Within the framework of a comprehensive debate between researchers and practitioners, it should consider whether, given their structural starting position and the distorted world food markets, the LDCs can forgo a minimum of tariff protection for both primary and processed foodstuffs if they intend to develop economically.

3   Development cooperation partners should think about the incompatibility of their present allocation priorities (physical and social infrastructure in urban areas) with the overriding objective of development policy (poverty reduction).

4   They should ask themselves whether the present policy of supporting unbalanced urbanization rates – especially in the sub-Saharan African countries – can be sustained financially and politically in the longer term.

5   They should take a far greater interest in the recipient countries' agricultural policy environment than they did in the past decade and take significantly greater account of agriculture and rural areas in the poverty-stricken regions (sub-Saharan Africa and South Asia) when allocating development cooperation resources.

6   In view of the rather high income elasticities of demand for food among the rural poor and the pronounced multiplier effects of agricultural growth, the donors should make it clear that agricultural promotion targeted on the aforementioned poverty-stricken regions of the world would have hardly any impact on the world food markets.

7   In the context of a policy of this kind, development cooperation partners should not resort to the old patterns of centrally planned implementation – along the lines of the old IRD, for example – but address the task with a decentralized, subsidiarity-based approach, in which district administrations and farmers' cooperatives have a central role to play.

8   In this context, there should be a move away from development cooperation's new urban bias in sub-Saharan Africa on the basis of an agricultural policy concept which is feasible in terms of its profitability and risk implications and with which aid should equally comply.

9   Rural infrastructure, agricultural research and extension, adult education, health care and primary schools in rural areas should be permanent priorities

for development cooperation in the sub-Saharan African and South Asian countries with a view to reducing poverty.

10 Land reforms – especially in southern Africa – should be stabilized through the development of infrastructure and the promotion of support services and possibly through the refinancing of land reform banks.

11 In southern Africa land reform processes that began some 10 years ago are accelerating. Where these processes have assumed revolutionary traits and amount to the radical redistribution of land to the benefit of small and medium-sized holdings (as in Zimbabwe), they deserve the donors' prompt and full support so that the outcome may be structurally stabilized. Such support measures are likely to have a broad and sustained poverty-reducing effect if they culminate in a small- to medium-scale agrarian structure. On the other hand, land reforms which merely change the colour of the landowners' skin but leave the distribution of farm land untouched can do little to help reduce poverty. They do not therefore represent an appropriate starting point for development cooperation and should not be promoted for that reason.

Notes

Part I: Background to the problem: world food question

1   With a daily per capita income of <US$ 1 PPP.

2   In view of the low price elasticities of supply and demand, annual surplus demand (as defined above) of 40 million tonnes causes a real price rise of 10 per cent. The present 20 per cent cyclical fall in prices must be offset against this. For the elasticities of supply see Rosegrant *et al.* (2001a), p. 141 ff.

3   A doubling of the price of energy increases the CIF cost of cereals by about 40 per cent. Extensive internal transport in the importing country may lead to a further substantial increase in energy costs.

Part II: Motive for the study: new urban bias in development cooperation

1   'In the real world of politics the focus is not only, and by no means primarily, on public welfare, but on the actors' interest in power, positions and money.' See von Arnim (2001), p. 34. This observation concerns the problem of degeneration of institutions (in relation to the separation of powers, political competition, viable opposition, national sovereignty) in a representative democracy. Under the conditions of a dictatorship or a regime without democratic competition it becomes the absolute maxim.

2   Market equilibrium is given as: $S1 \cdot En - dp \cdot En = -dp \cdot Ea$;
solved for dp and with S2 substituted for S1:

$$dp = -S_2 \ \frac{E_n}{E_n - E_a}$$

where: S_1 = unit subsidies
               S_2 = total subsidies
               E_n = direct price elasticity of demand
               E_a = direct price elasticity of supply
               dp = correction factor
               $S_2 - dp$ = corrected distortion margin.

3   At least in the urban coastal areas, where some 80 per cent of the sub-Saharan urban population live. Inland the price ratios are different because of the high transformation costs.

4   This can be illustrated with the following rough calculation:

$dNw = EN \cdot dPw$;
$dAw = EA \cdot dPw(1 - R) + dAa \cdot R$;
$dNw = dAw$;

$$dP_w = \frac{Aa \cdot R}{EN - EA(1 - R)};$$

$$dU_a = dP_w + dA_a;$$

where:
dNw	=	percentage change in world demand
EN	=	direct price elasticity of world demand
dPw	=	percentage change in world market prices
EA	=	long-term supply elasticity of non-African suppliers
dAw	=	percentage change in world supply
dAa	=	percentage change in (an) African or competing supplier(s)
R	=	world market share of (the) African supplier(s) before its/their change in supply.

Let the share of an African supplier R of the market in a raw material be 5 per cent, the direct price elasticity of world demand (EN) –0.20 and the price elasticity of competing suppliers (EA) 0.40. The doubling of supply by the African supplier will then lead, *ceteris paribus*, to a 17.2 per cent reduction in the world market price. His turnover thus rises by $100 - 17.2 = 82.8$ per cent. This increase in turnover should be compared to the corresponding increase in costs.

Part III: Poverty reduction in the conceptual experience of agricultural development

3 This approach, as applied, for example, to Ethiopia's agricultural development policy, was recently described as 'narrative', and for the purpose of irony, a handful of other, similarly plausible explanations were offered for the failed 'narrative'. See Hoben (1997).

4 The classical contributions cited here are joined by others in the more recent debate on agricultural policy under the general heading of multifunctionality:

- Social contributions:
  - The agricultural sector provides employment directly and, through its demand, indirectly.
  - It is a social reinsurance institution for migrants.
  - It is a nursery for industrialization as regards informal institutions and gainful activity (housekeeping, saving, investing, working).
- Ecological contributions:
  - It contributes to the stabilization of natural resources, which is becoming a (social and economic) necessity as the rural and urban population grow, each in its respective area.

This list is by no means exhaustive. Various aspects will be referred to again in the course of the study. In the strictly economic context discussed here they are mentioned at this stage merely to complete the picture.

3 It was found that, at 2.5 to 5.0, the agricultural sector's c/o ratios were no lower than the industrial sector's (see Krishna, 1982).

4 For the interrelated effects of the instruments see Chapter 13.

5 A number of earlier criticisms are noted in Hayami and Ruttan (1984), p. 44.

6 In South Asian villages the value-added multiplier was 1.87 – see Hazell and Ramasamy (1991), p. 244.

7 Another important factor is undoubtedly the economic scarcity of land compared to the shares of land, labour and capital in agricultural value added.

8 The theoretical assimilation maximum is about 50 tonnes/ha p.a. of organic dry matter. Of this, some 15 to 18 tonnes GE/ha could be used for human consumption. At present, only about 8 to 10 tonnes/ha of spelt rice is harvested in intensive wet rice growing.
9 Following part of the paragraph from Brandt and Neubert (2000), p. 46.

Part IV: Economic growth, agricultural development, poverty reduction

1 Including capital intensification, technical progress, productivity and income growth, and deconcentration of land ownership.
2 Overviews can be found in: World Bank (1982, 1986); Mellor (1995a); Timmer (1998); Sarris (2001).
3 Summaries of the findings can be found in Binswanger (1990) and Mundlak et al. (1997).
4 'Short-term' signifies a time lag in the regression analyses of a year between aggregate sectoral output and previous sectoral terms of trade.
5 Mundlak makes a similar comment on his finding of low aggregate price elasticities: '... a major channel for the effect of prices on productivity is through the effect on stock of inputs.' Mundlak (1999), p. 33.
6 This finding is, moreover, extremely old and backed by centuries of empirical agricultural experience. After examining the whole breadth of European data, Abel concludes: 'Whether the development of farm technology, yields, expenditure or operating systems is considered, the decisive advances occurred at times of long-term upward price movements.' See Abel (1978), p. 287.
7 Organizational intensity describes the weight carried by specifically intensive branches of farming in relation to total expenditure or yield.
8 An overview of the recent empirical process can be found in Deininger and Squire (1998) and Dollar and Kraay (2001).
9 Urbanization rates of 4 to 5 per cent have compared in the past five or six years with rates of urban economic growth of only 3.5 per cent.

Bibliography

Abel, W. (1978): Agrarkrisen und Agrarkonjunktur, Hamburg und Berlin

Adams, M. / H. Howell (2001): Restributive Land Reform in Southern Africa, in: *ODI, Natural Resource Perspective*, No 64

Adams, R.H. / J.Y. He (1995): Sources of Income Inequality and Poverty in Rural Pakistan, in: *IFPRI Research Report Abstract*, No 102

Aereboe, F. (1919): Bewirtschaftung von Landgütern und Grundstücken, Berlin

Aereboe, F. (1923): Allgemeine landwirtschaftliche Betriebslehre, Berlin

Aereboe, F. (1925): Das Ernährungsproblem der Völker und die Produktionssteigerung der Landwirtschaft, in: *Weltwirtschaftliches Archiv*, Vol. 21

Aereboe, F. (1928): Agrarpolitik, Berlin

Agrawal, R.C. (1991): Green Revolution and Sustainable Development: Competitors or Complements?, in: *Nord–Süd aktuell*, 3rd quarter

Ake, C. (1996): Development Strategy for Nigeria After the Structural Adjustment Programme, in: *DPC Lecture Series*, No 2, Ibadan

Akindes, F. (1999): Food Strategies of Urban Households in Côte d'Ivoire Following the 1994 CFA Franc Devaluation, in: *Food Policy*, Vol. 24, No 5, p. 479 ff.

Alexander, M. (2002): Opium Poppy Cultivation in Afghanistan: Can Alternative Development Offer Viable Options?, in: *Entwicklung und ländlicher Raum*, Vol. 36, No 3, p. 15 ff.

Alexandratos, N. (2001): World Food and Agriculture: Outlook for the Medium and Longer Term, in: Proceedings of the National Academy of Sciences (USA), Vol. 96, No 11, p. 5908 ff.

Amis, P. / C. Rakodi (1994): Urban Poverty: Issues for Research and Policy, in: *Journal of International Development*, Vol. 6, No 5

Anderson, K. *et al.* (2001): Agriculture and the WTO, in: *Review of International Economics*, Vol. 9, No 2, p. 192 ff.

Andreae, B. (1972): Landwirtschaftliche Betriebsformen in den Tropen, Hamburg, Berlin

Antle, J.M. (1983): Infrastructure and Aggregate Agricultural Productivity: International Evidence, in: *Economic Development and Cultural Change*, Vol. 31, p. 609 ff.

Arnim, H.H. von (2001): Das System, Ulm

Askari, H. / J.Th. Cummings (1976): Agricultural Supply Response, New York

Atkins, F. (1988): Land Reform: A Failure of Neoclassical Theorization?, in: *World Development*, Vol. 16, No 8, p. 935 ff.

Badiane, O. / C.L. Delgado (rapporteurs, 2002): A 2020 Vision for Food, Agriculture, and the Environment in Sub-Saharan Africa: A Synthesis, Washington, D.C.

Bairoch, P. (1976): Agriculture and the Industrial Revolution 1700–1914, in: Cipolla, C.M. (ed.): The Industrial Revolution 1700–1914, New York

Bates, R.H. (1981): Markets and States in Tropical Africa: The Political Basis of Agricultural Policies, Berkeley

Bates, R.H. (1998): The Political Framework for Agricultural Policy Decisions, in: Eicher, C.K. / Staatz, J.M. (eds.): International Agricultural Development, Baltimore, p. 234 ff.

Benavides, M.A. (1987): Análysis del uso de tierras registrado en las visitas de los siglos XVI y XVII a los Yanquecollaguas, in: W.M. Denevan (ed.), Pre-hispanic Agricultural Fields in the Andean Region, Oxford, p. 129 ff.

Benn, G. (1992): Gebührt Carleton ein Denkmal?, in: *Essays und Reden*, Wiesbaden und München

Bensing, F. (1897): Der Einfluss der Landwirtschaftlichen Maschinen auf Volks- und Privatwirtschaft, dissertation, Breslau

Berg, E.J. (1993): Rethinking Technical Cooperation. Reforms for Capacity Building in Africa. New York

Besley, T. / R. Burgess (1998): Land Reform, Poverty Reduction and Growth: Evidence from India, London

Besley, T. / R. Burgess (2000): Land Reform, Poverty Reduction and Growth: Evidence from India, in: *Quarterly Journal of Economics*, Vol. 115, No 2, p. 389 ff.

Bierschenk, T. *et al.* (1991): Langzeitfolgen der Entwicklungshilfe. Empirische Untersuchungen im ländlichen Westafrika, in: *Afrika Spektrum*, Vol. 1991, No 2

Bigsten, A. (1983): What Do Smallholders Do for a Living? Some Evidence from Kenya, University of Göteborg, Göteborg

Binswanger, H. (1989): The Policy Response of Agriculture, Washington, D.C.

Binswanger, H.P. / M. Elgin (1998): Reflections on Land Reform and Farm Size, in: Eicher, C.K. / J. M. Staatz (eds.): International Agricultural Development, p. 316 ff., Baltimore

Birdsall, N. / J.L. Londono (1997): Asset Inequality Matters: An Assessment of the World Bank's Approach to Poverty Reduction, in: *American Economic Review*, Vol. 87, No 2, p. 32 ff

Bittermann, E. (1956): Die landwirtschaftliche Produktion in Deutschland 1800–1950, in: *Kühn-Archiv*, No. 70, Halle

BMZ (1996): Entwicklungspolitische Konzeption des BMZ, in: *BMZ aktuell*, Bonn

BMZ (1999): Land Policy – Tenure Rights in Development Cooperation, Challenges and Opportunities, in: *BMZ spezial*, No 002

BMZ (2001): Ländliche Entwicklung, Bonn

Boeke, J. (1953): Economics and Economic Policy of Dual Societies, New York

Bond, E.M. (1983): Agricultural Response to Prices in Subsaharan-Africa, in: *IMF Staff Papers*, Vol. 30, No 4, p. 703 ff., Washington, D.C.

Booth, A. (1988): Agricultural Development in Indonesia, Singapore

Borrell, B. / D. Pearce (1999): Sugar: The Taste Test of Trade Liberalization, Centre for International Economics, Canberra & Sydney

Boserup, E. (1965): The Conditions of Agricultural Growth, Chicago

Brandt, H. (1971): Die Organisation bäuerlicher Betriebe unter dem Einfluss der Entwicklung einer Industriestadt, in: *Zeitschrift für Ausländische Landwirtschaft*, Materialsammlung, Frankfurt

Brandt, H. (1974): Rahmenanalyse Ghana, Berlin

Brandt, H. (1984): Food Security Programmes in the Sudano-Sahel, Berlin

Brandt, H. (1985): Ernährungssicherungsprogramme im Sudano-Sahel, Berlin

Brandt, H. (1991): Zu Thaers ökonomischer Lehre aus heutiger Sicht, Möglin

Brandt, H. (1994): Von Thaer bis Tschajanow

Brandt, H. (1995a): Auswirkungen von Exporterstattungen der Europäischen Union auf die Rindfleischsektoren westafrikanischer Länder, Berlin

Brandt, H. (1995b): Zur Betriebslehre Johann Heinrich von Thünens, in: *Berichte über Landwirtschaft*, 210. Sonderheft, p. 171 ff.

Brandt, H. (1997): Zur agrarpolitischen Debatte, Berlin

Brandt, H. / S. Neubert (2000): Ressourcenmanagement im Sahel als politische Herausforderung an die Entwicklungszusammenarbeit, in: DSE, Fachkonferenz 'Ressourcenmanagement im Sahel', p. 39 ff., Zschertau

Brandt, H. *et al.* (1986): Afrika in Bedrängnis, Vol. I und II, in: *Deutsche Welthungerhilfe*. Reihe Problem, Nos 15 und 16, Bonn

Brandt, H. *et al.* (1993): Die Wirtschaftlichkeit der Flachserzeugung in der Republik Estland, Berlin

Brandt, K. (1965): Friedrich Aereboes Beitrag zum agrarpolitischen und ernährungswirtschaftlichen Wissen der Welt, in: A. Hanau *et al.* (eds): Friedrich Aereboe, Würdigung und Auswahl aus seinen Werken aus Anlass der 100. Wiederkehr seines Geburtstages, Hamburg und Berlin

Braun, J. von *et al.* (1998): Verbesserung der Ernährung in Entwicklungsländern, Bonn

Braun, J. von *et al.* (2001): Agrarhandel und Agrarpolitik in der WTO, Bonn

Britz, W. / J. Schmidhuber (2002): The Impact of OECD Policy Reform on International Agricultural Commodity Markets, in: Schriften der GEWISULA, Vol. 37, p. 95 ff.

Brown, L. (1996): Tough Choices: Facing the Challenge of Food Scarcity, New York

Chenery, H. *et al* (1974): Redistribution with Growth, New York

Chibber, A. (1988): Steigerung der Agrarproduktion – Preise und andere Einflussfaktoren, in: *Finanzierung und Entwicklung*, p. 44 ff.

Christiaensen, L. *et al.* (2002): Growth, Distribution and Poverty in Africa. Messages from the 1990s, Washington, D.C.

Clark, C. (1957): The Conditions of Economic Progress, London

Clark, C. (1960): The Conditions of Economic Progress, London

Clark, C. (1968): Population Growth and Land Use, New York

Clark, C. / M. Haswell (1964): The Economics of Subsistence Agriculture, London

Cleaver, K.M. (1985): The Impact of Price and Exchange Rate Policies on Agriculture in Sub-Saharan Africa, in: *World Bank Staff Working Papers*, No 728, Washington, D.C.

Congress of the United States (1995): Agriculture, Trade, and Environment, Washington, D.C.

Coombs, P.H. / M. Ahmed (1974): Attacking Rural Poverty, Baltimore und London

Crosson, P. / Anderson, J.R. (1992): Resources and Global Food Prospects, Washington, D.C.

Datt, G. / M. Ravallion (1998): Farm Productivity and Rural Poverty in India, in: *Journal of Development Studies*, Vol. 34, No 4, p. 62 ff.

Davies, T.J. (1986): Development of Rainfed Agriculture under Arid and Semiarid Conditions, Washington, D.C.

Deiniger, K. / H. Binswanger (1999): The Evolution of the World Bank's Land Policy: Principles, Experience and Future Challenges, in: *The World Bank Research Observer*, Vol. 14, No 2

Deininger, K. / L. Squire (1996): A New Data Set Measuring Income Inequality, in: *The World Bank Economic Review*, Vol. 10, No 3, p. 565 ff.

Deininger, K. / L. Squire (1998): New Ways of Looking at old issues: Inequality and Growth, in: *Journal of Development Economics*, Vol. 57, Vol. 2, p. 259 ff.

De Haan, A. (1997): Urban Poverty and its Alleviation: Introduction, in: *IDS Bulletin*, Vol. 28. No 2

De Janvry, A. (1984): The Role of Land Reform in Economic Development, in: Eicher, C.K. / J.M. Staatz: Agricultural Development in the Third World, Baltimore

De Janvry, A. / E. Sadoulet (2000): Growth, Poverty and Inequality in Latin America: A Causal Analysis, 1970–94, in: *Review of Income and Wealth*, Series 46, No 3

Delgado, Ch.L. *et al.* (1998): Agricultural Growth Linkages in Sub-Saharan Africa, in: *IFPRI Research Report*, No 107, Washington, D.C.

Deutsche Welthungerhilfe (2001): Hunger, Bonn

DFID (2002): Better Livelihoods for Poor People: The Role of Agricultre, London

Dollar, K. / A. Kraay (2001): Growth is Good for the Poor, Washington, D.C.

Donkin, R.A. (1979): Agricultural terracing in the Aboriginal New World, Tucson

Drechsel, P. *et al.* (2001): Population Density, Soil Nutrient Depletion, and Economic Growth in Sub-Saharan Africa, in: *Ecological Economics*, No 31, p. 251 ff.

Dumont, R. (1962): L'Afrique noire est mal partie, Paris

Duncan, A. / J. Howell (1992): Structural Adjustment and the African Farmer, London and Portsmouth

Dyson, T. (1999): World Food Trends and Prospects to 2025, in: Proceedings of the National Academy of Sciences (USA), Vol. 96, No 11, p. 5929 ff.

ECDPM (2002): Some Basic Facts, in: *Cotonou Infokit*, No 5, Brussels

Eicher, C.K. (1995): Zimbabwe's Maize-Based Green Revolution: Preconditions for Replication, in: *World Development*, Vol. 23, p. 805 ff.

Elvin, M. (1973): The Pattern of the Chinese Past: A Social and Economic Interpretation, Stanford

Engberg-Pedersen, P. / L. Udsholt (1997): Limits of Adjustment Programs in Africa, in: *Entwicklung und ländlicher Raum*, Vol. 31, No 1

Eurostep (1999a): Coherence in EU policies towards Developing Countries, Brussels

Eurostep (1999b): Dumping in Jamaica. Dairy Farming undermined by subsidized EU exports, Brussels

Fan S. / P. Hazell (2000): Promoting Sustainable Development in Less-Favoured Areas, Washington, D.C.

Fan, S. / P. Hazell / S. Thorat (1999): Linkages Between Government Spending, Growth, and Poverty in Rural India, IFPRI-Research Report, No 110

Fan, S. *et al.* (2000): Growth and Poverty in Rural China: The Role of Public Investments, in: *EPTD Discussion Paper*, No 66

FAO (1995a): Investment in Agriculture: Evolution and Prospects, Rome

FAO (1995b): Lessons from the Green Revlution – Towards a New Green Revolution, Rome

FAO (1996): World Food Summit, Vol. 2, p. 41

FAO (1997): The Impact of the Rise in International Grain Prices in 1995–96 on Domestic Prices in Selected Importing and Exporting Countries, Rome

FAO (2001a): Food Insecurity in the World, Rome

FAO (2001b): The State of Food and Agriculture, Rome

FAO (2002): The State of Food Insecurity in the World, Rome

Feder, G. / A. Keck (2001): Increasing Competition for Land and Water Resources: A Global Perspective, Washington, D.C.

Fei, J.C.H. / G. Ranis (1964): Development of the Labour Surplus Economy, Homewood

Finck, A. (1963): Tropische Böden, Hamburg, Berlin

Foster, M. *et al.* (2001): Sector Programme Approaches: Will They Work in Agriculture, in: *Development Policy Review*, Vol. 19. No 3

Garibay, A.H. (1999): New Approaches to Land Reform, in: BMZ, *BMZ spezial*, No 002, p. 29 ff.

Geertz, C. (1963): Agricultural Involution, Berkeley

Gellner, E. (1995): Pflug, Schwert und Feder, Nördlingen

Gerhart, J. (1975): The Diffusion of Hybrid Maize in Western Kenia, Mexico City

Gläsel, E. (1916): Die Entwicklung der Preise landwirtschaftlicher Produkte und Produktionsmittel während der letzten 50 Jahre und deren Einfluss auf Bodennutzung und Viehhaltung im Deutschen Reich, in: *Landwirtschaftliche Jahrbücher*, Vol. 50, Berlin

Goldin, I. / D. Knudsen (1993): Trade Liberalization: Global Economic Implications, Paris

Goreux, L.M. (1959): Income Elasticity of the Demand for Food, Rome

Griffith, K. (1979): The Political Economy of Agrarian Change, London

Gsänger, H. (1994): The Future of Rural Development, in: *GDI Book Series*, No 2

Guttenberg-Jacobi, M. (1993): Lage und Perspektiven auf dem Welttextilmarkt, in: *Bulletin / Deutsche Bank Research*, p. 18 ff.

Haggblade, S. / P. Hazell (1989): Agricultural Technology and Farm-Nonfarm Growth Linkages, in: *Agricultural Economics*, No 3, p. 345 ff.

Haggblade, S. *et al.* (1989): Farm-Nonfarm Linkages in Rural Sub-Saharan Africa, in: *World Development*, Vol. 17, No 8, p. 1173 ff.

Hailey, S. (1971): Magoye Unit Farm 1966–71, Magoye, nimeo

Harrold, P. (1995): The Broad Sector Approach to Investment Lending, Washington, D.C.

Hassan, H.A. (1993): Organization and Performance of the Marketing System of Sorghum in the Sudan, dissertation, Berlin

Hauser, E. (2001): Agrarhandel: Stärkung der LDC's bei der Integration in die Weltwirtschaft, Frankfurt/Main.

Hayami, Y. (2000): An Ecological and Historical Perspective on Agricultural Development in Southeast Asia, in: *IBRD Policy Research Working Paper*, No 2296

Hayami, Y. / V.W. Ruttan (1971): Agricultural Development: An International Perspective, Baltimore

Hayami, Y. / V.W. Ruttan (1984): The Green Revolution: Inducement and Distribution, in: *Pakistan Development Review*, Vol. 23, No 1

Hayami, Y. / V.W. Ruttan (1985): Agricultural Development, Baltimore and London

Hazell, B.R. / C. Ramasamy (eds., 1991): The Green Revolution Reconsidered, Baltimore and London

Herlemann, H.-H. (1954): Technisierungsstufen der Landwirtschaft, in: *Agrarwirtschaft*, Vol. 32, No 1

Herlemann, H.H. / H. Stamer (1958): Produktionsgestaltung und Betriebsgröße in der Landwirtschaft unter dem Einfluss der wirtschaftlich-technischen Entwicklung, in: *Kieler Studien*, No 44

Hirschmann, A.O. (1958): The Strategy of Economic Development, New Haven, Connecticut

Hoben, A. (1997): The Cultural Construction of Environmental Policy. Paradigms and Politics in Ethiopia, in: *The Ecologist*, Vol. 27, No 2, p. 55 ff.

Hofmann, W. (1956): Die Arbeitsverfassung der Sowjetunion, Berlin

Holdcroft, L.E. (1978): The Rise and Fall of Community Development in Developing Countries, 1950–65: A Critical Analysis and an Annotated Bibliography, in: MSV rural development papers, No 2, East Lansing

Holliday, R.H. (1976): The Efficiency of Solar Energy Conversion by Whole Crops, in: Buckham, A.N. *et al.* (eds.), Food Production and Consumption, Amsterdam, Oxford

Hussein, H.A. (2002) Rural Financial Markets in the Sudan with Emphasis on Shail and Salam in Sorghum Subsector, dissertation, Berlin

Hyden, G. (1983): No Shortcuts to Progress – African Development Management in Perspective, Berkeley

IBRD (1988): Rural Development. World Bank Experience, Washington, D.C., p. 16 ff.

IBRD (2002): Reaching the Rural Poor – An Updated Strategy for Rural Development, Washington, D.C.

IFAD (2001): Rural Poverty Report 2001, Oxford

IFPRI (2001): Global Food Projections to 2020, Washington, D.C.

Ingco, M.D. (1990): Changes in Food Consumption Patterns in the Republic of Korea, in: *IBRD Working Papers*, WSP 506, Washington, D.C.

Irz, X. (2001): Agricultural Productivity Growth and Poverty Alleviation, in: *Development Policy Review*, Vol. 19, No 4, p. 449 ff.

Järvesoo, E. (1939): Voraussetzungen und Richtlinien zur Mechanisierung der Landwirtschaft in Estland, Berlin

Jaycox, V.K. (Vice-President of the World Bank, 1993): Capacity Building: The Missing Link in African Development, address given on 20 May 1993, in: *Courier*, No 141, September, Reston/Virginia

Jayne, T.S. (1996): Trends in Real Food Prices in Six Sub-Saharan African Countries, in: SD Publication Series, Technical Paper, No 39, Washington, D.C.

Jayne, T.S. *et al.* (1996): Estimating Consumer Response to Food Market Reform Using Stated Preference Data: Evidence from Eastern and Southern Africa, in: *American Journal of Agricultural Economics*, Vol. 78, p. 820 ff., Ames

Johnson, G. (1999): The Growth of Demand will Limit Output Growth for Food over the next Quarter Century, in: Proceedings of the National Academy of Sciences (USA), Vol. 96, No 11, p. 5915 ff.

Johnston, B.F. / P. Kilby (1975): Agriculture and Structural Transformation: Economic Strategies in Late-Developing Countries, New York

Kabou, A. (1991): Et si l'Afrique refusait le développement, Paris

Kabou, A. (1993): Weder arm noch ohnmächtig, Basle

Kherallah, M. *et al.* (2000): The Road Half Travelled, Washington

King, R.P. *et al.* (1977): Income Distribution, Consumption Patterns and Consumption Linkages in Rural Sierra Leone, in: *African Rural Company Paper*, No 16, East Lansing

King, R.P. / G.E. Oamek (1983): Generalized risk-efficient Monte-Carlo programming: a technique for farm planning under uncertainty, in: Modeling farm decisions for policy analysis: (Papers), Boulder, Colo.

Kirk, M. (1998): Summary and Recommendations, in: *BMZ spezial 1999*, No 002, p. 38 ff.

Koester, U. / J. von Braun *et al.* (1995): Assessing Coherence Between the Common Agricultural Policy and the EU's Development Policy, Kiel

Kolonko, P. (2002): Verlierer des Aufschwungs, in: *Frankfurter Allgemeine Zeitung* vom 08.06.02, p. 3

Kopelew, L. (1996): Im Widerspruch zur Geschichte, in: *Die Zeit*, No 40, 27 October 1996

Körner, M. (1996): Sozialwissenschaftlicher als Projektmanager, in: *Entwicklung und Zusammenarbeit*, Vol. 37, No 4

Kreditanstalt für Wiederaufbau (2000): Sektorprogramme mit deutscher Beteiligung. Eine Auswertung im Rahmen der Strategic Partnership with Africa, Frankfurt am Main

Kreditanstalt für Wiederaufbau (2002): Transportinfrastruktur, in: Diskussionsbeiträge, Frankfurt am Main

Krishna, R. (1967): Agricultural Price Policy and Economic Development, in: Southworth, H.M. / B.F. Johnston (eds.): Agricultural Development and Economic Growth, Ithaca

Krishna, R. (1982): Some Aspects of Agricultural Growth, Price Policy and Equity in Developing Countries, in: *Food Research Institute Studies*, Vol. 18, No 3, Washington, D.C.

Kumar, J. (1987): Integrated Rural Development. Perspectives and Prospects (1952–82), Delhi

Kuznets, S. (1955): Economic Growth and Income Inequality, in: *The American Economic Review*, Vol. 45, No 1, p. 1 ff.

Laur, E. (1927): Landwirtschaftliche Betriebslehre für bäuerliche Verhältnisse, Aarau

Leibenstein, H. (1957): Economic Badwardness and Economic Growth, New York

Lewis, W.A. (1954): Economic Development with Unlimited Supplies of Labour, in: *The Manchester School*, Vol. 22. No 2, p. 139 ff.

Lewis, W.A. (1955): Theory of Economic Growth, London

Lindert, P.H. (1996): Soil Degradation and Agricultural Change in Two Developing Countries, Adelaide

Lipton, M. (1977): Why Poor People Stay Poor. A Study of Urban Bias in World Development, London

Lipton, M. (1997): Why Poor People Stay Poor. A Study of Urban Bias in World Development, London

Lluch, C. *et al.* (1977): Patterns in Household Demand and Saving, Washington, D.C.

Lucius, R. von (2001): Der Ruf nach Umverteilung, in: *FAZ* vom 15.03.01, p. 16

Ludwig, H.D. (1967): Ukara – Ein Sonderfall tropischer Bodennutzung im Raum des Victoriasees, München

Marx, K. (1962): Das Kapital, Vol. 1, Darmstadt

Masson Meiss, L. (1984): La recuperación de los andenes para la amplificación de la frontera agrícola en la sierra, Lima

Mellor, J.W. (1995a): Agriculture on the Road to Industrialization, Baltimore and London

Mellor, J.W. (1995b): Introduction, in: Mellor, J.W. (ed.): Agriculture on the Road to Industrialization, p. 1 ff., Baltimore and London

Mellor, J.W. (1998a): Foreign Aid and Agricultural Development, in: Eicher, C.K. / Staatz, J.M., International Agricultural Development, Baltimore

Mellor, J.W. (1998b): Agriculture on the Road to Industrialization, in: *International Agricultural Development*, Baltimore

Mellor, J.W. / G.M. Desai (1985): Agricultural Change and Rural Poverty: Variations on a Theme by Dharm Narain, Baltimore

Metschies, G. (1988): Transportplanung im ländlichen Raum, in: *GTZ-Info*, No 1, p. 39

Mundlak, J. (1999): Elmhurst Memorial Lecture, in: Peters, G.H. (ed.): Food Security, Diversification and Ressource Management, Aldershot

Mundlak, J. / D.F. Larson (1992): On the Transmission of World Agricultural Prices, in: *The World Bank Economic Review*, Vol. 6, p. 399 ff.

Mundlak, J. *et al.* (1989): Agriculture and Economic Growth in Argentina, 1913–84, in: *IFPRI Research Reports*, No 76, Washington, D.C.

Mundlak, J. *et al.* (1997): The Determinants of Agricultural Production, in: *IBRD-Policy Research Working Papers*, No 1827, Washington, D.C.

Munro, J.M. (1987): Cotton, New York

Münzinger, A. (1929): Der Arbeitstag der bäuerlichen Familienwirtschaft, Berlin

Murgai, R. (1999): The Green Revolution and the Productivity Paradox, in: *IBRD Policy Research Working Paper*, No 2234

Nagy, J.G. / H.W. Ohm (1985a): Economic Analysis of Tied Ridges and Fertilization in Farmer-Managed Sorghum Trials in Burkina Faso, West Lafayette

Nagy, J.G. / H.W. Ohm (1985b): Appropriate Technologies to Farmers in Semi-Arid West Africa, West Lafayette

Naumann, A. (1911): Die Bewegung der Löhne der ländlichen 'freien Arbeiter', Berlin

Neunhäuser, P. (2000): More People, Less Erosion. Nutzung Fragiler Ökosysteme am Beispiel Machakos/Kenia, in: Fachkonferenz 'Ressourcenmanagement im Sahel', 6–8.11.2000, Zschortau

Netting, R. (1968): Hill Farmers of Nigeria: Cultural Ecology of the Kofyar Plateau, Seattle

OECD (2001a): Entwicklungszusammenarbeit-Bericht 2000, Paris

OECD (2001b): Agricultural Policies in OECD Countries, Paris

Ohm, H.W. / J.G. Nagy (1986): Appropriate Technologies for Farmers in Semi-Prid West Africa, West Lafayette

Otzen, U. (1992): Stabilization of Agricultural Resources, Berlin

Otzen, U. (2000): Warum scheitert Simbabwe an der Landfrage?, in: *Namibia Magazin*, No 4

OXFAM (2001a): The Future of the Common Agricultural Policy: Implications for Developing Countries, Oxford

OXFAM (2001b): Impact of the CAP on the Development of Value Added Food Processing Industries in Southern Afrika, Oxford

Paarlberg, R. (2000): The Global Food Fight, in: *Foreign Affairs,* Vol. 79, No 3, p. 24 ff.

Park, A. / B. Johnston (1997): Rural Development and Dynamic Externalities in Taiwan's Structural Transformation, in: *Economic Development and Cultural Change*, Vol. 44, No 1

Peter, B.R. *et al.* (1983): Rural Growth Linkages, in: *IFPRI Research Report*, No 41, New York

Peterson, W.L. (1997): Are Large Farms More Efficient?, in: Staff Paper Series, *Staff Paper*, No P97-2, Department of Applied Economics, College of Agricultural, Food and Environmental Sciences, University of Minnesota, St. Paul

Picciotto, R. / R. Wearing (1997): Structural Adjustment Programs – An Assessment, in: *Entwicklung und ländlicher Raum*, Vol. 31, No 1

Pieri, Ch. (1989): Fertilité des terres en Savannes, Paris

Pimentel, D. (1998): Immer weniger für immer mehr, in: *Politische Ökologie*, Sonderheft 10

Pimentel, D. (undated): Environmentally and Economically Sound Energy Strategies for a Sustainable Agriculture (unpublished manuscript)

Pimentel, D. *et al.* (1987): World Agriculture and Soil Erosion, in: *BioScience*, Vol. 37, No 4

Pingali, P.L. *et al.* (1997): Asian Rice Bowls, Wallingford and New York

Pinstrup-Andersen, P. / J. Babinard (2000): The Global Food Situation: The EU Agricultural Policy and Developing Countries, in: *Farm Management*, Vol. 10, No 9, p. 551 ff.

Prebisch, R. (1950): The Economic Development of Latin America and its Principal Problems, New York

Prebisch, R. (1959): Commercial Policy in Underdeveloped Countries, in: *American Economic Review*, May 1959, p. 251 ff.

Priebe, H. / W. Hankel (1980): Der Agrarsektor im Entwicklungsprozess, Frankfurt/Main

Ravallion, M. (2000): Prices, Wages and Poverty in Rural India: What Lessons Do the Time Series Data Hold for Policy?, in: *Food Policy*, No 25, p. 351 ff.

Ravallion, M. / G. Datt (1996): How Important to India's Poor is the Sectoral Composition of Economic Growth ?, in: *World Bank Economic Review*, Vol. 10, No 1, p. 1 ff.

Ravallion, M. / G. Datt (1999): When is Growth Pro-Poor, in: *IBRD-Policy Research Working Paper*, No 2263

Rehbein, F. (1911): Das Leben eines Landarbeiters, Jena

Rosegrant, M.W. *et al.* (2001a): Global Food Projections to 2020, Washington, D.C.

Rosegrant, M.W. *et al.* (2001b): 2020 Food Outlook, Washington, D.C.

Rosset, P.M. (1999): The Multiple Functions and Benefits of Small Farm Agriculture, in: *Food First – Policy Brief*, No 4, Oakland

Rümker, A. von (1972): Die Organisation bäuerlicher Betriebe in der Zentralregion Malawi, in: *Zeitschrift für Ausländische Landwirtschaft*, Materialsammlung, Frankfurt

Runge, C.F. / B. Senauer (2000): A Removable Feast, in: *Foreign Affairs*, Vol. 79, No 3, p. 39 ff.

Ruthenberg, H. (1980): Farming Systems in the Tropics, Oxford

Sanchez, P.A. (1979): Soil Management in Oxisol Savannahs and Ultisol Jungles of Tropical South America, in: Greenland, H.H. (ed.), Characteristics of Soils in Relation to their Classification and Management, London

Sanders, J.H. *et al.* (1996): The Economics of Agricultural Technology in Semiarid Subsaharan Africa, Baltimore

Sarris, A.H. (2001): The Role of Agriculture in Economic Development and Poverty Reduction: An Empirical and Conceptual Foundation, Athens

Savadogo, K. / H. Kazianga (1999): Substitution Between Domestic and Imported Food in Urban Consumption in Burkina Faso: Assessing the Impact of Devaluation, in: *Food Policy*, Vol. 24, No 5, p. 535 ff.

Savaget, C. (1981): Bona-Village de Kondè en terrotr Kabye, in: *ORSTOM-Atlas des Structures Agraires au Sud de Sahara*, No 16, Paris

Schadek, H.-P. (1992): Entwicklungsmöglichkeiten kleinbäuerlicher Betriebssysteme in der Zentralregion Togos, Berlin

Scherr, S.J. (1999): Soil Degradation, Washington, D.C.

Schug, W. (1996): Welternährung, Darmstadt

Schultz, Th. W. (1964): Transforming Traditional Agriculture, New Haven and London

Schultz-Lupitz, A. (1885): Reinerträge auf leichtem Boden, ein Wort der Erfahrung zur Abwehr wirtschaftlicher Noth, in: *Landwirtschaftliche Jahrbücher, Zeitschrift für wissenschaftliche Landwirtschaft*, Vol. 10, p. 807 ff., Berlin

Schwarz, M. (2002): Landreform in Simbabwe, in: *Internationales Afrikaforum*, Vol. 38, No 1

Sen, A. (1981): Poverty and Families, Oxford

Seppälä, P. (1996): Food Marketing Reconsidered, in: WIDER-Research for Action 34, Helsinki

Singh, I. (1990): The Great Ascent. The Rural Poor in South Asia, Baltimore and London

Smith, Th. C. (1959): The Agrarian Origin of Modern Japan, Stanford

Sobhan, R. (1993): Agrarian Reform and Social Transformation: Preconditions for Development, London

Steinich, M. (1997): Dezentralisierung und Entwicklung: Licht in der entwicklungspolitischen Dunkelheit, in: *Nord-Süd aktuell*, Vol. 11, No 1

Stern, N. (1994): Growth Theories, Old and New, and the Role of Agriculture in Economic Development (mimeo. FAO, Policy Analysis Division)

Stevens, R.D. (1965): Elasticity of Food Consumption Associated with Changes in Income in Developing Countries, Washington, D.C.

Stryker, J.D. *et al.* (1990): Trade Exchange Rate and Agricultural Pricing Policies in Ghana, Washington, D.C.

Tangermann, S. (1999): Europe's Agricultural Policies and the Millennium Round, in: *World Economy*, Vol. 22, p. 1155 ff.

Teklu, T. (1996): Food Demand Studies in Sub-Saharan Africa: A Survey of Empirical Evidence, in: *Food Policy*, Vol. 21, No 6, p. 479 ff.

Thaer, A.D. (1815): Leitfaden zur allgemeinen landwirtschaftlichen Gewerbelehre, Berlin

Thaer, A.D. (1809–12): Grundsätze der rationellen Landwirtschaft, Berlin

Thumer, C.P. (1998): The Agricultural Transformation, in: Eicher, C.K. / J.J. Staatz (eds): International Agricultural Development, p. 113 ff, Baltimore

Thünen, J.H. von (1990): Der isolierte Staat in Beziehung auf Landwirtschaft und Nationalökonomie, Berlin

Tiffen, M. *et al.* (1995): More People, Less Erosion, Chichester

Timmer, C.P. (1997): How Well Do the Poor Connect to the Growth Process, in: *HIID-CCCCAER II Discussion Paper*, No 17

Timmer, C.P. (1998): The Agricultural Transformation, in: Eicher, C.K. / J.M. Staatz (eds.): International Agricultural Development, Baltimore

Todaro, M.P. (1981): Economic Development in the Third World, New York

Totter, B. / A. Gordon (2000): Charting Change in Official Assistance to Agriculture, in: *Food Policy*, Vol. 25

Tschajanow, A.V. (1923): Die Lehre von der bäuerlichen Wirtschaft, Berlin

Tyers, R. / K. Anderson (1992): Disarray in World Food Markets, Melbourne

Ullerich, C. (1979): Rural Employment and Manpower Problems in China, Hamburg

United Nations (1996): World Urbanization Prospects. The 1996 Revision, New York

United Nations (1998): World Population Prospects, The 1998 Revision, New York

United Nations (2000): World Population Prospects, The 2000 Revision, New York

United Nations (2001): Population, Environment and Development, New York

USDA (2001): USDA Agricultural Baseline Projections to 2010, Washington, D.C.

USDA/ERS (2001): The Road Ahead: Agricultural Policy Reform in the WTO-Summary Report, Washington, D.C.

Valdes, A. / J. Zietz (1995): Distortions in World Food markets in the Wake of GATT: Evidence and Policy Implications, in: *World Development*, Vol. 23, No 6, p. 913 ff.

Verheye, W.H. (2001): Food Production or Food Aid? An African Challenge, in: *World Bank Series*: Environment, Rural and Social Development, No 190, Washington, D.C.

Wagemann, E. (1935): Die Großhandelspreise in Deutschland von 1792 bis 1934, Berlin

Waller, P.P. / H. Lingnau (1995): Evaluierung von Positionsmaßnahmen der Europäischen Kommission zur Forderung von Menschenrechten und Demokratie, Berlin

Weber, A. (1973): Productivity Growth in German Agriculture, 1850 to 1970, in: *Staff Paper*, p. 73-1, University of Minnesota, Economic Development Center, Wisconsin

Wehrheim, P. / von Cramon-Taubadel (1997): Assessing Coherence between the Common Agricultural Policy and the EU's Development Policy: Principles and Case Study, in: *Quarterly Journal of International Agriculture*, Vol. 36, No 1

Wellner, G. (1998): Die Auswirkungen der externen EU-Rindfleischpolitik auf die kommunalen Bauern in Namibia, Stuttgart

Wencong, Lu (2001): Chinese Agriculture After the WTO Accession: Competitiveness and Policy, in: *Quarterly Journal of International Agriculture*, Vol. 40, No 3, p. 251 ff.

Wiesmann, P. *et al.* (2000): An International Nutrition Index, in: *ZEF-Discussion Papers on Development Policy*, Bonn

Wiggins, S. (1995): Change in African Farming Systems between Mid-1970s and Mid-1980s, in: *Journal of International Development*, Vol. 7, No 6

Windfuhr, M. (2002): Everything but Farms ..., in: *E+Z*, Vol. 43, No 3, p. 82 ff.

Witzke, H. von (1999): Getreideweltmärkte im Jahr 2010, Berlin

Wolff, P. (1997): Sector Investment Programs in Africa, Berlin

World Bank (1981): Accelerated Development in Sub-Saharan Africa. An Agenda for Action, Washington, D.C.

World Bank (1982): World Development Report 1982, New York

World Bank (1986): World Development Report 1986, New York

World Bank (1988): Rural Development. World Bank Experience 1965–86, Washington, D.C.

World Bank (1997): Weltentwicklungsbericht 1997, Washington, D.C.

World Bank (2000a): World Development Indicators, Washington, D.C.

World Bank (2000b): Desertification in the Sahelian and Sudanian Zones, Washington, D.C.

World Resource Institute (1994): World Resources 1994–95: People and the Environment, Washington, D.C.

Appendix

Table A1 Growth rates in rice yields in rural practice in Asian countries (in % p.a.)

High-intensity regions				Low-intensity regions		
Bangladesh	**1970–80**	**1980–87**			**1970–80**	**1980–87**
Dhaka	2.09	0.18	Faridpur		1.15	3.43
Camilla	1.12	1.87	Dinajpur		0.85	2.29
India	**1970–80**	**1980–88**			**1970–80**	**1980–88**
Andhra Pradesh	2.61	1.94	Madhya Pradesh		0.06	2.86
Haryana	4.46	–0.85	Orissa		3.63	2.34
Punjab	4.60	0.70	West Bengal		1.28	4.53
			Bihar		0.51	4.02
Philippines	**1970–80**	**1980–91**			**1970–80**	**1980–91**
Luzon	4.96	1.02	North Mindanao		2.24	2.84
Bicor	3.68	1.60	West Mindanao		8.36	2.17
Tagalong	2.94	2.79				

Source: Pingali *et al.* (1997), p. 72.

Table A2 Percentage of peasant family household income spent on food in Sierra Leone, by income deciles

Income deciles	<10	30–50	50–70	90–100	Average
Subsistence	68	50	50	29	45
Food bought in	15	20	22	26	22
Other household expenditure	17	30	32	35	33

Source: Peter *et al.* (1983).

Table A3   Percentage of peasant family household income spent on food in sub-
Saharan African countries, by income deciles

	Uganda 1969	Malawi 1972	Northern Nigeria 1976/77	Sierra Leone 1977
Subsistence	35–40 %	28–49 %	44–59 %	29–68 %
Food bought in	26–31 %	11–15 %	19–32 %	15–26 %
Other household expenditure	28–30 %	27–32 %	22–24 %	17–35 %

Sources: Brandt (1971); von Rümker (1972); King *et al.* (1997); Peter *et al.* (1983).

Table A4   Income elasticities of demand for food in the regions of the world, 1997

Product	South Asia	East Asia	South-East Asia	West Asia North Africa	Sub-Saharan Africa	Latin America	Industrial-ized countries
Beef	0.57	0.82	0.81	0.45	0.84	0.38	0.17
Poultry	0.91	0.91	0.81	0.72	0.72	0.81	0.64
Eggs	0.56	0.51	0.51	0.41	0.46	0.21	0.03
Milk	0.50	0.63	0.59	0.32	0.73	0.30	0.27
Wheat	0.18	0.26	0.32	0.10	0.50	0.09	0.17
Rice	0.18	0.05	0.14	0.20	0.38	0.22	0.33
Maize	0.02	–0.16	0.04	–0.14	0.30	0.05	–0.05
Other fodder cereals	0.01	–0.09	–0.04	–0.12	0.33	–0.10	–0.18
Sweet pota-toes and yams	–0.08	–0.06	0.00	0.10	0.26	–0.05	–0.10
Cassava and other root vegetables	0.06	–0.05	0.04	0.08	0.31	–0.06	–0.18

Source: Rosegrant *et al.* (2001a).

Table A5 Producer subsidy equivalents[a] in agriculture by regions of the world and products, 1999–2000

Regions	Wheat	Maize	Rice	Soya	Edible oil	Beef	Milk
USA	0.17	0.06	0.14	0.10	0.10	0.04	0.60
EU 15	0.46	0.29	0.46	0.38	0.38	0.63	0.57
Japan	0.86	0.84	0.68	0.36	0.36	0.32	0.80
OECD	0.49	0.38	0.17	0.27	–	0.76	0.48
Eastern Europe	0.07	0.00	0.05	−0.09	−0.09	0.14	0.29
Central Asia	−0.15	0.20	0.20	−0.04	−0.04	0.23	0.37
Other former USSR	−0.15	−0.30	0.00	−0.04	−0.04	0.39	0.45
Mexico	0.29	0.01	0.10	0.06	0.06	0.04	0.44
Brazil	0.24	0.20	0.05	0.09	0.05	0.12	0.20
Argentina	0.04	0.06	0.05	0.01	0.00	0.07	0.17
Other Latin America	0.05	0.11	0.05	0.16	0.28	0.06	0.18
Nigeria	−0.30	0.30	−0.10	−0.10	−0.10	0.25	0.00
Northern SS Africa	−0.29	−0.17	−0.17	−0.03	−0.03	0.28	0.00
Central and western SS Africa	−0.20	0.41	−0.23	−0.07	−0.07	0.43	0.00
Southern SS Africa	−0.25	0.12	−0.20	−0.07	−0.07	0.24	−0.29
Eastern SS Africa	−0.23	0.30	−0.06	−0.02	−0.02	0.50	−0.10
Egypt	0.46	0.12	0.03	0.30	0.04	0.15	0.30
Turkey	0.42	0.05	0.46	0.45	0.45	0.34	0.54
India	0.10	0.18	0.02	0.30	0.20	0.29	0.26
Pakistan	0.15	0.10	0.28	0.30	0.18	0.10	0.22
Bangladesh	0.10	0.20	0.20	0.20	0.12	0.10	0.22
Indonesia	0.10	0.09	0.04	0.38	0.19	0.11	0.15
Thailand	0.60	0.10	0.10	0.24	0.10	0.13	0.50
Malaysia	0.28	0.49	0.25	0.05	0.17	0.13	0.50
Philippines	0.28	0.27	0.60	0.29	0.10	0.25	0.50
Vietnam	0.05	0.25	0.09	0.10	0.17	0.27	0.27
Myanmar	0.10	0.20	0.09	0.10	0.10	0.15	0.08
China	0.07	0.07	0.08	0.02	0.02	0.22	0.25
Rep. Korea	0.13	0.71	0.70	0.77	0.77	–	–

[a] PSE = (direct + indirect subsidies/gross return) multi. 100; no account taken of general taxes and subsidies or of exchange rate distortions and distortions of world market prices.

Source: IFPRI (2001); OECD (2001b).

Table A6   Percentage of peasant family household income spent on food in rural regions of Southern India

Source of income	1973/74	1982/83	1983/84
Small paddy farm	82.5	76.5	77.0
Large paddy farm	74.7	69.4	78.1
Other farms	75.6	77.5	70.2
Landless households	84.0	79.0	75.9
Non-agricultural households	83.7	79.1	75.1

Source: Hazell and Ramasamy (1991), p. 48.

Table A7   Agricultural worker's wages in France, 1700–1872

Year	kg GE/day
1700	2.6
1788	2.8
1813	3.5
1840	4.6
1852	6.1
1862	6.1
1872	6.1

Source: Clark and Haswell (1964), p. 92.

Table A8 Structure of average annual expenditure and revenue of 30 peasant households in the central region of Malawi, 1972, in DM and %

Expenditure group	Cotton farms[a]		Subsistence farms[b]	
	DM	%	DM	%
Subsistence	315	28	171	49
Purchase of food and semi-luxuries	119	11	52	15
Other private expenditures	305	27	111	32
Cash wages (agric.)	284	25	10	3
Expenditure on materials (agric.)	106	9	7	2
Total expenditure	1129	100	352	101
Subsistence	315	27	171	46
Agricultural sales	488	42	39	11
Off-farm revenue	358	31	160	43
Total revenue	1161	100	370	100

[a] n = 19; [b] n = 11.

Source: von Rümker (1972).

Table A9 Structure of average annual expenditure and revenue of 25 peasant households in two Ugandan villages, February 1968 to January 1969, in Shs and %

Expenditure group[c]	Buwenda[a]		Kibibi[b]	
	Shs	%	Shs	%
Subsistence	905	35	1171	40
Purchase of food and semi-luxuries	811	31	754	26
Other private expenditure	780	30	831	28
Cash wages (agric.)	96	4	170	6
Expenditure on materials (agric.)	29	1	15	1
Total expenditure	2621	101	2941	101
Subsistence	905	35	1171	34
Agricultural sales	792	30	1972	57
Home-made alcoholic beverages	198	8	62	2
Off-farm revenue[d]	724	28	269	8
Total revenue	2619	101	3474	101

[a]   Village of Buwenda, on the outskirts of the town of Jnija, n = 13;
[b]   Village of Kibibi, about 20 km north of Jnija, n = 12;
[c]   broken down further in source document;
[d]   almost entirely agricultural and non-agricultural wage labour.

Source: Brandt (1971).

Table A10 Breakdown of marginal and average expenditure by peasant households in Sierra Leone and Northern Nigeria, in % per capita

Expenditure group	Gusau (northern Nigeria) 1976/77 Expenditure deciles					Sierra Leone 1977 Expenditure deciles				
	1st	5th	6th	10th	Average[a]	1st	4th+5th	6th+7th	10th	Average[b]
Food	78	76	76	76	81	84	70	72	55	67
thereof subsistence	59	50	50	44	57	68	50	50	29	45
local purchases	15	21	20	25	19					
imported purchases	4	6	6	7	5	15	20	22	26	22
Non-food	22	24	24	24	19	17	30	32	35	33
thereof locally produced	11	11	111	11	8	2	14	16	28	17
thereof regional imports	11	13	13	13	11	15	16	16	17	16

[a] average budget shares of 5th decile;
[b] average budget shares of total of total sample.

Sources: King *et al.* (1977): Income Distribution, Consumption Patterns and Consumption Linkages in Rural Sierra Leone, in: *African Rural Economy Paper*, No 16, East Lansing; Peter *et al.* (1983): Rural Growth Linkages, in: *IFPRI Research Report*, No 41, New York.

Table A11 Sources of income of peasant family farms, by income categories, Kenya, 1974–75, % of total income

Income category (in KShs)	0–999	1000–1999	2000–2999	3000–3999	4000–5999	6000–7999	>8000	Total
Farm income	23	44	53	56	61	61	64	57
Wage labour	29	24	24	20	15	25	21	22
Transfer income	31	21	18	13	12	8	4	10
Non-agricultural gainful activity	16	11	10	12	12	6	11	10

Source: Bigsten (1983): What Do Smallholders Do For a Living? Some Evidence from Kenya, University of Göteborg, p. 17, Göteborg.

Table A12 Selected price ratios in German agriculture, 1801/10–1955/59

Period	Land[a] Labour	Machines[b] Labour	Land[c] Com. fert.	Rye[d] Labour	Rye[e] Com. fert.	Animal products[f] Plant products	Agricultural products[g] Industrial products
1800–09	–	–	–	249 (1999) (h)	–	(76) (h)	(58) (h)
1810–19	–	–	–	190 (152)	–	(80)	(50)
1820–29	–	–	–	126 (101)	–	(88)	(39)
1830–39	–	–	–	147 (118)	–	(91)	(48)
1840–49	–	–	–	176 (141)	–	(70)	(61)
1850–59	948 (98)[h]	(228)	–	276 (221)	–	(78)	(67)
1860–69	898 (92)	(149)	–	118 (94)	–	(98)	(70)
1870–74	982 (95)	(162)	–	122 (98)	–	(96)	(71)
1875–79	882 (91)	(98)	–	103 (82)	–	(104)	(87)
1880–84	972 (100)	(100)	631 (100)[h]	125 (100)	0.20 (100)[h]	(100)	(100)
1885–89	987 (102)	(90)	442 (146)	103 (82)	0.23 (115)	(101)	(92)
1890–94	909 (94)	(99)	394 (152)	114 (91)	0.29 (145)	(94)	(101)
1895–99	832 (86)	(93)	251 (215)	90 (72)	0.36 (180)	(96)	(90)
1900–04	828 (85)	(94)	253 (213)	81 (65)	0.32 (160)	(106)	(83)

Table A12 (cont.)

Period	Land[a] Labour	Machines[b] Labour	Land[c] Com.fert.	Rye[d] Labour	Rye[e] Com.fert.	Animal products[f] Plant products	Agricultural products[g] Industrial products
1905–09	870 (90)	(86)	223 (257)	89 (71)	0.40 (200)	(100)	(91)
1910–13	914 (94)	(78)	199 (294)	78 (62)	0.39 (195)	(108)	(95)
1925–29	768 (79)	(69)	125 (395)	62 (50)	0.50 (250)	(113)	(87)
1930–34	536 (55)	(60)	104 (344)	48 (38)	0.46 (230)	(96)	(92)
1935–38	622 (64)	(60)	94 (427)	58 (46)	0.62 (310)	–	–
1950–54	465 (48)	(42)	56 (533)	37 (30)	0.66 (330)	–	–
1955–59	419 (43)	(34)	36 (717)	30 (24)	0.83 (415)	–	–

[a] Man-days/hectare; [b] Daily wage index/machine price index; [c] kg/hectare; [d] man-days/tonne; [e,f,g] wholesale stage; [h] ratios in 1880–84 = 100.

Sources: Weber (1973): Productivity Growth in German Agriculture: 1850 to 1970, in: *Staff Paper*, p. 73-1, University of Minnesota, Economic Development Center, Wisconsin; Wagemann (1935): Die Großhandelspreise in Deutschland von 1792 bis 1934, Berlin; Naumann (1911): Die Bewegung der Löhne der ländlichen 'freien Arbeiter', Berlin; Gläsel (1916): Die Entwicklung der Preise landwirtschaftlicher Produkte und Produktionsmittel während der letzten 50 Jahre und deren Einfluss auf Bodennutzung und Viehhaltung im Deutschen Reich, in: *Landwirtschaftliche Jahrbücher*, Vol. 50, Berlin.

Table A13 Trend in intensity indicators and physical yields in German agriculture, 1800–1965

Year	Labour density (workers/ha UAA)		Livestock density (LU/ha UAA)		Pure nutrient application (kg/ha UAA)		Rye yield (kg/ha)		Milk yield (kg/cow/year)	
	abs.	%	abs.	%	abs.	%	abs.	%	abs.	%
1800	0.28	100	0.25	100	11.3	16	1030	100	860	100
1865	–	–	–	–	28.9	42	1400	136	1225	142
1885	0.27	93	0.46	184	69.1	100	1500	147	1450	169
1895	0.29	100	0.54	216	–	–	1690	176	1800	209
1905	0.28	97	0.60	240	–	–	1980	164	–	–
1913	0.31	107	0.61	244	113.1	164	2100	204	2200	256
1925	0.34	117	0.71	284	–	–	1840	179	2100	244
1935	0.31	107	0.76	304	179.7	260	2220	216	2500	291
1955	0.30	103	–	–	–	–	–	–	–	–
1965	0.21	72	–	–	316.5	458	–	–	–	–

UAA = utilized agricultural area; LV = lifestock.

Source: Bittermann, E. (1956): Die landwirtschaftliche Produktion ..., loc. cit.; Weber, A. (1973): Productivity Growth ..., loc. cit.

Table A14 Application of plant nutrients in German agriculture, 1800–1968, in kg/ha UAA

				Consumption/ha			
	1800	1878/89	1898/00	1911/13	1936/38	1961/62[a]	1968/69[a]
Nitrogen (N) total kg	3.9	10.8	20.7	31.0	54.3	81.6	118.9
Stable manure	3.9	10.1	18.5	24.6	29.3	43.9	50.5
Com. fertilizers kg	0.0	0.7	2.2	6.4	25.0	43.7	68.4
Stable manure as %	100.0	93.5	89.4	79.4	54.0	50.1	42.5
Phosphorus (PO) total kg	2.2	7.2	20.6	32.6	42.5	66.6	84.0
Stable manure kg	2.2	5.6	10.3	13.7	16.3	22.0	25.2
Com. fertilizers kg	0.0	1.6	10.3	18.9	26.2	44.6	58.8
Stable manure as %	100.0	77.8	50.0	42.0	38.4	30.3	30.3
Potash (KO) total kg	5.2	10.9	27.8	49.5	82.9	134.4	147.4
Stable manure kg	5.2	10.1	24.7	32.8	39.2	61.5	70.7
Com. fertilizers kg	0.0	0.8	3.1	16.7	43.7	72.9	76.6
Stable manure as %	100.0	92.7	88.9	66.3	47.3	45.8	48.0

[a] Federal Republic of Germany

Source: Weber, A. (1973): Productivity Growth ..., p. 16, loc. cit.

Table A15 Labour substitution on the transition from manual methods to animal-powered mechanization, 1890–1900

Operation	Volume of work	Time needed for manual labour		Machine	Time needed with animal power[a]		
		TWD	MD		HD	WD	MD
Cutting straw	10 tonnes	–	42.5	Gin chopper	2.9	–	2.9
Cutting beet	10 tonnes	–	3.3	Gin cutter	0.8	–	1.2
Breaking oilcake	10 tonnes	–	10.1	Gin cake breaker	2.7	–	2.7
Sowing cereals	10 ha	–	2.7	Drilling machine[b]	6.0	–	6.0
Spreading manure	10 ha	–	2.5	Manure spreader	2.0	–	3.0
Sowing beet	10 ha	10.0	–	Drilling machine	4.0	0.0	6.0
Planting potatoes	10 ha	50.0	–	Potato planter	6.7	0.0	10.9
Hoeing beet	10 ha	169.2	–	Hoeing machine	3.6	0.0	3.6
Cutting and tying cereals	10 ha	20.0	20.0	Reaping and binding machine	7.6	0.0	5.0
Mowing clover	10 ha	–	20.0	Mower	5.0	–	2.0
Turning hay	10 ha	100.0	–	Hay turner	2.9	0.0	2.1
Threshing	10 tonnes	–	67.0	Steam thresher	–	–	20.0
Harvesting potatoes	10 ha	350.0	–	Potato lifter	30.0	100.0	20.0
Harvesting beet	10 ha	350.0	–	Beet lifter	20.0	150.0	20.0

[a] TWD = total work days; HD = horse-days; WD = woman-days; MD = man-days; [b] mainly has the effect of saving seed and increasing yield

Source: Calculated from F. Bensing (1897): Der Einfluss der Landwirtschaftlichen Maschinen auf Volks- und Privatwirtschaft, dissertation, Breslau.

Table A16 Income shares of different quintiles, by decade and region

Quintile and region	Overall average	1960s	1970s	1980s	1990s
Lowest quintile					
Sub-Saharan Africa	5.26	2.76	5.10	5.70	5.15
East Asia and the Pacific	6.34	6.44	6.00	6.27	6.84
South Asia	7.74	7.39	7.84	7.91	8.76
Eastern Europe	9.34	9.67	9.76	9.81	8.83
Middle East and North Africa	6.66	5.70	–	6.64	6.90
Latin America and the Caribbean	3.86	3.42	3.69	3.67	4.52
Industrial countries and high-income developing countries	6.42	6.42	6.31	6.68	6.26
Middle class (third and fourth quintiles)					
Sub-Saharan Africa	34.06	32.72	32.15	35.40	33.54
East Asia and the Pacific	37.92	36.29	36.88	37.18	37.53
South Asia	37.25	37.95	37.89	37.17	38.42
Eastern Europe	40.65	39.69	41.59	41.25	40.01
Middle East and North Africa	36.28	35.30	–	35.88	36.84
Latin America and the Caribbean	33.21	28.13	34.59	33.58	33.84
Industrial countries and high-income developing countries	40.99	39.89	40.61	41.21	41.80
Top quintile					
Sub-Saharan Africa	51.79	61.97	55.82	48.86	52.37
East Asia and the Pacific	45.73	45.90	46.50	45.51	44.33
South Asia	43.01	44.05	42.19	42.57	39.91
Eastern Europe	36.11	36.30	34.51	34.64	37.80
Middle East and North Africa	46.32	49.00	–	46.72	45.35
Latin America and the Caribbean	55.12	61.62	54.18	54.86	52.94
Industrial countries and high-income developing countries	40.42	41.22	41.11	39.89	39.79

– Not available.

Source: Deininger and Squire (1996), p. 585.

Table A17 Effects on poverty and productivity of additional government expenditures in India

Expenditure variable	Elasticities		Marginal impact of spending Rs 100 billion at 1993 prices		Number of poor reduced per Rs million spent
	Poverty	TFP[a]	Poverty	TFP	
			(per cent)		
R&D	−0.065*	0.296*	−0.48*	6.98*	91.4*
Irrigation	−0.007	0.034*	−0.04	0.56	7.4
Roads	−0.066*	0.072*	0.87*	3.03*	165.0*
Education	−0.054*	0.045*	−0.17*	0.43*	31.7*
Power	−0.002	0.0007	−0.015	0.02	2.9
Soil and water	−0.0004	0	−0.035*	0	6.7*
Rural development	−0.019*	n.a.	−0.15*	n.a.	27.8*
Health	−0.0007	n.a.	−0.02	n.a.	4.0

[a] TFP = total factor productivity (ratio of total farm output value to total costs).

Source: Fan *et al.* (1999), p. 37.

Table A18 Agricultural production and productivity growth in the People's Republic of China

Year	Production	Land productivity	Labour productivity	Total factor productivity	Policy phase
			Annual growth rates (%)		
1952–77	2.10	1.87	0.12	−0.42	centrally administered production and distribution
1978–84	6.63	7.37	5.07	4.72	household production responsibility system[a]
1985–89	3.17	2.64	1.39	0.95	curtailment of price incentives[b]
1990–95	6.89	6.64	7.50	5.85	abolition of quotas, incipient subsidization[c]
1952–95	3.72	3.57	2.22	1.50	

[a] minimum delivery quotas at fixed prices;

[b] inflation of input prices, repression of output prices;

[c] 90% of agricultural output freely marketed, incipient subsidization of the agricultural sector.

Source: Fan *et al.* (2000), p. 20.

Table A19 Effects on poverty and growth of additional government expenditures, by type of investment and region

	Coastal region	Central region	Western region	China
Returns to agricultural production	(Yuan additional Yuan investment)			
R&D	7.33	8.53	9.23	7.97
Irrigation	1.40	0.98	0.93	1.15
Roads	3.69	6.90	6.71	4.91
Education	6.06	8.45	6.20	6.68
Electricity	3.67	4.89	3.33	3.90
Rural telephone	4.14	8.05	6.57	5.29
Returns to poverty reduction	(Number of poor reduced per additional 10,000 Yuan)			
R&D	0.97	2.42	14.03	3.36
Irrigation	0.15	0.23	1.14	0.39
Roads	0.70	2.80	14.60	2.96
Education	1.79	5.35	21.09	6.40
Electricity	0.92	2.64	9.62	2.92
Rural telephone	0.98	4.11	17.99	4.02

Source: Fan *et al.* (2000), p. 40.

Table A20 Freight rates by various methods of transport, in €/tonne/km

Human head (hired)	abt. 5.00
Beast of burden (camel, donkey)	1.50–2.00
Ox or donkey cart, bicycle (own)	0.40–0.60
Tractor + trailer, pick-pp on track	0.60–0.85
Lorry (7 tonne payload, on metalled road)[a]	0.20–0.35
HGV[b] (on asphalt)	0.10–0.15

[a] high estimate;
[b] at optimum load – if empty, freight rates almost double.

Source: Metschies (1988).

Table A21 Grain prices, agricultural wages and wage–price ratio, Bangladesh, 1973/74

Month	Wages		Grain prices		Wage–price ratio[a]	
	1973	1974	1973	1974	1973	1974
January	4.78	6.22	72.37	92.11	100	102
February	4.91	6.36	76.68	98.93	97	97
March	5.14	7.17	83.84	117.33	93	93
April	5.35	8.22	96.49	136.98	84	91
May	5.47	8.72	96.29	135.68	86	97
June	5.83	8.26	91.11	139.04	97	90
July	6.02	8.61	87.06	141.78	105	92
August	5.81	8.82	85.92	171.25	102	78
September	5.72	8.80	89.47	212.80	97	63
October	5.85	8.64	94.11	251.78	94	52
November	6.00	8.39	89.65	213.73	101	50
December	6.32	8.70	80.90	188.98	118	51

[a] Index: January 1973 = 100.

Source: Sen (1981), p. 145.

Table A22 Rural household expenditure behaviour in sub-Saharan rural areas

Expen- diture item	Burkina Faso, 1984/85		Niger, 1989/90		Senegal, 1989/90				Zambia, 1985/85	
					South-eastern Groundnut Basin		Central Groundnut Basis			
	ABS[a]	MBS[b]	ABS[a]	MBS[b]	ABS[a]	MBS[b]	ABS[a]	MBS[b]	ABS[a]	MBS[b]
(per cent)										
All food and drink[c]	85	75	75	62	72	55	78	62	84	74
Non-food com-modi-ties	9	14	15	22	27	44	20	38	12	19
Ser-vices	6	11	10	16	1	1	2	0	3	7
By tradability and sector[d]										
Farm nontrad-ables	57	45	10	17	35	11	28	15	73	60
Non-farm nontrad-ables	13	22	21	39	15	24	12	17	3	7
All trad-ables	29	33	69	53	59	65	69	68	24	33

[a] Average budget share (ABS) is the percentage of total consumption expenditures on that item.

[b] Marginal budget share (MBS) is the percentage of total increments to expenditure on that item. The expenditure elasticity of demand (often used as proxy for the income elasticity of demand) is MBS/ABS.

[c] Includes processed foods.

[d] Processed farm items are included in nonfarm. Tradability is defined at the national level, meaning that non-tradables are rarely exported to or from the (non-African) world market.

Source: Delgado, Ch. L. *et al.* (1998), p. 123.

Table A23 Average budget shares for household expenditure, Southern Indian villages
(per cent)

	1973/74					1982/83				
	Small paddy farms	Large paddy farms	Non-paddy farms	Land-less	Non-agric.	Small paddy farms	Large paddy farms	Non-paddy farms	Land-less	Non-agric.
Total foods	82.5	74.7	75.6	84.0	83.7	76.5	69.4	77.5	79.0	79.1
Alcohol & tobacco	4.5	5.4	4.2	4.3	5.3	3.4	3.0	3.9	5.2	5.2
Clothing & foot-wear	4.4	7.1	4.2	3.1	3.2	3.7	4.4	2.5	2.4	4.3
Religious & social functions	1.2	2.7	1.5	0.7	0.9	7.8	7.8	2.5	3.1	1.6
Other items	6.0	8.8	119	7.9	5.2	7.0	13.9	11.0	8.3	7.6

Source: Hazell, B. R. and C. Ramasamy (1991), p. 48.

Table A24 International comparison of commodity-specific average production costs and yields in China for the period 1996–98

Item	Wheat[a]			Rice				Maize		
	CN-N	CN-S	USA	D-SH	CN-N	CN-S	USA	CN-N	CN-S	USA
Yield (ton/ha)	4.48	2.53	2.41	8.50	7.19	8.21	6.56	5.68	4.28	8.74
Production costs (US $/ ton)	156.24	243.97	140.45	155.00	173.18	134.74	207.15	109.83	158.23	77.84
Direct costs	57.27	61.16	42.90	43.24	44.42	34.31	87.66	34.36	41.49	33.35
Machinery and labour costs	81.52	157.62	65.06	94.83	82.18	78.62	84.00	64.02	102.48	39.03
Fixed costs	17.44	25.19	32.44	16.93	46.54	21.86	35.49	11.47	14.25	5.45
Producer price (US $/ ton)	161.00	158.00	128.00	163.00	178.00	163.00	126.00	119.00	159.00	92.00

Table A24 (cont.)

Item	Soybean			Cotton			Rape seed		
	CN-N	CN-S	USA	CN-N	CN-S	USA	CN-N	CN-S	D-SH
Yield (ton/ha)	1.84	1.75	2.91	1.16	0.83	0.78	1.73	1.27	3.32
Production costs (US $/ton)	264.59	299.48	143.47	994.40	1896.10	1438.70	262.10	425.50	310.00
Direct costs	64.80	59.97	53.41	449.70	413.90	483.20	61.93	97.48	86.48
Machinery and labour costs	144.65	191.41	72.73	386.50	1398.20	858.20	174.96	293.56	189.66
Fixed costs	55.14	48.10	17.33	158.10	83.90	97.30	25.21	34.45	33.86
Producer price (US $/ton)	330.00	346.00	240.00	1520.00	1754.00	1521.00	327.00	299.00	282.00

[a] CN-N = North China; CN-S = South China; USA = United States of America; D-SH = Schleswig-Holstein in Germany.

Source: Wencong, Lu (2001), p. 261.

Table A25 Changes in the nutrient content and pH value of the uppermost
0–45 cm of soil in well-ordered ley farming in Uganda, 1963–69

Nutrients	after three years of fallow (kg/ha)[a]	after three years of cultivation (kg/ha)
organic carbon	+ 15.950	− 19.700
total nitrogen	+ 769	− 968
total phosphorus	+ 85	− 88
total sulphur	+ 45	− 86
pH value (in CaCl$_2$)	+ 0.26	− 0.31
exchangeable K	+ 471	− 461
exchangeable Ca	+ 971	− 1.897
exchangeable Mg	+ 465	− 420

[a]   including the nutrient content of the fallow vegetation.

Source: Munro (1987), p. 110.

Table A26 Changes in the distribution of land ownership in Latin America

Country	Year	Gini-coefficient
Bolivia	1978	0.55
	1952	0.79
Chile	1987	0.64
	1965	0.70
Colombia	1983	0.70
	1970	0.74
Dominican Republic	1981	0.70
	1971	0.68
Ecuador	1987	0.69
	1954	0.70
El Salvador	1985	0.57
	1971	0.62
Guatemala	1979	0.72
	1950	0.71
Honduras	1980	0.64
	1952	0.65
Mexico	1970	0.58
	1923	0.78
Peru	1984	0.61
	1961	0.74

Source: BMZ (1999), p. 37.

Table A27 Current distribution of land ownership and state of land reform in Southern Africa, 2000

Country	Utilized agricultural area (10^3 km^2)	Privately owned and/or farmed (%)	In traditional joint ownership (%)	Redistribution completed (%)	Currently settled households
RSA	1221	72	14	1.0	53950
Namibia	824	44	43	1.4	3400
Zimbabwe[a]	391	41	42	22.5	75000

[a] excluding land occupied in 2000/2001.

Source: Adams and Howell (2001).

Table A28 Price elasticities of production in Ghanaian agriculture

Price of product	Elasticities[a]			
	Cocoa	Maize	Cassava	Rice
Cocoa	+0.22	−0.14	−	−
Maize	−0.27	+0.79	−0.44	−
Rice	−0.39	−	−	+0.43

[a]   Minimum level of significance 10%.

Source: Stryker *et al.* (1990), p. 166.

Part B

Institutional and organizational ways for rural communities of sub-Saharan Africa to reduce poverty

Uwe Otzen

Poverty has always been indigenous to Greece, but competence had first to be imported and acquired through wisdom and strict law. By using it, Greece defends itself against poverty and tyranny.

Herdotus, 450 BC

Introduction

In the 1990s the international community of UN Member States, using unparalleled organizational, financial and human resources and with considerable support from international development research institutions, created an unprecedented framework for sustainable development and thus for sustainable agricultural and rural development. This alone signifies a major advance in the search for an international consensus on development policy. Furthermore, remarkable conceptual work was done to give structure to the analysis of local, national and regional problems, to problem-solving approaches and to policy recommendations. This framework has henceforth formed a comprehensive construct for the perception of the global problems that have accumulated over the years with regard to *food security*, the *improvement of rural incomes* and the *stabilization of natural resources*. It also forms a normative basis for individual national and joint efforts to cope with precisely these three tasks, which have, of course, been the global guide for sustainable agricultural and rural development since UNCED '92.

The creation of a long-term conceptual framework of this kind and the jointly proclaimed political will to change the circumstances peculiar to each country so that the three objectives may be achieved are, however, subject to extremely varied constraints and trends. Different problem-solving approaches will have to be sought to suit the history of each country's development, the level of development and technology it has reached and its soil and climatic conditions. The inhibitory factors and the resistance will also differ from one country to another. What emerged only after the conclusion of the negotiation process and especially towards the end of the decade was the realization that adding more and more development objectives to the list, however wellfounded they may be, is one thing; achieving tangible results is another, and it will be far more difficult.

Simply lining up such objectives as food security, income improvement and natural resource stabilization and commitments to promote participation and democracy and achieve gender fairness, agricultural reform and the abolition of international agricultural protectionism is unlikely on its own to contain the problem of hunger and poverty effectively. It is not the absence of adequately integrated concepts to cope with the complex problem situation that characterizes the current dilemma in development policy, but rather the fact that merely adding objectives, action programmes and measures, however justified they may be, is doomed to failure because most countries have limited implementation capacities

The UN Programme of Action 2015 for halving the number of the extremely poor, which must be seen as the logical conclusion of this process of establishing a global framework, faces the same dilemma. Although it takes up the relevant cross-references to the precursor programmes, such as Agenda 21, the Convention to Combat Desertification, the World Food Summit Plan of Action and the World Conference on Agrarian Reform and Rural Development, it is confronted with the same urgent questions about implementation capacity. Consequently, with a view to the implementation of all the global projects referred to here and the integration of their programme objectives and action programmes into national poverty reduction strategies, far greater account will have to be taken in the future of the capacity for political, institutional, organizational and practical implementation. This concerns both the partner countries, whose implementation structures are usually inadequate, and the OECD countries, with their differing and, in some cases, overly complicated development cooperation structures.

This global debate on sustainable agricultural and rural development and the contribution it can make to the reduction of global poverty is bound to be followed by the sobering, but unavoidable, debate on feasibility. A solution now needs to be found to the problem of organizing and financing implementation at national, intermediate and local level. In this, all natural, financial and human resources will have to be used innovatively and efficiently, and all political, civil and international actors will have to cooperate effectively. The debate on how sustainable and poverty-reducing development should be achieved can no longer be conducted in non-committal, general terms, especially as the African states, for their part, are giving the highest priority to agricultural and rural development in their declaration of commitment to the new development partnership with the OECD countries, NEPAD, and would like to mobilize all available resources for this purpose.

Since the 2000/2001 Millennium Summit in New York the OECD countries have similarly embarked on a process of rethinking how the underlying poverty reduction strategies might be swiftly implemented by 2015. It is to be feared that, along with numerous complex aspects of the restructuring of the development cooperation mechanisms, a crucial missing link is again being overlooked: the level of mediation between central government and the local grass-roots level, where food insecurity, hunger, poverty, shared responsibility and involvement manifest themselves in a very practical form – the level of local authorities and municipalities. This, then, is the level on which the study focuses.

Against the background of international development policy commitments, the study begins (Part I) by examining the whole question of programmes of action for its relevance to sustainable, poverty-reducing agricultural and rural development. The second step (Part II) is to attempt to come closer to realistic problem-solving approaches, and culminates with the promising option of decentralized implementation. In Part III reference is made to the importance for and effect on broad-based socio-economic development of the decentralization of government. Part IV then undertakes the conceptually difficult process of bringing together the decentralization approach, the setting of development policy priorities, private-sector development and the integration of these three components into intersectoral reform programmes, which are now seen in the context of national poverty reduction strategies. In view of the complexity of the question, some simple principles, such as subsidiarity, division of labour and least possible government intervention, must be applied. A number of countries are then taken as examples to demonstrate this. The last step (Part V) is to indicate institutional and organizational options for achieving poverty reduction, with agriculturally based rural development taken as the example. Finally, some new ways in which development cooperation organizations might support efforts to achieve political, institutional and fiscal decentralization are suggested.

This study emphasizes the complementary role which African local authorities can play in the institutional and organizational achievement of agriculturally based rural development. As some 80 per cent of the poor in sub-Saharan Africa live in rural areas, the gradual development and constant strengthening of subnational government structures is an essential precondition for poverty reduction. Only then can there be broad-based socio-economic development, processes of democratization from the bottom up and integrated support measures on the part of the international development cooperation community. This may be the ideal course for a new, more efficient partnership with the countries of Africa. The study thus deliberately addresses the tension that exists between the desirable and the feasible. However, this has been done because all these countries must in any case take the course of strengthening the intermediate levels if poverty-reducing policies are to be widely implemented.

Summary

Global development framework

According to international development policy standards, the reduction of rural poverty through sustainable agricultural and rural development can be achieved only within the framework of global action programmes, which will have to be implemented at district and local level. The global action programmes emerging from international commitments between UNCED '92 and the UN Millennium Summit of 2000/2001, such as Agenda 21, the plan of action to implement the Desertification Convention, the World Food Summit Plan of Action and the implementation of the poverty reduction strategies to achieve the Millennium Development Goals, all cover the whole range of national development policies; they are complex in nature and, if they are to be successfully implemented, they will usually require comprehensive sectoral or macropolitical reforms. This will not be achieved with the conventional approaches of project-based or subsectoral development. The concept of setting development policy priorities and establishing programmes accordingly, on the other hand, will be more helpful, especially where the aim is to pool resources and use them more effectively.

Within this framework international development cooperation must now seek out efficient forms of implementation for cooperation in partnership as advocated in the G8 Africa Action Plan for New Partnership for African Development (NEPAD). It should be remembered in this context that

- all the main groups of actors are involved (participation requirement);
- all levels of government are involved (subsidiarity requirement);
- all relevant sectors can make their complementary contributions to development (integration requirement); and
- the private sector can accept the challenge to cooperate in its own economic interests (market requirement).

On the whole, this is also true of agricultural and rural development, which has waned in importance in international development policy since the 1980s. Nor, unfortunately, has it yet found, after decades of failed attempts (Community Development, Package Deal Approach, Integrated Rural Development), really viable structural foundations on which broad-based economic and social development might occur in the national context. This weighs all the more heavily as it has prevented – not least with international support – rural communities in sub-Saharan Africa, where some 80 per cent of the poor live predominantly on agricultural and subsistence incomes, from adopting their own, effective pattern of development within the framework of traditional territorial and decision-making structures.

On the other hand, it is sufficiently well known that in many countries of sub-Saharan Africa the requirements of participation, subsidiarity and market orientation have been repeatedly ignored. This has led to more or less serious distortions of the various aid approaches, by which the structural adjustment programmes have not been left untouched either. On the whole, inappropriate national development policies, suboptimal forms of external support, generally declining ODA flows for agricultural and rural development and the infringement of the subsidiarity principle have exacerbated the 'urban bias', which reflects the neglect of the development of the rural economic area in the past few decades, including the failure of donor and partner countries to provide sufficient public funds for agriculture and rural development.

Promoting agriculturally based development of benefit to the mass of the population

Empirical findings now clearly indicate that poverty reduction in the agricultural countries of Africa can be achieved primarily through agriculturally based growth. Agricultural development can, in turn, succeed only where it is integrated into a spatial development concept which is in balance with national, local and urban development. Thus sustained poverty reduction can be achieved only through broad-based agricultural and social development combined with politically, structurally and fiscally strengthened rural communities.

A positive sign is the growing realization during the global debate on development policy since UNCED '92 and the 1996 World Food Summit that the emphasis must be placed on the following aspects of development if there is to be sustainable agricultural and rural development:

- *Agricultural development*, including (a) price, market and trade policy, (b) the development of agricultural innovations and technology, (c) the improvement of agricultural services and (d) support for agrarian reforms;
- *Social development* in the areas of (a) primary education, (b) initial and advanced vocational training and (c) primary health care and measures to combat HIV/AIDS;
- *Institution-building and capacity improvement* in the areas of (a) local democratic structures, (b) local services and development coordination and (c) regulatory mechanisms to ensure the administration of justice and the setting of appropriate standards;
- *Development of rural infrastructure* in the areas of (a) road-building, (b) transport and communications, (c) energy, (d) local markets, (e) irrigation and drinking water and (f) refuse disposal.

Initiating decentralization

It is becoming increasingly clear in the development debate that the extremely ambitious approaches to solving national cross-section problems will hardly be possible in the future unless steps are taken beforehand or in parallel to decentralize government. This is as true of rural development as it is of the implementation of sectoral programmes and reforms. It is most certainly true of the implementation of global policies that now have to be transformed downwards to local level. The question of the implementation of poverty reduction strategies merely provides the latest proof in this respect: international development cooperation will be able to provide lasting support for implementation throughout a country only if it can be based on political, institutional and fiscal structures that can be used at a decentralized level. Only then will the result be broad-based development and the development of democracy from the bottom up.

The aim here is to bid farewell to approaches to development which have hitherto been too dirigistic and complex and of which too much has been expected. What is being sought, in the final analysis, is an optimum alliance between the public and private sectors, represented by the main groups of actors at the various levels of government. This optimum alliance is most likely to evolve in a state structure in which the subsidiarity principle is applied. It includes two aspects: (a) the creation of conditions for the gradual emergence of political, institutional and fiscal decentralization and (b) the creation of an economic environment that enables private-sector development and local economic linkages to become more dynamic.

The changes of direction in development policy to be deduced from this for poverty-reducing development should be made gradually: where the provision of public funds is concerned, towards the sectors with the best prospect of successfully reducing poverty; in the institutional and organizational sphere, towards the strengthening of rural communities; and in the area of private-sector development, towards the creation of legal and investment conditions conducive to local economic development.

Taking institutional and organizational precautions

In general, national poverty reduction strategies can be implemented only if

- the targets referred to above are fully integrated into development policy and competently guided by central government (Comprehensive Development Framework);
- the various forms of assistance are provided by central government, local government, organized civil society or the private sector in accordance with the subsidiarity principle;
- the development measures can be implemented in a decentralized and participatory manner; and
- they receive sustained support under the financial and fiscal policies.

Thus poverty-reducing agriculturally based rural development undoubtedly needs politically, institutionally and fiscally strengthened rural authorities capable of combining sectoral integration with responsibility delegated to them in accordance with the subsidiarity principle. If (a) participatory planning processes, (b) decision-making processes over which the local authorities have sole jurisdiction and (c) intersectoral coordination processes are eventually to lead to (d) development measures ready for financing, efficient and transparent steering mechanisms will be needed at local government level. They are most likely to be established in systems of local administration that are able to harmonize political and technical/financial interests and options. Such twin-track systems have already been installed in many local government administrations, especially in the English-speaking countries of Africa; they should be revived under development policies. Such countries as South Africa, Ghana and Uganda are already making good progress in this direction, while such countries as Malawi and Tanzania are just beginning.

The idea behind such systems – notwithstanding a number of problem cases, foremost among them Zimbabwe, Sudan and Nigeria – is that provincial, district and local councils should use the political track to develop their own guiding development policy function, while the administrative track is designed to make intersectoral coordination possible, to draw on local expertise and to prepare the budgeting of development measures. The political mandate held by the councils (in elected local and district assemblies) for a set term should enable them to call at any time on the expertise summoned by the local administration and provided by the line ministries, the private sector and organized civil society. As a rule, this is achieved through technical subcommittees. Local government decisions coordinated politically and technically in this way form the basis on which viable development schemes and measures can then be launched. They can be supported jointly by the public authorities, the private sector and international development cooperation within the framework of a programme that is consistent in itself.

Unfortunately, reality in many sub-Saharan African countries still differs from this ideal. The missing link between central government and the people, which the local or district administrations ought really to have forged long since, is now supplied by organized civil society in many cases. But NGOs and community-based organizations are not a permanent substitute for a development-oriented local administration integrated into the state, which should be capable of performing even long-term and intersectoral development tasks. South Africa has accepted this challenge in exemplary fashion with its 'developmental local government' approach.

Strengthening fiscal autonomy

If broad-based rural development is to have the backing of financial policy, the fiscal autonomy of the lower territorial authorities must be strengthened. For the decentralized development of rural areas to benefit from an increase in fiscal autonomy, local financial management must be gradually improved and form part of a general fiscal policy framework. This can be achieved only on the basis of four pillars of fiscal decentralization, which usually have still to be developed: (1) improving the local revenue base, (2) securing and increasing intergovernmental transfers, (3) gearing expenditure to development and (4) where appropriate, local borrowing, which should be handled with extreme caution.

Increasing fiscal autonomy is in itself a very laborious and lengthy process; it should be viewed from the angle of the joint financing of the decentralized rural development by means of intergovernmental transfers and local resources and – where public–private partnerships evolve – with the private sector involved; it should also be coordinated with sectoral development financing and with the provision of external financial flows, where this can be negotiated with the international donor organizations.

These three components (local joint financing, sectoral financing and external development financing) together create the financial framework for decentralized development in accordance with the subsidiarity principle. Within this framework contributions to the establishment of programmes could be made, firstly, by central government (through the financing of the local administration, the intergovernmental transfers and the sectoral contributions), secondly, by the local authorities (from local revenue and, possibly, by borrowing), thirdly, by the private sector (from its own funds or from public–private partnership resources) and, fourthly, by international development cooperation. The gradual institutionalization and improvement of this financing framework is one of the most important basic requirements for sustained and broad-based development. It cannot therefore be rated highly enough in national and international promotion policies. Development cooperation will thus need to use new forms of development financing, such as sectoral budget financing and decentralized budget financing.

Integrating rural communities into the state as a whole

Against the background of largely positive global experience of the decentralization of government, in contrast to the largely unsuccessful efforts to implement complex, cross-section development projects effectively, attempts should now be made to develop a framework of practical action from these two positions. It should seek to combine one with the other. This will be possible only if the general principles of simplification and subsidiarity are made to apply both in national development policy and in international development cooperation.

On the basis of the subsidiarity principle and the tried and tested arguments for political, institutional and fiscal decentralization, the structure within which complex development policy tasks should be performed in the future becomes clear: a graduated division of labour between central government, local government, organized civil society, the private sector and the organizations of international development cooperation. Thus the long-term aim should be an organizational framework which

- ensures that core government functions are performed by central government;
- provides for an appropriate delegation of development tasks to local government;
- makes private-sector participation possible; and
- can also be used for external support without creating parallel structures.

On the whole, this is a challenge of the first order when related to the practical side of development policy. What will be needed is a long-term, gradual process guided by its internal logic of coming closer to a form of internal development that is based on a division of labour. In this process the funding agencies at the various levels may have reached widely different stages in their own development, which is an entirely realistic scenario. It will be crucial to apply the principle of the graduated division of labour at each level of funding with the aim of reducing poverty. With its principle of 'cooperative governance' and the constitutional requirement of 'developmental local government', South Africa has created almost ideal conditions for development. It will be important to ensure that, once launched, this process is irreversible. It should therefore be able to survive political turbulence and not, as has happened all too often in the past, become bogged down in feeble approaches that repeatedly fall short of what is needed.

Realigning development cooperation

With partner countries facing such challenges, international development cooperation too should adopt a new position, of course. This applies both to planning, development coordination and procedures and to programming. Fortunately, recent approaches already anticipate this in such important areas as the setting of development priorities, donor coordination, efforts to achieve coherence between development and other policies, the establishment of coherent programmes, budget financing and even the promotion of decentralization. Presumably, this marks the beginning of the evolution of a conception of international development cooperation that remains viable in the long term. This might be ideal inasmuch as it would be capable of combining sustainability and broad-based development with the promotion of democracy.

The above considerations and the conclusions drawn from them enable a number of recommendations to be made. They are largely in the nature of long-term prospects of a gradual change of direction in development policy. The measures recommended could be taken in various sequences: consecutively, simultaneously or before they are actually needed; what is decisive is that they are integrated into an overall plan of implementation that focuses on increasing agricultural productivity, improving rural infrastructure, promoting local economic development and decentralizing governments' social and support services and features an effective division of labour. This might be supported by international development cooperation as follows:

1   Helping partner governments to (further) develop national decentralization policies and such regulatory, legal and fiscal mechanisms as local government, supervisory control over local authorities, joint functional authorities, etc.

2   Helping partner governments to develop and expand the local administration and the most important sectoral ministries for poverty reduction, and especially the agriculture, health, education, training and public works ministries.

3   Helping partner governments to establish long-term cooperation between central government and its sectoral ministries, organized civil society, the organized private sector and the local authorities in accordance with the subsidiarity principle.

4   Helping partner governments to reform their financial administrations with a view to both strengthening the fiscal autonomy of the lower territorial authorities and introducing new forms of external development financing.

5   Both sectoral budget financing and decentralized budget financing can be considered in this context; the latter could use either the mechanisms of intergovernmental transfers or decentralized development funds; at district level district development funds might be formed; these would have to include help to establish an effective independent financial control system.

6   Helping partner governments to train experts and managers in the local government administrations and to establish development-oriented local planning and coordinating units.

7   Helping partner governments and local authorities to expand and maintain the rural road network with the aid of innovative forms of joint financing and participation embracing central government, local government and the private sector.

8   Helping partner governments to improve the performance of their agricultural administrations with a view to deconcentration and orientation towards poverty-reducing services.

9   Helping partner governments with the decentralized implementation of agricultural reforms with a view to a division of labour between central government (agriculture ministry and its external offices), local authorities and the private sector.

10 Helping partner governments to develop a cooperative savings and credit system on the model of the Raiffeisen purchasing and credit cooperatives with a view to overcoming the chronic undercapitalization of the farming and small business sector in the medium term.

11 Helping partner governments to deconcentrate and enhance the effect of government agricultural research with a view to focusing on poverty-reducing research efforts.

The financial risk attached to decentralized funding mechanisms, such as district development funds, taken as a whole, is probably no greater than that inherent in the conventional development financing of public-sector investment projects through the treasury. When such risks as weak financial control, waste of resources and nepotism are weighed up against the potential benefits for decentralized development, such as ownership, avoidance of parallel structures and the achievement of wider-ranging development, the latter must be rated higher.

Part I   Global framework for sustainable and poverty-reducing agricultural and rural development

1   Agenda 21

1.1   Sustainable agricultural and rural development

Agenda 21 in 1992 was the first attempt to provide a concept for sustainable development that was binding on all the signatory states of the United Nations Conference on Environment and Development (UNCED).[1] In this concept agricultural development plays a very important role. Each of the four sections[2] of the Agenda, with its 40 chapters, includes a number of chapters with references to areas of action of fundamental importance for sustainable agricultural development. They are: combating poverty, population dynamics and sustainable development, an integrated approach to the planning and management of land resources, local authorities' initiatives in support of Agenda 21 and strengthening the role of farmers.

Chapter 14 in particular, under the heading *Promoting sustainable agricultural and rural development*, refers to the following programme areas (see Figure 1):

1 Agricultural policy review, planning and integrated programming in the light of the multifunctional aspect of agriculture, particularly with regard to food security and sustainable development;
2 Ensuring people's participation and promoting human resource development for sustainable agriculture;
3 Improving farm production and farming systems through diversification of farm and non-farm employment and infrastructure development;
4 Land-resource planning information and education for agriculture;
5 Land conservation and rehabilitation;
6 Water for sustainable food production and sustainable rural development;
7 Conservation and sustainable utilization of plant genetic resources for food and sustainable agriculture;

UNCED '92	UNCED '92
Agenda 21, Chapter 1	**Convention to combat desertification**
Programme areas:	**Obligations**:

1 Agricultural policy review, planning and integrated programming in the light of the multifunctional aspect of agriculture, particularly with regard to food security and sustainable development	1 Integrated approach addressing the physical, biological and socio-economic processes of desertification
	2 Establishment of an enabling international economic environment
2 Ensuring people's participation and promoting human resource development for sustainable agriculture	3 Integration of poverty eradication strategies into efforts to combat desertification
3 Improving farm production and farming systems through diversification of farm and non-farm employment and infrastructure development	4 Cooperation in the fields of environmental protection and the conservation of land and water resources
4 Land-resource planning information and education for agriculture	5 Strengthening of subregional, regional and international cooperation
5 Land conservation and rehabilitation	6 Strengthening of international cooperation with a view, inter alia, to
6 Water for sustainable food production and sustainable rural development	7 Avoiding duplication
7 Conservation and sustainable utilization of plant genetic resources for food and sustainable agriculture	8 Use of existing bilateral and multilateral financial mechanisms
8 Conservation and sustainable utilization of animal genetic resources for sustainable agriculture	
9 Integrated pest management and control in agriculture	
10 Sustainable plant nutrition to increase food production	
11 Rural energy transition to enhance productivity	
Aims: To promote sustainable agricultural and rural development	To alleviate and combat the consequences of drought and desertification with effective measures at all levels

Figure 1 Normative framework for global agricultural and rural development in the light of international agreements

World Food Summit '96	Millennium Summit 2000
World Food Summit Plan of Action	**National Programme of Action 2015**

Obligations:

Actions of the Federal German Government:

1 Ensure an enabling political, social and economic environment based on equal participation of women and men	1 Removal of European and international agricultural protectionism and export subsidies
2 Eradicating poverty and improving physical and economic access to safe food	2 Support for agricultural and land reforms
3 Pursue sustainable food, agriculture, fisheries, forestry and rural development policies, considering the multifunctional character of agriculture	3 Support for needs-oriented agricultural research
4 Strive for a fair and market-oriented world trade system	4 Promotion of capacity-building, development of organizations and increases in the efficiency of public servants
5 Meet transitory and emergency food requirements	5 Promotion of national and regional food security
6 Promote optimal allocation of public and private investments to foster human resources, sustainable food, agriculture, fisheries and forestry systems, and rural development	6 Safeguarding access to plant genetic resources
7 Implement the Plan of Action in co-operation with the international community	7 Support for partner countries in affording protection against risks inherent in genetic engineering
Aims: To halve the number of the chronically hungry by 2015, improve agricultural incomes, ensure food security and conserve natural resources	To halve the proportion of the extremely poor by 2015

Figure 1 (cont.)

8   Conservation and sustainable utilization of animal genetic resources for sustainable agriculture;
9   Integrated pest management and control in agriculture;
10   Sustainable plant nutrition to increase food production;
11   Rural energy transition to enhance productivity.

Each of the programme areas referred to above is broken down by such operational aspects as (a) the clarification of the bases for action on which the programmes can be implemented, (b) the definition of programme objectives and (c) measures and instruments for the implementation of programmes. In its conception, Agenda 21 is entirely geared, normatively at least, to implementation. It names possible financial resources and mechanisms, refers to the need for the transfer of environmentally sound technologies, underlines human resource development and the strengthening of institutional capacities and emphasizes in particular the improvement of national mechanisms and international cooperation for strengthening developing countries' implementation capacity. Nonetheless, it lacks recommendations for institutional and organizational action to harmonize sustainable agricultural and rural development and achieve it at a country's various levels.

Even Part IV of Agenda 21, which concerns the means of implementation, has very little to say on this aspect. Only Chapter 37 discusses, in very general terms, national mechanisms and international cooperation for human resource development and the strengthening of institutional capacities in developing countries. Capacity-building in this context relates to each country's human resource and scientific, technological, organizational, institutional and financial potential. It thus touches on the requirements for the achievement of sustainable agricultural and rural development in no more than very general terms.

1.2   Sustainable development of local communities

With the inclusion of local communities in the Agenda 21 follow-up process, the *local Agenda 21*, it became clear that the global concept must have its local counterpart if the concepts of environment and development were not to remain stuck in the vagueness of an international standard-setting process. On the basis of Chapter 28 of Agenda 21[3] the *Commission for Sustainable Development* (CSD) sought in the mid-1990s to persuade the governments of the contracting states to adopt political and practical methods to convert the global objectives through their respective national environmental action plans into local targets and eventually to identify programmes and projects geared to specific local communities. With this decisive step (decisive in the sense of the 'think-global–act-local' principle) an almost global concept for the active participation of *local communities* was first launched. '*With the local Agenda 21, cities and local authorities throughout the world commit themselves to taking practical action to put sustainable development guidelines into practice at local level.*'[4]

In accordance with the basis for action agreed in Chapter 28 the following is to be achieved: the local authorities are to

> construct, operate and maintain economic, social and environmental infrastructure, oversee planning processes, establish local environmental policies and regulations, and assist in implementing national and subnational environmental policies.
>
> (UNCED 1992, p. 231)

Although it should be borne in mind from the outset that this basis for action does not yet exist in most rural African communities, what is decisive here is the objective to which sustainable rural development should be geared, namely that most local authorities in each country should undertake a consultative process with their populations and achieve a consensus on 'a local Agenda 21' for the community (UNCED 1992, loc. cit.).

For structurally and financially weak local communities, as most African rural communities undoubtedly are, this process will require long-term support from central government, international development cooperation or any partner communities in industrialized countries. Great expectations should not, however, be pinned on support of this kind while such immediate elementary problems as food insecurity, income inequality and poverty are deemed to be more important than environmental issues. This is true even where there is awareness of the causal links between environmental degradation, poverty and development.

The Rio plus 10 conference in Johannesburg in 2002 tried to determine how far national governments, cities and local authorities had been able to integrate and implement the various programme areas by means of national and local environmental action projects. Where agricultural and rural development is concerned, it must be established how central, local and private resource-stabilizing measures, such as environmentally sound farming and land improvement objectives, have been implemented and what groups in society they have primarily benefited. It is not surprising that the central coordinating role of the local authorities has also been mentioned in this context.

2   World food summit plan of action

2.1   Objectives

The signatory states of the *Rome Declaration on World Food Security and the World Food Summit Plan of Action 1996*[5] set themselves the goal of halving the number of chronically undernourished people of currently some 800 million by 2015. For this objective there is a positive and a negative scenario, the negative scenario tending to be regarded as realistic, according to an interim statement.[6] This shows that the number of hungry people in 2015 will probably still be 600 million, rather than 400 million.

Irrespective of the prospects of one or other objective being achieved, the *Rome Declaration* is based on the assumption that only peaceful and politically stable development and a beneficial legal, social and macroeconomic environment will form a favourable basis for the implementation of the Plan of Action. It also realistically assumes that the pattern of agricultural and rural development in regions with agricultural potential will differ from that in regions which are agriculturally marginal. However, it emphasizes the need for greater importance to be attached to rural areas in development policy as a whole so that economic revitalization may be achieved.

In view of the well-known fact that food security, agricultural development and rural development are interdependent and highly complex tasks, clear reference is made to the involvement and shared responsibility of an organized rural population, central government, the public administration, the private sector and NGOs. In addition, emphasis is again placed on what was realized years ago, that peasant farming is multifunctional: it combines the food security, employment and income, environmental conservation, social security and capital-forming functions in a way that is specific to each culture. Against this background seven internationally binding obligations are listed (see Table 1):

1 Ensuring an enabling political, social and economic environment based on equal participation of women and men;
2 Eradicating poverty and improving physical and economic access to safe food;
3 Pursuing sustainable food, agriculture, fisheries, forestry and rural development policies, considering the multifunctional character of agriculture;
4 Striving for a fair and market-oriented world trade system;
5 Meeting transitory and emergency food requirements;
6 Promoting optimal allocation of public and private investments to foster human resources, sustainable food, agriculture, fisheries and forestry systems, and rural development;
7 Implementing the Plan of Action in cooperation with the international community.

2.2   Framework for action

As the statements of the seven-part Plan of Action cannot be discussed in detail, all that will be considered here is how the *Rome Declaration* and the *World Food Summit Plan of Action* rate the chances of their being implemented. Besides the objectives and actions that are normative in terms of binding sustainability criteria, those which concern methodology and techniques in terms of general efficiency criteria and those which are appellative in terms of general fairness criteria, vague approaches to the institutional and organizational attainment of sustainable agricultural and rural development are outlined only under Obligation 3. They are largely related to the obligations of previous international agreements, and especially Agenda 21 (see Chapter 1), the *Climate Convention*, the *Desertification Convention* (see Chapter 3), the *Leipzig Declaration on the Sustainable Utilization of Plant Genetic Resources*, the commitments to the *Consultative Group on International Agricultural Research* (CGIAR) and the call for the reinforcement of the standing *World Conference on Agrarian Reform and Rural Development* (WCARRD).

This broad framework for action already makes it clear that food security at regional or national level and sustainable agricultural and rural development can be achieved only within a comprehensive system based on mutual support. Only then does the question of institutional and organizational implementation become a key issue. It covers not only what is in itself the complex sphere of international and national agricultural price, market and trade policy (see Part A, Chapter 13.1) but, above all, aspects of agricultural structural reforms and of microeconomic and technological adjustment (see Part A, Chapter 13.2), political participation, increases in the efficiency of extension and financial services, the improvement of rural infrastructure and the integration of all these areas into local development.

Since development cooperation first came into being, the key issue of institutional and organizational implementation has only ever been addressed in part and from a different angle on each occasion. It has never been seen in terms of local and national developments being processes which are both mutually dependent (complementarity) and must coordinate and guide intersectoral development, each in its own way (policy coherence). The necessary vertical and horizontal integration of agricultural and rural development has thus been impossible hitherto because the key function of decentralized regional authorities has not been appreciated either by the international donor community or by the partner countries. How futile past efforts have been is evident from the following synoptic overview, which is discussed in greater detail in Chapter 9 of Part A:

In the 1960s the sole aim was to modernize traditional agriculture with the resources of a rather socio-technical approach, *Community Development*, the level at which action was taken being the village community. In the 1970s the main aim was to increase agricultural production with the resources of the combined deployment of packages of inputs and technology, which then sparked the *Green Revolution*, primarily in India and South-East Asia; the level at which action was taken in this case was the peasant target group. From the late 1970s until the late 1980s this key issue was addressed with the concept of *Integrated Rural Development* (IRD); the action taken consisted in the alignment of various sectoral policies and the integration of extension services; both were achieved for the purpose of target-group-oriented development with, for the most part, expensive and parallel structures. In the early 1990s the aim was primarily capacity- and institution-building and the mobilization of self-help organizations; action was taken at the level of governmental and non-governmental organizations. Since the mid-1990s the focus has been on the institutional and organizational implementation of *Sector Investment Programmes* (SIPs), which are now viewed from the angle of improved sectoral policies and reforms; action is taken at the level of deconcentrated sectoral administrations (e.g. area agricultural offices), which do not yet, as a rule, cooperate with the local authorities.

The Plan of Action itself still implicitly follows on from the old concept of integrated rural development (IRD), simply adding the attribute *sustainable* (*Sustainable Agricultural and Rural Development* – SARD).[7] The framework established for this is a widely branched network of macroeconomic, institutional, programmatic and technical relationships, which are not suitable for implementation (see Figure A1). The only reference to the importance of local development for the achievement of sustainable agricultural and rural development is a brief comment under Objective 36b (*Strengthen local government institutions in rural areas and provide them with adequate resources, decision making authority and mechanisms for grassroots participation*). What is already discernible here is the threefold implementation problem: (a) the question of the mobilization of financial resources, (b) the question of institutional decision-making mechanisms and (c) the question of political participation. These very issues are considered again in Section III of this part of the study in the context of institutional, political and fiscal decentralization. Unfortunately, the follow-up conference to the 1996 World Food Summit, *Rome plus 5,* that was held in June 2002, did not shed any fresh light on these questions or on the implementation of the Plan of Action.

3   UN Convention to combat desertification

3.1   Evolution

Against the background of the economic, social and environmental problems of the anthropogenic and climatogenic degradation of arable, pasture and forest land, especially in the arid areas of Africa, which had been known since the *Conference on Desertification* (UNCOD) in 1972, it was proposed at the *United Nations Conference on Environment and Development* (UNCED) in 1992 that an integrated approach to the sustainable development of natural resources should be developed. This proposal was adopted. An international negotiating committee prepared the *Convention to Combat Desertification in Those Countries Experiencing Serious Drought and/or Desertification, Particularly in Africa* (CCD), which was ready for signing in 1994 and entered into force in 1996. More than 150 countries (CCD signatory states) have meanwhile acceded to the convention. The Conference of the Parties of the UNCOD meets every two years.

3.2   Provisions of the convention

The provisions of the CCD[8] of importance for this study include Article 3 (Principles), Article 7 (Priority for Africa), Article 10 (National action programmes), Article 12 (International cooperation), Article 13 (Support for the elaboration and implementation of action programmes), Article 14 (Coordination in the elaboration and implementation of action programmes), Article 17 (Research and development), Article 19 (Capacity building, education and public awareness), Article 20 (Financial resources) and Article 21 (Financial mechanisms).

From this brief summary of the wide range of objectives, obligations and provisions (see Figure 1) it is already clear how difficult it will be to perform cross-section tasks of the nature of sustainable agricultural and rural development in a national, let alone a regional, context. This task must therefore ultimately be performed – and this is clearly expressed in Article 3(a) concerning the principles underlying the convention – by the local communities; it is here that the degradation problems manifest themselves, whether caused by the local communities themselves or by some external agent, and it is at this level that action must be taken, entirely in keeping with Chapter 28 of Agenda 21 (see Chapter 1).

Alongside the local Agenda 21, the CCD is thus a second global indication that the conservation and economic use of common goods must be very much a matter both for the international community and for individual signatory states; however, both – national and supranational responsibility – will continue to be fruitless without the shared responsibility and involvement of local communities. The CCD has therefore taken the precaution in Article 14 (Coordination of action programmes) and Article 19 (Capacity building) of insisting that an operational mechanism in whatever form must and, in the long term, can be developed between the international community, the individual signatory states and local communities.

What the CCD fails to make clear, however, is not only that local communities will be the most important sponsors of sectorally integrated, cross-section and grass-roots common tasks but that greater political and fiscal importance must be attached to them if they are to cope with this task. This vital precondition can in turn be fulfilled only by means of long-term national policies of political, institutional and fiscal decentralization, as conceived in Section III of this part of the study for the intersectoral cross-section task of rural development. The protection of the natural environment and agricultural and rural development could and should therefore be promoted with the same policy measures and guiding mechanisms. One of the win-win opportunities often cited during the environmental debate might emerge here in the future: development of local authorities can have positive effects on the environment, agriculture and poverty reduction.[9]

3.3   Regional implementation in Africa

What is special about the issue of the regional implementation of the CCD, and thus of sustainable agricultural and rural development in Africa, are not only the agro-economic, structural and trade policy obstacles, as described in particular in Part A, Chapter 6, but also the difficulties due to settlement structures and institutional organization. Given the wide variety (and thus cultural wealth) of settlement structures in African agricultural societies, it can be said that the ability of rural communities to organize and help themselves is developed to very different degrees. While the determinants of this will not be discussed here, the conclusion must be that this variety is bound to have implications for the problem-solving ability of local communities. This very largely depends on the following scales of area organization:

1   The degree of the development of local authorities, local constitutionality and institutionalization, ranging from (a) open, unregulated organization with features of gathering and nomadism to (b) the closed, locally regulated, modern village or community, as an individual or extended community;
2   The degree of settlement density, ranging from (a) a completely dispersed, transhumant to (b) a permanent, compact settlement structure;
3   The degree of market integration, ranging from (a) a pure subsistence economy to (b) a commercialized and completely integrated peasant and commercial village community with a distinct division of labour.

According to the point on these scales at which local communities currently find themselves in their evolution, their initial requirements for the ability to integrate into society and the economy as a whole differ. The question is therefore how nomadic economies in northern Niger, for example, comprising a mix of types 1(a), 2(a) and 3(a) or arable-commercial societies in the highlands of Kenya consisting of a mix of types 1(b), 2(b) and 3(b) are able to organize themselves with a view to solving their environmental, economic and social problems with the support of central government. It hardly needs to be mentioned here that there is every conceivable intermediate stage of structural and socio-economic problem in this context. What is involved here is, generally, a change of highly complex cultural systems and economies over time – a change which cannot be predetermined and can be guided only with difficulty.

What will be decisive is that, starting from the current situation of a local community in country x or y, central government and local authorities endeavour to use the existing intermediary structures for the implementation of national CCD action programmes in such a way that account can be taken of any weaknesses due to structural and regional factors. Where local communities are incapable of overcoming these weaknesses by their own efforts in the long run, support from outside, possibly through international development cooperation, will be necessary. In favourable circumstances it may be needed for a limited period; in unfavourable circumstances it may be needed for a long time. From these deliberations it is already evident that sustainable agricultural and rural development will probably take a limited period to achieve in African regions with high agricultural potential, but will be unattainable in marginal agricultural regions unless long-term external support is provided.

Most attempts hitherto made to provide international support for the implementation of national CCD action programmes have suffered from having paid too little attention to these basic considerations in the past. They have not yet been able to develop any viable support structures which grant the local communities, or enable them to acquire, greater political, institutional and fiscal power and thus a genuine lever in coping with their local environmental and economic development tasks. The coordination of international support is correspondingly difficult, because an international consensus on local community development has yet to be found (Konrad-Adenauer-Stiftung 1999, p. 5).

4   UN Millennium Declaration and poverty reduction strategies

4.1   UN Millennium Declaration

Section III of the UN General Assembly's Millennium Declaration of 8 September 2000 (*Development and poverty eradication*) refers to ten points, section IV (*Protecting our common environment*) to three points, section V (*Human rights, democracy and good governance*) to two points and section VII (*Meeting the special needs of Africa*) to two points intended to substantiate the international commitment to halve global poverty by 2015.[10] Various elements of earlier commitments at past UN world summits are included (UNCED 1992, World Social Summit 1994, World Summit on Gender and Development 1995, World Food Summit 1996). Taken together, these UN processes have engendered a situation in the development debate where the problem of global poverty has now become central to all aspects of societal, social and economic development. This may in fact mark the end of the debate on development concepts, for the moment at least, since henceforth the emphasis must surely be placed on actual implementation.

The points of the UN Millennium Declaration mentioned above also refer, of course, to the decisive demands for the area of agricultural and rural development being considered here, which the UN member countries and the international community should be seeking to meet unilaterally or together: creation of a conducive environment at the national and global levels alike (III.12), good governance (III.13), mobilization of national and international resources (III.14), consideration of the special status of least developed countries (III.15), solving the debt problem (III.16), problems of the landlocked developing countries (III.18), need for partnerships between the private and public sectors (III.20), sustainable resource management (IV.21, 22 and 23) and capacity- and institution-building for the establishment and strengthening of democracy, the rule of law and good governance (V.24 and 25), especially in Africa (VII.27 and 28).

Together with the other, here unmentioned obligations set out in this and other UN declarations, the Millennium Declaration forms for the first time a broad development policy basis for an undertaking which marks the end of a decade of the globalization of development policy, which has come to be known in Germany as *Globale Strukturpolitik*, or global structural policy:[11] every form of development in the poor countries of the South, and especially of sub-Saharan Africa, should be focused on poverty reduction; the policies of the international community must also be geared to this (orientation of the development policies of all countries towards the *Millennium Development Goals* – MDGs). For its part, the Federal German Government has reacted with its *Programme of Action 2015* as its contribution to the global halving of extreme poverty (see Figure 1).[12] The Programme of Action is summarized in seven points:

1   Removal of European and international agricultural protectionism and of export subsidies;
2   Support for agricultural and land reforms;
3   Support for needs-oriented agricultural research;
4   Promotion of capacity-building, the development of organizations and improvement of the efficiency of the public service;
5   Promotion of national and regional food security;
6   Safeguarding access to plant genetic resources;
7   Support for partner countries in affording protection against risks inherent in genetic engineering.

In this case too, development policy approaches that concentrate on local community development might be identified at best in section IV.21, 22 and 23 of the Millennium Declaration and point 4 of the corresponding German Programme of Action. Unfortunately, however, neither considers further the question of how measures to reduce poverty are to be implemented institutionally and organizationally.

4.2   Poverty reduction strategy of the IMF and World Bank

In 1999 the IMF and World Bank decided that *Poverty Reduction Strategy Papers* (PRSPs) relating to the IDA partner countries (some 70 low-income countries throughout the world) were to form the basis of all new loan commitments and of debt relief in the context of the accelerated *Initiative for Heavily Indebted Poor Countries* (HIPC II). This approach is based on the principles previously adopted for the establishment of *Comprehensive Development Frameworks* (CDFs) for the overall national policies underlying the future development of the LDCs. These principles are: (a) taking a long-term national and holistic view of development as the basis, (b) the partners countries' assumption of responsibility for the CDF, (c) partnership between donor and recipient countries and (d) orientation towards political action geared to development.

Both the poverty-oriented strategy approach and the underlying comprehensive development principles were elevated to form the new basis of aid programmes. The latter are now gradually to replace the Structural Adjustment Programmes (SAPs) of the old type. The PRSPs to be drawn up by the partner countries themselves are to meet the following criteria in this context:[13]

- Country-driven, involving broad-based participation by civil society and the private sector in all operational steps;
- Results-oriented, and focused on outcomes that would benefit the poor;
- Comprehensive in recognizing the multidimensional nature of poverty;
- Prioritized so that implementation is feasible, in both fiscal and institutional terms;
- Partnership-oriented, involving coordinated participation of development partners (bilateral, multilateral and non-governmental);
- Based on a long-term perspective for poverty reduction.

According to IMF and World Bank assessments, initial experience with the PRSP approach is promising (IMF / IDA 2001, p. 20 ff.). By the end of 2001, 24 of the sub-Saharan African countries had already drawn up interim PRSPs. A growing number of countries are now able to present a comprehensive PRSP.

The partner countries are urged – and many have complied – to ensure that, as a rule, not only central government but also (where they exist) national and subnational parliaments or other representative bodies, representatives of civil society, including the poor, and external partners (usually development cooperation representatives) are involved in the drafting of PRSPs. On this basis overriding national objectives for the long-term reduction of poverty are selected and then serve as the basis for a growth- and poverty-reducing strategy, from which poverty-oriented macro, structural and sectoral policies are in turn derived. On the basis of the (usually very sobering) prospects outlined in the CDF, an assessment of the quality of governance and of the country's financial and fiscal situation, realistic cost estimates and financing proposals are then made or called for. Only then can programmes and reform policies aimed at direct or indirect poverty reduction be established (see Figure A2).

What is already discernible in this conception for the establishment of PRSPs, which is already in practice in some cases, is highly relevant to implementation:

1　The participation of national and subnational parliaments or other representative bodies, and especially, therefore, local councils;
2　A realistic assessment of costs and necessary financial resources;
3　The notification of possibly unavoidable sectoral and structural reforms; and
4　the continuous participation of all main groups of actors.

All these points are repeatedly mentioned in this study too and form, as it were, the underlying tone of the deliberations on the institutional and organizational implementation of poverty-reducing agricultural and rural development (see Chapters 21 to 23): the strengthening of subnational structures and the examination of the financial basis for poverty-oriented development. From points 2, 3 and 4 it is clear that the World Bank's experience of the Sector Investment Programmes (SIPs) in the late 1990s has had some influence here. It is also evident that SIPs can be effective to only a limited degree as separate programmes within poverty-reduction strategies, as will be shown later (see Chapter 21).

Of crucial importance for the implementation of PRSPs will be the question of cost and financing. The *PRSP Sourcebook* therefore devotes a lengthy passage to this issue,[14] linked to the call for an improvement in financial management as a whole:

> It is important that the PRSP build on and provide consistency with other current government documents that set forth national or sectoral development plans and/or budgets. There are important linkages between implementation of the strategy and the annual budget cycle, medium term expenditure frameworks (MTEF) where there exist, and the iterative process by which results from the preceding year and ongoing dialogue are fed into policy and program redesign and annual progress reports. It is important that the PRSP become institutionalized in domestic budget preparation and policy and program formulation practices.[15]

This very important issue is also considered here. This cannot be done quantitatively, of course: the discussion focuses on new decentralized public financing mechanisms (see Chapter 17) and new forms of development cooperation financing (see Chapter 22).

4.3   New World Bank strategy for reducing rural poverty

As a logical consequence of its interest in the Comprehensive Development Framework (CDF), the Poverty Reduction Strategy (PRS) and the Millennium Declaration and on the basis of its many years of experience of rural development projects, the World Bank has now initiated a decisive step in development policy: it intends to take a renewed interest in rural areas and agricultural development as the real driving force of income generation and poverty reduction. Its President justifies this with the following words:

> ... the Bank's future direction for rural development and poverty reduction is the culmination of thinking on how the Bank will contribute to the ... Millennium Development Goals.
>
> (World Bank 2002a, p. 1)

The World Bank strategy for rural development is consequently based on three pillars:

1   It is geared to the poor in rural areas, adopts a holistic approach (*holistic pro-poor rural development*) and seeks a sustainable increase in the productivity of land and labour in agriculture;

2   It adopts a *suprasectoral approach* and so departs from the old sector approach; the old SIP approach should therefore be integrated into the national poverty-reduction strategy;

3   It endeavours to forge *development alliances* among the main groups of actors, comprising all groups in society of functional importance to rural development (see Figure A3). They may potentially influence the following developments: human capital formation, social capital formation, agricultural capital formation, management of the economy to reduce poverty, private-sector and infrastructure development and conservation of common goods.

It is assumed that national peculiarities and regional distinctions – like those described in Chapter 3.3 – will have a strong influence on implementation. Each country's development priorities within the poverty reduction objective and the appropriate mix of policy instruments in each case will be determined by the following factors: (a) the progress of sectoral reforms, (b) the economic strength of a country as a whole, (c) the state of development of the rural economy and its degree of linkage with the economy as a whole and (d) access to external markets and financial resources. Furthermore, a clear reference is made – as emphasized on several occasions in both parts of this study – to now well-documented links between increases in agricultural productivity and direct poverty reduction and between per capita agricultural growth and the improvement of rural incomes, especially in the low-income countries (World Bank 2002b, p. XII).

Against the background of these findings and given the effects on employment and incomes of linkages between rural and urban economic areas, a broad-based growth approach is propagated.[16] To trigger agriculturally based economic dynamism in rural areas, the World Bank believes there is a need for (a) the development of innovative rural financial infrastructure tailored to the smallholding sector (small and micro credit institutions), (b) greatly improved social infrastructure (health, education, water, sanitation), (c) physical infrastructure reaching the length and breadth of rural areas (roads, energy, markets, communications) and (d) public and private institution- and capacity-building. The last of these must ensure that civil and private-sector interests and service requirements are able to engage in a productive exchange. The individual areas of priority action for the implementation of an agriculturally based growth strategy of this kind are summarized for the various regions in Figure 2.

This strategic view is gaining in importance in the international development debate. What the World Bank lacks, however, is the conceptual conclusion drawn from this for the long-term development of a national structural framework that combines the three strategic objectives of (a) agricultural growth, (b) integrated sectoral development and (c) the formation of development alliances at national and subnational levels. Here again – as in the case of the World Food Summit Plan of Action, the implementation of the Desertification Convention and the poverty reduction strategy – the missing link between central government and the grass roots can be identified: a development-oriented local government system.

The institutional and organizational framework needed for this at central government, subnational and local level, between these levels and between organized civil society, the state and the organized private sector, and so between rural communities, districts and central government, is not to be seen. In this new context too, then, a forward-looking approach of a broadly effective and long-term transmission belt is lacking for the implementation of the World Bank poverty-reduction strategy. This is all the more surprising as the World Bank had already placed clear emphasis on decentralization in its 1997 World Development Report under the heading 'Bringing the State Closer to the People' (World Bank 1997a, p. 128 ff.). What is missing is the framework of donor organizations and institutions that is appropriate to a country's level of development (see Chapter 3.3) and takes effective advantage of the mutual links between central government, organized civil society, the private sector and the local communities so that innovative, reconciling and productive forces may be released. According to Amartya Sen (1999), the institutional environment for economic options, political freedoms and social conditions is influenced by the extent to which people are able to exercise their freedoms, i.e. by their freedom to participate in economic, social and public decisions that promote progress (Sen 1999, p. 15). It is in this sense that the introductory quotation from Herodotus should be understood.

Objective	Theme	AFR	EAP	ECA	MNA	LCR	SAR
Fostering broad-based rural growth	Land reform and administration	S		S		S	
	Research and extension	S					
	Rural non-farm economy incl. business development	I	I	I	I	I	I
	Rural–urban linkages, incl. small rural towns	I	I		I	I	
	Private sector role in service provision					S	
	Support for producer organizations/user groups	I		S			
	Food safety and agribusiness	I	I	I			
	Micro-finance	S	S	S	S	S	S
	Information technology – marketing and knowledge	I		I			I
	Rural infrastructure	S	S			S	S
	Irrigation and drainage	S		S			S
Strengthening social services and reducing risk and vulnerability	Participatory planning tools		S		S		
	Health and education: specific issues in rural areas	I	I	I	I	I	I
	Community-driven development / district programmes	S	S				S
	Commodity, climate and disaster risk management	I	I	I		I	
	Social inclusion incl. women and girls				I	I	I
	Rural water supply						S
Sustainable natural resource management	Watershed development		S				
	Community natural resource management			I	S	S	
	Community forestry						S

Note: S = Scaling-up of good practice activities
         I = Development and adoption of innovative approaches

Regions: AFR = Africa, EAP = East Asia and Pacific, ECA = Eastern Europe and Central Asia, MNA = Middle East and North Africa, LCR = Latin America and Caribbean, SAR = South Africa Region

Figure 2 Regional priorities for early action in scaling-up good practices and innovative approaches

Source: World Bank (2002b), p. XVII.

5   Effects of, difficulties with the implementation of and lessons to be learnt from the structural adjustment programmes

5.1   Effects

Between 1982 and 1992 macroeconomic adjustment programmes and structural reforms were adopted in 30 sub-Saharan African countries with the support of the IMF and World Bank and of a number of bilateral donors within the framework of the Structural Adjustment Facility (SAF) and the Enhanced Structural Adjustment Facility (ESAF). They were implemented until the late 1990s and are now being replaced by the Poverty Reduction Strategy as part of the Debt Relief Initiative for Heavily Indebted Poor Countries (HIPC) (see Chapter 4). The aim of the structural adjustment programmes was '*to address the deep-rooted internal structural problems and financial imbalances and to counteract the unfavourable effects of a difficult external environment.*' (Saleh 1993, p. 21) The programmes sought to reduce budget deficits by cutting public spending, to restrict government activities in the service and business sectors, to support institutional reforms, to initiate price and trade liberalization in order to release market forces and to bring about realistic exchange rates.

Of the many studies of the effects of structural adjustment measures on the economic and social development of the adjusting countries (World Bank 1988, Corbo and Webb 1991, Duncan and Howell 1992, Nsouli 1993, World Bank 1994a, Abaza 1996, Reed 1996, White 1996), two views will be discussed here, a summary by the IMF and World Bank based on indicators of macroeconomic success (Table A1) and a synopsis of various country evaluations (Table A2). The findings of the summary assessment by the IMF and World Bank are as follows:

- In two-thirds of the countries an improvement in growth performance, a reduction of inflation and a rise in foreign currency reserves were identified;
- In two-fifths of the countries only foreign currency reserves rose;
- The Gambia, Malawi, Mozambique and Togo in particular were successful in reducing their debt/GDP ratios;
- Ghana, Guinea, Kenya and Mauritania were able to stabilize their debt ratios;
- Half of the countries had to suspend their structural adjustment programmes for some time because of internal opposition;
- In a number of countries unfavourable climatic conditions and losses of crops had result-distorting effects (Burundi, the Gambia, Ghana, Kenya, Lesotho, Mozambique, Rwanda, São Tomé e Príncipe, Senegal, Uganda and the Central African Republic);
- In Equatorial Guinea, Ghana, Guinea-Bissau, Kenya, Madagascar, Mauritania, Mozambique and Uganda the terms of trade worsened;
- In many countries the implementation of the structural adjustment programmes was hampered by poor administrative practice combined with weak institutional and organizational infrastructure;

- In some countries the programmes were obstructed by delays and failures in the transfer of external financial aid to the budget;
- In some countries the inefficiency of ministerial administrations resulted in delays and even in ineffectiveness in the implementation of certain sectoral programme loans;
- Five countries were affected by political instability and by internal and border conflicts, resulting in programme errors.

As regards the effects of the structural adjustment programmes on government assistance and the effectiveness of public services for agricultural development, the following summary can be given in respect of Ghana, Kenya, Madagascar, Malawi, Niger and Zambia (Duncan and Howell 1992):

- The public marketing boards were the main target of reforms and privatization, which proved, however, to be extremely complicated and problematical because private agencies could not be substituted directly for government marketing services, especially in remote rural areas; the result was a service vacuum;
- Much the same was true of the rural transport system; in remote rural areas poor transport infrastructure hampered the supply of inputs and the marketing of agricultural produce;
- Another important target for structural reform was the government-assisted agricultural credit sector; its downsizing and the removal of subsidies led to serious financing constraints in the peasant farming sector;
- The service areas of agricultural extension, training and research were not substantially but gradually affected by the structural adjustment measures; cuts in public budgets led in this case to a dilution of extension services, training constraints and falling expenditure on agricultural research; it was principally the poorer segments of the agricultural population who were directly affected by these measures;
- Government veterinary services were least affected by the structural adjustment measures; their major importance for general animal health, peasant income generation and the export of animal products means that the veterinary services continue to be an essential component of government agricultural assistance; nonetheless, a tendency to privatize these services is already to be seen in such countries as Ghana, Kenya and Zambia.

5.2　Implementation difficulties

Both the World Bank and the authors of many country evaluations refer to the serious difficulties encountered in the implementation of the structural reforms. This is especially true of Burundi, Cameroon, Malawi, Zambia, Zimbabwe and Uganda (see Table A2). It is known that structural reforms usually require comprehensive packages of measures, which place considerable demands on the public budget and the public administration and often entail a whole string of follow-up measures. Structural reforms are therefore said to have a layer effect that makes it necessary to undertake reforms at several levels of development simultaneously if the required effect is to be achieved.

All this has inevitably resulted in structural reforms always taking a long time to reach maturity. In some countries it proved impossible to determine the whole range of effects of adjustment programmes in addition to the indicators of macroeconomic success even after ten years. Where obvious constraints or supply gaps occurred in the public service sector (agricultural extension, credit, marketing, health, food), measures were subsequently taken to provide for the social cushioning of adverse effects of adjustment (*social dimension of adjustment*). But this too inevitably required additional public funds, administration, logistics and monitoring.

A further difficulty, which has yet to be overcome, is the fact that, after existing imbalances in the public sector had been reduced (removal of subsidies, downsizing and privatization of state-owned enterprises, restriction of public services) and foreign trade had been partly liberalized, the problems connected with the provision of financial services for the private sector became very serious indeed. This is particularly true of the agricultural credit sector, but the commercial sector and the maintenance of rural infrastructure are also affected. It is not therefore surprising that more comprehensive development financing solutions are now being sought, especially for the rural areas (*rural financial system*).

5.3   Lessons

From experience with structural adjustment programmes in sub-Saharan Africa, and particularly from the difficulties encountered in implementing them, it has been possible to learn a number of lessons (Nsouli 1993, p. 23). They should similarly be taken into account in efforts to implement sectoral programmes, sectoral reforms and even poverty-reduction strategies; according to Nsouli (1993), the following lessons should be learnt:

1   Macroeconomic adjustment and structural reforms must be addressed as a *comprehensive package of measures*; only then can private investment be mobilized and production incentives created through the removal of economic distortions.
2   Only an appropriate *sequence* of macro policy measures (exchange rate measures, liberalization of foreign currency movements, removal of trade restrictions) and of structural reforms can increase the effectiveness of structural adjustment programmes.
3   Of crucial importance for the success of structural reforms is the *continuity of policy-making*; because of the aforementioned layer effect and the long lead-in periods, reforms, once initiated, need to be steadfastly maintained by the government in office and by the public administration; as national and

local policies are often in danger of being breached and as donor interests change, this is a serious problem.

4 Continuous *improvement of administration and institutions* is a basic requirement for the success of complex structural reforms; it is less vital in this context to create 'optimum capacities' in the shortest possible time than to achieve gradual and continual improvement in quality at decisive focal points; this is not, of course, helped by the high staff turnover hitherto to be seen in many African administrations.

5 Careful *collection of important core data* on structural changes and ongoing *monitoring of progress* based on such data must accompany all reform projects and be centralized for control purposes; here again, it is not the desire to create 'optimum data analyses' that is important but the need for important key data to be handled in an appropriate and generally comprehensible manner.

A further lesson, the need to install social safety nets to cushion any adverse consequences of structural adjustment measures, will not be considered in greater depth. The problems associated with this need have, after all, been one of the main reasons for abandoning traditional structural adjustment programmes. It has simply been swallowed up in the now general call for poverty reduction. The former social dimension of adjustment was increasingly perceived as a typical add-on function attached to the structural adjustment programme; it is now to become an integral part of virtually all sectoral programmes and sectoral reforms. Agricultural development and reform and rural development too will have to have a social dimension in the future if they are to be regarded as part of a national poverty-reduction strategy. Within this social dimension the gender equality strategy will play a growing role because poverty in sub-Saharan Africa is defined not only as a rural problem but also, in many areas, as a woman's problem. The social dimension of agricultural and rural development will therefore have to be considered in keeping with the – now internationally acknowledged – gender mainstreaming approach.

Part II Realistic problem-solving approaches

6 Requirements to be met by development cooperation

If, as claimed in Chapter 2.2 in particular, international development cooperation has constantly viewed the problem area of agricultural and rural development and the associated task of poverty reduction 'from the wrong angle' in the past, the question now has to be what, then, would be the 'right angle' and where might realistic problem-solving approaches be found? To get to grips with this difficult issue, five notional steps will first be taken, culminating in another idea: what structures of government and society would be most likely to support the performance of complex development tasks of this kind?

When the case is put here for the decentralization of government, it should be remembered that this approach has not only assumed considerable importance in theory and practice throughout the world, but is also repeatedly adopted for specific areas of development policy. In some newly industrializing countries too there has already been a change of direction, with major strides being taken towards decentralization (as in Brazil, India, Indonesia and Mexico). A question that has yet to be analysed, on the other hand, is why decentralization has not been consistently and comprehensively sought or achieved for rural development in more than a few instances. Regardless of whether, in the end, a decentralization option in comprehensive or weakened form is pursued (see Chapter 13), it is true to say that realistic problem-solving approaches will be possible only if the following requirements are progressively satisfied in development cooperation:

1 The focusing of government, the business community and society on key areas of development policy, according to whether public tasks or tasks of civil society are concerned;
2 The sequencing of development steps, with clear priorities set;
3 The jettisoning of development cooperation ballast from previous development decades;
4 The pooling of human and financial resources and the setting of development policy priorities, combined with new forms of technical support and development financing; and
5 Donor coordination and the creation of opportunities for an international division of labour in development cooperation.

Some of these requirements (the first, fourth and fifth) are now finding more favour in the international development debate: development cooperation practitioners are already preparing for and, in some cases, taking the steps concerned (Bohnet 2000). Moderate sequencing of development steps that is not beyond the capabilities of development policy and the jettisoning of development cooperation ballast, on the other hand, have not yet been singled out for discussion. In view of the need to integrate sectoral reforms and rural development into poverty reduction strategies, however, giving these requirements serious consideration in the future cannot be avoided.

7   Focusing on key areas of development policy

In the context of agricultural and rural development, concentration on key areas of development policy first means, with regard to the decentralization option, endeavouring to achieve a *division of labour* in development policy appropriate to the level of development reached by the country concerned. This applies to (a) tasks for which central government takes sole responsibility, (b) the private sector's tasks, (c) tasks of the local authorities (however structured), (d) tasks of organized civil society and (e) supplementary tasks of international development organizations. In any such approach to a division of labour the country's political, civil and professional/technical actors should concentrate, in accordance with the subsidiarity principle, on the tasks in which their competence gives them comparative advantages (see Chapter 13). According to conclusions drawn in a decade-long, often heated international debate on development policy,[1] the key areas, related to the division of labour theorem, are the following:

Tasks for which central government takes sole responsibility

1 *Establishment of long-term strategies* for reducing poverty, combating desertification and alleviating the consequences of drought and for sustained agricultural and rural development within a comprehensive development framework (CDF);
2 *Establishment and adoption of sectoral policies and policies for strengthening* institutional *framework structures*, which coordinate development cooperation at all levels in a spirit of partnership between the main actors and the donor community;
3 *Creation of participatory structures* at local and subnational level to enable local population groups and non-governmental organizations to participate effectively, with due regard for men and women, resource-users and their professional organizations;
4 *Creation or strengthening of early warning systems to guarantee food security*, including local and national facilities and joint systems at regional level, and of mechanisms for assisting people displaced by environmental conditions;
5 *Creation or strengthening of systems to ensure food supplies*, including storage and distribution facilities in rural and urban areas;

6 *Creation or strengthening of systems to prevent or contain animal epidemics*, including facilities for monitoring compliance with international export requirements;

7 *Political, legal and administrative arrangements to implement land and land management reforms*, including the guarantee of socially compatible access to agricultural, forestry and fishery resources;

8 *Financing, provision and maintenance of economically viable rural infrastructure*, including rural roads and energy supply, communications, marketing, water supply, sanitation and veterinary monitoring facilities;

9 *Creation* or *strengthening of national agricultural research, training and extension facilities* geared primarily to peasant user groups;

10 Promotion *of a rural financial system* that takes account of the special circumstances of producer groups in agriculture and the sectors up- and downstream who have little capital and are exposed to risks.

The private sector's tasks

11 *Self-help organization* of agricultural production, processing, insurance, input purchasing, product marketing, machinery and accountancy associations to improve farm performance and strengthen markets;

12 *Formation of agricultural purchasing, marketing and credit cooperatives* (on the Raiffeisen model, for example) or of microfinancing institutions (like the Grameen Bank) for short-term borrowing to bridge shortfalls in farmers' own capital;

13 *Cooperative or inter-farm organization and control of irrigation schemes* and their sustainable management and maintenance;

14 *Formation* of *craft and trade associations* to promote rural and peri-urban agro-industrial development.

Tasks of organized civil society

15 *Organization by villages of their own participatory structures* for maintaining local community and infrastructure facilities and jointly managing water catchment areas, communal forests or communal grazing land;

16 *Local organization of agricultural, forestry and fishery interest groups* to bring professional and political influence to bear at local and national level;

17 *Organization of domestic economy self-help structures* for local food security, product processing or the manufacture of consumer goods.

Tasks of local authorities

18 *Development and strengthening of efficient local organizational and service structures* to bring about institutional, political and fiscal decentralization

with a view to promoting local social and economic development (see Chapter 12).

Supplementary tasks of development cooperation organizations

19 *Technical assistance for partner governments with the establishment of long-term strategies* (CDFs, PRSPs, CCD, SARD, etc.) and with the strengthening of institutional structures that improve development cooperation at all levels in a spirit of partnership with the donor community;

20 *Technical and financial assistance for partner governments during government decentralization projects* according to the country's level of development, its size and the political acceptance of such schemes;

21 *Technical assistance for partner governments with the creation of an international environment conducive to development*, and especially of a fair world agricultural trade system during the WTO negotiations;

22 *Financial and technical assistance for partner governments with the strategic orientation* and implementation of national *agricultural research programmes* within the CGIAR framework;

23 *Financial and technical assistance for partner governments and their local authorities* with the development of rural physical *infrastructure*;

24 *Financial and technical assistance for partner governments and their local authorities* with the management of the stabilization of *natural resources and common goods* in keeping with Agenda 21 and the CCD.

8   Sequencing of development steps

In international development cooperation, especially since the introduction of the goal-oriented project planning (GOPP) method in the 1970s, it has repeatedly been suggested that economic and social development can be stimulated on the basis of goal-directed planned projects and programmes and may lead to self-sustaining development. When the history of development cooperation is considered, this is exceedingly naïve and confusing. We have only to agree that broad-based regional development presupposes decentralization for it to be clear that such development can gain ground only over generations and in long-term sequences. A striking example is the gradual revival of the societal, economic and cultural development of many Central European principalities and communities after the Napoleonic Wars. In Prussia, for example, it was only on the basis of the comprehensive *Stein-Hardenberg reforms* of the early nineteenth century that the self-sustaining development of local government became possible; even then it was only over the next one to two generations that this gradually released dynamic economic, social and cultural forces.[2]

From such successful examples and others, including some from outside Europe (especially India), it can thus be inferred that broad-based economic development not only presupposes decentralization, but can probably be achieved only in very moderate sequences. What will be decisive is not the 'goal-oriented fine-tuning' but *consistently paving the way for an appropriate sequence of development steps within the framework of reforms that build on one another.* Appropriate sequencing will differ from one country to another. What is crucial is that the development steps initiated today are such that they continue to be viable tomorrow and the day after. Decentralization for the promotion of broad-based regional economic development is, as the historical evidence shows, very likely to be a step of this kind.

Against the background of the division of labour among the various principal actors that has been described above for coping with key areas of development policy (see Chapter 7), a sequence of realistic development steps for the agricultural countries of sub-Saharan Africa will now be outlined; it should, of course, be noted in this context that it is impossible and unnecessary for one step to follow another in strict order: depending on the institutional and manpower capacity and political assertiveness of bodies representing central government, the private sector, civil society and local authorities, sequences may take longer, or they may run in parallel or in tandem; this probably comes closest to the reality of complex socio-political reform projects. Even moderate sequences will be impossible unless the national government's capacity for reform, the financial and human resources it has for implementing such projects and the willingness of its citizens to accept reforms are taken into account. In addition, a danger that must always be addressed is that such negative features of a ruling class as clientelism, nepotism and corruption may be transferred to local levels of government with decentralization.

Given the reform and development steps already prepared or taken in previous development decades, it is realistic to assume that the reform and development projects referred to in Chapter 7 are unlikely to be implemented 'all at once' in any African country. Individual countries will not be considered in depth at this stage (this is done in Chapter 19); reference will simply be made to *essential steps* to be taken by their principal actors. As, moreover, all relevant political, economic, institutional, organizational, financial policy and fiscal policy problem areas are discussed in both Part A and Part B of the study, there is no need for further explanations here. A distinction must, however, be made between two groups of countries as regards their capacity for reform:

Essential steps for *countries with incipient or already advanced democratic structures*, governments ready for reform, liberal economic systems and growing economies (of the South African, Botswana, Ghanaian and Ugandan type) should be taken in the key areas which have hitherto been neglected by the partner countries and by international development cooperation. In the 24 areas referred to in Chapter 7 this may take very different forms, possibly having a greater impact on central government's, the local authorities' or the private sector's area of responsibilities or on organized civil society's. In the case of agricultural reform projects it would be appropriate, for example, to proceed sequentially in such a way that a start was made, of course, with the legislative process, the introduction of a land register followed, extension services were professionalized on this basis and, at the same time, an agricultural credit system was developed. This sequence should be backed by measures to promote local economic development, the private sector possibly taking over, say, the agricultural marketing services.

Essential steps for *countries with weak democratic structures*, governments unwilling to undertake reforms, centralist economic systems and stagnating to shrinking economies (of the Zimbabwean type) should be taken in the key areas which, all political factors considered, are still capable of being promoted within the development cooperation framework. In the 24 areas referred to in Chapter 7 this is more likely to affect civil society's and the private sector's areas than central government's and the local authorities'. Even for the latter there are opportunities to become involved, as described in the cases of Zambia and Zimbabwe (see Chapter 19), in promoting democratization and decentralization as preconditions for broad-based development virtually 'by the backdoor'. Where, however, democratization and decentralization are definitely not wanted, there is, in any case, no place for development cooperation.

9   Jettisoning of ballast inherent in development cooperation

With the aforementioned reservations (promoting key areas of development policy, following moderate development sequences, setting priorities), perceptible adjustments within development cooperation are imperative. The concepts, approaches and instruments emerging with the various development policy 'fashions' must be cut back to a level that is justifiable by the criteria of restricted capacity for action: justifiable given the partners' limited absorptive capacities, justifiable when seen from the angle of permanently scarce human, financial and development management resources, justifiable in view of the reservations referred to above and justifiable when it is remembered that targeting in development policy is essential.

The criteria for determining an 'excess of development cooperation organization', known here as ballast inherent in development cooperation, can be deduced from the key areas of development policy referred to in Chapter 7 and from the assignment of the tasks involved. As the supplementary development cooperation tasks are increasingly shifted from the project sphere to the programme level, it will become easier to assign and integrate the procedures. Parallel structures do not occur at all. It goes without saying that catharsis can be achieved only country by country, sector by sector. There is no denying, however, that the reservations mentioned above indicate that a number of measures are now overdue, because they have been 'carried forward' from past development cooperation periods and their approaches are now outdated.

While it is impossible to consider the general context of the development theories on which all development cooperation projects are based, reference will be made to some areas which, in view of the previous deliberations, might simply be described as ballast. They are:

- Escalating, time-consuming, labour-intensive, detail-loving and, moreover, as a rule highly bureaucratic planning methods (e.g. staggered GOPP procedures);
- Inappropriate, gender- or target-group-specific, overly statistical methodological approaches to advisory projects (e.g. GPEA);
- Parallel organizational and administrative structures which have been developed and expanded in the course of many development cooperation projects, except CIM projects, to maintain a high degree of effectiveness, to signal their own importance, to gain influence or to ensure their own employment;
- Adherence to less important areas of development policy, which have become obsolete with the consolidation and decentralization of government structures and the integration of functions into newly emerging systems (for example, institutionalized development committees are able to take over decision-making mechanisms that once formed part of externally funded projects; see Chapter 19);
- Escalating use of consulting services by external technical cooperation experts for internal tasks and procedures, which, moreover, usually entail considerable monitoring and often serve to justify the experts' existence;
- Excessively stringent evaluation requirements, which unduly burden the partner: one expert mission often follows another; they can be significantly reduced in number if – as described here – financing and participatory structures integrated into the system are used through the development and financing of local government and budget aid (see Chapter 22);
- 'Networking' activities, which are becoming increasingly fashionable, often concealing sound development work and encouraging a flow of information that can no longer be handled.

Practical examples of all these general symptoms can be found in specific countries. They are also criticized by Lancaster (1999, p. 47 ff.), among others.

10   Pooling human and financial resources and setting priorities

The general consensus supporting this demand addressed to development cooperation cannot conceal the fact that it has rarely been met. The processes relating on both sides to the development of Comprehensive Development Frameworks (CDFs) (World Bank 2001b), the ongoing adjustment of existing country concepts (Kennweg 2000) or country strategy papers and the drafting of priority strategy papers (*Schwerpunktstrategiepapiere,* SSP) (BMZ 2000) are well under way. All this, taken together, represents a major step forward in the steering of development cooperation, but it also ties down enormous human resources at development cooperation headquarters. It remains to be seen how this progress now leads on to practical development steps aimed at reducing poverty.

One thing can, however, be said at this juncture: if all this conceptually lavish preliminary work on the achievement of poverty-reducing development under likewise extremely ambitious Poverty Reduction Strategy Papers (PRSPs) is to have any impact, new ways of organizing civil participation, implementation, coordination and financing will be needed. They will have to internalize the demand voiced here for the pooling of human and financial resources and for the setting of priorities in development policy, and this functionally, politically and financially.

There will eventually have to be structures that include 'good governance', however defined and shaped. Though it will never be perfect, it should at least not be dysfunctional with respect to the poverty reduction task; it should be appropriate in order to encourage the necessary minimum of democratization, human capital development and broad-based economic and social development in each case. Such governance has several tasks to perform, and development cooperation should make its contribution in keeping with the functional division of labour referred to above:

1   It should be focused on the relevant development priorities by means of a resolute poverty-oriented *budgetary policy*, which means, in this context, that national financial and international ODA resources should be increasingly geared to the agricultural sector, rural infrastructure, the implementation of agricultural reforms and the development of human capital in rural areas (see Part A, Chapters 14 and 15, and Part B, Chapter 12) (Otzen 2001).

2   As these comments indicate, it should consistently and gradually develop a *permanent decentralized* organizational *and institutional framework* capable of encouraging the performance of the aforementioned development tasks in a division of labour and in accordance with the subsidiarity principle; unless the local government structures that have evolved are integrated as a whole into the forthcoming task of implementing the World Food Summit Plan of Action and other, national action programmes, there will be no striking successes in poverty reduction (see Chapter 21).

3   Where necessary, it should establish a *legally binding and transparent framework* for land reforms and for the socially compatible and sustainable use of natural resources, with account taken of the gender issue (see Part A, Chapter 13.3).

4   It should give precedence to the development of *rural infrastructure* in keeping with the poverty-oriented setting of priorities, and in this the maintenance of local infrastructure should also form part of the local population's own contribution.

5   It should pay greater attention to *agricultural research, training and extension* geared to poverty reduction than it has in the past, with innovative forms of private-sector participation being given a progressively growing role to play.

6   It should leave room for decision-making and action relating to the *development of the private sector* in rural and peri-urban areas on the basis of price and service incentives in conjunction with government or joint safeguards against investment risks (see Chapter 18).

7   It should ensure that private (cooperative or commercial) or publicly assisted *rural financial systems* emerge to meet the growing saving and bor-

rowing requirements of hitherto severely undercapitalized farming and business sectors.

These demands were repeatedly voiced (in one form or another) by leading representatives of the international development cooperation community in the past decade; some of them were also mentioned in the document on the new development partnership between the African and the OECD countries, NEPAD, along with the call for good governance.[3] While it is gratifying to see this international consensus evolve, the extent to which these demands are met will differ widely from one country to another. The essential factor, however, will be the partner governments' ability in principle so to set their development priorities that there is a prospect of poverty reduction in the medium to long term. The priorities are currently being set or reviewed in a growing number of bi- and multilateral cooperation agreements.

In German development cooperation with the partner countries in sub-Saharan Africa the following development priorities have been set (as at July 2002) (BMZ 2002):

1   Decentralized rural development (Zambia, Lesotho);
2   Decentralization / development of local government (Benin, Burkina Faso, Cameroon, Malawi, Mali, South Africa);
3   Regional concentration of rural development (Mozambique, Senegal, Guinea, Niger, Chad);
4   Promotion of democracy / civil society / public administration (Ethiopia, Ghana, Rwanda);
5   Private-sector promotion / agriculture (Kenya, Côte d'Ivoire);
6   Natural resource protection / rural development (Namibia, Tanzania, Madagascar);
7   Development of water resources (Uganda, Eritrea);
8   Development of peace / crisis prevention (Burundi).

This orientation already indicates the importance which German development cooperation attaches to decentralization in future agricultural and rural development. It may also indicate a change of trend to take greater account of rural areas again.

11   Donor coordination and international division of labour

In the context of international development efforts to achieve *territorially integrated development*, with the focus on poverty reduction, donor coordination and the division of labour within the donor community play a decisive role. These efforts will have to be rated by reference less to the level of ODA contributions than to their effectiveness (degree of goal achievement), significance (influence on the environment) and sustainability (creation of lasting structures).

Donor coordination and an international division of labour in development cooperation were only recently demanded again during the implementation of Sector Investment Programmes (SIPs), for which they are major requirements. In the past, however, they have unfortunately failed to have any striking success. The reasons for this are that the partner governments themselves were, as a rule, hopelessly overextended by the task of programme coordination, that *joint financing* was not consistently adopted by the donors in the shape of *basket funding* and that the sectoral deconcentration needed for implementation seriously hampered the coordination work. It can generally be said of the issue of donor coordination and the division of labour that

> ... the demands which complex development programmes make on the technical, political and moral competence of partner administrations are far greater than those made by the old project-based development cooperation.
>
> (Asche 2002)

Donor coordination and the division of labour are now given a new direction to follow by the territorially integrated development cooperation favoured here. It is not the wide range of individual projects (as in the first generation of development cooperation) or the individual components of programmes (as in the second generation of development cooperation) that must be coordinated by the central governments of the partner countries: coordination must instead be taken to mean that the donor organizations' supplementary contributions must adapt to the configuration of territorially integrated development cooperation. What does this mean for agricultural and rural development?

In this context technical and financial cooperation are no longer addressed solely to individual counterpart bodies – central government, sectoral ministries, parastatal organizations and NGOs – but also, and now above all, to the rural authorities. They are primarily responsible for broad-based democratic, intersectoral, economic and social development. This new direction – graduated, based on a division of labour and in accordance with the subsidiarity principle in keeping with Chapters 13 and 20 – also requires of the donor organizations a strict division of labour among themselves. They will have to decide in the future what level they are prepared to support: the central government, sectoral, parastatal, NGO or local government level.

Within these levels clear agreements should be reached on who supports which component (international division of labour). On the whole, all external contributions, whether in the form of technical or financial cooperation, should now be seen as components of this integrated territorial development. As regards the form of financing, the donors' contributions could be used, as in the past, as sectoral financial aid for sectoral programme projects, as NGO support for non-governmental development projects or as budgetary aid for integrated territorial development (see Chapter 22).

Territorially integrated rural development in accordance with the subsidiarity principle, the resulting call for decentralization and the implications for donor conduct based on a division of labour obviate the need for any separately organized coordination. The new configuration gives rise to coordination virtually on its own (see Figure 3). This would be the responsibility of:

1   The finance ministry through interdepartmental coordination of general development financing (coordination of budget policy and external financial contributions through general budget financing);
2   The sectoral ministries through the inter-divisional coordination of programme components (coordination of the sectoral policy and external financial contributions through sectoral budget financing);
3   The local authorities through the coordination of intersectoral development projects at district level (coordination of the territorial development policy with contributions from internal and external development financing, i.e. internal transfers and external decentralized budget financing).

Further comments on this difficult aspect, some relating to individual countries, are to be found in Chapter 19; it is comprehensively reviewed when new ways in which development cooperation can lend support are considered in Chapter 22. This also reveals how new forms of donor coordination and the international division of labour and of development financing differ from the inadequate approaches hitherto adopted.

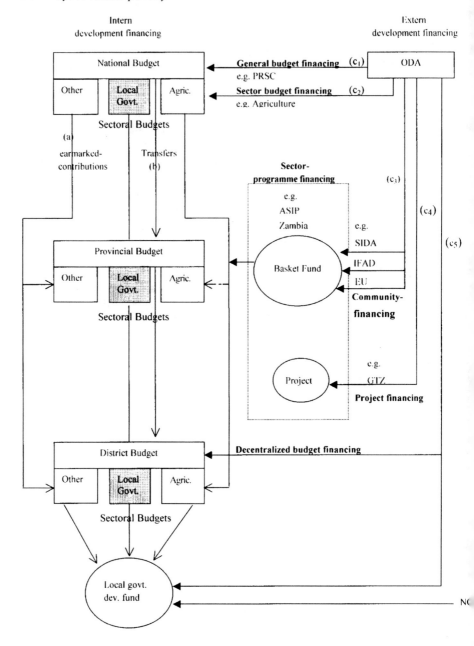

Figure 3: Forms of development financing through the integrated allocation of resources (a, b, c)

Key: → intern financing ← extern financing

Source: own design (2002).

12 Performance of multifunctional agricultural and rural development tasks through decentralization

12.1 Rural development as a cross-section task

Rural development has always been a cross-section task, and this will not change. There will thus be no escaping this unalterable challenge to development policy. In the majority of African countries, moreover, it will continue to have the highest priority in development policy for the next few decades. This will be true at least as long as the majority of the population continues to live in rural areas. But even if the ratio of rural to urban population should change to the advantage of the latter from about 2020 (Ashley and Maxwell 2001b, p. 400), a difference in development and incomes is likely to persist between urban centres and rural areas. This would then justify a continuation of the priority treatment of rural development in the national context (see Part A, Chapters 6 and 7).

The aim of this cross-section task will thus continue to be so to improve the living conditions of the population in rural areas so that they remain attractive enough compared to the urban centres to prevent mass rural–urban migration. This can be achieved only through agriculturally based economic, social and infrastructure development, as postulated in Part A, Chapter 15. In the course of this development efforts must be made to strengthen the linkages between agricultural primary production, marketing and trade and commercial and industrial processing and to improve such agricultural services as extension, research, training and financial services. These expanding linkages may give rise to new employment and income-generating opportunities, which may absorb at least some of the workers who are bound to become redundant as a result of the gains in agricultural productivity. As a complement to this, crafts, small-scale industry and manufacturing should develop to support the agriculturally based growth process with technology and innovations.

It continues to be generally agreed that during poverty-reducing agriculturally based economic development such social components as primary education, primary health care and housing and the development of such basic rural infrastructure as roads, electricity, communications, water, drainage and irrigation form part of integrated development. Nor is this consensus threatened by the fact that most attempts at *integrated rural development* in the past have failed because of its considerable complexity, the difficulty of organizing it and its underfunding (see Part A, Chapter 9). In the future, then, the aim will be less to achieve integrated rural development holistically and systematically than to decide how to achieve it sequentially (see Chapter 8). A question that needs to be asked in this context is how deep the graduation of the basic social and infrastructure components must go. This question should be asked regardless of the economic strength of a given rural region in the case of the social components and as a function of its economic strength in the case of the infrastructure components.

This aspect has been considered in an IFPRI study (Shenggen and Hazell 2000; Focus 4, Brief 5) on India and China, in which investments in agricultural development, infrastructure and social measures in irrigated and high-yielding regions and in marginal regions were compared and their effects on output and poverty reduction were examined (Tables A3 and A4). The findings show that investments in both cases produced the highest marginal returns and also had the greatest poverty-reducing effect at less favourable agricultural locations. The conclusions drawn from this study read: *'The results do suggest that attractive opportunities exist for reducing poverty through additional investment in less-favored areas and that rather than sacrificing growth, many of these investments actually offer win-win opportunities for achieving more production growth and greater poverty reduction.'* As a cross-section task, rural development can thus successively stimulate the fundamental subsectors of agricultural development, development of rural infrastructure and the social service infrastructure in an effective way (which will be described later); this is equally true of strong and marginal agricultural regions.

In economically dichotomized countries (Kenya, Zimbabwe, Zambia, Malawi and Namibia being particular examples), where subsistence agriculture continues to exist side by side with modern agriculture, largely without any links between them, it must be ensured that rural development also results in the integration of the two subsectors. Experience shows that African farmers, male and female, have considerable integrative strength and adaptability, given a favourable macro-economic and regulatory framework (see Part A, Chapter 8).

To stimulate agriculturally based growth in both modern and subsistence agriculture, there is also a need to overcome the chronic weakness of African agricultural development, namely its undercapitalization compared to the considerable potential it has in some areas for intensification, diversification and value added (World Bank 2000a, p. 170 ff.) (see Part A, Chapter 12). If it is to be possible to use existing productivity reserves, to make progress with integration into the market and to establish sectoral linkages, financial services tailored to peasant agriculture must be provided. Agricultural banks or agricultural purchasing, marketing and credit cooperatives (on the Raiffeisen model, for example) can meet this need, but they must be prepared for the contribution they have to make to supporting the cross-section task. The development of a rural financial system is a complex and difficult task in itself, as will be shown later (Chapter 21).

All past experience shows that a cross-section task of the breadth outlined here is unlikely to be successfully performed by central government in a national context, let alone accomplished by means of donor-assisted programmes. It becomes even less likely where individual sectors or parts of the civil service have to undergo reform processes. Agricultural development, infrastructure development, social development and sectoral integration and reform can consequently be achieved only through decentralized steering structures, into which the donor programmes might then be integrated. As a cross-section task, rural development thus requires, first and foremost, *institutional decentralization* if it is to be successfully achieved.

12.2 Rural development as a joint task

Rural development can only be seen as a joint task for all the actors concerned (see Chapters 7 and 19): all social groups in rural areas should be involved through their representatives in non-governmental organizations (NGOs), community-based organizations (CBOs) and civil society organizations (CSOs). Rural development is also a joint task for the representatives of all political parties in the provincial, district and local parliaments (where they exist). The representatives of parastatal organizations, where they operate in rural areas, should also be involved. It is also a joint task for the representatives of private-sector interest groups, and especially of farmers', craft and traders' organizations. Finally, the representatives of the traditional groups, which play a particularly significant role in the African context, should participate in this joint task.

In Africa in particular there is considerable potential for self-help in the performance of this joint task. This is due to the local community structures that are still largely intact in predominantly agricultural societies and to their ability to form social capital (Gsänger 2001b, p. 261 ff.; World Bank 2001c, p. 128 ff.). This especially concerns the level of primary production (neighbourhood help, joint field work, etc.), subsistence safeguards (shared food security) and social security (help for the elderly and in emergencies).

Unfortunately, the structures for government involvement and formal decision-making processes are not yet sufficiently advanced in most sub-Saharan African countries for the joint task to be performed by representatives of the various groups of actors referred to above. The tragedy of the many externally financed rural development programmes is that they have failed, and indeed were bound to fail, because of the absence of institutional integration and political decentralization. All attempts to create expansive counterpart organizations, most of them acting in parallel, that were meant to bring about participation and involvement and to assume responsibility for intersectoral coordination have failed (see Part A, Chapter 9). Nor would it have been possible to finance them in the long term.

Where any provision was made for the involvement of the local population in the administrative structures originally established in former colonies, local government structures emerged in the English-speaking sphere, *collectivités locales* structures in the French-speaking sphere. What these structures had in common was that they were geared primarily to the exercise of colonial control and the maintenance of colonial power and to steering the colonial economy; only as an afterthought were they used to involve sections of the population in the development of the hinterland. Nonetheless, wide-ranging administrative structures capable of acting as a basis for institutional decentralization did emerge there.

When such structures were transferred to the post-colonial period, the local government system in particular was able to assume a guiding role in development policy, if not explicitly, then at least indirectly. However, when it came to the implementation of rural development concepts, the stigmatization of the colonial legacy meant that these systems were discredited both in the eyes of the new sub-Saharan African governments and in the international debate on development policy. As a result, they have not been used in the past, or only to a limited degree. Every donor has thus tried to reinvent the wheel for involvement structures and to devise its own conceptual approach. This has given rise to inflated and also, in many cases, parallel counterpart structures defined by the donor, which the partner country did not, in the end, have the human or financial resources to maintain ('white elephants').

South Africa is a commendable exception in this respect. It has skipped practically all stages of the rural development that eventually failed (see Part A, Chapter 9) and, with considerable self-assurance, had the courage to make a new start of its own. It has even created the government conditions for integrated rural and urban development and so for broad-based economic and social development in a country deeply divided by apartheid: the conditions for political, institutional and fiscal decentralization. The constitution (Republic of South Africa 1996), which is geared to a federal system of government, allocates clearly defined powers and development tasks to the 850 municipalities (as at 2000)[4] in the nine provinces. This is intended to guarantee the process of involving all the social groups concerned, the political parties, the private sector and the traditional leaders (see Figure A4). Furthermore, the constitution already provides for the municipalities to coordinate the process of development cooperation among all governmental and non-governmental actors. To this end, the term *developmental local government* has been specially coined. This new quality in African constitutional history cannot be rated highly enough, as was true of the Stein-Hardenberg reforms in their day and of the political and economic strengthening of the municipalities in post-Napoleonic Germany (see Chapter 8).

This would not have been possible if the old centralized, or apartheid, state had not been completely abandoned to make way for the constitutional foundations for the development of a decentralized state, in which the principle of *cooperative government* applies. This suggests a multi-layered form of cooperation that is essential for the national process of reconstruction and development (R&D). There is to be cooperation between:

- All spheres of government and all organs of state within each sphere, national, provincial and municipal;
- The various political parties;
- The governmental and non-governmental actors;
- The various ethnic groups;
- The various sectoral ministries of relevance to development policy.

Having laid these foundations, South Africa is probably the most up-to-date and interesting advocate of the decentralized performance of a joint task in the development policy sphere, as it sees rural development. It has yet to take the third essential hurdle, fiscal decentralization, which is intended to provide the financial underpinning of this joint, cross-section task. If it is to do so – and it has already gone a considerable way down this road – development policy has another difficult step to take: at least in the provinces with a large rural population, rural development should be seen as a non-party national task and challenge that is not restricted by parliamentary terms. Rural development may have its first chance in South Africa to take the important place that is its due in the country's overall development through *political decentralization*.

12.3 Rural development as a national task

If rural development is to be elevated to the rank of a national task, all political actors must be willing to give priority in development policy to the current problems in rural areas. In sub-Saharan Africa these problems are due to the fact that:

- Some 80 per cent of the poor live in rural areas (IFAD 2001, p. 20 ff.);
- The proportion of chronically undernourished children under the age of five has continued to rise in sub-Saharan Africa, unlike all other regions of the world; they now number about 37 million, the vast majority living in rural areas (IFPRI 2001, p. 14);
- Only 39 per cent of the rural population have access to clean drinking water, as compared to 68 per cent of the urban population (IFAD 2001, p. 36);
- Adequate sanitary facilities are available to only 33 per cent of the rural population, as compared to 65 per cent in urban areas (IFAD 2001, p. 36);
- The literacy rate of the population over the age of 15 averages 58 per cent; (UNDP 2001, p. 206 ff.); in rural areas it is estimated to be 41 per cent (ECA 2001, p. 6 ff.);
- The most important economic sector in rural areas, agriculture, has been neglected in the past two decades both by the national governments and by the international donor organizations (see Part A, Chapter 7);
- The improvement of the rural road, transport and communications infrastructure has lagged well behind improvement in rural areas; paved roads accounted for less than 19 per cent of the total road network in the low-income African countries in 1996 (World Bank 1998, p. 47).

The causes and consequences of this unequal development must be ascribed to the familiar phenomenon of urban bias (see Part A, Chapter 6). Urban bias reflects the neglect of the development of the rural economic area, including agriculture, for the past few decades. As a result, major development opportunities have not been seized; the potential for development, especially as regards agriculture, social capital and demand, has remained untapped; the rural–urban linkages that would make for broad-based economic and social development have largely failed to materialize; it has been impossible to prevent migration to the towns and cities because the most important and often only sector of the economy could not be made more attractive. The conclusion that must be drawn from this for development policy is expressed by an old GTZ campaigner as follows:

> Agricultural development can only succeed where it forms part of a rural development concept which is in balance with national, local and urban development.

(Lampe 2001, p. 31)

If anything like a balance is to be struck in development between rural areas and urban centres, far more should be done in the future to ensure that budget policies concentrate more of the national human and financial resources available on rural areas and specifically on those with the potential for economic development (see Chapter 22). This will, however, require a change of mind in society and on development policy, which can be neither decreed nor simply brought about by central government. Instead, the following basic regulatory requirement should be met: to persist with the image of rural development as a cross-section, joint and national task, institutional and political decentralization should now be joined by *fiscal decentralization*.

In the long term at least this might ensure that financial resources based on sectoral policy and channelled through sectoral budget allocations (vertical financial flows) are joined by resources channelled through horizontal financial flows to give a regional balance. These funds may come from various sources (local tax revenue, national financial transfers, ODA contributions, etc.) and/or result from the reallocation of funds from national and/or international provisions (see Chapter 16). In any case, fiscal decentralization is an effective development policy tool for striking a balance in development in the national context between urban and rural areas. It is only when fiscal decentralization takes root that rural development becomes a factor in its own right, provided that

> it is integrated into a set of rules that ensures the protection of overriding national interests.

> (Djafari 2001, p. 185)

Part III Importance for development policy of, preconditions for and effects of decentralization

13 Decentralization as a recurrent challenge to development policy

According to many international authors,[1] decentralization (for forms and a definition see Box 1) must be seen as one of the most important recent development policy approaches to pushing through reforms of government and administration with the aim of (a) achieving better government performance, (b) perpetuating the promotion of local democracy, (c) supporting broad-based regional development and (d) promoting national integration. For Simon (Simon 2001, p. 151), therefore,

> there is no alternative to decentralization as a development strategy today: it is being propagated everywhere and introduced even in developing countries, as well as it can be. This does not alter the fact that it is constantly the subject of critical analysis. This criticism may quite rightly refer to numerous problems associated with the decentralization concept and most certainly to even more numerous shortcomings of decentralization in practice. But if the two aspects are not measured against some ideal or other, but compared to the other available options for reforming government and administration, the conclusion is obvious: there is practically no proposal that can be taken seriously for reverting to and introducing centralist structures rather than resorting to decentralization. As a general rule, then, it is no longer a question of whether decentralization should be the goal in developing countries, but simply how it can be achieved, and what insights in this respect can be gained from past experience.

It cannot be generally inferred from the global experience of decentralization that there is a close correlation between decentralization and the development of society; nor, according to a number of authors (Moore and Putzel 1999, p. 8; World Bank 2000b; Crook and Sverrisson 2001), is it clear what will be the long-term effects of political decentralization (also known to some authors as democratic decentralization) on general economic and social development and thus, indirectly, on poverty reduction. Despite this, it can be firmly stated

---

***Box 1* Forms of decentralization**

As a rule, the following terms are used in connection with decentralization to define more precisely the various forms and intensities of decentralization and a specific context in which action is taken:

Deconcentration: transfer of responsibilities and powers to lower levels within the administrative hierarchy of central government.

Delegation: transfer of specific tasks to usually non-governmental or parastatal bodies in civil society.

Devolution: actual transfer of legislative and executive functions to local authorities.

Privatization: transfer of functions to the private sector, the difference from delegation being that central government does not continue to perform supervisory and monitoring functions.

Source: Thomi (2001), p. 17 ff.

---

that decentralization can evidently be said to perform a kind of catalytic function. In other words, it would appear to be an area of strategic intervention the effects of which extend far into government and civil society and the promotion of which therefore seems to be attractive and to promise success.

(Thomi 2001, p. 20)

Decentralization is an inherently political process: although it can be supported by development policy, it must emerge as such from the process of national political decision-making. The fact that the horizontal division of power (legislature, executive, judiciary) is joined by a vertical division of power (graduated jurisdiction) makes decentralization a difficult political coordination project. This nonetheless gives rise to further opportunities for the essential political checks and balances and for political competition both among the various levels of government and between provinces, districts and local authorities. Decentralization is also an expensive process that countries on the verge of fiscal crisis cannot afford. All this makes it clear how difficult it will be for quite a number of African countries to take the path of decentralization successfully, how high the risks will be in this context and how cautiously and selectively international development cooperation must proceed with its support measures. For some partner countries support is (currently) out of the question (e.g. PR Congo and Sudan), for others it comes at just the right time (e.g. South Africa, Ghana, Zambia and Uganda), and for yet others it is not an option (excessively small economies).

The effects which decentralization is expected to have on development policy and which obviously account for its considerable attractiveness and prospects of success are undoubtedly based on the subsidiarity principle. This concept, which stems from Catholic social teaching, was defined by Nell-Breuning in 1955 as follows:

> What can be done in the village, in the local community, should not be left to that large public entity the state; what can be accomplished within the family circle should not be entrusted to the public.
>
> (Nell-Breuning 1955, p. 55)

Conversely and related to developing African societies, it might be said today: the state should concern itself with those development tasks which cannot (yet) be performed by the local authorities; what cannot (yet) be accomplished within the circle of the extended African family needs the support of the public sector. The fact that under African conditions the public sector – as in the years of reconstruction in post-war Europe – has more tasks to perform is irrelevant to the application of the principle.

Within the framework of the decentralization of government and administration subsidiarity can be achieved through deconcentration, delegation, devolution and privatization. To ensure the systematic pervasion of the principle, Simon (Simon 2001, p. 151) recommends the following breakdown:

- *Vertical subsidiarity* through the decentralization of public tasks and resources and of processes of legitimation at local levels;
- *Horizontal subsidiarity* through cooperation among the public, private and joint sectors in accordance with comparative advantages;
- *Cooperative subsidiarity* through support from the upper level(s) for the lower level.

The great challenge for African development policy now consists in so attaining decentralization with the three goal directions referred to above that the widest possible application of the subsidiarity principle corresponding to the level of development reached by the country concerned is possible. It is generally assumed that this would have both a catalytic effect and the effect inherent in the subsidiarity principle of mobilizing local human resources. To enable this challenge to be met, it has proved extremely helpful in the development debate of the past two decades to assign decentralization to three development policy strands that affect society as a whole:

- The *political strand*, which extends from central government to local government level; it covers political or democratic decentralization; it includes the promotion of political and civil tasks and the exercise of state controls;
- The *public administration strand*, which extends from central government to district and, in some countries, even local government level; it covers institutional decentralization; it includes the organization and administration of subnational governments and corresponds to the German principle of *kommunale Selbstverwaltung* (local self-government);

- The *strand of the public financing* of development, which in most African countries extends only from central government to district level; it covers fiscal decentralization; it includes the development of capacities for the mobilization and use of local, national and external financial resources.

Figure A5 summarizes these thoughts very impressively. It also provides a methodological insight into how the effects of decentralization projects can be evaluated and relates this to rural development. Decentralization is likely to be able to promote rural and any kind of intersectoral development when (a) decentralization projects involve the local population duly in development (participation), (b) decentralization enables sufficient financial resources to be mobilized for local social and economic development (resource mobilization), (c) local institutional capacities operate efficiently (institutional capacity) and (d) the representatives of district and/or local administrations and deconcentrated ministerial offices act responsibly (accountability). Fully in keeping with the South African approach of *developmental local government*, institutional and financial sustainability, effectiveness of resource use and participation can then be achieved and the responsiveness of government services to needs ensured. The idea of political, institutional and fiscal decentralization imbues all the following chapters. It is of fundamental importance for the performance of complex development policy tasks.

14   Importance for broad-based socio-economic development

Decentralization is never an end in itself. This is evident from the very fact that, if introduced consistently, the decentralization of government and administration is a complicated, institution-intensive and, therefore, expensive undertaking. Logically, only fairly large, comparatively sophisticated economies with a sizeable population can afford it at first. Measured against these criteria, such countries as the USA, Brazil, India and Germany are, then, the classical representatives. In the course of their recent history, these federal countries have created for themselves a comprehensive three-tier administrative and government structure at national, subnational and local level. Historically, this was a laborious, but largely worthwhile process. India took advantage of the local government structures imposed on it during its colonial period.

In sub-Saharan Africa only Nigeria and – in somewhat modified form – South Africa opted for a federal state structure on gaining their independence. In South Africa's case, however, this has not led to independent federal states being formed, merely provinces with independent jurisdiction over planning in specific spheres. But in both the classical federal states and in Nigeria and South Africa the third level of government plays a very decisive role in these countries' capacity for development; it consists of the variously graduated public bodies, the urban authorities (municipalities), districts and amalgamated local authorities. As a rule, the constitution has assigned them a locally restricted but, within the set limits, independent governing and self-governing role.

Decentralization of government has three objectives: efficiency, participation and quality assurance related to public measures; according to Cheema and Rondinelli (Cheema and Rondinelli 1983, p. 14 ff.), it may therefore offer three options for economic, social and societal development through the structures and procedures it creates:

1   It may increase the efficiency of government administration, this being achieved through *institutional decentralization*;
2   It may promote political participation and public involvement, this being achieved through *political decentralization*; and
3   it may lay the organizational foundations for balanced social and economic territorial development by deliberately steering central government funding to underdeveloped territorial authorities, this being achieved through *fiscal decentralization* (see Figure A5).

The sub-Saharan African countries have largely failed to recognize the fundamental importance of decentralization for their development in contrast to the classical federal system. *'The existing local government systems have remained dormant bodies with respect to their developmental role.'*[1] Put more clearly, the potential and the catalytic effect of decentralization where broad-based socio-economic development is concerned have been largely ignored by all but a few countries, such as Nigeria, Uganda, Ghana and South Africa.

Since the 1980s, however, there has been a tendency towards more decentralization throughout Africa. This has a number of causes: for one thing, the Structural Adjustment Programmes were not as successful as had been hoped, partly because the reform projects associated with them hopelessly overextended the central administration (see Chapter 5.2). For another, the required democratization processes called for the growing participation of both the people and the *stakeholder groups* in the development process. This was, moreover, to be done on the basis of *good governance* and *development-oriented administration*, however these terms might be defined. This had implications for government administrative and participatory structures: the pattern of development that had hitherto been largely determined statistically was increasingly questioned, without any regulatory alternatives being explicitly demanded. Eventually, the list of demands for globally based development programmes, which was outlined in Part I of this part of the study and has unfortunately been seen thus far as no more than an 'add-on', made a decisive contribution to the implementation of holistically designed projects. This could no longer be achieved by central government alone. With the Millennium Summit and the poverty reduction tasks arising from it, it finally became abundantly clear that the national structural reforms which were the target and which extended to all sections of society, politics and the business community would be too much for all the centrally governed African states (and not only them) and their governments.

From all this it can be inferred that the crucial link between the often overextended, weak, but in any case inefficient central administration and a motivated and often well-organized population base is missing: the territorial administration that is development-oriented and familiar with local conditions. Provided that it is accountable to a democratically legitimized local government for the action it takes in important development issues, it can become a strong link between central government and the people. This is clearly reflected in the phrase 'bringing government nearer to the people'.

A development-oriented local government system is in a far better position to bring about the formal integration of the representatives of the private sector, the informal sector, the NGO sector, CSOs and CBOs. It can achieve a stronger upward and downward bonding effect than a central administration. A firmly institutionalized framework for a development dialogue between (a) representatives of the people in the local governments, (b) NGO/CSO/CBO representatives, (c) representatives of central government at local level (where they exist) and (d) representatives of the private sector is more likely to lay the ground for participatory development planning and realistic implementation than the central government is able to do. The latter can come nearer to the people at best where it extends down to field level through its deconcentrated sectoral ministries and their staff, as is usually the case with the health, education, agricultural extension and veterinary services.

It should be pointed out in this context that, if there is to be effective coordination of central government services (like those listed in Chapter 7), only firmly institutionalized administrative structures can serve their development policy purpose. This can never be achieved, or even started, by the 'freely floating segment' comprising the NGOs, CSOs, CBOs and interest groups. This important segment of civil society in state activities naturally occupies a special position, standing for what we generally know as civil participation, protection of interests and lobbying. But it cannot replace decentralized government that stretches down to local level. For cooperation geared to the long term between central government, the organized private sector and organized civil society, then, firmly installed decentralized administrative structures for representative participation are essential. Although this has been appreciated since the 1980s, it has unfortunately not been given anything like its due in the debate on development policy. Only now is it beginning to re-enter the consciousness of the development cooperation community. It is to be hoped that the same will apply to rural development.

15   Effects on and risks for development policy

According to Cheema and Rondinelli (1983), Conyers (1985), Silverman (1992), Fuhr (1999) and Thomi (2001), the potential effects to be expected of decentralization are of major relevance to development policy. They also concern all areas regarded as particularly critical for the improvement of the effectiveness of development cooperation, such as:

- The widening and deepening of political participation in the development process;
- The more efficient provision of public goods and services;

- A service-oriented and accountable administration;
- A general improvement in development results through the involvement of local knowledge and the mobilization of endogenous potential;
- The improvement of conditions for greater political stability;
- The creation of a government tool for achieving fairer distribution of resources (see Box 2).

Box 2 Opportunities and risks inherent in decentralization

Opportunities	Risks
Better performance:	Threats to performance:
• Closer to problems	• **Decentralization of corruption**
• More flexible	• Unbridled spending
• More innovative	• Withdrawal of central government
• Cheaper	
• **Mobilizes the comparative advantages** of local enterprises and the local public sector	• Unqualified, dependent personnel averse to risk-taking
Promotion of local democracy:	*'Local politics is still politics'*:
• Greater opportunities for participation	• **Reproduction/re-labelling of local elites**
• Opportunities for joint and private-sector organizations to express themselves	• Inability of poor to express and assert themselves
• **School for democracy**	• Clientelism
• Protection of minorities	
National integration:	Danger of separatism:
• **Fairer distribution of resources**	• Institutionalization of **ethnic fragmentation**
• **Vertical division of power**	
• Joint decision-making bodies and performance of tasks	• Reproduction of majority party's discriminatory policies

Source: Steinich (2001), p. 190.

On the other hand, decentralization also exposes development policy to certain risks. According to Steinich (2001, p. 190), they concern not only the area of government performance and the development of local democracy but also national integration. It may lead to the decentralization of corruption, to unbridled spending by local elites, to the withdrawal of central government, to the strengthening of local elites, combined with local clientelism, and to the institutionalization of ethnic fragmentation. Furthermore, there is with decentralization the associated problem of administrative, political and financial implementation when it comes to the details, in which the adversaries often get bogged down. All this should be weighed up against the potential positive effects when countries opt for more decentralization in the service of their development policies.

Given such opportunities and risks on the one hand and the global experience of decentralization policies successfully pursued (as in India, Brazil, the Philippines and Indonesia) on the other hand, it is surprising that the vast majority of African countries have so far failed to recognize the potential that lies in decentralization. It is also surprising to learn that it has never yet been seriously considered for the performance of such complex cross-section and national joint tasks as rural development, the implementation of Agenda 21 and the poverty reduction strategy. One exception, as mentioned above, is South Africa, the 'last African country to gain independence', which adopted the decentralization approach for the country's broad-based development from the outset.

South Africa and even countries with unitarily constituted government structures, such as Ghana, Uganda and Malawi, expect much of the effects of decentralization on development. It is known from experience that the effects do not become apparent primarily in the general system of administration (central administration, local administration) but rather at sectoral level. This is quite understandable because it is at this level, whether in the agricultural, health or edu-cation sector, that government services must be conveyed down directly to the grass roots and so become capable of being experienced by everyone. Unlike a general administration, sectoral administrations never stand on their own, but should always be at the service of the general public.

Decentralization projects usually take several years; up to 20 years is a realistic time frame, which may therefore cover the terms of several governments. Steps towards decentralization may, as in Zimbabwe's case, be followed by steps towards recentralization. This is often accompanied by seriously adverse effects not only for the internal administration but also for the sectoral levels; indeed, they may impede the whole of economic development. In a process of forward and backward steps of this kind decentralization never really comes to an end. It continues to be a recurrent challenge to development policy.

In the context of the effects or benefits of decentralization, its costs must also be considered. What is important here is less the absolute level of costs, which is in any case difficult to calculate: of greater interest is the question whether decentralization has been achieved efficiently, i.e. how far down the public administration system should be decentralized. In this, of course, the size of a community or sector is an important factor. Another question is whether the costs should be borne by the sector concerned or distributed by central government. In general, the question of the cost of decentralization should never be considered without the potential effects being assessed. They usually extend well into society, although the benefit cannot be easily quantified. A very decisive factor where decentralization is concerned, and one whose cost cannot be determined, is the effect it has on the complex commonly known as the 'ownership' of development, i.e. the people's awareness of the benefits they will derive from and their identification with, say, the development of their local community (civil pride).

16   Importance of fiscal decentralization for development

Fiscal decentralization is a devolutionary process in which powers relating to public revenue and expenditure are transferred from central government to a lower level (province, city, local community). It covers all fiscal measures that generally help to strengthen or establish the autonomy of the lower territorial authorities. Subnational territorial authorities account for a far larger proportion of a country's total revenue and expenditure in federal countries than in semi-federal and unitary countries. The degree of autonomy enjoyed by the lower territorial authorities varies accordingly (see Table A5).

> *Autonomy* in general includes the right and the obligation to take full responsibility for all matters concerning the regional and local community. *Fiscal autonomy* in particular means action taken with full responsibility – not independently – in determining the tasks to be performed and in connection with the associated revenue and expenditure.
>
> (GTZ 2000, p. 1)

The four pillars of fiscal decentralization for achieving greater fiscal autonomy are:

- The delegation of responsibility for public expenditure to subnational territorial authorities;
- The transfer of the power to levy taxes and the right to spend revenue to subnational territorial authorities;
- Measures to make intergovernmental fiscal transfers possible; and
- the authorization of subnational territorial authorities to borrow and to incur limited debt.

These pillars are extremely unequally developed in the sub-Saharan African countries because post-colonial developments and decentralization and democratization processes have been very different. Most commonly encountered is the delegation of central government's responsibility for expenditure to lower territorial authorities within the framework of local government, less so the *transfer of the right to spend revenue freely*. Both these pillars, however, represent an important mechanism for financing service functions delegated by central government to the local authorities. But they have not yet performed an explicit development function in any country except South Africa.

Intergovernmental transfers, similarly still far from common, are, on the other hand, particularly important for development. As vertical financial transfers, they can be guided to the level of government where they have the widest comparative impact. As horizontal transfers, they may help to bring about fiscal equivalence among the various provinces or local authorities. They may also be used specifically to promote national development priorities. Finally, they may provide the funds for payments to compensate for particular regionally specific burdens (Bahl *et al.* 2001).

Local government borrowing is another important pillar for development, but it is one that can be employed for development purposes only where local government structures are more advanced. Apart from the fact that the uncertainty attached to and, especially in rural communities, the very limited nature of public revenue from local taxes, user fees, levies and licences leave little room for local government debt, there are only a few national financial institutions capable of funding sizeable investments by local government. In the African context, then, public borrowing (through municipal bonds, for example) does not yet play a major part in fiscal decentralization; nor should it do so for the time being. In the future this might, however, become an important area of activity for development, and one in which national and regional development banks and international financial cooperation will take a growing interest (Djafari 2001, p. 185).

The rules on local government's responsibility for expenditure, the structure of taxes and revenue and internal equalization mechanisms thus differ significantly with a country's size and the extent to which government is decentralized. The sectors in which the territorial authorities have sole responsibility for revenue and expenditure range from regional transport infrastructure, water supply, sanitation and refuse disposal to education and health care (Djafari 2001, p. 174). Related to African rural areas, this covers the part of rural development for which the public sector should at present be primarily responsible. There won't be any sudden change in this respect.

Fiscal decentralization is also particularly important because it can in itself lend effective support to such cross-section tasks as the implementation of Agenda 21 and the CCD and achievement of rural development and poverty reduction at local level. However, this presupposes institutionalized local financial and development management, as outlined in Chapter 21.3. In this, a special part is played by the fiscal aspects, such as financial allocations to local authorities, financial equalization among the provinces and targeted intergovernmental transfers.

> An appropriately arranged intergovernmental financial system can serve a number of political purposes. For example, it can be used to fill financial gaps, to compensate for benefit spillovers, to ensure compliance with minimum standards in the supply of public goods and services, to implement central redistribution policies and to coordinate the stabilization policy.
>
> (GTZ 2000, p. 14)

In accordance with the subsidiarity principle, it is also true to say in this context that – by analogy with political and institutional decentralization – public financial services should be provided at the (central, regional or local government) level at which they produce the most favourable results when judged by the criteria of efficiency and significance. Government revenue from taxes, levies, fees and licences should accordingly be spent where it is collected and where it can be used most effectively.

The structure and level of public revenue from various sources (local taxes, levies, fees, licences, transfers from central government, etc.) and the degree of responsibility for expenditure (fiscal autonomy) thus form a decisive framework for local government's ability to develop itself. The discretion assigned by law with respect to public revenue and expenditure (local discretion) may differ widely from one country and one task to another, as is again illustrated in Box 3 (see also Table A6).

Box 3 **Policy guidelines for fiscal decentralization**

Fiscal decentralization covers two interrelated issues: the division of *spending responsibilities* and *revenue sources* across levels of government (national, regional, local) and the *amount of discretion* given to regional and local governments to determine their own expenditures and revenues. These combined dimensions have a significant impact on the reality of decentralization in its broad political and administrative sense. How much power and responsibility regional and local governments actually exercise depends crucially on what range of public services they finance, whether their revenues are commensurate with their responsibilities, how much real choice they have in allocating their budget to individual services, and whether they can determine the rates of their taxes and charges.

Spending responsibilities
There is wide diversity across states in terms of the scale of tasks devolved to local government. In most countries, local government is responsible for what are often called communal services: local roads and lighting, water supply and sanitation, waste management, parks and sports facilities, cemeteries, low-income housing. What varies greatly is the extent of local responsibility for the social sector, chiefly comprising education, health, and social assistance. In some cases, these services are funded by the state budget; in some, costs are split between levels of government, and, in others, local budgets meet all costs except central supervision. Cost splitting may be by function (the state pays for secondary education, hospitals, and social benefits, and local government pays for basic education, primary health care, and social services) or by cost factor (the state provides professional salaries, while local government pays all other operating costs). The degree to which local budget responsibility for the social sector varies has an important effect on the nature and scale of decentralization. Without devolution of such responsibility, local government expenditure is unlikely to exceed 5–6 percent of GDP.

It is customary to distinguish between current and capital expenditure. Current expenditure covers such operating costs as salaries, repairs, energy and other utilities, travel, materials, and debt service. Capital expenditure covers investment in new construction, major renovations, and purchase of land and durable equipment. It is also customary to distinguish between the financial sources for these two types of expenditure. Operating costs are normally covered by a combination of local taxes, user fees, intergovernmental transfers (either grants or subsidies), or shares of state taxes.

Local discretion
Clearly, the structure of local government responsibilities and resources affects the local government's discretionary power – its ability to make decisions about the nature and levels of local services. If local government obtains a significant proportion of local taxes and charges, it is in a much better position to determine how it spends the money. Revenue shares and block grants should provide more freedom of allocation than targeted grants. In practice, local discretion depends on a more complex set of factors. Sharing a well-established national tax may support more budgetary choice than dependence on a politically sensitive and administratively burdensome local tax.

Source: Davey (2000).

17 Opportunities for development cooperation to promote decentralization

With the instruments it has for financial, technical and human resources development cooperation and for assisting NGOs, development cooperation has a wide range of opportunities for supporting national decentralization policies. They extend from high-level advice given to bodies drawing up constitutions establishing federal government structures (as the German political foundations have done for South Africa) through advice given to existing local government administrations in support of political decentralization projects (as the GTZ has done for Malawi) and technical and financial assistance given to decentralized institutions with the implementation of sectoral investment programmes (as the GTZ has done for Zambia) to the work of the German Voluntary Service (DED) at village level to strengthen local participatory structures.

All current development cooperation projects can be functionally assigned to the three strands of political, institutional and fiscal decentralization. Their implementation is most likely to be most appropriately supported by development cooperation if the general social and development policy framework in the partner country has been prepared for this or if there is at least a long-term prospect of a national political consensus in support of greater decentralization. But even where the conditions are less favourable and central government has for the moment set its sights on recentralization (as currently in Zimbabwe and other African countries), the institutional decentralization strand can certainly be pursued together with the development of the private sector. This is happening at present in Zambia as part of the support which development cooperation is providing for the Agricultural Sector Investment Programme (ASIP). In both situations, then, development cooperation can promote decentralization processes in the long term: in the former case, with targeted policy advice, institution-building, human resources development and capacity-building, in the latter case, by means of sectoral reform programmes, the promotion of the private sector or the strengthening of the local level.[3]

There is a growing realization in the development policy debate that it will be virtually impossible to cope with national cross-section tasks unless steps are taken in advance or simultaneously to decentralize government. This is equally true of rural development and of the implementation of sectoral programmes. There is absolutely no doubt that it is true of the implementation of globally formulated policies which now have to be transformed down to national and, eventually, local level. The question of the implementation of poverty reduction strategies furnishes the latest evidence in this respect: development cooperation will be able to support implementation country-wide and sustainably only if it can rely on political, institutional and fiscal structures that can be used in a de-centralized way. Only then can this lead to broad-based development and the promotion of democracy from the bottom up. Seen in this light, the promotion of decentralization by development cooperation might be regarded as an ideal path to take.

Of German development cooperation it can be said, according to Gräfe (2001) and other authors (Hinrichs 2001; Meyer 2001), that support for decentralization projects provided by a donor country 'with a federal system of government and a high degree of decentralization in many areas of society has a comparative ad-vantage over many other donor countries.' According to Hinrichs (2001, p. 282),

> in 1999 alone the BMZ approved over DM 400 million for projects that promote reforms of the public sector in developing countries. A large pro-portion of these projects seek directly or indirectly to support decentraliza-tion processes.

In multilateral development cooperation too, support for decentralization pro-jects is playing a growing role, whether at the World Bank or UNDP or in the EU. From 1997 to 1999 UNDP assisted programmes and projects relating to the promotion of local governance with some US\$ 90 million (Hinrichs 2001, p. 283). The German political foundations have similarly been giving priority to decentralization and the promotion of local government for some considerable time (Friedrich-Ebert-Stiftung 1999; Konrad-Adenauer-Stiftung 1999). The pro-motion of the development of local government also plays a special part in part-nerships between individual German *Länder* and partner provinces in develop-ing countries (e.g. in South Africa: North Rhine-Westphalia with Mpumalanga, Lower Saxony with Eastern Cape, Bavaria with Western Cape, Baden-Württemberg with KwaZulu-Natal and Saxony with Northern Cape).[4]

Part IV Decentralization and development cooperation priorities

18   Cooperation between the private and public sectors

18.1   Functionality and efficiency

Rural development is based predominantly on activities in agriculture and its up- and downstream sectors and in the craft and commercial sectors. They are undertaken by either the private or the parastatal sector and they are supported or coordinated by the public sector as and when the need arises. In general, all such activities can be broken down functionally into (a) primary agricultural production, (b) the processing of agricultural products, (c) agricultural and non-agricultural services and (d) the commercial activities of micro, small and medium-sized enterprises (SMEs). According to the usual effect criteria, economic efficiency, social compatibility and environmental sustainability are expected.

The first functional group includes forms of farm and enterprise ranging from subsistence farms through semi- and fully commercialized farms to cooperative and state farms. Among the most important service enterprises in rural areas are public and private banking and credit institutions, private money-lenders, public or private extension and veterinary services, still predominantly government research service providers, cooperative or private agricultural machinery service providers and public or private providers of land use and regional planning services. The most important rural SME group includes transport and marketing enterprises, input suppliers, agricultural processing enterprises, local traders and firms making and repairing agricultural machinery and equipment, where these functions are not performed by government or parastatal bodies.

All four functional groups differ within themselves to a greater or lesser extent depending on the level of development the economy has reached, the distance from the market and the natural and economic conditions at the location concerned. This is true both of the farming systems (from subsistence farms to mixed arable farms with integrated animal husbandry) and of the trend in farm size. The breakdown into small, medium-sized and large farms during agricultural development is of decisive importance for the development of employment in agriculture and income generation and for the development of economic linkages between the agricultural and non-agricultural sectors (see Part A, Chapter 8). The legal form varies as a function of level of development, regulatory prescriptions and land tenure system, examples being (a) family farms, (b) communal farms, (c) farms that join forces for various production purposes, (d) cooperative farms and (e) state farms.

Whatever the legal form, the degree of integration of farming activities, the functional diversity or the division of labour between farms and commercial enterprises, the ability to achieve economic efficiency and positive linkages will largely depend on smooth interaction between the private and public sectors. This is true of interaction both between primary agricultural production and the service sector and between primary agricultural production and up- and downstream SMEs. The decisive factors if this interaction is to occur are the state and composition of (a) physical infrastructure in the road, water, energy and communications spheres, (b) rural financial infrastructure and (c) the institutional infrastructure that exists for public service, coordination and political mediation purposes.

The modernization and reform of the agricultural sector thus depend entirely on efficient cooperation between the private and public sectors. This, in turn, depends entirely on the integrated and balanced development of primary agricultural production and the service and SME sectors (see Part A, Chapter 13). The most promising instruments or approaches in this interaction are still considered to be the four approaches formulated by Chambers (1983) to the creation of economic incentives (prices, taxes, subsidies), the provision of technical innovations (inputs, machinery and equipment), the development of physical infrastructure (rural roads, water supply, electricity) and the creation of efficient public institutions (extension services, veterinary services, agricultural research, agricultural credit institutions). In the Anglo-Saxon literature these approaches are known by the four familiar terms *incentives, innovations, infrastructure and institutions* (Chambers 1983, p. 190 ff.).

18.2   Dysfunctionalities and weaknesses

The interaction between the private and public sectors does not, of course, occur in any society without frictions. An added difficulty in the sub-Saharan African countries is that (with few exceptions) the level at which this interaction is normally organized, the level of interest groups, associations and cooperatives, is not yet very well developed. Their development is, however, one of the most important requirements for the implementation of poverty-reducing economic, social and structural policies. For just as these policies should gradually take shape in the public sector, their most important sectoral and functional elements should come into being at local and private-sector level. Decentralization policies are likely to be the most suitable transmission belt for this purpose.

The most obvious dysfunctionalities in the interaction between African public and private entities today are mainly to be found in the areas of (a) agricultural price, market and trade policy, (b) agricultural structural policy, (c) agricultural service and innovation policy, (d) rural infrastructure and (e) SME policy. As the macro and sectoral economic links between agricultural and rural development cannot be considered in this part of the study (for this see Part A, Chapters 4, 10 and 11), the focus here will be on the institutional and organizational weaknesses of the aforementioned policies.

The lack of development-promoting *agricultural price and market policies* with calculable price assumptions is one of the most sensitive weaknesses affecting producers, service providers and sectors up- and downstream from agriculture alike. The transition initiated at the time of market liberalization and structural adjustment from state-controlled price policies and their implementation through parastatal marketing boards to the privatization of agricultural trade has yet to be completed in many African countries. In most cases it has resulted in serious constraints in the marketing of products and in the supply of inputs and credit. This is particularly true of the peripheral disadvantaged areas of production, where the private sector has been unable to take on the role of marketing agricultural products previously played by the state because of the difficulty of meeting the costs involved (see Chapter 5.2).

In the area of *agricultural structural policy* too, the necessary reform and adjustment processes have not yet been completed in all African countries, especially those with dualistic agricultural structures inherited from the former colonial economies. In some cases they have not even been initiated. Sub-Saharan Africa is currently experiencing processes of change in two directions: on the one hand, in countries where land is scarce there is a call for a socially compatible balance between the large farm structures shaped during the colonial period and the African land use systems that have evolved throughout history. Here property rights imposed by the colonists face traditional communal rights of use. The reforms sought in these cases are redistributive in nature, the aim being both to preserve efficient medium-sized to large farm structures and to create new small farms. They are currently concentrated on Zimbabwe, Namibia and South Africa. On the other hand, commercialization and modernization are exerting considerable pressure on peasant farming to change. Innovative agricultural reforms that are compatible with the market provide for the gradual modernization of land tenure systems entailing mostly still usual rights of usufruct in common property and rights of use and tenancy that are guaranteed in the long term. Only the latter are acceptable as the collateral for loans that is constantly demanded. Both processes require well-planned and carefully controlled reform programmes, which should be backed by measures to strengthen the supply of government and private services (see Part A, Chapter 13.3).

In *agricultural service and innovation policy* the most serious weaknesses continue to lie in the financing of loans and of agricultural extension and research, despite decades of promotion by international development cooperation in this very area. Where credit services can no longer be subsidized by the state in the wake of the structural adjustment policies, small farmers have little chance of using them to finance technical innovations. This particularly affects the use of machinery and equipment that increase productivity and the financing of innovations that stabilize resources and of technologies that improve quality. In these areas in particular interaction between the private and public sectors, either through a division of labour or through public–private partnerships, is of the utmost importance for rapid development.

In this context, a particularly critical mention must be made of the obvious *undercapitalization* of African farming (World Bank 2000a, p. 170). The degree of capitalization and thus of mechanization and intensification in farming can be determined microeconomically only by reference to the ratio of the two factors of production land and labour one to the other in the country concerned, or macroeconomically by reference to the ratio of total resource endowment to agricultural population. Undercapitalization exists where endowment with capital in the form of fixed assets and stock is too low in relation to the farm's potential for intensification, diversification and value added and so impedes economic development. This is true of much of farming in sub-Saharan Africa. It is especially true of the potential agricultural areas in the sub-humid regions, the belt of arable land stretching from Angola through Zambia, Malawi and Tanzania to Mozambique, but also of large areas of Sudan and the Democratic Republic of Congo. In these countries mechanization should be used primarily to increase the productivity of the land, to make work easier and to improve quality: it should not lead to the redundancy of workers; only then can rural unemployment be avoided and poverty sustainably reduced.

A further obvious dysfunctionality in the interaction between the rural commercial and public sectors concerns *rural infrastructure*. Owing to what has been branded since 1977 as urban bias, mainly by Lipton (Lipton 1977), it has repeatedly been pointed out that infrastructure undersupply in areas of production, particularly in the rural hinterland, is one of the main causes of their poor economic and social development. For broad-based agricultural development that taps the potential for linkages, the widening and deepening of the rural economic infrastructure is thus of the utmost importance. This includes not only road-building, rural water and energy supply, the development of local markets, the improvement of veterinary stations and irrigation infrastructure but also the improvement of the rural financial infrastructure. The latter often begins with the development of small mobile saving and loan facilities as branches of commercial banking institutions. In general, the rural economic infrastructure should be tailored to farming as the real potential source of productivity increases, diversification and quality improvement. This orientation would undoubtedly increase the significance of investment in infrastructure and thus its influence on broad-based economic development (see Tables A3 and A4).

18.3 Problem-solving approaches

Problem-solving approaches aimed at ensuring effective interaction between the private and public sectors in agricultural and rural development will be neither regional nor national in scale, least of all if all the criteria for success – efficiency (profitability of the measures taken), effectiveness (degree of goal achievement), significance (influence of the measures on the environment), financial sustainability (ability to cover current costs) and environmental compatibility – are taken as a basis at once. What may be possible, on the other hand, are steps towards realistic problem-solving approaches (as called for in Part II), towards minimum solutions, so to speak, which are, in certain circumstances, restricted to subregions. But even this demand would have to be based on three principles:

1 Simplification through the setting of development policy priorities (see Chapter 10);
2 Subsidiarity as the basis of a graduated division of labour in society (see Chapter 13);
3 The least possible government intervention (see Chapter 20).

These principles can be applied not only to internal cooperation between the public and private sectors in the partner countries but also to international development cooperation in general. If this is borne in mind, the errors of the past decades, for which development cooperation is largely to blame and which it has introduced into the partner countries' development policy conceptions, will be recalled. They are:

1 The excessive functional complexity of development projects;
2 The rapid change of development policy conceptions and 'fashions';
3 The excessive commitment of local financial and human resources to complex development projects;
4 The creation of 'insular solutions' without any national integration or broad-based impact;
5 The impossibility of recurrent costs being financed by partner countries until project/programme completion;
6 The partner countries' lack of ownership of development projects.

In view of these frequently recurring errors and weaknesses in international development cooperation,[1] it should now be decided how the main groups of actors in development cooperation can collaborate most effectively with a view to gradually finding realistic minimum solutions. These main groups of actors are:

1 Organized civil society, represented by its spokesmen in NGOs, CSOs and CBOs and by traditional leaders;
2 Democratically legitimized representatives (where they exist) in national and subnational parliaments of central and local government;
3 The representatives of the public administration in sectoral and intersectoral ministries and their subordinate offices and divisions;
4 The representatives of the organized business community in chambers of commerce, industry, etc., associations and interest groups; and
5 the representatives of the international development cooperation organizations and NGOs.

Given the considerable inherent diversity of the tasks of these groups of actors in society as a whole, the highly disparate consequences of their decisions and the opportunities for exercising influence, it is imperative that ways be sought to achieve a graduated division of labour, again in accordance with the subsidiarity principle. The identification of tasks which are of joint interest and may therefore be seen as a priority in the development of a rural community, municipality or region is also appropriate and promising. Finally, in view of the wide range of tasks to be performed, it is essential to minimize government intervention. This is appropriate for very obvious reasons: first, it enables potential and initiative to develop at local level; second, it eases the human and financial burden on the administrative apparatus, and third, it gives central government the freedom to concentrate on core government functions (see Chapter 7).

In the search for national, subnational and local problem-solving approaches it must now be asked where the comparative strengths and advantages of the various main groups of actors lie in a graduated division of labour of this kind. What can one group do that the others cannot? These questions also need to be raised particularly with respect to tasks which are marked by complexity, diversity and their cross-section nature, as is the case with rural development. The answers will be provided in the next chapter with reference to various examples.

19 Integration of intersectoral programmes into poverty reduction strategies

On the basis of the previous deliberations, questions concerning the conceptual integration of national agricultural and rural development programmes can now be answered. The same is true of other intersectoral programmes, such as the implementation of Agenda 21, the World Food Summit Plan of Action, the CCD and national poverty reduction strategies. Most, if not all, intersectoral reform programmes can be broken down into their component parts. Zambia's Agricultural Sector Investment Programme (see Chapter 19.1), for example, consists of 13 ASIP subprogrammes (MAFF 1994, p. 12 ff.). It is usually impossible for all these component parts to be developed or publicly assisted at the same time. Nor is this necessary; what is important, however, is acceptance of the need to combine functionally related activities and to avoid the possibility of mutual 'development blockades'. To ensure this,

- the public and private sectors;
- all the main groups of actors referred to in Chapter 18.3; and
- all levels of government administration.

need to participate actively and cooperatively. If feasible solutions are to be found for integrated national tasks which are complex in development policy terms, they must undoubtedly be broken down functionally, the implementation of their component parts must be staggered, and they must be arranged in a way that is clear and understandable to all groups of actors. We are helped in this by the consistent application of the principles (referred to in Chapter 6) of simplification, subsidiarity and the least possible government intervention.

The aim here is no less than to abandon overly etatist, dirigistic and complex approaches to development of which too much is expected. The ultimate objective is to find an *optimum level of interaction between the public and private sectors*, represented by the main groups of actors at the various levels of government. As will be shown later, this optimum level of interaction can emerge only in a decentralized government structure in which the subsidiarity principle is applied. It entails two things: (a) the creation of conditions for the gradual achievement of political, institutional and fiscal decentralization and (b) the creation of an economic environment which leaves room for private-sector development to become more dynamic. That this structure is still in its infancy in most African countries does not detract from the fact that prompt action needs to be taken to ensure that these conditions can be created. The implementation of the forthcoming reform programmes and the gradual emergence of this level of interaction may well, and indeed, given global experience, should, occur at the same time, fully in keeping with the learning-by-doing approach. The implementation of intersectoral programmes might also be accompanied by appropriate institution-building.

What specific form this might take, which African countries might be predestined for this and how this development might best be promoted and financially and technically assisted by international development cooperation will be shown in the following chapters. To ensure systematic pervasion, the three principles of *simplification, subsidiarity* and *least possible government intervention* will be applied across the three levels of government (vertical view) and the sectors relevant to intersectoral development (horizontal view). It should also be pointed out that these considerations may equally apply to all cross-section national development policies, and especially to the implementation of poverty reduction strategies.

19.1   National government tasks (The case of Zambia)

Let us begin with a programme for the development of the agricultural sector as a whole. The report on the evaluation of Zambia's Agricultural Sector Investment Programme (ASIP) (GTZ 2001b) has the following to say:

1   The conception, planning and implementation of a sector-wide approach (SWAP) can succeed only if they are coordinated at all three levels (in this case, the national, provincial and district levels).
2   In a typical agricultural country like Zambia an agricultural sector programme has a very strong impact on many areas of the public administration at national and subnational levels; it therefore challenges other sectors to a greater or lesser degree to adjust (in this case, road infrastructure, water, health and social services and, of course, the whole of the local administra-

tion); consequently, horizontal coordination mechanisms are essential at national and district level.

3   To make such mechanisms effective, the agricultural administration must be deconcentrated. At provincial and district level it must establish efficient administrative units that can cooperate with the other sectoral administrations at these levels, these being the District Agricultural Offices (DAOs) in the present case.

4   The deconcentration of the agricultural administration should be achieved with the existing staff of the Agriculture Ministry and should not lead to staff increases; for fiscal reasons the sectoral service apparatus should, in fact, be slimmed down.

5   The involvement of the private sector is a basic requirement if the ASIP is to succeed; the greatest difficulty here (as in many other sub-Saharan African countries) is still due to the business community's lack of willingness to become involved and to invest in such risky economic activities as agricultural marketing, veterinary services and road maintenance.

6   The public administration at national level is overextended by the coordination and steering of the ASIP and should therefore be relieved of this task; one consequence of this would be that central government should focus on the tasks over which it in fact has exclusive jurisdiction and on the reforms that are important for agricultural development (core functions); programme tasks over which central government has exclusive jurisdiction should remain at national level, while programme coordination and implementation tasks should be transferred to district level.

7   As a countermove, the private sector should progressively take over government services for agriculture which it is able to provide either more cheaply or more appropriately; but this will entail a lengthy privatization process, which the state should nonetheless support.

8   International development cooperation can support the sectoral investment programme appropriately with complementary activities or by sharing the workload only if all the donor organizations involved[2] adapt themselves to the agricultural administration's coordinating framework (integrated donor coordination) and gradually help to promote institutional decentralization.

9   It is becoming clear from the ASIP that success in the long term will be possible only if (a) the Agriculture Ministry clearly concentrates on functions over which it has exclusive jurisdiction, such as agricultural market, price and trade policy measures and the formulation of development priorities and programme control (simplification), (b) a comprehensible division of labour between the sectoral ministries involved, the private sector and the NGOs emerges from this (subsidiarity) and (c) the business community and the private service sector are able to develop freely (least possible government intervention).

Tasks over which central government typically has exclusive jurisdiction would be the following in Zambia's case (as under other sectoral reform programmes as part of rural development; see Chapter 7):

- Negotiating national development priorities and formulating sectoral policies at cabinet, provincial and district level, steering them politically and ensuring their institutional and organizational implementation;
- Improving public financial management by establishing a Medium Term Expenditure Framework (MTEF);
- Creating laws, regulations and implementing provisions on environmentally appropriate land use, animal production with veterinary hygiene safeguards, product processing, storage and distribution conforming to market trends, supervision of food safety and the control of food security as a whole;
- Financing rural emergency aid programmes related to specific sectors, e.g. combating animal epidemics, food security and disasters due to fire or flooding;
- Providing and financing state agricultural services, which – commensurate with the country's level of development – should support necessary reform processes, but which it should be possible to reduce at an advanced stage, such as extension, veterinary services, agricultural marketing and provision of market information;
- Providing and financing advanced agricultural training and agricultural research.

This list can, of course, be extended for a number of countries, shortened for others; this will depend on the importance of the agricultural sector to the economy and its degree of diversity and integration into the economy as a whole. Regardless of this, however, there will be, on the one hand, a gradual shift in the importance of the public administration and the private sector in favour of the latter during any modernization or reform process; on the other hand, the need for coordination and mediation in decision-making between the interests of the various groups of actors will grow.

This factor will, as a rule, be equally true of all levels of government. The process of decentralization should therefore run parallel to the modernization and reform processes in the various sectors. This dual task of sectoral reform and modernization on the one hand and the decentralization of government on the other poses probably the greatest difficulty and challenge for development policy, as South Africa, Zambia,[3] Malawi, Ghana and Uganda in particular are finding at present. Nonetheless, there would seem to be hardly any alternative if such complex national programmes as sectoral reform programmes and the implementation of Agenda 21, the CCD and the World Food Summit Plan of Action are to be implemented. It is in the nature of things that the problem-solving concepts too will now become more comprehensive. This makes the consistent application of the principles of simplification and subsidiarity all the more necessary. In practical terms, this might now mean one element after another being reformed and modernized step by step at the various levels, rather than complete programmes being implemented. And this might mean in practice:

- Both making progress with the sectoral reform programme by implementing certain subprogrammes or measures; and

- making gradual improvements to human resources development (advanced training) and building institutions through decentralization;
- Progressively privatizing state veterinary services, for example, during the development of the private sector;
- Gradually undertaking training measures during the reform of the public administration.

All these steps could certainly be staggered in such a way that their financing from the annual budget and their implementation continues to be possible. The crucial factor is that the objective of each reform should be guided in the long term by the overriding objective of development policy, poverty reduction. In this case, the intersectoral national ministries (Finance, Local Government) and the appropriate sectoral ministries should assume responsibility for overall control of their respective elements. For the implementation of complex programmes of this kind, then, central government with a strong leadership is needed, but it should concentrate on the core functions listed above.

As long as this is not possible, and at present that is unfortunately true of the majority of African countries, there is a danger that sectoral reform programmes will come to a halt in their early stages. Reform projects are, moreover, often interrupted or disintegrate into individual measures when governments or departmental responsibilities change; later it is difficult to reassemble the measures concerned. Without a minimum of public financial control and monitoring, corruption, waste of resources and misallocation of funds may also become prevalent. Without central programme control, donor coordination too is hardly possible. The losses that occur when financial and human resources are misallocated may exceed what is acceptable, and disappointment and frustration may overtake all groups of actors, and especially the people.

It is therefore important that the three principles referred to above for realistic problem-solving approaches (see Chapter 18.3) are applied consistently not only at national and, if appropriate, provincial level but especially at local level. What looks extremely complex at national level, such as the control of sectoral reform projects, the formation of national or sectoral priority strategies or the implementation of national action programmes, may be more straightforward at local level, where it usually breaks down into very specific, feasible measures. What is important is that the focus remains on the overriding objective of development policy, poverty reduction, so that the danger of the national and local views drifting apart may be averted.

19.2   Local government tasks

19.2.1 Integration into the state as a whole (The case of South Africa)

Even if sectoral and cross-section programmes have enjoyed full political and financial support at national level, their general implementation at local level is not a foregone conclusion. For this the obstacles at the subnational levels are too diverse and unpredictable, the mechanisms and procedures of the processes of political negotiation, especially with traditional leaders, still too irregular, the processes of intersectoral coordination too rudimentary and the financial and fiscal constraints, not to mention the technical difficulties encountered during implementation, too great. Because this is so, it seems necessary to ask, fully in keeping with the subsidiarity principle, where local government has genuine room for manoeuvre and where the comparative advantages lie at local level. Where is this level more deserving of national or international support than the provincial level?

Three diagrams (Figures A6, A7 and A8) may help to reveal the interaction between the public and private sectors at local level, taking South Africa as an example. Figure A6 shows the situation as it has existed in the municipalities since the local elections and the legislative process to establish a developmental local government in 2000.[4] It provides an overview of the interaction between legislative, executive and development-coordinating bodies and authorities at the three levels of government. In this the private sector is assigned a specific role in the development of local government.

Of the five main groups of actors named in Chapter 18.3, four are shown in Figure A7: (a) representatives of civil society (citizens and community groups, private-sector representatives and organized interests), (b) central government officials, (c) local government officials and (d) the elected representatives of the people (councillors). Any process of negotiation on development policy affect-ing the local community must ultimately take place among these four groups (spheres of mediation) if it is to result in fruitful cooperation in local economic, social and structural development. This is then portrayed again in an enlarged context in Figure A8 and seen as a dual challenge to the local authorities:

- Exercising municipal functions to maximize the impact on social develop-ment and economic growth; and
- playing an integrating and coordinating role to ensure alignment between public and private investment.

The first challenge is seen here to be to advance democratization of the de-velopment of local government in a way that is fully in keeping with *political decentralization*; the second challenge is seen as a leadership and coordination task in keeping with *institutional decentralization*. On the whole, then, local government is expected eventually to develop democratic, transparent and insti-tutionalized mechanisms for advancing local economic and social development in agreement with the representatives of the main groups of actors (stake-holders).

A very decisive role in this is played by the members of the municipal coun-cils. However, a study conducted in Mpumalanga Province in 1999 (Otzen *et al.* 1999, p. 54 ff.) shows that these councillors are still inexperienced and have still to grow into their responsible role. They are, after all, increasingly expected – as greater emphasis is placed on the principle of developmental local government – (a) to help promote change at local level, (b) to negotiate and mediate on the substance and the social policy aspects, (c) collectively to find solutions to challenges relating to local economic and social development and (d) to shape and sustain the new developmental role assigned to them by the constitution.

This clear assignment of tasks, backed by a political mandate brought about by local elections, forms the basis for the planning and achievement of *democratically shaped, decentralized territorial development*; this, in turn, must be seen in the context of the national strategy for Growth, Employment and Redistribution (GEAR) and the national Reconstruction and Development Programme (RDP). Besides this purely municipal task, central government, represented by the Ministry of Local Government and Provincial Affairs (MLGPA) and by the sectoral ministries, has four other important tasks to perform:

1 The provision of municipal administrative and service infrastructure

    a to permit institutionalized political decision-making (democratic decentralization through local elections) and

    b for the delivery of general central government services;

2 The provision of public services

    a in support of the tasks of the political office-holders (councillors) in the areas of social and development policy and

    b for the planning, coordination and control of local development policy tasks by the developmental local authorities;

3 The provision of sectorally structured, deconcentrated administrative infrastructure

    a for intersectoral coordination (sector alignment) and

    b for the delivery of sectorally deconcentrated services;

4 The provision of local administrative infrastructure for the mobilization and coordination of financial resources from

    a national financial transfers to the municipalities (intergovernmental transfers),

    b regular revenue from local taxes, fees and levies (fiscal decentralization) and their development-oriented use,

    c public–private partnerships and

    d financial transfers by international donor organizations (ODA transfers).

This multi-layered structure of local tasks, as is currently emerging in South Africa, may, of course, differ from one country to another, depending on the levels of democratic development and decentralization achieved (see Chapter 12). It is possible to consider how far South Africa will be capable of performing the major development policy tasks it faces, such as overcoming apartheid and regional disparities and achieving rural development and poverty reduction at local level with the developmental local government system. By courageously employing a model of government that is held in high esteem throughout the world, decentralized government, South Africa has at least been able to leapfrog all the laborious, resource-intensive and ultimately unsuccessful development concepts and intermediate stages (see Part A, Chapter 9).

19.2.2 Planning the development of local government (The case of South Africa)

With the commitment based on constitutional law to *cooperative governance* (cooperative both vertically among municipalities, provinces and central government and horizontally among the various municipalities, ethnic groups and sectors) and to *developmental local government*, the South African municipalities have been assigned a prominent role in development activities. The instrument they have been given by law to perform these tasks is Integrated Development Planning (IDP). Despite the conceptual similarity to the Integrated Rural Development (IRD) of the 1970s and 1980s, efforts are made to preclude this connotation. In any event, the mistakes of conceptual overstretching and planning fetishism of the old IRD approach are to be avoided.

What is decisive about the IDP instrument is that it is meant to help break up the separate structures within the municipalities, government institutions and ethnic groups that stem from the apartheid era. The plan is to integrate (a) formerly separate municipal areas to form large new municipalities (municipal area reform), (b) various government services in support of sectorally coordinated development measures (administrative reform) and (c) the various population groups so that they may undertake joint development efforts. This instrument is also to be used (d) to combine the various needs of the people to form development priorities which are accepted by the majority. The approach is intended in this way to help overcome the blocking of development decisions that has repeatedly occurred in the past owing to ethnic differences.

On the basis of this integrated and participatory planning approach, which has been adopted in 20 pilot municipalities since 1998, primarily with German assistance, the development of organization for integrated territorial development has made a highly successful start (Otzen 1999, p. I). Even though the planning effort during the pilot phase still seems excessive (too time-consuming and too expensive for the municipalities themselves), the approach is understandable and unavoidable for a post-apartheid South Africa. After the withdrawal of German technical cooperation, the planning procedures in the pilot municipalities, which form part of the various provincial development strategies, will in any case have to continue in simplified form.

A difficult step in the organization of the integrated development of local government – and this not only in South Africa – is the transformation of planning results into clear decisions for action at local level. It is important in this context that the central or deconcentrated government services provided by the sectoral ministries and the decentralized demands voiced by the local population should be reconciled to some extent. This means:

- Institutionalizing and steering the process of negotiation between government representatives and the people; as sectoral service capacities and financial resources are limited, priorities must now be selected from among even grass-roots development decisions arrived at through participation; bringing about these decisions is a task over which local government must have exclusive jurisdiction;
- Coordinating the process of implementation consistently; this is done against the background of a given set of physical resources and a given financing framework; this is a task that can only be performed by intersectoral task forces and working parties.

Both processes, like the participatory planning procedures, may well be organized differently in different countries. Which of the lower levels of government – district, municipality or ward – undertakes the process of negotiation and coordination depends on which has exclusive jurisdiction over planning in the development policy field. What is decisive in the case of integrated municipal development is that:

- It is possible for a planning process that is participatory in line with the specific features of the culture and society of the municipality to take place at grass-roots level (democratization of development planning);
- Realistic development decisions can be taken by the elected municipal council, given the existing sectoral service capacities and limited financial resources (decision-making over which the municipality has exclusive jurisdiction); and
- Professional and motivated expert bodies are able to calculate and coordinate the necessary physical inputs, financial volumes and schedules (public and private competence).

Where one or more of these conditions is not satisfied or has not yet developed, external support can be provided with the help of development cooperation; this is true of capacity-building, the training of specialists, institution-building and the scheduling of development sequences. On the whole, then, participatory planning of municipal development, institutionalized decision-making over which the municipality has exclusive jurisdiction and the strengthening of competence are the three main tasks for municipal development.

19.2.3 Steering local development (The case of Zimbabwe)

If participatory planning processes, decision-making processes over which local authorities have exclusive jurisdiction and intersectoral coordination processes are to lead to development measures which are ready for financing and implementation at the local grass-roots level, there must be efficient and transparent steering mechanisms in place. Unfortunately, the administrative infrastructure needed for this exists in only a few sub-Saharan African countries. The more advanced countries include South Africa, Ghana, Uganda and Rwanda; Malawi is just making a new start in this respect; in Zimbabwe these mechanisms have been significantly weakened again by the current political tendency to recentralize government.

Wherever the various countries may stand in this respect, whether decentralized steering mechanisms do not seem opportune at present on political grounds (as in Zimbabwe), whether it has not yet been possible to establish them for financial and capacity reasons (as in Zambia) or whether countries have not yet been able to introduce them by their own efforts because of strong intervention by development cooperation (as in Malawi), one thing can be predicted with certainty: none of these countries will be able to forgo the elements of public participation, delegation of decision-making and sectoral coordination in the long term if there is to be democratically endorsed, efficiently managed and sustainable territorial development.

What form might such structures and mechanisms take, or what can we learn from the experience of countries with already established (or even again weakened) decentralized structures? In this context, the case of Zimbabwe should be mentioned. Immediately after gaining independence in 1980 on the basis of the transitional constitution agreed between the United Kingdom and the now independent Rhodesia in the Lancaster House Agreement of 1979, Zimbabwe was in an extremely favourable position to launch political and institutional decentralization. This it had, as it were, inherited with the local government system of the colonial period. Until 1984 the eight provinces and 54 districts had extensive planning powers and important coordinating functions in the implementation of the Reconstruction and Development Programme (RDP) (Government of the Republic of Zimbabwe 1981b), for which donors provided massive financial support. The Provincial Councils and Administration Act 1984 and the Rural District Councils Act 1985 initiated the decentralization of development planning and the merging of rural councils (former white farming areas) and district councils (communal African rural areas, known as communal lands).

In 1984 the posts of eight provincial governors were created under the Provincial Councils and Administration Act and filled by decree with members of the ruling ZANU (PF) party.[5] It has always been their formal task to coordinate all development projects at provincial level and to strengthen local government structures. However, these statutory tasks were soon joined by party-political tasks, principal among them being the strengthening of the party structures down to village level and the representation of central government in all matters at provincial level. Although this formally laid the foundations for political and institutional decentralization, it was in fact so designed as to be manipulable for party-political purposes.

When the transitional constitution expired in 1989, a clear move towards recentralization began, not least under the growing pressure of the unsolved problems connected with the distribution of land between former white farming areas and the communal lands (Otzen 2000). The aforementioned local government and land reform legislation had also been passed to establish an institutional and organizational framework for the elimination of the dualism and the integration of former white farming areas and the communal lands surrounding them. For the integrated rural development of both areas a process of decentralization, not renewed political centralism, was essential. Unfortunately, the latter occurred and deprived the former of its momentum.

What form is now taken by the structures and mechanisms for municipal and district development with whose help a whole package of agricultural and rural development programmes and projects have been implemented under the Reconstruction and Development Programme (RDP)?[6] They are, in particular, (a) the development mandate of the District Development Fund (DDF),[7] (b) the rural Resettlement Programme,[8] (c) the Communal Lands Development Programme (CLDP)[9] and (d) the implementation of some 130 individual agricultural and rural development projects throughout the country.[10]

From national level through provincial and district level down to ward level there are two vertically linked institutional strands under the umbrella of the Ministry of Local Government and Town Planning (MLGTP) (see Figure A9): one strand is designed to regulate the political organization of urban, district and ward matters under the legislation passed by the bicameral parliament (House of Assembly and House of Senate); it runs through the provincial, district and ward councils and forms part of political decentralization. The other strand is designed to promote the planning and organizational and technical achievement of general and sectoral development; it is overseen by the central government's Ministry of Finance, Economic Planning and Development (MFEPD) and in the sectoral ministries. It forms part of institutional decentralization.

The two strands are linked at all levels by coordinating bodies: the Cabinet Committee on Development (CCD) at national level, the eight Provincial Development Committees (PDCs), the 54 District Development Committees (DDCs) and the many Ward and Village Development Committees (WADCOs and VIDCOs). Their work is crucially important for the quality of intersectoral cooperation, the degree of development policy coherence and the effectiveness of cooperation between the public and private sectors and organized civil society.

Since the late 1980s party-political interference by ZANU (PF) in this two-strand system has increased sharply, and this has had an adverse influence on decision-making processes at all levels of government. This has also had implications for the second strand, especially as the party now has a considerable say in the appointment of the chairmen of what are in effect technical bodies for development coordination. Despite this, the steering and operating mechanisms for rural and regional development have remained largely intact. They have, however, lost a great deal of their development policy momentum because:

- It has so far proved impossible to clarify the division of ministerial responsibilities for rural development between the MLGTP and the sectoral ministries;
- The rural and agricultural development aspects have been overshadowed by the muddled situation as regards land reform and the unsolved resettlement problem; and

- international development cooperation has therefore withdrawn from the promotion of institution- and capacity-building for rural development.

Nonetheless, it can be seen even from a system that has come under party-political pressure, but is meant to be decentralized, how important its operation is for broad-based territorial development. By the early 1990s it had been possible to find solutions near to the people to a number of problems relating to rural infrastructure development, resettlement, socially compatible land distribution, the tailoring of agricultural services and the participation of NGOs and the private sector in individual rural development projects. This was done conceptually through the politically led ward councils and organizationally through the Village Development Committees (Otzen *et al.* 1991, p. 26 ff.). Both institutions have their counterparts at the next higher level in the shape of the district councils and the District Development Committees and their sectorally oriented technical subcommittees, which are convened as the need arises (see Figure A9). At the lowest levels, the ward and district levels, civil society may be represented either through political mandates (councillors) or through technical mandates (committee members). Transparency and dialogue between the political and technical bodies and among the various levels are maintained through regular meetings and the minutes of these meetings, to which the public have access. The representatives of the private sector and the local CBOs, CSOs and NGOs are also involved in this process.

Irrespective of the current problems, the conclusion to be drawn from the *two-strand system* is that the provincial, district and ward councils should be assigned a guiding function in development policy. The political mandate held by the councillors (sitting in ward and district assemblies) for a fixed period should be brought into contact with the collective expertise provided by the sectoral ministries and the private sector. This has been achieved through technical subcommittees. On the basis of local government decisions politically and technically coordinated in this way viable development projects can then be launched. If appropriate, they can also be supported with technical and financial assistance from the private sector or international development cooperation within a well-ordered framework. This basic, two-strand pattern of *democratically legitimized and intersectorally coordinated local development* is also to be found in South Africa, Uganda, Rwanda and Ghana (see Figure A10). Consequently, it also forms the basis on which the implementation of poverty reduction strategies is organized (see Figure A11).

19.3   Requirements and opportunities for private-sector development

19.3.1 Requirements and starting conditions

In the context of the theory of decentralization the most radical step is the privatization of public tasks. If private-sector activities and initiatives are to evolve and if the private sector is to participate in or take over public tasks, there is a need for (a) economic incentives, (b) government willingness to reform and legal certainty and (c) a favourable institutional environment at national and especially local level (see Chapter 19.2). In this, sub-Saharan Africa is no different from other parts of the world where the first steps towards deregulation and market-economy reforms have been taken. According to North (1995, p. 17–26) and Kydd (2002, p. 6 f.) there also continue to be, without a doubt, differences of degree between liberal market economies (LMEs) and coordinated market economies (CMEs), the group of African countries falling into the latter category.

The evolution of private-sector activities would have been inconceivable if the structural adjustment measures had not been taken in the early 1980s. Despite the modest success of many adjustment policies in a total of 80 African countries (see Chapter 5), the steps so far taken towards liberalization and deregulation can still be regarded as an essential requirement for the private sector's increasing involvement in economic development. The interaction of agricultural and non-agricultural activities in the private agricultural and non-agricultural sectors forms, as has been emphasized on several occasions (see Chapter 18), the backbone of broad-based rural development.

Recent studies have shown that 40 to 45 per cent of rural household incomes in sub-Saharan Africa is generated by non-agricultural activities, the largest proportion originating from local rural sources of work, not from urban transfers (Bryceson and Jamal 1997; Reardon 1997, p. 735–748; Seddon and Subedi 2000; Barrett *et al.* 2001, p. 315–332; Lanjouw and Shariff 2001). The current ratio (of 40 to 45 per cent non-agricultural income to 55 to 60 per cent agricultural income) forms an important empirical basis for further theoretical and practical deliberations on intersectoral rural and urban development (see Part A, Chapter 10). This is based on the assumption of growing linkages and diversification of peasant agriculture and business activities. Productivity gains and diversification in the farming sector lead, of course, to rising demand for inputs and consumer goods produced by the commercial sector. A dynamically developing commercial sector can then increasingly take on the processing and marketing of agricultural products. These up- and downstream linkages between the farm and non-farm private sectors have, in turn, implications for the tertiary sector, which is able to become more differentiated (see Figure 4).

The diversification of production, the achievement of productivity gains and the emergence of linkages between the agricultural and non-agricultural sectors based on a division of labour are thus important components of a policy that has repeatedly been demanded for Africa since the mid-1980s. This policy should lead to balanced growth of agriculture and industry (Kuznets 1966; Hayami and Ruttan 1985; Chenery *et al.* 1986; Syrquin and Chenery 1989, p. 114 ff.). Experience shows that this situation cannot be achieved without at least some government intervention to guide public and private investment flows (see Part A, Chapter 11).

Linkage to agriculture	Secondary sector (Construction and manufacturing)	Tertiary sector (Trading and services)
Production: Forward linkage	Processing & packaging industries Construction of storage & marketing facilities	Transportation & trade Credit services
Production: Backward linkage	Agricultural inputs, tools & equipment	Agricultural & veterinary services Input supply information services Insurance services
Consumption linkage	Household items Home improvements Consumer goods	Domestic services Transportation services Sale of consumer goods

Figure 4 Rural non-farm activities linked to agricultural growth, by sector

Source: Start (2001), p. 493.

There cannot, of course, be a generally valid approach to a policy for promoting balanced rural–urban economic growth. After all, the liberalization policies of the past two decades have clearly shown that the private sector in particular is reluctant to invest heavily in remote rural areas (Start 2001, p. 500). All the more reason, then, for targeted public investment to ensure that the high transaction costs to private businessmen can be reduced in the long term. Important areas of investment in this context would be the improvement of transport and communications infrastructure and of local marketing facilities. However the priorities are set for public investment in a country that has opted for balanced rural and urban development, Start (2001, p. 502) believes that the following considerations must be weighed up one against the other:

- What are the comparative returns of rural versus urban investments? Should investment be directed towards low-potential regions at the expense of higher returns in more favourable regions? Or should private capital flow unhindered, allowing increasing rural–urban inequality and migration to run their 'natural' course?
- Does the administrative framework and capacity for the development of the rural non-farm economy exist? Given the local specificities and the cross-cutting nature of many elements of the rural non-farm economy, local governments are clearly the agency of choice in a climate of decentralisation. However, serious questions remain as to their ability to support development and manage a local economy, given their weak administrative, technical and financial resources.

- Does the political calculus add-up? Where will the political will for rural investment come from, given that rural people in remote areas have very little political voice?

Here Start is again referring very clearly to the major role that the rural authorities should play in the promotion of local economic development. However, he is also aware of their administrative, professional, technical and financial weaknesses. They are nevertheless the ones that are able to lay the foundations and create the conditions for agricultural–commercial linkages, for private-sector investment in the sectors up- and downstream from agriculture and for appropriate local infrastructure development. The general complaint that small municipalities and rural authorities are overstretched by all these tasks does not alter the fact that other public bodies are not available and the NGO sector is certainly not capable of performing them.

19.3.2 Obstacles to private-sector development

Unfortunately, there are always numerous obstacles preventing the private sector from developing in areas with the potential for the establishment of economic linkages between peasant agriculture and commerce. The following comments are based on the conclusions drawn at a regional forum of experts representing agriculture ministries, international development organizations and research institutions in 14 African countries, who considered the question: *Sector Wide Approaches – Do They Really Help the Poor?* (MFA, IFAD, GTZ and SNRD 2001).

The main obstacles on the *government side* are caused by the absence of framework legislative guidelines and regulations governing, for example, the private-sector's land transactions and long-term land use, which, in turn, adversely influences the creditworthiness of enterprises and so makes it virtually impossible to raise loans for capital investments; in countries such as Malawi and Zimbabwe marketing boards still have the effect of distorting the local pricing of agricultural products; hardly any of the countries represented at the forum of experts has an effective law on cooperatives that permits the formation of combined purchasing/marketing and credit cooperatives, which might, after all, support the linkages between the primary sector, agriculture, and the secondary and tertiary sectors; economic and export policies that lack clarity and transparency impede private willingness to invest in such important spheres as agricultural processing and the manufacture of inputs; hardly any of the countries (the exception being South Africa; see Chapter 19.2.1) have authorities at local level that might promote local economic development specifically at intersectoral level.

Where the *private sector* is concerned, dynamic development is hampered, especially in rural areas, not only by such sufficiently well-known weaknesses as the lack of operating capital and of access to credit, extension services and training but also by the limited organizational skills of enterprises; this affects both the development of individual firms and cooperatives and cooperation among firms in the purchase of inputs, the marketing of products and the joint use of machinery and equipment; the formation of professional interest groups is also still in its infancy in most countries; where, for example, there are associations of farmers or craftsmen at local level, they are poorly represented or fail to form a united front at national level; at present, the private sector is also badly represented as a partner in the provision of financial assistance for the maintenance of public facilities or common goods, such as local roads, dams, energy supply facilities and waste water purification plant.

19.3.3 Overcoming the obstacles: examples from Malawi, Zambia and Zimbabwe

A number of examples will now be given to show how government services that can no longer be fully provided for budget and reform policy reasons can be taken over by private-sector initiatives. In Malawi Road Maintenance Authorities (RMAs) (MFA, IFAD and GTZ 2001, p. 25) have been established to maintain and improve minor roads. On presentation of evidence of work they have done, government funds from transport tax revenue are transferred to the RMAs to cover expenditure on materials and personnel. In this, the district administrations and the local representatives of the Public Works Departments play a supporting, coordinating and monitoring role.

Attempts are also being made in various sub-Saharan African countries to privatize agricultural services; under its ASIP, Zambia, for example, is trying to privatize veterinary services where improved marketing and income-generating opportunities in livestock farming are gradually giving rise to demand for such services backed by purchasing power. To this end, veterinary assistants who can no longer be employed by the state because of budget cuts are given a small government loan with which to obtain vaccines, simple medical equipment and a motorcycle. However, as these veterinarians cannot cover the whole area from which the government veterinary service is withdrawing, 'community livestock auxiliaries' (CLAs) selected from the ranks of interested livestock farmers are also being trained so that they can fill the gap. With this kind of privatization, then, three things can be achieved:

- The easing of pressure on the national budget;
- The creation of additional income-generating opportunities both for the veterinarians and for the livestock farmers; and
- on the whole, the continued provision of veterinary services for livestock farming.

In dualistic economies, in which subsistence farms and commercial farms have hitherto existed side by side without any links between them, another way of pressing ahead with privatization and commercialization in peasant agriculture is to form cooperative associations. They can consist, for example, in the exchange of the large farms' machinery for manual labour available on the peasant farms to their mutual benefit, in the marketing facilities of the large farm sector being used by nearby peasant farms if they can offer an equivalent quantity of manual labour, in private extension services of the commercial farm sector being used for the peasant sector, or in credit in kind in the form of inputs or machine hours being exchanged with nearby peasant farmers for a portion of their harvest or for work.

In Zimbabwe a Farmers Development Trust (FDT) has been established as a result of the standstill in land reform. The FDT's aim is to ensure the continuation of the support no longer provided by the government for the settlement of new farmers on large farms purchased by the state. This is done under an agreement reached by central government, the local authority, the small farmers' association and the private sector. The FDT has set itself the task of making good the withdrawal of government support by undertaking planning work itself, forming partnerships with the government agricultural services and providing credit guarantees secured by international development cooperation organizations. The long-term objective is to have the private sector make a contribution to an orderly process of land reform once the general political situation in Zimbabwe permits. This would be an example of decentralized local development supported by the private sector at 'times when development is difficult'.

These opportunities present themselves only where the general atmosphere between the two segments of the economy is politically relaxed and forms part of an overall concept for long-term integration. This can be achieved within the framework of a reform of agricultural services or land management based on market-economy principles. But it can also be achieved under legislation on taxes and levies that enables the development of the backward peasant farming segment to be financed with tax revenue and levies from the modern, export-oriented large farm sector. In all these cases the local authorities would have important planning and coordinating tasks to perform, tasks which could be combined – as in South Africa – under the heading of *developmental local government*.

19.3.4 Local government's role in local economic development

Until the late 1990s the development policy role played by local authorities throughout Africa in the development of the areas over which they have jurisdiction was restricted to delivering administrative and social services provided by central government and supporting the maintenance and improvement of local infrastructure. Only recently has it been realized that they could also have played a major part in local economic development. The main reasons for this belated recognition are that (a) the local authorities' potential in this respect was simply overlooked or disparaged on all sides; (b) the limited impact of the Structural Adjustment Programmes could be ascribed, among other things, to the institutional weaknesses at local authority level (see Chapter 5.2); this missing link has only now been recognized; and (c) the international call for increased political participation was late in focusing on decentralization as an appropriate develop-ment policy approach.

During the first three decades development cooperation practitioners were thus unaware that broad-based economic and social development cannot be achieved unless local government plays an active and clearly defined role. It therefore now seems necessary for local government to perform not only the conventional task of delivering central government services but also the task of mediating between the public and private sectors. However, only a functioning and development-oriented local authority is capable of this. As many sub-Saharan African countries are characterized by inadequate professional, financial and organizational preparation for these tasks, national public service reform programmes (Presidential Review Commission 1988, p. 229 ff.) and – where desired – international assistance with capacity- and institution-building are needed.

Local economic development based on an intersectoral division of labour thus very much depends on the efficiency and innovativeness of authorities at district or local level. In cooperation with the central government services provided by the appropriate sectoral ministries, the following tasks should be performed with the private sector: (a) the development policy field should be rigorously pre-pared for integrated territorial development under a local development concept; (b) the local authority should act as an entrepreneur in the management of public goods; (c) it should act as the promoter of local economic development; (d) it should perform the function of development policy catalyst; and (e) the local council should lobby central government with the support of associations of lo-cal authorities formed for specific purposes. In South Africa's case (IRI and NBI 1998, p. 2 ff.) this package of tasks is described as follows (see Box 4).

Box 4 **The role of local authorities in South Africa**

Local authorities will play a central role in economic development by virtue of their constitutionally determined powers and functions. They influence the economic environment of the locality through the policies and by-laws they pass, the programmes they support, the tendering practices they follow and a wide range of other activities. However, ensuring that these powers and functions are harnessed strategically to promote economic growth and job creation requires local authorities to understand the specific roles they play. Local authorities must develop a clear understanding of the economic conditions and comparative advantages in their locality. Strategic decisions will be required on budget priorities and revenue levels, and the ability to imbue pride, generate public support and community ownership of economic development will be very important. To provide leadership, important roles for local authorities in the South African concept of local economic development (LED) include:

- **Policy-maker** – Through their ability to make policy, local authorities can help ensure that small businesses have access to the tender process, prevent regulations and by-laws from becoming barriers to growth and investment, create streamlined approval processes for investment and development projects, and assist the training and capacity-building projects of local NGOs.
- **Entrepreneur** – As owners of land and buildings, local authorities can explore the commercial potential of these assets. Often these assets are left vacant or under-utilised without calculations of the cost to the local economy. Local authorities can act as entrepreneurs to maximise the commercial potential of their land and buildings, multi-storey car parks, open public spaces, beaches, caravan parks, roads, reserves and pavements. Local authorities can explore this potential by involving the private sector and other stakeholders.
- **Promoter** – Local authorities can promote economic development by creating a positive image of their locality. An effective way to do this is to establish a team of key councillors and officials to meet investors, businesses, trade delegations and others to highlight the strengths and opportunities of your locality.
- **Catalyst** – Local authorities can take actions to catalyse new development initiatives. For example, by releasing land and planning infrastructure programmes, they can encourage developments in deteriorating and underdeveloped areas. New business location and expansion can be catalysed by providing serviced sites. In addition, local authorities can creatively utilise their facilities for major sporting and cultural events to maximise and increase the locality's visibility and image.
- **Lobbyist** – Local authorities can also lobby national and provincial government for policies and programmes that benefit their localities. These lobby activities can often be conducted through local government associations.

Source: IRI / NBI, 1998.

19.4   Local implementation of Agenda 21 (The case of Zimbabwe)

The local Agenda 21 is the equivalent of the global Agenda 21 at the territorial level of a district, rural or urban authority (see Chapter 1.2). It is at this level that the overarching principle of 'think global – act local' should take practical form in all environmental spheres in agreement with the business community, trade, transport, education and training, etc. The detail involved must be worked out with the various interest groups concerned in processes of political negotiation at district or local level and under national environmental legislation on a case-by-case basis. As a rule, this will require an institutionalized process that takes place both between the groups of those concerned and government representatives and within the appropriate official framework (district or local council, environment committee, expert body, etc.).

Both national environmental legislation and the regulations and official decision-making to which it gives rise are still poorly developed in most African rural communities. Outside this official framework, however, there is a wide range of civil participation through NGOs, CBOs and CSOs. As a rule, this includes the traditional leaders. Increasingly, steps are also taken to ensure that indigenous knowledge can be involved in the processes of political negotiation.

The local organizational framework should thus be used particularly for matters of relevance to the environment that come under the international agreements discussed above (in Part I). Otherwise, the local implementation of Agenda 21 will be virtually impossible, whether in Africa or elsewhere. Here again, it has to be asked whether local authorities which are only just being developed are at all capable of performing these coordinating and organizational tasks. To prevent this undertaking from proceeding in accordance with the principle of management by chaos and from degenerating into a set of purely dirigistic rules, tried and tested regulatory principles must be applied. They are equivalent to the principles of *subsidiarity, division of labour* and *economic incentives*. Sustainable land use in several rural communities in Zimbabwe has been studied to determine how these principles can be applied (Otzen *et al.* 1994).

The question in this context is how measures to stabilize agricultural resources which have been tried and tested throughout the world can be undertaken at farm, local and national level in accordance with the subsidiarity principle. Another question is how this can be done in a division of labour between the private sector, the local authorities and central government; and finally, it was felt it would be interesting to establish what economic incentives exist, or should be created, to encourage environmentally appropriate farming.

For a more detailed explanation of this, reference should be made to Figure A12. All measures with the aforementioned goal direction can be organized by the private sector, the local authority or central government, as individual examples show (e.g. tie-ridging at farm level, land terracing at local authority level, land use planning in water catchment areas at national level, etc.). Each of these measures is characterized by a need for a different economic factor (labour-intensive, capital-intensive, land-extensive, organization-intensive or regulation-intensive). Seen from a market-economy angle, the implementation of all these measures is, of course, possible to only a limited degree owing to factor restrictions at farm, local or national level. If, despite this, it is to be possible for all these measures to be widely taken in compliance with environmental requirements, central government must establish a system of incentives and support in the long term. This is normally reflected in an environmental policy requiring intersectoral and territorial coordination.

It is here that the aforementioned process of political negotiation and technical organization begins for the Zimbabwean government and for each local authority and each farm. This process should, as a rule, take place at three levels simultaneously, as a cooperative procedure integrated into the system (*cooperative governance*). That this has so far been done in hardly any country, let alone Zimbabwe, does not detract from the significance of the organizational framework described here. It just needs to be borne in mind that complex development processes (a particular example being the implementation of Agenda 21 at local level) can be undertaken only if the long-term goal is a functioning politico-economic regulatory framework that distributes the wide range of tasks appropriately. In Zimbabwe, as in any country, this is a difficult, lengthy and usually organization-intensive process. It requires institution-building, the achievement of transparency, the training of skilled personnel and financial resources to match.

In the 1980s, Zimbabwe had a comparatively favourable starting position in this respect, one that was essentially able to rely on the decentralized structures mentioned above (see Chapter 19.2.3 and Figure A9). The market-economy conditions for price incentives, for the support of extension and credit services and for land use planning related to the environment certainly existed. What was undoubtedly missing was a coherent agricultural and land reform policy that also took account of environmental interests at the various levels of government.

It is here that international development cooperation should have stepped in, but it was unable to do so for a number of reasons: the government did not yet have a coherent framework as outlined here for technical and financial assistance; it was not clear to the representatives of the development cooperation organizations how they should assist the country appropriately and in a coordinated way; Zimbabwe has not yet advanced beyond the initial stage of a national environmental action plan (National Conservation Strategy).[11] The political attempt to force through an implementation plan[12] intersectorally has similarly had very little success. All this eventually resulted in the support for the implementation of Agenda 21 disintegrating into a highly complicated array of unconnected public and, in particular, NGO measures. There is as yet no evidence of the impact they have had. It must be assumed that most of the national and international efforts and financial resources devoted to supporting the implementation of a national environmental action plan have been wasted.

Part V   Institutional and organizational implementation options

20   Attempt at a conceptual approach

Against the background, on the one hand, of a predominantly positive global experience of the decentralization of government and, on the other hand, of the efforts made in the past, unfortunately with little success, to implement complex development and cross-section reform projects effectively, an attempt will now be made to derive a comprehensible and logical approach to action from these two positions, combining one with the other. This will depend on the general application of the principles of *simplification, subsidiarity* and *least possible government intervention* referred to above.

With this borne in mind, the second step will be to define, on the basis of the subsidiarity principle and the arguments concerning *political, institutional* and *fiscal decentralization,* which have proved themselves in theory and practice, the structure within which complex development policy tasks should be performed in the future, a graduated division of tasks between *central government, civil society, the private sector* and *development cooperation organizations* and the main groups of actors in each case.

The final step will be to design an organizational framework which can be used in the long term (a) for the performance of central government's *core functions,* (b) for the appropriate delegation and devolution of development tasks, (c) for the involvement of the private sector and (d) for external support from development cooperation organizations, and which manages without parallel structures.

On the whole, related to development policy practice, this is a challenge of the first order for sectoral, local government and fiscal policy. It cannot possibly be met with individual projects, however well coordinated. What will be needed, on the other hand, is a long-term *process of coming closer to graduated development based on a division of labour* that is guided by its internal logic. Once this process begins, it is important that it should be irreversible. It should therefore be able to survive political rejection and not, as so often in the past, become bogged down in lame approaches that constantly fall short of what is needed.

Faced with such challenges to the partner countries, the international development cooperation community should, of course, adopt a new position. This applies both to planning and coordination procedures and to the allocation structure. Fortunately, recent approaches have already anticipated this in such important areas as the *setting of priorities, demands for coherence, the programme approach and budget financing* in development policy or, indeed, the *promotion of decentralization.* This probably marks the beginning of the evolution of what will be, it is to be hoped, a conception of development cooperation that remains viable in the long term. This might be an ideal course inasmuch as it could combine sustainability and broad-based development with the promotion of democracy from the bottom up.

To enable the reader to keep track of this attempt at an approach, *agriculturally based rural development* will be taken as the example in all the intellectual and empirically proven steps involved in the conceptualization. As emphasized on several occasions, however, the same could be demonstrated for any other cross-section spheres.

21   Poverty reduction through agriculturally based rural development

21.1   Sectoral integration

Authors engaged in the recent development debate[1] unanimously agree that for the sub-Saharan Africa countries with agricultural resource potential agriculturally based growth and rural development integrated into the economy as a whole are a basic requirement and one of the main levers for reducing poverty (see Part A, Chapters 10, 11 and 12). This growing realization is, as a rule, associated with follow-up developments and processes of making economic and social trends more dynamic. However, they can have a broad impact only if they are decentralized and involve the sections of the population living in the peripheral areas.

This view not only reflects long-known tenets of development theory that require balanced rural and urban, agricultural and industrial development (Hayami and Ruttan 1985, p. 40 ff.) but is also increasingly emphasized by development policy practitioners. Thus more than sixty representatives of government, international development cooperation organizations and NGOs from eleven African countries attending a conference on poverty in sub-Saharan Africa stated that:[2]

- Labour-intensive agricultural growth is particularly important for poverty reduction in Africa because agriculture provides employment for up to 70 per cent of the labour force, and up to 70 per cent of the poor live in rural areas;
- In most of Sub-Saharan Africa ... resources and decision-making are still heavily concentrated in central ministries, not at the local government or community level where the poor come in direct contact with available services;
- Many African governments still have ... political difficulty ... reallocating resources away from the better-off towards the poor;

- Poverty alleviation cannot be successfully addressed by African governments alone; experience has demonstrated that it must combine the complementary efforts of domestic private and non-governmental actors, the international donor community, international private investment, and, most important, the poor themselves;
- Governments should examine the elements of public regulations that have the most direct impact on the poor with a view to minimize such rules and regulations that hamper the poor in their daily economic and income-earning activities;
- Government should accord high priority to the potential for generating more resources for poverty alleviation through expenditure switching between and within sectors;
- Much greater attention should be given to ways of shifting government decision-making to the local level where the poor can actively participate and be encouraged to form civic and self-help organisations.

What is again clearly discernible in these findings is that the governments concerned and all the main groups of actors, including the private sector and the international donor community, are urged not to delay in charting the most important development policy courses for future poverty-reducing development. The focus is clearly indicated: (a) on the sectors with the greatest prospect of effective poverty reduction, and especially agricultural and rural development, where the national allocation of financial resources is concerned; (b) on decentralization and measures to ensure effective interaction among all the main groups of actors where the institutional and organizational sphere is concerned; (c) on the creation of favourable legal and investment conditions in the area of private-sector development.

It has also become clear from the practical experience of development gained by the World Bank (World Bank 1997b, p. 64 ff.) in 21 African countries that agricultural growth and the improvement of primary education and primary health care are the main pillars of any poverty-reducing development (see Figure A13). For most of these countries, however, it has also become clear that, besides an improvement in transport infrastructure, the promotion of non-agricultural income-generating measures is an important area of development policy action to reduce poverty.

The G8's Africa Action Plan (Kananaskis Summit 2002, p. 17 ff.), which takes up the African initiative of the *New Partnership for Africa's Development* (NEPAD), calls for a clear sign of the integration of agricultural and rural development into the national poverty reduction strategies.[3] It makes an equally clear reference to the most important strategic components, such as increases in agricultural productivity, sustainable management of natural resources, the improvement of entrepreneurial skills in farming, the clarification of rights of usufruct in natural resources, the promotion of gender-neutral technology development and the development of rural infrastructure.

On the whole, this reveals, from the angle of development policy practice and research, the range of policies that are decisive for poverty-reducing development. It requires of each and every country an institutional and organizational framework within which implementation appears realistic and is geared to the long term. All previous deliberations and past experience of decentralization in practice throughout the world indicate that this can be achieved only within the framework of a staggered, gradual and graduated development process based on a division of labour. Experience again shows that this process will take place in the countries concerned in different ways and in different sequences, stretching over several decades, during which it may well suffer repeated setbacks. Nevertheless, the principles taken as a basis here will have to be applied in one form or another if anything like justice is to be done to this complex task.

21.2 Graduated development based on a division of labour

Graduated development based on a division of labour in the area of relevance to poverty reduction and agricultural and rural development, thus needs to be geared to a clear strategy for political, institutional and fiscal decentralization; it also requires the participation of all the main groups of actors; and finally, it requires the concentration of public financial resources on or their reallocation to the priorities, which are agricultural development, primary education, primary health care and the development of rural infrastructure. How can this complex 'minimum demand' on a national government be met by political and organizational means in agreement with the main groups of actors?

Zambia is again an appropriate example. It clearly shows how the Agricultural Sector Investment Programme (ASIP), which was launched in 1996, must now be integrated into Zambia's Poverty Reduction Strategy (PRS) from 2001/2002. The Ministry of Finance and Economic Development (MFED 2001), which is responsible for the conception of the Poverty Reduction Strategy, requires all current ASIP subprogrammes (see Chapter 19.1) to be incorporated into a programme structure that contributes to food security and income generation and so to poverty reduction. The sectoral approach is not changed by this, but it is unambiguously related to a specific objective. This will be reviewed at regular intervals to see what progress has been made towards its achievement, this being the task of the Monitoring and Evaluation System which has meanwhile been established (but is still weak). This refocusing will have implications for the whole structure of MAFF services and expenditure. Central government has already taken appropriate preliminary political decisions and steps, including:

1   The revision of the decentralization policy,[4] with the aim of entrusting the intersectoral coordination of development at district and provincial level to the Ministry of Local Government and Housing (MLGH);
2   The deconcentration of the relevant sectoral ministries: Agriculture,[5] Roads, Health and Education;
3   The reform of the ministerial administration in the agricultural sector, together with a recommendation from the independent Agricultural Consultative

Forum (ACF) that it should concentrate on core development policy functions (see Chapter 19.1);

4   Privatization and private-sector development in such areas as agricultural marketing and input supply;

5   Donor coordination, together with a call to all development cooperation organizations involved to adopt a new position with a view to preparing themselves for a coordinated approach based on a division of labour to the implementation of the national Poverty Reduction Strategy.

These far-reaching steps are naturally accompanied by fierce political debate and by organizational and financial frictions. Where decentralization is concerned, for example, these frictions can be described as follows: the present legal requirement is that major public investment, as effected under the ASIP, for instance, be agreed with other important ministries, and especially the Ministry of Finance and Economic Development (MFED), the Ministry of Environment and Natural Resources (MENR), the Ministry of Communication and Transport (MCT), the Ministry of Lands (MOL), the Ministry of Community Development and Social Services (MCDSS) and, of course, the MLGH. At provincial and district level the bodies formally responsible are the Provincial Development Coordination Committees (PDCCs) and the District Development Coordination Committees (DDCCs). At district level primary responsibility for the coordination and guidance of development rests with the democratically legitimized District Councils.[6] The MLGH assists the Councils with this task in the rural communities through the Council Secretaries. Until 2000 the latter still chaired the DDCCs. The District Administrators appointed by the President for party-political reasons have now taken over as chairmen on the ground that 'inadequacies and weakness in the coordination of district development must be eliminated quickly.' Zambia's efforts to decentralize government have thus been disrupted. Rather than independent MLGH officials (Council Secretaries) chairing the DDCCs and so supporting the assembly of democratically legitimized District Councils, confidants of the President now exercise decentralized party rule over the district authorities. It must be assumed that this development will have a generally adverse effect on the implementation of current sectoral investment programmes. As this kind of development is unfortunately no exception in the sub-Saharan African countries, the process of political and institutional decentralization should be continued unwaveringly, with the long-term goals of democratization and poverty reduction borne in mind.

Frictions also occur in the area of privatization policy and private-sector development. The private sector's participation in the implementation of the ASIP forms an integral part of the sectoral programme, the underlying Zambian agricultural policy and the macroeconomic approach to the deregulation of the Zambian economy. At the meetings held by the donors to discuss their financial cooperation in the ASIP a distinction was therefore made from the outset between donor contributions to assist (a) the public sector, (b) the private sector through MAFF and (c) the private sector by the direct route (see Table A9). Of the donor organizations, SIDA, NEDA, USAID, the EU and NORAD make both a direct and an indirect financial contribution to private-sector development in agriculture. Direct contributions are made to enterprises in the agricultural trade and service sectors, while the indirect contributions go towards promotional measures through the ministry. But not even this differentiated approach has so far resulted in the service gap being closed in remote rural areas. In the difficult sphere of the privatization of agricultural marketing and input supply the ASIP will be more dependent in the future on support from central government, the provincial and district authorities and the organized private sector, the main goals here being (a) the rapid implementation of a national rural road programme, (b) the development of a national strategy for local economic development and (c) the development of a rural financial system.

Frictions of this and other kinds should be treated as perfectly normal difficulties caused by development; on no account should they be seen as a reason for depriving the process of graduated development based on a division of labour, once begun, of the important components which have been described above. One of the key components is the reallocation of public financial resources in conjunction with the progressive introduction of fiscal decentralization, and it is probably the most difficult requirement to meet. It therefore merits special attention.

21.3 Integrated local development

21.3.1 Expansion of fiscal autonomy

The gradual expansion of fiscal autonomy (see Chapter 16 and Table A5) is a major requirement if local authorities are to be able to co-finance intersectoral development programmes and cross-section programmes and so to stimulate self-sustaining local economic development. Unfortunately, the fiscal autonomy of local authorities in most sub-Saharan African countries is still extremely limited. Local taxes account for only 2.2 per cent of total tax revenue in Kenya and 5.5 per cent in South Africa, for example. The equivalent figure in the USA is about 14 per cent (see Table A7). Local authorities' budgets still consist predominantly of transfers from central government. Such transfers account for between 2 and 13 per cent of the total budgets of the sub-Saharan African countries, the proportion being 3.9 per cent in Kenya and 8.3 per cent in South Africa (see Table A8). Countries with (quasi-)federal structures, such as Nigeria and South Africa, lie at the upper end of the scale, countries with poorly developed decentralized structures at the lower end.

The ratio of local revenue (from local taxes, levies, fees, licences and rents) to central government transfers (recurrent and block grants) is about 1:3 in Uganda, as a study of 20 municipalities and districts shows (Livingstone and Charlton 2001, p. 83) (see Table A6). Block grants account for about 13 per cent of central government transfers. On the revenue side, local taxes are the largest item, at about 50 per cent, followed by market fees (20 per cent) and trade licences and other fees (8 per cent). Another interesting factor in Uganda's case is that fiscal decentralization has already made a certain degree of fiscal autonomy possible. This has also resulted in development cooperation contributions towards the financing of local development projects being received through local authority budgets.

The local taxation of rural households, farms and small businesses is still very difficult for most sub-Saharan African countries for economic, social and political reasons. The main problems are, of course, widespread poverty, the associated small or non-existent economic tax base, the general absence of wage labour and generally low tax rates. A relatively costly tax collection system would, moreover, have to be maintained for so little tax revenue. Both the widening of the rural tax base and the improvement of the tax collection system are therefore important preconditions for the strengthening of local fiscal autonomy in the long term.

It can be assumed that, as peasant agriculture begins to develop more dynamically, business activities increase and sectoral linkages grow, the general income, property and service situation will so improve that a more viable tax base may eventually emerge. If this tax base is to be used to reduce poverty, some basic questions need to be answered: what kind of tax is particularly conducive to development, what kind inhibits development, what kind might have a direct poverty-reducing effect, and what kind might have an indirect poverty-reducing effect?

The kind of tax which least inhibits development and which might be levied at the beginning of an initially modest fiscal attempt to support local economic development is a tax on land, cattle and business (Prudhomme 2001). Under a development-oriented fiscal policy other kinds of tax might then be extended to include rural areas, examples being wage tax, income tax and property transaction tax. The decisive factor in establishing a fiscal policy that focuses on poverty will be to choose a tax and a basis of assessment which do not curb local economic development.

It is also important to decide which level of government should have the power to levy taxes and how much of this power it should have to enable it to promote rural development with the instrument of fiscal decentralization. Decisions on this are of a far-reaching nature in social and development policy terms, but are at the centre of any effort to achieve decentralization. All that is certain in this context is that, while the lower territorial authorities have no appreciable tax revenue of their own, their position in negotiations with central government will remain weak.

21.3.2 Enlargement of the basis for local development financing

If the expansion of fiscal autonomy is to do more for integrated local development that is capable of performing cross-section development policy tasks, local financial management must be gradually improved and placed within a general development policy framework. This can only be done on the basis of the aforementioned four pillars of fiscal decentralization, which have usually still to be developed (see Chapter 16): (1) improving the revenue side, (2) securing central government transfers, (3) gearing the expenditure side more to development and (4) borrowing by local authorities. The expansion of fiscal autonomy will be a very laborious and lengthy process in itself. It should be viewed, on the whole, from the angle of co-financing using the local authorities' own revenue and central government transfers; it should also be accomplished in coherence with sectoral development financing and with the provision of external financial flows where this can be negotiated with the international development cooperation organizations.

It is only with these three components together (co-financing, sectoral financing and financing by the development cooperation community) that the financial base for local development in accordance with the subsidiarity principle will be created. Within this framework,

- first, central government should make its contribution by financing the local administration as such, the government transfers and the earmarked sectoral contributions,
- second, the local authorities should make their contribution from local revenue and (where possible) by borrowing,
- third, the private sector should make its contribution for its own account or through public–private partnership projects; and
- fourth, international development cooperation organizations should make their contributions in the form of technical cooperation, financial cooperation or NGO resources

(see Figures 3 and A11). The gradual institutionalization of this financing framework that complies with the subsidiarity principle is an important basic requirement for sustainable and broad-based development. It cannot be rated highly enough in national and international development policy. Once a certain degree of institutionalization has been achieved and a minimum of public financial control is guaranteed, it may also act as a special incentive to external financial donors, such as the international development cooperation community and local authority partnerships; this is particularly true where political decentralization is accompanied by fiscal decentralization, where, then, 'democracy and development' can occur on a sound financial basis of 'financing and development'. But there is a long way to go before that stage is reached.

In the meantime, transitional solutions, such as sector programme financing, must be used. Sector programme financing is, however, based on a complicated mechanism, which very often runs parallel to internal development financing, for instance via a basket fund. It cannot therefore be seen as a permanent solution. Consequently, external development financing should eventually be integrated into the internal financing mechanism in the form of general, sector-related or decentralized budget financing (see Figure 3). But this is bound to be followed by a call for an improvement in public financial management and for joint public financial control. The latter is problematical because it touches on national sovereign rights.

21.3.3 Integration into government as a whole

According to the subsidiarity principle, local development integrated into government as a whole is a task for various of the levels of government and the main groups of actors. The graduated responsibility for development based on a division of labour in accordance with the subsidiarity principle which applies to the local level must also apply to the higher levels in the long term. Hence the desirability of 'coherent development policy'. Where it cannot be achieved in the long term for internal reasons, there are likely to be development blockades between levels of government, a lack of simultaneity in development, regional disintegration or even political conflicts. To counteract this, significant compensatory payments would have to be made from the public purse, for example, or in the form of disproportionately high intergovernmental transfers.

There is, of course, hardly a country in which this 'coherent development policy' can be sustained. It must be constantly sought nonetheless. In keeping with the minimum requirement referred to above a gradual approach should therefore be adopted, but it should be irreversible in itself, as in South Africa's case. South Africa is able to pursue this objective because it has placed its local development on a sound constitutional footing from the outset, as the following quotation proves:

> ... Central government is now exploring different national settings for co-ordinating policies in a decentralized government system. Currently, national policies are being set by central line ministries, but financing and implementation are in the hands of subnational governments. The coordination of national policies with an emerging multi-tiered system of governance is an important issue in the development and execution of the inter-governmental system as prescribed by the constitution.[7]

In other, non-federal countries legal preparations should first be made for decentralization policies, or laws should be appropriately amended. Where this is not (immediately) politically possible, preliminary steps should at least be taken through the preparation of existing local government structures specifically for their development mandate. As in the cases of Zambia, Malawi and some other countries referred to above (see Chapter 10), provision can also be made for this to be supported by development cooperation organizations. This would mean that, under the prescriptions of political, institutional and fiscal decentralization and a division of labour between central government, civil society, the private sector and international development cooperation organizations in accordance with the subsidiarity principle, the organizational and institutional conditions for graduated development should be created over a fairly long period at all levels of government. This process cannot, however, succeed without the binding force of a strong central government (Presidential Review Commission 1998, p. 5). It may run the risk of weakening the nation state as a whole.[8] In some cases, this may result in disintegration (Somalia). It is therefore important for decentralization and graduated development based on a division of labour to be seen as a long-term process, in which the integration of local communities into government as a whole must always be borne in mind.

In addition, it should be accepted that decentralization and integrated local development proceed at different speeds and with the backing of bodies whose efficiency differs (local authorities, provincial authorities, central government, individual groups of actors). They may encourage each other's development, occasionally compete with one another or even stand in each other's way. There may well be periods in which local development is slowed down while the development of central government dominates, or vice versa. In Zambia, for example, massive support from development cooperation organizations under the Agricultural Sector Investment Programme has resulted in the newly established, deconcentrated District Agricultural Offices disputing the district authorities' competence for development (GTZ 2001b, p. 4 ff.). Most sub-Saharan African countries currently find themselves at stages where their decentralization projects are proceeding at varying speeds and have reached varying levels of maturity. According to many experts,[9] this is a normal course for development to follow. It should, in any case, be promoted as long as it is remembered that the goal is to integrate the local authorities firmly into government as a whole in development policy and fiscal terms and to involve them in general development.

This integration into government as a whole, which must be the objective and must be constantly promoted, is the real challenge if any intersectoral development or cross-section development policy task is to be successfully achieved or performed. Whether this integration effort occurs at the same time as sectoral development, in advance of administrative reform or subsequently will not determine the success of the project as a whole (see Chapter 8). What is decisive is that vertical integration (from central government through provincial to local level) and horizontal integration (across the various sectors) are progressively consolidated, thus enabling due account to be taken of the hybrid nature of decentralization (political and socio-economic) (Silverman 1992, p. 17). The institutional and organizational mechanisms that can support this are discussed below along two lines of argument, as taken as the basis in Part A, Section IV, and in Figure A11.

Agricultural development and sustainable food security, health care (including measures to combat HIV-AIDS), the promotion of initial and advanced training and the development of physical infrastructure are the sectoral, vertically structured pillars of agriculturally based and poverty-reducing rural development. The local government system (in its various country-specific forms) is similarly a vertical structure of central government. It is designed to be able to link sector-wide development programmes and cross-section programmes (environment, gender, poverty reduction, etc.) to one another horizontally. The institutional and organizational mechanism that promotes this process of integration and should therefore be gradually expanded manifests itself primarily in the intersectoral planning and coordinating bodies and their respective technical committees at central government, provincial, district and possibly local level (see Chapter 19.2). It is of the utmost importance for the long-term process of the development of society as a whole that the control of this process become increasingly democratic. As emphasized on a number of occasions, this is taking place within the framework of the process of political decentralization and the promotion of democracy, which is in constant need of fresh stimulation and, where appropriate, external support (see Chapter 12).

Under the premises adopted in this study that

- poverty reduction in most African countries is most likely to be achieved through agriculturally based rural development backed by the development of social safeguards, training and infrastructure;
- the necessary broad-based development can, however, be achieved only in a gradual process of integrating sectoral priorities and territorial development into government as a whole through decentralized structures,

it can be inferred that national Poverty Reduction Strategies can be implemented only if they

1   are comprehensively integrated into development policy and are competently overseen by central government;
2   are sectorally related one to another (integrated) and prioritized;
3   can be implemented in a decentralized way; and, finally
4   are sustainably supported by fiscal policy.

The support of fiscal policy is, as has been emphasized on several occasions, of primary importance both for sector-wide programmes and for cross-section development policy tasks. The levers that can be used at local level in this context – which are only effective, of course, in conjunction with the sectorally based budget allocations from the central administration – are:

- Changes in expenditure on local government tasks in favour of agriculturally based poverty-reducing rural development (*accountability* under development policy);
- Improvement of the revenue structure in favour of local economic development (*devolution of power* to collect taxes and levies for development policy purposes);
- Use of intergovernmental transfers for local measures to promote poverty-reducing rural development (*redistribution* under development policy) and
- participation in *public borrowing* and *public–private partnerships* for the development and improvement of local infrastructure.

The general integration of the Poverty Reduction Strategy into development policy, its control by financial policy and the setting of sectoral priorities can only be done at central government level. This, however, requires the *checks and balances* of local representative bodies and their umbrella associations (e.g. SALGA in South Africa), bodies representing the private sector and their trade associations and the CSOs, CBOs and NGOs. There is also a need for internal monitoring, which can be achieved through the decentralized coordinating mechanisms themselves (M&E systems) (see Chapter 19.1). The most important area of planning that requires coordination is the allocation of resources in line with a medium-term financial policy. This is true both of the central government level and of the subnational levels, provided that there is any possibility of intersectoral negotiation on financial allocations at these lower levels. In such cases, the proportion set aside in the budget estimates for the sectors which together contribute to agriculturally based poverty-reducing rural development is the decisive factor. Related solely to agricultural development, it is currently well below the appropriate percentage in most sub-Saharan African countries (see Part A, Chapter 7).[10]

21.3.4 Medium-term financial planning

From the organizational diagrams in Figures 3 and A11 it is evident that, seen from the partner countries' point of view, there are two options for steering cross-section programmes towards poverty reduction: (a) a central, budget policy option, whereby the allocation (or reallocation) of public funds would have to be negotiated intersectorally in keeping with a nationally defined Poverty Reduction Strategy, and (b) a decentralized option supported by fiscal policy; in this case, local expenditure and government transfers would have to be guided to accord with a subnationally defined Poverty Reduction Strategy; this could be done both vertically and horizontally.

All these various factors presuppose, however, the existence of a set of financial and fiscal policy instruments which guide national and local revenue and central government expenditure on earmarked grants (sectoral resources) and untied budget allocations (block grants) and prepare them for a medium-term planning framework. What is needed, then, is a Medium-Term Income and Expenditure Framework (MTIEF). With its help public financial resources for sectoral development and decentralized territorial development which have to be provided for poverty reduction purposes can be integrated into a general framework. Only then will it be possible and appropriate for the resources from (c), external development financing, to be so integrated that their centralized or decentralized inclusion in an overall coherent concept of development financing becomes feasible. In this, as Figure 3 shows, different forms of development financing can well be used: general budget financing (c_1), sectoral budget financing (c_2) or decentralized budget financing (c_5). The implications this may have for international development cooperation are considered in Chapter 22.

In Uganda public revenue from local taxes, levies, fees and licences accounted in the 1995–96 financial year for an average of 31 per cent and central government transfers for 69 per cent of the budgets of 20 districts or municipalities studied; 13 per cent of the government transfers consisted of block grants. Contributions from international donor organizations amounted to 10 per cent of revenue and were included either in the block grants or the transfers (see Table A9). At that time, however, donors' funds did not yet figure in the medium-term financial planning, but took the form of untied or earmarked funds. It will be for countries with similarly temporary financial structures to integrate such funds into a coherent public budget system in the future so as to create for both sides procedures which are transparent and binding.

The argument that fiscal decentralization also leads to the 'decentralization of corruption' cannot be simply dismissed, but does not in principle rule out decentralization. The financing risk associated with decentralized local development funds is probably no greater *in summa* than the conventional approach to the financing of public capital projects through a central finance department. When the risks (such as poor financial control, waste of resources and nepotism) are weighed up against the benefits for development (such as ownership, the avoidance of parallel structures, transparent procedures and the achievement of broad-based development), the latter must be rated more highly.

21.3.5 Local development management

The difficulties facing the governments of the 22 sub-Saharan African countries currently implementing agricultural and other sector-wide investment programmes with international assistance have been evaluated in an initial study within the framework of the Strategic Partnership with Africa (KfW 2000, p. 3 ff.). Surveys of 30 sector programmes in 18 countries clearly revealed the following:

- 'National and sectoral implementation capacity' with respect to sectoral programmes and their integration into development policy is difficult to achieve.
- 'National, sectoral and decentralized budget management' generally causes serious difficulties.
- 'Decentralized implementation capacity', i.e. local development management, similarly causes serious difficulties.

These findings (which are also very familiar from other contexts) basically endorse the observations on integrated development in the previous chapters: although sectoral programmes appear theoretically and conceptually plausible, they can be implemented only if they are combined with steps towards institutional and fiscal decentralization. With these conclusions borne in mind, what needs to be clarified is how current sectoral programmes can be continued or, if appropriate, integrated into the national Poverty Reduction Strategies. According to everything that this study has so far been able to do to help answer these questions, there are two approaches that should be adopted in the long term:

1   Adaptation of the sector-wide approach on the basis of a structural reform that sets simultaneous or subsequent decentralization in motion; and
2   creation of clear and manageable mechanisms for rural development to be financially supported by central government, local government and interna-

tional development cooperation organizations in accordance with the subsidiarity principle.

Unless these two approaches are adopted, the sectoral programmes are likely to continue in the suboptimal range or, indeed, to peter out. The instruments hitherto created, such as joint financing through a basket fund, are no more than interim solutions, which should eventually be abandoned. The question that still needs to be considered here, then, is how the sustainable institutional and organizational integration of agriculturally based rural development (and other cross-section tasks) into local development is to be achieved. Let us begin by examining the extremely troublesome issue of the management of local development financing. From the sectoral programmes, we know that it has not yet been possible to find a satisfactory solution to the problem of financial management either through the basket fund or within the framework of internal sectoral management. One reason for this is undoubtedly that the established financial management systems (FMSs) are not integrated into the local structure of development financing, but continue to be attached to the line structures of the sectoral ministries. This is due to the fact that in most cases fiscal decentralization has not yet advanced very far.

In the long term the sectoral (central government) and local (decentralized) financing strands should thus be united. The financial contributions made by a public works ministry to rural road-building (capital expenditure), for example, might be combined with the financial transfers of a local government ministry for road maintenance (recurrent expenditure), and this might, in turn, be combined with the spending of an agriculture ministry on a food-for-work programme (payments in kind) to form expenditure on poverty-reducing rural development. To make this approach amenable to the law, a fund for targeted poverty-reducing local development could be established. It might act as a structure for receiving decentralized transfers from international development cooperation organizations. In this way the foundations might be laid for joint financing for a specific purpose (see Chapter 22).

If individual local authorities are one day to be able to improve their local revenue situation to about one-quarter of their total revenue as the local economy develops, there might also be an incentive for development cooperation organizations to support them directly. Or, to put it the other way round, the prospect of financial support from international development cooperation organizations might encourage the local authorities to improve their local revenue situation. They might at least ensure that they concentrate revenue from local taxes, fees and licences on priority development measures in keeping with the goal of poverty reduction. From the mix of (a) financial contributions from local revenue, (b) central government transfers and (c) external grants, a new financial basis for self-sustaining growth might be created at local level. On this basis such complementary sectoral development as the modernization of farming, the development of business activities and the improvement of infrastructure, with the private sector involved, would then be particularly effective. If these developments are to succeed, there is no doubt that it is extremely important for a locally generated development fund for public measures to be established. Before this important question can be answered, however, further financial policy explanations would be needed, and they should be devoted specifically to the area of agricultural credit and rural finance (Giehler 1999, p. 35 ff.).

Against the background of such multi-layered structures, local financial management is possible only within the framework of soundly assembled local co-ordinating structures (see Figure A12). Experience shows that achieving this usually involves a tough process of negotiation and adjustment. It is vital that it be made absolutely clear in these structures (from local councils through technical committees to interest and self-help groups):

- what the local government priorities are and how they are to be pursued (local development strategy);
- what financial resources are available, from what sources and in what time frame (incoming receipts budget);
- how the financial resources are to be spent (outgoing payments budget);
- what human, financial and physical resources the private sector and the self-help groups have and how they are to be integrated into local development (operations plan);
- what estimated benefit is likely to accrue from local development financing, sectoral contributions and private-sector involvement (cost–benefit estimate).

This transparency can only and must be ensured by a local council, however elected. To this end, it should use various technical committees, the number of which can, however, only be very small for capacity reasons. Local financial and development planning is undoubtedly one of the most important tasks for these committees. It goes without saying that it is a task which can be performed satisfactorily by few rural authorities in sub-Saharan Africa at present. This, then, is a large and worthwhile area of activity in the long term for international development cooperation in the context of institution- and capacity-building and especially local financial management. Measures to reform administrative structures should begin in the next five to ten years, initially at provincial level. On this basis, the district levels should then be expanded in keeping with a system of developmental local government. Both can only be done against the background of a reasonably balanced national budget, perceptible rural economic growth and significant tax revenue.

22   New ways for development cooperation support

22.1   Financial requirements for poverty-oriented rural development

Given the circumstances indicated above, the support that international development cooperation organizations give to poverty-oriented rural development should be restructured. The requirements for long-term structural development, which will undoubtedly take decades in some countries, primarily concern the core areas, which can again be summarized as follows:

- *Agricultural development* comprising the areas of (a) price, market and trade policy, (b) agricultural innovation and technology development, (c) improvement of agricultural services and (d) support for agricultural reforms (see Part A, Chapter 15);
- *Promotion of social development* in the main areas of (a) primary education, (b) vocational training and (c) primary health case and measures to combat HIV/AIDS;
- *Promotion of institution- and capacity-building* in the areas of (a) grass-roots and local democratic structures, (b) local development financing and coordination and (c) rules on the administration of justice and the setting of standards;
- *Promotion of rural infrastructure development* in the areas of (a) roads, (b) transport and communications, (c) energy, (d) local markets, (e) irrigation and drinking water and (f) refuse disposal.

In some of these areas project approaches may well still be appropriate here and there, especially where the development cooperation projects are complete in themselves, such as advanced agricultural training and local general accounting. Nonetheless, the tendency should now be for integrated programme approaches to be adopted. But, as in the case of the current Sector Investment Programmes, they too should eventually be anchored at local authority level and integrated into government as a whole, as has been suggested above. These portents indicate that the international development cooperation community can look forward to a call for support in three areas:

1 Institution-building culminating in efficient decentralized sectoral and government administration structures;
2 Capacity-building to produce personnel skilled in the areas of development management, sectoral coordination and financial planning;
3 Budget management based on gradual fiscal decentralization.

The first and second points have been discussed at length in the previous chapters, and to conclude, the third will now be considered in greater depth. The issue examined in this context will be the currently much discussed question of the financial instruments most suitable for supporting programmes which are anchored at local authority level and integrated into government as a whole. Of primary concern here is the further development of basket funding and budget aid.

22.2   Budget aid

We begin with a statement by Wiemann (2001) on the appropriateness in development policy terms of the transition from project to budget aid, which does, however, address the need for reform in the direction of fiscal decentralization (Wiemann 2001, p. 3):

> The major challenge for the donors will be to agree on the countries which satisfy the internal requirements for the introduction of programme and budget aid. Only where the internal situation favours reforms is it realistic to expect that budget aid will help to increase the recipient countries' feeling of ownership, to gear their policies more to poverty, to make the partners' development strategies coherent, to make programmes and the external support they receive more effective and to improve donor coordination.

This said, budget aid will be considered here in the form not of general budget financing (balance-of-payments financing) but of decentralized budget financing, that is to say the *budget financing of sectoral budgets* and of *government transfers to local authorities for local development tasks aimed at reducing poverty*, which needs to be examined on a country-by-country basis. Related to the above statement, this would mean (a) supporting the partner countries' willingness to undertake reforms with a view to achieving more fiscal autonomy and (b) dovetailing the process of public revenue and expenditure planning with the process of decision-making on development policy at central and local government level. It would also mean (c) helping to develop the overall national financial framework for integrated sectoral development and for decentralized territorial development.

If these three processes are to be set in motion in the medium to long term, the introduction of *medium-term financial planning* is unavoidable. It might be undertaken after prior political decision-making before the end of each financial year and come into effect at the beginning of the next financial year. Where agriculturally based rural development is concerned, it should establish a Medium-Term Expenditure Framework (MTEF) for the four core requirements listed in Chapter 22.1 (promotion of agriculture, social development, institution-building and infrastructure development). It goes without saying that this expenditure framework – divided into recurrent and capital expenditure – can be established only against the background of the medium-term national estimate of revenue, including new borrowings in compliance with financial policy. External financial contributions from the various development cooperation institutions, including World Bank funds for the Poverty Reduction Support Credit (PRSC), should now appear in this expenditure framework. The PRSC would be entered under general budget financing, but could be used for decentralized budgeting.

So far we have unfortunately been moving in largely uncharted territory in financial, fiscal and development policy terms. With the inclusion of the financing of the local government system (which differs from one country to another) as a sponsor of regional development (*developmental local government*) we are treading new ground, but ground that is very important where development policy is concerned. The conventional sectoral ministries are now joined in medium-term financial planning by the internal administration, with local government as a sponsor of development. Besides its function of mediating between government and civil society (through political and institutional decentralization), local government performs a complementary, development-financing function (through fiscal decentralization). In this dual function it might now also be supported by development cooperation institutions in a relatively simple, but above all coherent way by means of the established (or still to be established) lever of government financial transfers to the local authorities. In plain language, the development cooperation institutions might deliberately use the government transfer mechanism to support poverty-oriented local government projects; the PRSCs provided by the World Bank might also be used for this purpose.

The development cooperation organizations should not, in this context, finance the recurrent costs either of the sectoral ministries or of the local government system, but focus on poverty-reducing development investments at local level. This could be done without costly and usually parallel counterpart structures being created. Where, however, poverty-reducing development investments become necessary in a sectoral context, they could still be planned by the appropriate ministerial administration as the body responsible and co-financed by the development cooperation institution concerned by means of sectoral budget financing (see Figure 3).

The subsidization of government financial transfers by the international donor community undoubtedly requires a functioning supervisory and monitoring system. Where this system does not yet exist or is inadequately endowed, it should be established or improved. Here again, the development cooperation organizations can participate in various ways. It might also usefully combine the necessary auditing with programme evaluation. At regular intervals joint budget audits might reveal whether budget funds from external sources had been used in keeping with the national Poverty Reduction Strategy.

22.3 Joint financing as an interim solution

The joint financing of current Sector Investment Programmes cannot be seen as anything other than an interim solution, given the development policy prospects described here. It will continue only until the permanent institutional and fiscal decentralization mechanisms take effect. For quite a number of sub-Saharan African countries programme financing by means of a basket fund will therefore continue to be the appropriate, though suboptimal, mechanism for a transitional period.

Unlike budget financing through a given sectoral budget (sectoral budget financing) or by means of an existing transfer mechanism of the local administration (decentralized budget financing), conventional programme financing is an administratively complex mechanism, because it occupies structures alongside the budget finance system (see Figure 3). For both sides, donor and recipient organizations, this means that additional checks are necessary and that the co-ordination question can never be answered unambiguously.

The question of the co-financing of local development funds by means of a basket fund alongside the budget finance system is again problematical. If a fund of this kind is to be effective, after all, the highest level of local financial control must come from within the supervisory jurisdiction of a democratically legiti-mized municipal or district council; furthermore, financial management must be subordinated to the professional budgeting of an independent treasurer or chief accountant. Both bodies form part of the local government system. For a local development fund fed from a basket fund, extensive monitoring and procedural mechanisms should first be created.

Finally, it is only with the aid of integrated local development funds that pub-lic–private partnership projects can be launched. This kind of cooperation be-tween the public and private sectors calls for clearly defined responsibilities and rules on liability. These cannot be achieved with parallel financing mechanisms. A local development fund must be subject to clear audit criteria. There is also a need for a regular financial check by the external investors, including representa-tives of the international development cooperation community. It is hoped that the mix of (a) the local authorities' development investments, (b) the participa-tion of their representatives in planning and monitoring, (c) the participation of the local private sector, (d) the development orientation of intergovernmental transfers and (e) supplementary assistance from international development co-operation will create far more favourable conditions for broad-based develop-ment than has hitherto been the case with centrally planned investments in rural development.

Part VI Conclusions and recommendations

23 Conclusions

The general conclusion to be drawn from this part of the study is that prominence should be given to the complementary development policy role to be played by African local authorities in the achievement of agriculturally based economic development. As some 80 per cent of the poor in sub-Saharan Africa live in rural areas, the gradual creation or the strengthening of development-oriented community structures is an essential precondition for poverty reduction. Only through decentralized development, achieved on the basis of political, institutional and fiscal decentralization, can broad-based socio-economic development and processes of democratization from the bottom up take place simultaneously. Within this framework international measures in support of intersectoral development programmes can also be more effectively integrated in accordance with the principle of the graduated division of labour and responsibility for development between the local population, the private sector, the local authorities and central government.

This being the case, the local authorities must do far more than in the past to face up to the challenge of making efficient use of their own assets and external financing for local economic development with a view to reducing poverty; they are also repeatedly urged to practise democracy and development on specific projects by eliciting democratic decisions on the use of the scarce resources provided by themselves and obtained from external sources. Both having constantly to deal with the hard realities of development financing constraints democratically and implementing majority decisions on development in a decentralized structure governed by the subsidiarity principle probably form the ideal course for future poverty-oriented development. Following this course successfully will undoubtedly require staying power of all concerned, both in the partner countries and in the international development cooperation community.

This staying power is, however, already heralded in the new ACP-EU Partnership Agreement. In this connection, much is expected not only of the conventional central government actors but also of the provincial and local authorities as future complementary development partners who should be taken seriously.[1]

24 Recommendations

The deliberations in Parts A and B and the conclusions drawn from them now enable a number of practical recommendations to be made. They are very largely in the nature of long-term prospects for development sequences. The measures involved could be implemented in different sequences, consecutively, simultaneously or in advance; what is decisive is that they comply with the premise of implementation that focuses on agricultural and rural development, is decentralized and is based on a division of labour. This could be supported by the development cooperation community in the following ways:

1   Helping partner governments to improve the performance of their agricultural administrations with the prospect of deconcentration and orientation towards poverty-reducing services for the subsistence and small-scale farming sector and of privatization for the commercial farming sector.

2   Helping partner governments to conceive and plan decentralized agricultural reforms; they should be undertaken with the prospect of achieving a division of labour between central government (the agriculture ministry and its subnational offices), local authorities, the private sector and the development cooperation organizations; in this, central government would be responsible for overall planning and guidance and for sectoral financing, the local authorities for regional and land use planning and for the co-financing of the local cost components, the private farming sector for farm development planning and cost-sharing by farms and the development cooperation organizations for reform policy back-stopping and co-financing by means of the decentralized financing mechanisms (see point 12).

3   Helping partner governments to develop national land registers, with the prospect of different land use and property titles being allocated, in accordance with the land tenure system of the country concerned; if land markets emerge, they should be so regulated that they do not aggravate the poverty situation.

4   Helping partner governments to develop a cooperative savings and loan system for agriculture and small-scale business on the model of the Raiffeisen purchasing, marketing and credit cooperatives, with the prospect of overcoming the farming and small business sectors' chronic undercapitalization in the medium term.

5   Helping partner governments to increase the effect of state agricultural research, with the prospect of its being focused on poverty-reducing research efforts (innovations that increase productivity, protect the environment and make work easier) on the one hand and privatization (formation of private research and extension schemes) on the other.

6   Helping partner governments and local authorities to improve and maintain the rural road network with the help of innovative forms of co-financing and participation involving central government, local authorities and the private sector; the commitment to reduce poverty in peripheral areas should be taken

into account through targeted transfers from central government to the local authorities concerned.

7 Helping partner governments to (further) develop national decentralization policies in the regulatory and fiscal policy spheres.

8 Helping partner governments to develop and expand decentralized organizational structures in the areas of local administration and the most important line ministries for poverty reduction, such as, in particular, the agriculture, health, education and training and public works ministries; the deconcentrated government subnational offices should recruit their staff from headquarters so as to avoid inflating the administration; on the whole, deconcentration should tend to result in a leaner apparatus of state.

9 Helping partner governments to train skilled and managerial staff in the decentralized offices and local administrations and to build development-oriented local planning and coordinating structures to improve local economic development management.

10 Helping partner governments to step up sustained cooperation between central government and its sectoral ministries, organized civil society and its NGOs, CBOs and CSOs, the organized private sector and its associations, the local authorities and PPP representatives in accordance with the subsidiarity principle; this cooperation should be achieved through institutionalized participation mechanisms of developmental local government.

11 Helping partner governments gradually to expand fiscal autonomy as a requirement for the local authorities to co-finance intersectoral development programmes and programmes of a cross-section nature and to be able to stimulate self-sustaining local economic development.

12 Helping partner governments to reform their financial administrations with a view both to strengthening the fiscal autonomy of the lower territorial authorities and to including new forms of external development financing; besides sectoral budget financing, decentralized budget financing can be considered in this context; the latter might use either the mechanisms of intergovernmental transfers or decentralized development funds; at district level *local development funds* might be established; this would also entail, of course, help with the development of effective independent financial control, which might also be used as a level of audit in the context of evaluation measures.

Notes

Part I: Global framework for sustainable and poverty-reducing agricultural and rural development

1 United Nations Conference on Environment and Development (UNCED), 1992, Agenda 21, Rio de Janeiro.
2 The four sections of Agenda 21 cover: 1. Social and economic dimensions, 2. Conservation and management of resources for development, 3. Strengthening the role of major groups and 4. Means of implementation.
3 Agenda 21, Chapter 28: Local authorities' initiatives in support of Agenda 21.
4 Federal Ministry for Economic Cooperation and Development (BMZ) (2000a): Wer braucht Entwicklung?, p. 24, Bonn.
5 World Food Summit (1996): Rome Declaration on World Food Security and the World Food Summit Plan of Action, Rome.
6 FAO (2000): Food insecurity: when people live with hunger and fear starvation. The state of food insecurity in the world 2000, Rome.
7 Rome Declaration on World Food Security and the World Food Summit Plan of Action (1996), p. 24, Objective 3.5: To formulate and implement integrated rural development strategies in low and high potential areas.
8 After the preamble, the CCD is divided into six parts and four annexes on regional implementation in Africa, Asia, Latin America and the northern Mediterranean region. Part I defines terms, objectives and principles for the achievement of the objectives of the convention, Part II contains general provisions and obligations entered into by the contracting parties, Part III sets out prescriptions for action programmes, scientific and technical cooperation and support measures, Part IV names the institutions and governs institutional proceedings, Part V specifies procedures, and Part VI consists of concluding provisions of international law.
9 Deutsche Gesellschaft für Technische Zusammenarbeit, GTZ (2001), Konventionsprojekt Desertifikationsbekämpfung, (CCD), p. 16 ff.
10 United Nations Resolution (2000), p. 5: 'To halve, by the year 2015, the proportion of the world's people whose income is less than one dollar a day and the proportion of people who suffer from hunger and, by the same date, to halve the proportion of people who are unable to reach or to afford safe drinking water.'
11 BMZ (2001a): Elfter Bericht zur Entwicklungspolitik der Bundesregierung, p. 59 ff.
12 BMZ (2001b): Armutsbekämpfung – eine globale Aufgabe. Aktionsprogramm 2015. Der Beitrag der Bundesregierung zur weltweiten Halbierung extremer Armut, Bonn.
13 The World Bank (2000): http://www.worldbank.org/poverty/strategies/overview.htm.
14 The World Bank (2001): PRSP Sourcebook (Public Spending for Poverty Reduction).
15 The World Bank (2001): PRSP Sourcebook (Overview), p. 6.
16 Results of a 1993 IFPRI study on the question of the financial support needed by the agricultural sector in 34 low- and middle-income countries shows that there is a 75

per cent correlation between agricultural and general economic growth in LDCs and a 21 per cent correlation in middle-income countries.

Part II: Realistic problem-solving approaches

1 This debate included a cross-section evaluation of the statements made in Agenda 21 (Chapter 14), the CCD and the new World Bank rural development strategy and at the IFPRI 20-20 Vision Conference, Bonn 2002.
2 The Stein-Hardenberg reforms resulted in the passing of state laws in Prussia which – combined with an appeal to the citizens to participate in their implementation – initiated the following reform projects and gradually led to success throughout Germany: (a) reform of public administration, (b) reform of the regulations governing rural authorities, of the district and provincial councils and of provincial government, (c) introduction of the freedom to engage in trade and other economic activity, (d) secularization of Church property and (e) emancipation of the peasantry and agricultural reform.

'Hardenberg yielded to agrarian liberalism, thus establishing rational agriculture and paving the way for agro-technical progress. Stein recognized the need for the historical foundations to be organically incorporated into the development tasks of the present.' (Brockhaus Enzyklopädie, 20th edition, 1999, Wiesbaden).
3 African Union (2002): The New Partnership for Africa's Development, NEPAD, and especially points 80, 82, 83, 88, 102, 117 and 154.
4 This situation is currently being changed by a reform of local government areas, the aim being to arrive at viable administrative units and reduce the number of municipalities to between 400 and 500.

Part III: Importance for development policy of, preconditions for and effects of decentralization

1 To name but a few: N. Djafari, M. Gräfe, C. von Haldenwang, K. Hinrichs, H.F. Illy, A. Mehler, W. Meyer, R. Pitschas, W. Polte, W. Rather, K. Simon, M. Steinich, W. Thomi, C. Twerenbold-Wippermann, R. Vaubel and M. Wieland.
2 Statement by representatives of South Africa at a regional forum on the question of Sector Wide Approaches: Do They Really Help the Poor?, Accra/Ghana, 13–16 November 2001.
3 The conclusion drawn in a cross-section evaluation of decentralization commissioned by the BMZ and a joint BMZ/UNDP evaluation of decentralization and local government is that '12 projects and programmes examined have certainly been able to lay the foundations for long-term political changes, e.g. by stimulating the formulation of a national decentralization strategy. The evaluated projects had succeeded in principle in developing capacities, especially at local level, and, perhaps even more importantly, in increasing awareness of the need for decentralization at all political levels. Highly commendable results have thus been achieved. However, it is reaffirmed in both evaluations that the projects and programmes often fail to achieve the goals set and to live up to the declarations of political intent by the partner governments.' (Hinrichs, K., 2001, p. 283 ff.).

4   Guidelines on development cooperation in which the German Länder engage are summarized in the decisions of the Prime Ministers of the Länder of 9 July 1998, 1 December 1994 and 28 October 1988.

Part IV: Decentralization and development cooperation priorities

1   In her book 'Aid to Africa. So Much to Do, So Little Done', C. Lancaster (1999) summarizes the errors and weaknesses that have so far accumulated in international development cooperation with the African countries as follows: 'inadequate owner-ship, overloading of local capacity to coordinate donor proliferation, lack of financial sustainability and institutional development, weak public sector management, patch-work management of development assistance' (p. 220 ff.).

2   In this case, the AfDB, EU, FAO, FINNIDA, GTZ, IDA, IFAD, JICA, NEDA, NORAD, SIDA, UNDP and USAID.

3   GTZ (2001b), p. 4: The evaluation report makes it clear: 'One of the essential findings of the evaluation of the ASIP is that sectoral programmes and decentralization should run in parallel: in its decentralization policy Zambia has only just begun to distinguish government at the national, provincial, district and ward levels. The distribution of po-litical and therefore development policy roles among these levels in accordance with the subsidiarity principle and the processes of negotiation among the representatives of politics, society and the private sector are still very poorly developed. The danger of an excessively powerful central government, a one-party state and clientelism re-emerging has not yet been averted. Sectoral programmes, however, require all-party central and local government steering structures capable of taking action to set in mo-tion the essential processes of democratic participation, the coordination of develop-ment policy and the development of the private sector. Sectoral programmes and de-centralization are thus mutually dependent. Where, then, development cooperation supports sectoral programmes, it would be well advised to promote decentralization as well, and where it strengthens local government structures, it also promotes the capac-ity for implementing sectoral programmes. Close collaboration within development cooperation in both areas of promotion is thus likely to be the ideal course in the fu-ture in broad-based territorial development and the promotion of local government and democracy.'

4   After a Green Paper on the subject had been submitted to wide-ranging consultations lasting over a year and embracing all sections of the population and discussed in depth at provincial workshops and conferences and at a national conference, a White Paper was presented to the cabinet for its approval in 1998. In the ensuing legislative proce-dure three related, but separate laws were passed: the Local Government Municipal Structures Act (1998), the Local Government Municipal Demarcation Act (1998) and the Local Government Systems Act (2000). The ministry responsible for the imple-mentation of these local government laws is the Ministry of Local Government and Provincial Affairs, so named in 2000.

5   ZANU (PF) stands for Zimbabwean African National Union (Patriotic Front).

6   The RDP is a national reconstruction and development programme which emerged from the Zimbabwe Conference on Reconstruction and Development (ZIMCORD) held in 1981 and has been implemented under the national strategy of 'growth with equity' by various government departments with the support of international devel-opment cooperation.

7 The DDF is a parastatal body which has implemented a programme financed by do-nors (mainly the KfW) for the reconstruction of rural infrastructure destroyed during the war of independence and is now responsible for the maintenance of district roads.

8 The resettlement programme was financed mainly by the United Kingdom, covered several phases and was overseen by the Ministry of Lands, Resettlement and Rural Development (MLRRD). It concerned the resettlement of landless people, subsistence farmers and former freedom fighters from the overpopulated communal lands to large farms that have been bought up. The resettlement was undertaken on the basis of three models: individual farm settlements, the establishment of cooperative farms and com-munal grazing schemes.

9 The CLDP was a programme of the Ministry of Lands, Resettlement and Rural De-velopment (MLRRD) for the development of disadvantaged peasant farming areas, in which the Coordinated Agricultural and Rural Development Programme (CARD) sup-ported by the GTZ until the late 1990s occupied a prominent position.

10 These 130 individual agricultural and rural development projects promoted by bi- and multilateral development cooperation and by NGOs were implemented under the Re-construction and Development Programme by the Ministry of Lands, Resettlement and Rural Development (MLRRD) together with the district authorities, local NGOs or parastatal bodies.

11 Government of the Republic of Zimbabwe, Ministry of National Resources and Tour-ism (1987): The National Conservation Strategy. Zimbabwe's Road to Survival, Ha-rare.

12 Government of the Republic of Zimbabwe, Ministry of Natural Resources and Tour-ism (1985): The Implementation of a National Conservation Strategy in Zimbabwe. Proceedings of the Conference Workshop, Harare.

Part V: Institutional and organizational implementation options

1 Mellor, J.W. (ed. 1995); Cleaver, K. (1997); World Bank (1997a / 2000b), p. 14 and p. 170 ff.; Delgado, C. *et al.* (1998); Gsänger, H. (2001b); Ashley, C. / S. Maxwell (eds. 2001a); De Haen, H. / K. Stamoulis / S. Broca (2001); Deutsches Institut für Entwicklungspolitik (2001)

2 The Blantyre Statement on Poverty Alleviation in Sub-Saharan Africa, 1997, in: De-velopment in Practice, Taking Action to Reduce Poverty in Sub-Saharan Africa, The World Bank, Washington D.C., p. 128 ff. (extract).

3 'The overwhelming majority of Africa's population is rural. Agriculture is therefore the principal economic preoccupation for most of Africa's people. Agriculture is cen-tral not only to the quality of life of most Africans, but also to the national economy of nearly all African states. Increased agricultural production, efficiency and diversifi-cation are central to the economic growth strategies of these countries. In support of the NEPAD's growth and sustainable development initiatives on agriculture, we commit to: ... develop sound agricultural policies that are integrated into Poverty Re-duction Strategies.'

4 The Zambian constitution and the existing legislative framework consisting of the Local Government Act, the Town and Country Planning Act, the Water Act and the Lands Development Act provide scope for the further development of the Zambian decentralization policy. An amendment of the Local Government Act has been sub-mitted to the cabinet.

5 The deconcentration of the Ministry of Agriculture, Food and Fisheries (MAFF) has been largely completed and will result in the medium term in 71 District Agricultural Offices, each with a District Agricultural Committee (DAC).

6 Important source references for the overriding importance of the District Councils for district development are:

Republic of Zambia, The Local Government Act, as amended by Act 30 of 1995, Part V, para. 31 (1): A council may establish standing and occasional committees consisting of such number of members as the council may determine, for the purpose of examining and reporting on any matter and of discharging any functions of the council delegated to them under this Act.

Republic of Zambia, Cabinet Office Circular on 3 January, 1995, establishing with immediate effect the following technical committees: (a) a District Development Coordination Committee (DDCC) in each district, (b) a Provincial Development Coordination Committee (PDCC) in each province, (c) a National Development Coordination Committee (NDCC) at the centre.

Republic of Zambia, Cabinet Office Circular of 28 November, 1995 on Institutional Framework for Planning, Co-ordination and Monitoring of Development in the District and Provinces, Appendix B, Functions of a Council: 1. The Council is responsible for the Socio-Economic Development Planning and Co-ordination of the implementation of programmes and projects.

Republic of Zambia, National Institute of Public Administration, The District Councillor's Handbook, Lusaka, 1981: The District Secretary is the chief government co-ordinating officer in the district, with particular reference to the work of economic development.

7 UNDP (2002): http://magnet.undp.org/Docs/dec/monograph/FiscalAdmin&CSR-SAF.htm.

8 Silverman, J.M. (1992), p. 17: 'In countries with weak central governments, decentralization is unlikely to be efficient or effective because too many opportunities exist to subvert program goals when the centre cannot impose the penalties necessary to elicit compliance.'

9 To name but one of the many: Silverman, J.M. (1992), p. 15 ff.

10 In recent years national public allocations to agricultural development have de facto declined and are currently below 10 per cent of the sector's contribution to national GDP; Otzen, U. (2001), p. 259.

Part VI: Conclusions and recommendations

1 'The specific identity of local government (as a separate sphere of government) and their role in promoting local (economic) development are increasingly recognized. Thus, the Cotonou Agreement considers local governments as distinct actors, to be associated to the formulation and implementation of ACP-EU cooperation. ... Therefore, they can also access National Indicative Programme, NIP, resources (a) where support to the decentralisation process is a focal sector (including in the country Support Strategy), (b) as an implementing agency for a sectoral programme (e.g. health), and (c) in the framework of decentralised cooperation programmes.' European Centre for Development Policy Management, ECDPM (2001), Cotonou, Infokit No 10, p. 3, and No 12, p. 2.

Bibliography

Abaza, H. (1996): Integration of Sustainable Objectives in Structural Adjustment Programmes. Using Strategic Environmental Assessment, in: *Project Appraisal*, Vol. 11, No 4, Guildford

Addison, T. / L. Ndikumana (2001): Overcoming the Fiscal Crisis of the African State, Wider Discussion Paper, World Institute for Development Economics Research, Helsinki

African Union (2002): The New Partnership for Africa's Development, NEPAD, s.l.

Ahmad, J. (1995): Kommunale Finanzordnung in Südafrika, in: *Finanzierung und Entwicklung*, No 9, Hamburg

Asche, H. (2002): Die zweite große historische Chance der Entwicklungspolitik. Von der Schwierigkeit, den richtigen 'strategischen Mix' gegen Armut und für nachholende demokratische Entwicklung zu finden, in: *Frankfurter Rundschau*, No 88, p. 7, Frankfurt/Main

Ashley, C. / Maxwell, S. (eds., 2001a): Rethinking Rural Development, Oxford

Ashley, C. / Maxwell, S. (eds., 2001b): Rethinking Rural Development, in: *Development Policy Review*, Vol. 19, No 4, p. 395–425, London

Bahl, R. *et al.* (2001): The Design and Implementation of Intergovernmental Fiscal Transfers, in: *Intergovernmental Transfers in Developing and Transition Countries: Principles and Practice*, p. 2 ff., Atlanta

Barrett, C. / T. Reardon / W. Patrick (2001): Non-farm Income Diversification and Household Livelihood Strategies in Rural Africa: Concepts, Dynamics and Policy Implications, in: *Food Policy*, Vol. 26, No 4, Wye, Kent

Bohnet, M. (2000): Regionale und sektorale Schwerpunktbildung in der EZ. Die Arbeit an der neuen Länderliste, in: *Entwicklung und Zusammenarbeit*, Vol. 41, No 7/8, p. 196 ff., Frankfurt/Main

Brockhaus (1999): Brockhaus Enzyklopädie, 20. Auflage, Wiesbaden

Bryceson, D. / V. Jamal (1997): Farewell to Farms: De-Agrarianisation and Employment in Africa, Aldershot, Ashgate

Bundesministerium für wirtschaftliche Zusammenarbeit und Entwicklung, BMZ (2000a): Wer braucht Entwicklung?, Bonn

Bundesministerium für wirtschaftliche Zusammenarbeit und Entwicklung, BMZ (2000b): Schwerpunktsetzung in der Entwicklungszusammenarbeit, Bonn

Bundesministerium für wirtschaftliche Zusammenarbeit und Entwicklung, BMZ (2001a): Elfter Bericht zur Entwicklungspolitik der Bundesregierung, Bonn

Bundesministerium für wirtschaftliche Zusammenarbeit und Entwicklung, BMZ (2001b): Armutsbekämpfung – eine globale Aufgabe, Aktionsprogramm 2015. Der Beitrag der

Bundesregierung zur weltweiten Halbierung der Armut, BMZ-Materialien No 106, Bonn

Bundesministerium für wirtschaftliche Zusammenarbeit und Entwicklung, BMZ (2001c): BMZ Konzepte: Ländliche Entwicklung – Ein Referenzrahmen, Bonn

Bundesministerium für wirtschaftliche Zusammenarbeit und Entwicklung, BMZ (2002): Schwerpunkte und Zeitplanung mit Kooperationsländern, Bonn

Chambers, R. (1983): Rural Development. Putting the Last First, London, Lagos, New York

Cheema, G.S. / Rondinelli, D.A. (eds., 1983): Decentralization and Development. Policy Implementation in Developing Countries, Beverly Hills / London / New Delhi

Chenery, H.B. / S. Robinson / M. Syrquin (eds., 1986): Industrialization and Growth: A Comparative Study, New York

Cleaver, K. (1997): Rural Development Strategies for Poverty Reduction and Environmental Protection in Subsaharan Africa, Directions in Development Series, World Bank, Washington, D.C.

Conyers, D. (1985): Decentralization: A Framework for Discussion, in: *Decentralization, Local Government Institutions and Resource Mobilisation*, Cornilla

Corbo, V. / S.B. Webb (1991): Adjustment Lending and the Restoration of Sustainable Growth, in: *Journal of International Development*, Vol. 3, No 2, Chichester

Crook, R.C. / A.S. Sverrisson (2001): Decentralisation and poverty-alleviation in developing-countries. A comparative analysis or, is WEST Bengal unique?, Brighton

Davey, K. (2000): Fiscal Decentralization. Basic Policy Guidelines for Practitioners, in: *Local* Government *Quarterly*, No 3/2000, Washington, D.C.

De Haen, H. / K. Stamoulis / S. Broca (2001): Reducing Hunger and Poverty Through Agricultural Growth. Dealing with Key Challenges, in: *Nord–Süd aktuell*, No 3, p. 461–473, Hamburg

Delgado, C. *et al.* (1998): Agricultural Growth Linkages in Subsahara Africa, International Food Policy Research Institute, IFPRI Report No 107, Washington, D.C.

Deutsche Gesellschaft für Technische Zusammenarbeit, GTZ (1999): Dezentralisierung in Afrika, in: *Akzente aus der Arbeit der GTZ*, Eschborn

Deutsche Gesellschaft für Technische Zusammenarbeit, GTZ (2000): Subsektorkonzept Fiskaldezentralisierung (Entwurf), Eschborn

Deutsche Gesellschaft für Technische Zusammenarbeit, GTZ (2001a): Konventionsprojekt Desertifikationsbekämpfung, (CCD), Desertifikation bekämpfen – Armut reduzieren. Überlegungen zum *mainstreaming* von Umwelt- und Entwicklungsstrategien (Diskussionspapier), Eschborn

Deutsche Gesellschaft für Technische Zusammenarbeit, GTZ (2001b): Projektevaluierung, Unterstützung des landwirtschaftlichen Sektorinvestitionsprogramms (ASIP) in der Südprovinz Sambias, Hauptbericht, Eschborn

Deutsches Institut für Entwicklungspolitik (2001): Herausforderungen und Ansätze für eine strategische Entwicklungspolitik in Sub-Sahara Afrika, Impulspapier zur Fachtagung des BMZ und DIE am 03.05.2001 in Bonn

Development Services and Initiatives, DSI / Deutsche Gesellschaft für Technische Zusammenarbeit, GTZ (2000): Financing the Agricultural Sector Investment Programme (ASIP) in Zambia. A GTZ Funded Study by DSI-Southern Africa, Lusaka

Djafari, N. (2001): Fiskalische Dezentralisierung und dezentrale Finanzierung in Entwicklungsländern, in: Thomi, W. / M. Steinich / W. Polte (eds), Dezentralisierung in Entwicklungsländern. Jüngere Ursachen, Ergebnisse und Perspektiven staatlicher Reformpolitik, p. 173–186, Baden-Baden

Dollar, D. / A. Kraay (2001): Growth Is Good for the Poor, in: Development Research Group, The World Bank, Washington, D.C.

Dreger, M. (2001): Territoriale Verwaltungsreform und lokale Entwicklung in Benin – rechtliche und entwicklungspolitische Rahmenbedingungen, in: *Bochumer Schriften zur Entwicklungsforschung und Entwicklungspolitik*, Vol. 48, Bochum

Duncan, A. / J. Howell (eds, 1992): Structural Adjustment and the African Farmer, London, Portsmouth

Economic Commission for Africa, ECA (2001): Compact for African Recovery, Operationalising the Millennium Partnership for the African Recovery Programme, Addis Ababa

Endom, E. (1997): Legal Constraints for Local Economic Development at Local Government Level, Paper Prepared for the Friedrich Ebert Foundation, Pretoria

Eriksen, S. (2002): Councils, Capacity Building and State. The Context of Local Government Reform in Tansania, in: *Journal für Entwicklungspolitik*, Vol. XVII, No 1, p. 9–29, Frankfurt am Main

European Centre for Development Policy Management, ECDPM, (2001): Cotonou Infokit. The New ACP–EU Partnership Agreement, Maastricht

FAO (1992): Sustainable development and the environment. FAO policies and actions, Stockholm 1972 – Rio 1992, Rome

Fan, S. / Hazell, P. (2000): Promoting Sustainable Development in Less-Favoured Areas. Returns to Public Investment. Evidence From India and China, IFPRI, Washington, D.C.

Friedrich-Ebert-Stiftung (1999): Dezentralisierung und kommunale Selbstverwaltung. Zur kommunalpolitischen Projektarbeit der Friedrich-Ebert-Stiftung in Afrika, Asien und Lateinamerika, Bonn

Fuhr, H. (1999): Institutional Change and New Incentive Structures for Development. Can Decentralization and Better Local Government Help?, in: *Welt Trends 25*, p. 21–74

Giehler, Th. (1999): Sources of Funds for Agricultural Lending, Agricultural Finance Revisited, No 4, Food and Agriculture Organization of the United Nations (FAO) / Deutsche Gesellschaft für Technische Zusammenarbeit (GTZ), Rome

Government of the Republic of Zimbabwe (1981a): Growth With Equity. An Economic Policy Statement, Harare

Government of the Republic of Zimbabwe (1981b): Let's Build Zimbabwe Together. Zimbabwe Conference on Reconstruction and Development, ZIMCORD, Salisbury

Government of the Republic of Zimbabwe (1982): Transitional National Development Plan 1982–85, Harare

Government of the Republic of Zimbabwe (1988): First Five-Year National Development Plan 1986–90, Harare

Government of the Republic of Zimbabwe, Ministry of Lands, Resettlement and Rural Development (1985): Communal Lands Development Plan, CLDP, Harare

Government of the Republic of Zimbabwe, Ministry of National Resources and Tourism (1985): The Implementation of a National Conservation Strategy in Zimbabwe. Proceedings of the Conference Workshop, Harare

Government of the Republic of Zimbabwe, Ministry of National Resources and Tourism (1987): The National Conservation Strategy. Zimbabwe's Road to Survival, Harare

Gräfe, M. (2001): Zivilgesellschaft und Dezentralisierung – Erfahrungen und Förderansätze der FES

Gsänger, H. (2001a): Überlegungen zu einer armutsmindernden agrargestützten Wachstumsstrategie, in: *Nord–Süd aktuell*, No 3, p. 481–485

Gsänger, H. (2001b): Sozialkapital als Baustein für Afrikas Entwicklung. Es mangelt an Vertrauen in gesellschaftliche Institutionen, in: *Entwicklung und Zusammenarbeit*, Vol. 42, No 42, Frankfurt/Main

Hayami, Y. / V. W. Ruttan (1985): Agricultural Development, Baltimore, London

Hinrichs, K. (2001): Dezentralisierung als Handlungsfeld der Entwicklungszusammenarbeit – Erfahrungen und Perspektiven, in: Thomi, W. / M. Steinich / W. Polte (eds), Dezentralisierung in Entwicklungsländern. Jüngere Ursachen, Ergebnisse und Perspektiven staatlicher Reformpolitik, p. 279–299, Baden-Baden

Hyden, G. (1983): No Shortcuts to Progress. African Development Management in Perspective, University of California Press, Berkeley, Los Angeles

International Fund for Agricultural Development, IFAD (2001): Rural Poverty Report 2001. The Challenge of Ending Rural Poverty, Oxford, New York

International Food Policy Research Institute, IFPRI (2001): 2020 Global Food Outlook. Trends, Alternatives, and Choices, Washington, D.C.

International Food Policy Research Institute, IFPRI (2002): Reaching Sustainable Food Security for All by 2020. Getting the Priorities and Responsibilities Right, Washington, D.C.

International Monetary Fund, IMF (1996): *Government Finance Statistics Yearbook*, Washington, D.C.

International Monetary Fund, IMF (1997): International Finance Statistics, Washington, D.C.

International Monetary Fund, IMF and International Development Association, IDA (2001): Poverty Reduction Strategy Papers – Progress in Implementation, Washington, D.C.

International Republican Institute, IRI / National Business Initiative for Growth, Development and Democracy, NBI (1998): The Local Authority's Role in Economic Development. A Handbook for Councillors and Officials, Durban

Internationale Bank für Wiederaufbau und Entwicklung / Weltbank (1997): Weltentwicklungsbericht 1997. Der Staat In Einer Sich Ändernden Welt, Bonn

Johnson, C. (2001): Local Democracy, Democratic Decentralisation and Rural Development. Theories, Challenges and Options for Policy, in: *Development Policy Review*, Vol. 19, No 4, p. 521 ff., Oxford

Kampffmeyer, Th. *et al.* (1998): Financing Local Development in the Decentralization Process of the Philippines. The Case of Cebu, German Development Institute, GDI, Reports and Working Papers 7/1998, Berlin

Kananaskis Summit (2002): G8 Africa Action Plan, Montreal

Kenneweg, J. (2000): Länderkonzepte und Förderstrategien. Zur Weiterentwicklung des Instruments des Bundesministeriums für wirtschaftliche Zusammenarbeit, BMZ, Bonn

Killick, T. (2001): Globalisation and the Rural Poor, in: *Development Policy Review*, Vol. 19, No 2, p. 155 ff., Oxford

Klugman, J. (2001): Poverty Reduction Strategy Source Book, The World Bank, Washington, D.C.

Konrad-Adenauer-Stiftung (1998): Auf dem Weg zu einer Weltcharta der Kommunalen Selbstverwaltung, Dokumente und Materialien, Sankt Augustin

Konrad-Adenauer-Stiftung (1999): Bürger und Kommunen im 21. Jahrhundert. Kommunalförderung in der internationalen Zusammenarbeit der Konrad-Adenauer-Stiftung, Sankt Augustin, Cologne

Kreditanstalt für Wiederaufbau (2000): Sektorprogramme mit deutscher Beteiligung. Eine Auswertung im Rahmen der *Strategic Partnership with Africa*, unpublished manuscript, Frankfurt/Main

Kuznets, S. (1966): Modern Economic Growth. Rat, Structure and Spread, New Haven: Yale University Press

Kydd, J. (2002): Liberalisation, Institutions and Agriculture, unpublished paper from the Centre for Development and Poverty Reduction of the Imperial College Wye, UK, presented at the Zentrum für Entwicklungsforschung, Bonn

Lampe, K. (2001): Biologie statt Ideologie. Grüne Gentechnik: Weshalb die Kritiker irren, in: *epd* Entwicklungspolitik, No 15/16, Frankfurt/Main

Lancaster, C. (1999): Aid to Africa. So Much to Do, So Little Done, Chicago, London

Lanjouw, P. / A. Shariff (2001): Rural Non-farm Employment in India: Access, Incomes and Poverty Impact. Paper presented at a workshop on Rural Transformation in India: The Role of the Non-Farm Sector, New Delhi

Lipton, M. (1977) Why Poor People Stay Poor: Urban Bias in World Development, London

Livingstone, I. / R. Charlton (2001): Financing Decentralized Development in a Low-Income Country: Raising Revenue of Local Government in Uganda, in: *Development and Change*, Vol. 32, p. 77–100, Oxford

Loquai, Ch. (2001): Strategic Priorities and Operational Challenges for European Support for Democratic Decentralisation in the Context of the New ACP–EU Partnership Agreement, ECDPM Discussion Paper No 24, Maastricht

Mellor, J.W. (ed., 1995): Agriculture on the Road to Industrialization, Baltimore

Meyer, W. (2001): Zur politischen Dimension von *Local Government Management* Reformen – Neuere Aspekte und Erfahrungen, in: Thomi, W. / M. Steinich / W. Polte (eds), Dezentralisierung in Entwicklungsländern. Jüngere Ursachen, Ergebnisse und Perspektiven staatlicher Reformpolitik, p. 73–98, Baden-Baden

Ministry of Agriculture, Food and Fisheries, MAFF, Republic of Zambia (1994): Agricultural Sector Investment Programme, A.S.I.P. Lusaka

Ministry of Finance and Economic Development, MFED, Republic of Zambia (2001): Poverty Reduction Strategies for the Agricultural Sector. Framework for Poverty Reduction in the Agricultural Sector, Lusaka

Ministry of Finance and National Planning, MFNP, Republic of Zambia (2002): Zambia Poverty Reduction Strategy Paper 2002–2004, Lusaka

Ministry of Finance, Planning and Economic Development, MFPED, Republic of Uganda (2001): Poverty Eradication Action Plan, Vol. 3, Kampala

Ministry for Food and Agriculture, MFA, Republic of Ghana, / International Fund for Agricultural Development, IFAD / Deutsche Gesellschaft für Technische Zusammenarbeit, GTZ / Sector Network Rural Development, SNRD (2001): Sector Wide Approaches: Do they Really Help the Poor? Proceedings of a Regional Forum, Accra

Moore, M. / J. Putzel (1999): Thinking strategically about politics and poverty, Brighton

National Business Initiative, for Growth, Development and Democracy, NBI (1997): Financial Management for Local Authorities: A Handbook for Local Government Councillors, Durban

Nell-Breuning, O. (1955): Gerechtigkeit und Freiheit. Grundzüge der katholischen Soziallehre, Munich

North, D.C. (1995): The New Institutional Economics and Third World Development, in: Harris, J. / C. Lewis (eds): The New Institutional Economics and Third World Development, Routledge, London

Nsouli, S.M. (1993): Strukturanpassung in Afrika südlich der Sahara, in: *Finanzierung und Entwicklung*, Hamburg

Organization for Economic Co-Operation and Development, OECD (2001): DAC Guidelines on Poverty Reduction, Paris

Otzen, U. *et al.* (1991): Development Management from Below. The Role of Village and Ward Development Committees in Rural Development in Zimbabwe, German Development Institute, GDI, Berlin

Otzen, U. (1993): Umwelt-Aktionspläne. Ein Handlungsrahmen zur Umsetzung von nachhaltiger Entwicklung?, DIE, Berlin

Otzen, U. *et al.* (1994): Facilitating Sustainable Agricultural Development in Zimbabwe. Key Factors and Necessary Incentives, German Development Institute, GDI, Environment and Development Activities Zimbabwe, ENDA, Berlin

Otzen, U. (1996): Nachhaltige Agrarentwicklung. Anpassungszwänge, Ziele, Konzepte und Förderpolitiken, Deutsches Institut für Entwicklungspolitik, DIE, Berlin

Otzen, U. (1998): Förderung nachhaltiger Agrarentwicklung durch Sektorinvestitionsprogramme. Fall Sambia, Deutsches Institut für Entwicklungspolitik, DIE, unpublished manuscript, Berlin

Otzen, U. *et al.* (1999): Integrated Development Planning. A New Task for Local Government in South Africa, German Development Institute, GDI, Berlin

Otzen, U. (2000): Ein sehr hoher Preis. Warum scheitert Simbabwe an der Landfrage?, in: *Entwicklungspolitik epd*, No 23/24, p. 56 ff, Frankfurt/Main

Otzen, U. (2001): Afrika braucht nachholende Agrarentwicklung. Bäuerliche Landwirtschaft kann armutsmindernde Dynamik schaffen, in: *Entwicklung und Zusammenarbeit*, Vol. 42, No 9, p. 257–260, Frankfurt/Main

Parker, A.N. (1995): Decentralization – The Way Forward for Rural Development?, Policy Research Working Paper, The World Bank, Washington, D.C.

Pinstrup-Andersen, P. (ed., 2001): The Unfinished Agenda. Perspectives on Overcoming Hunger, Poverty, and Environmental Degradation, Washington, D.C.

Presidential Review Commission (1998): Developing a Culture of Good Governance. Report of the Presidential Review Commission on the Reform and Transformation of the Republic Service in South Africa, Presented to the President of South Africa, Mr. N.R. Mandela, Pretoria

Prudhomme, R. (2001): Fiscal Decentralization and Intergovernmental Fiscal Relations, UNCDF Symposium on Decentralization Local Governance in Africa, Cape Town

Puncan, A. / Howell, J. (eds, 1992): Structural Adjustment and the African Farmer, London / Portsmouth

Reardon, T. (1997): Using Evidence of Household Income Deversification. A Study of the Rural Non-Farm Labour Market in Africa, in: *World Development*, Vol. 25, No 5, Oxford, New York, Tokyo

Reed, D. (ed., 1996): Structural Adjustment, the Environment, and Sustainable Development, London

Republic of South Africa (1996): The Constitution of the Republic of South Africa. One Land for One Nation, Pretoria

Republic of South Africa / Ministry of Provincial Affairs and Constitutional Development (1998): The White Paper on Local Government, Pretoria

Saleh, M. (1993): Enhancing Intra-Industry Linkages. The Role of Small and Medium Scale Industries, Kuala Lumpur

Seddon, D. / B.P. Subedi (2000): Labour Markets and the Poor. A Report to DFID, Overseas Development Group, University of East Anglia, Norwich

Sen, Amartya (1999): Ökonomie für den Menschen. Wege zu Gerechtigkeit und Solidarität in der Marktwirtschaft, Munich, Vienna

Shenggen, F. / Hazell, P. (2000): Promoting Sustainable Development in Less-Favored Areas. Returns to Public Investment. Evidence From India and China, International Food Policy Research Institute, IFPRI, Washington, D.C.

Silverman, J. (1992): Public Sector Decentralization. Economic Policy and Sector Investment Programs, World Bank Technical Paper 188, Washington, D.C.

Simon, K. (1994): Subsidiarität in die Entwicklungszusammenarbeit, in: *Entwicklung und Zusammenarbeit*, No 35, p. 11 ff., Frankfurt/Main

Simon, K. (2001): *Local Governance* als Lernprozess: Die Entwicklungszusammenarbeit vor postmodernen Tendenzen in Dezentralisierung und Verwaltungsreform, in: Thomi, W. / M. Steinich / W. Polte (eds), Dezentralisierung in Entwicklungsländern. Jüngere Ursachen, Ergebnisse und Perspektiven staatlicher Reformpolitik, p. 151–171, Baden-Baden

Start, D. (2001): The Rise and Fall of the Rural Non-Farm Economy: Poverty Impacts and Policy Options, in: *Development Policy Review*, Vol. 19, No 4

Steinich, M. (2001): Wirkungsbeobachtung im Vorhaben der Dezentralisierung, in: Thomi, W. / M. Steinich / W. Polte (eds), Dezentralisierung in Entwicklungsländern. Jüngere Ursachen, Ergebnisse und Perspektiven staatlicher Reformpolitik, p. 187–203, Baden-Baden

Sundar, N. (2001): Is Devolution Democratization?, in: *World Development*, Vol. 29, No 12, p. 2007 ff., Oxford

Syrquin, M. / H.B. Chenery (1989): Three Decades of Industrialization, in: *World Bank Economic Review*, Vol. 3, Washington, D.C.

Thomi, W. (2001): Hoffnungsträger Dezentralisierung?, in: Thomi, W. / Steinich, M. / Polte, W. (eds): Dezentralisierung in Entwicklungsländern. Jüngere Ursachen, Ergebnisse und Perspektiven staatlicher Reformpolitik, p. 17–41, Baden-Baden

UNCED (1992): Agenda 21, Rio de Janeiro

UNDP (2001): Bericht über die menschliche Entwicklung 2001, Bonn

United Nations (2000): Resolution Adopted by the General Assembly, United Nations Millennium Declaration, New York

United Republic of Tanzania (2001): Poverty Reduction Strategy Paper, Progress Report 2000/01, Dar-es-Salaam

Urban Sector Network, USN (1998): Developmental Local Government in South Africa, A Handbook for Urban Councillors and Community Members, Braamfontein

White, H. (1996): Adjustment in Africa, in: *Development and Change*, Vol. 27, p. 785–815, Oxford

Wiemann, J. (2001): Stellungnahme zur entwicklungspolitischen Sinnhaftigkeit des Übergangs von der Projekt- zur Budgethilfe, unpublished manuscript, Bonn

Wolff, P. *et al.* (2002): The Comprehensive Poverty Reduction Strategy in Vietnam. Process, Donor Contribution, and Implementation at the Local Level, German Development Institute, GDI, Bonn

World Bank (1988): Adjustment Lending: An Evaluation of Ten Year's Experience, Washington, D.C.

World Bank (1994a): Adjustment Lending: An Evaluation of Ten Year's Experience, Washington, D.C.

World Bank (1994b): Adjustment in Africa: Reforms, Results and the Road Ahead, Oxford

World Bank (1997a): World Development Report 1997. The State in a Changing World, Washington, D.C.

World Bank (1997b): Taking Action to Reduce Poverty in Sub-Saharan Africa, Washington, D.C.

World Bank (1997c):The Blantyre Statement on Poverty Alleviation in Sub-Saharan Africa, in: Development in Practice, Taking Action to Reduce Poverty in Sub-Saharan Africa, Washington, D.C.

World Bank (1999): World Development Report 1999/2000, New York

World Bank (1998a): The World Bank atlas 1998, Washington, D.C.

World Bank (1998b): Development of Micro, Small Enterprises and Rural Finance in Sub-Saharan Africa: The World Bank's Strategy, Findings No 106, Washington, D.C.

World Bank (2000a): Can Africa Claim the 21st Century?, Washington, D.C.

World Bank (2000b): Globalisierung und Lokalisierung. Neue Wege im entwicklungspolitischen Denken, Weltentwicklungsbericht 1999/2000, Washington, D.C.

World Bank (2001a): PRSP-Sourcebook on Public Spending for Poverty Reduction, Washington, D.C.

World Bank (2001b): Comprehensive Development Framework, CDF. Meeting the Promise? Early Experiences and Emerging Issues, Washington, D.C.

World Bank (2001c): World Development Report 2000/2001, Attacking Poverty, Washington, D.C.

World Bank (2002a): Reaching the Rural Poor – An Updated Strategy for Rural Development, Draft Final Report of a World Bank Strategy Paper, Washington, D.C.

World Bank (2002b): Toward Sharpening the Focus on Rural Poverty. A Review of World Bank Experience, World Bank Report No 24072, Washington, D.C.

Appendix

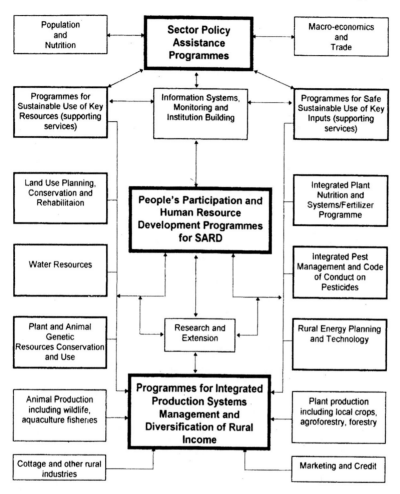

* Extra bold outlined boxes indicate programme and project groupings of an integrated, multi-disciplinary nature. Bold boxes indicate major programme and project groupings of a specialized nature; other boxes indicate related activities.

Figure A1 Framework for sustainable agriculture and rural development, SARD

Source: FAO (1992).

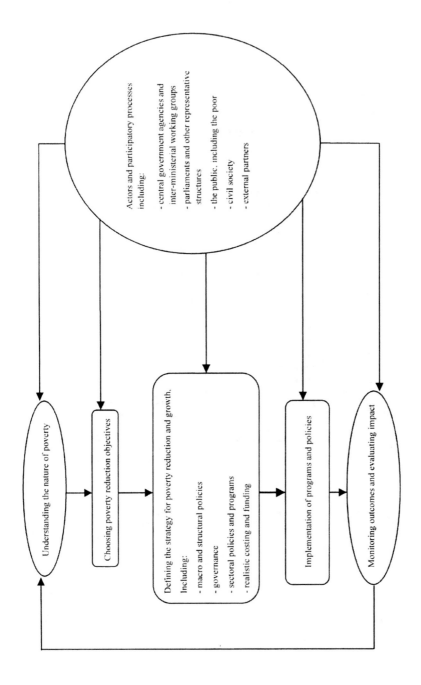

Figure A2 An illustration of how a PRSP can evolve at country level

Source: Klugman, J. (2001), p. 5

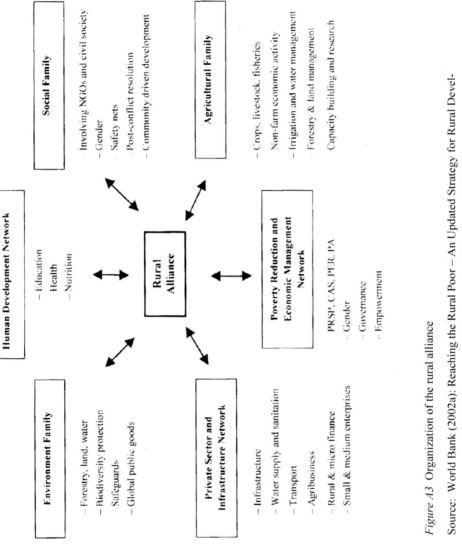

Figure A3 Organization of the rural alliance

Source: World Bank (2002a): Reaching the Rural Poor – An Updated Strategy for Rural Development, p. XX, slightly amended by the author, Washington, D.C.

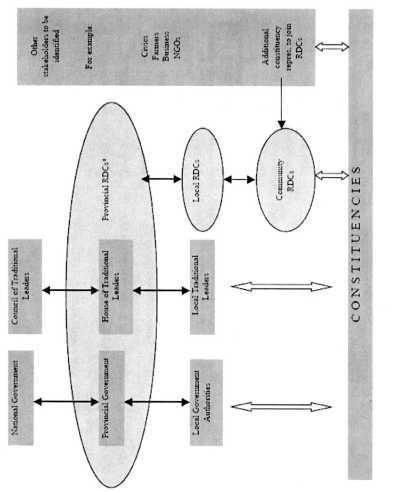

Figure A4 Participation of traditional leaders and good governance in South Africa

* Reconstruction and Development Committee

Source: Provincial Government of Mpumalanga (1998): Co-operative Governance, Development Strategy for Mpumalanga, p. 4.

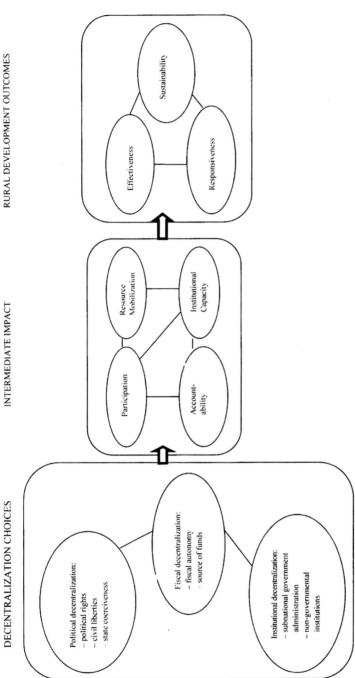

DECENTRALIZATION CHOICES · INTERMEDIATE IMPACT · RURAL DEVELOPMENT OUTCOMES

Political decentralization:
– political rights
– civil liberties
– state coerciveness

Fiscal decentralization:
– fiscal autonomy
– source of funds

Institutional decentralization:
– subnational government administration
– non-governmental institutions

Participation

Resource Mobilization

Institutional Capacity

Accountability

Effectiveness

Sustainability

Responsiveness

Figure A5 Conceptual model for analysing and developing decentralization

Source: Parker, A. N. (1995), p. 44.

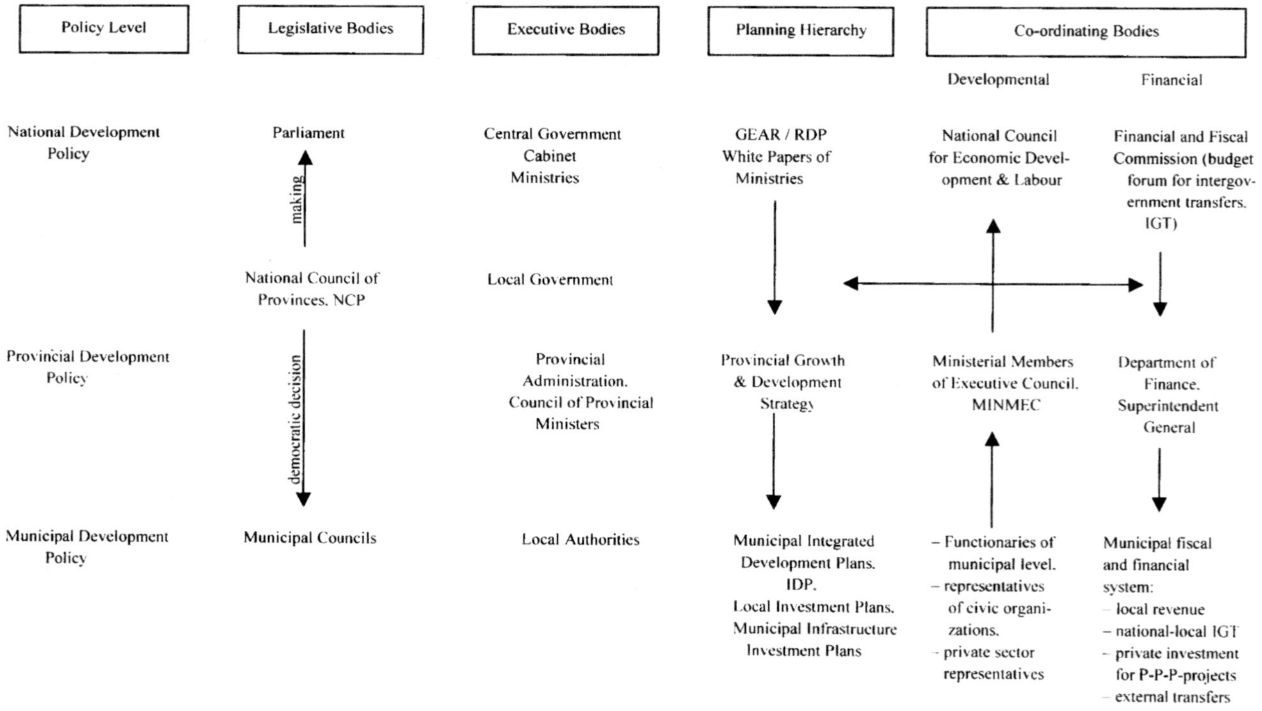

Policy Level	Legislative Bodies	Executive Bodies	Planning Hierarchy	Co-ordinating Bodies — Developmental	Co-ordinating Bodies — Financial
National Development Policy	Parliament	Central Government Cabinet Ministries	GEAR / RDP White Papers of Ministries	National Council for Economic Development & Labour	Financial and Fiscal Commission (budget forum for intergovernment transfers. IGT)
	National Council of Provinces. NCP	Local Government			
Provincial Development Policy		Provincial Administration. Council of Provincial Ministers	Provincial Growth & Development Strategy	Ministerial Members of Executive Council. MINMEC	Department of Finance. Superintendent General
Municipal Development Policy	Municipal Councils	Local Authorities	Municipal Integrated Development Plans. IDP. Local Investment Plans. Municipal Infrastructure Investment Plans	– Functionaries of municipal level. – representatives of civic organizations. – private sector representatives	Municipal fiscal and financial system: – local revenue – national-local IGT – private investment for P-P-P-projects – external transfers

making · democratic decision

Figure A6 Development planning pattern in the cooperative government system of South Africa

Source: DCD / DIE (1998).

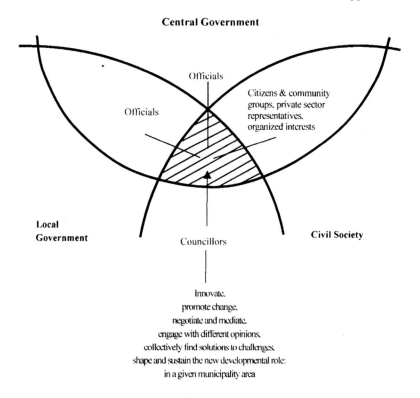

Figure A7 Spheres of mediation for developmental local government in South Africa

Source: MPACD and DIE (1998) – own design.

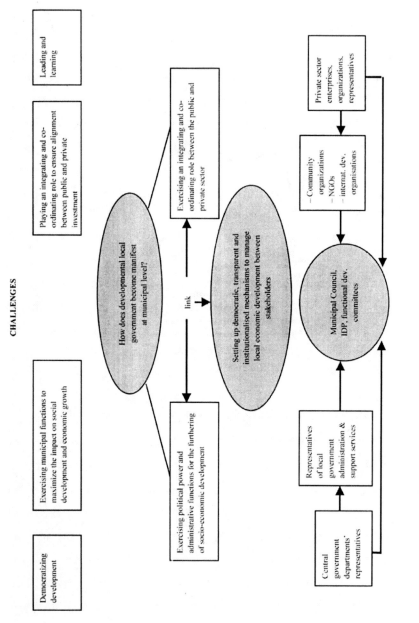

Figure A8 Challenges and appearance of developmental local government at municipal level in South Africa

Source: MPACD and DIE (1998) – own design.

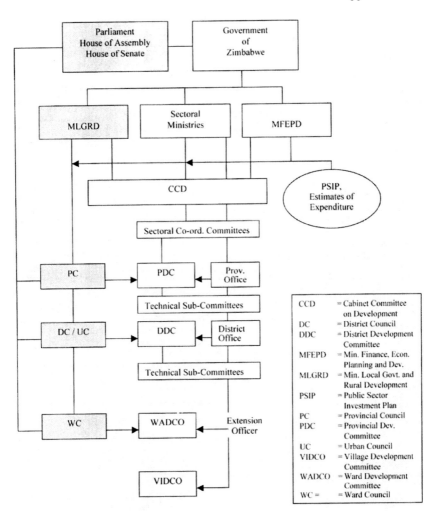

Figure A9 Frame for development planning and coordination in Zimbabwe since 1984

Legend: ▶ = political guidance   ◀ = fiscal / technical guidance

Source: own design (2002).

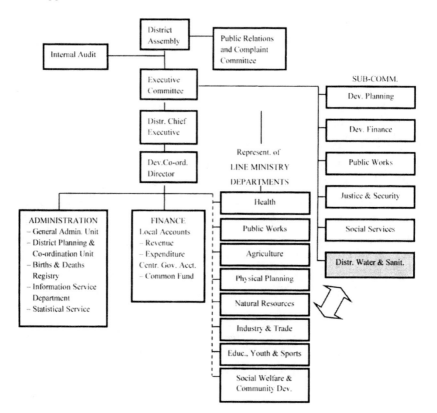

Figure A10 District assembly structure as implied by the Local Government Act
1993, Ghana

 advisory & consultative linkages   Legend: ▇▇▇ non-mandatory

Source: Ministry of Local Government and Rural Development (2002) (slightly
amended own design)

Poverty Reduction Strategy Paper (PRSP) requires new structures for development financing through allocation of resources via (a), (b), (c), (d)

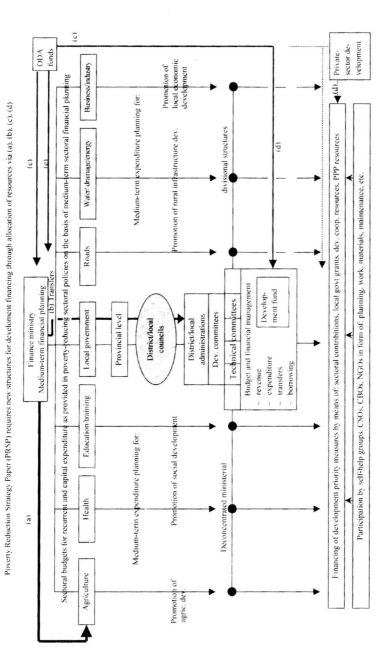

Figure A11 Organization chart for the implementation of poverty reduction strategies

Source: own design (2002).

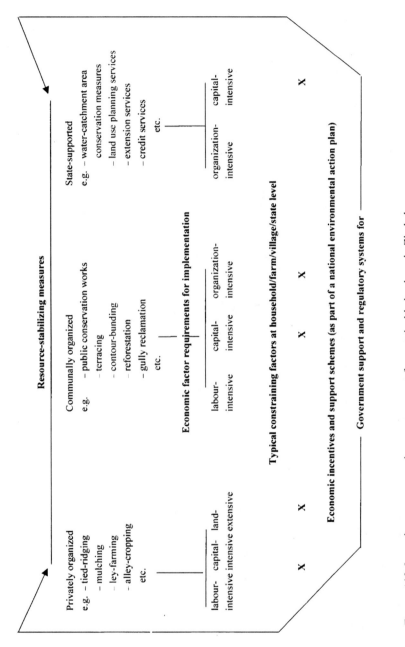

Figure A12 Incentive structure and support concept for sustainable land use in Zimbabwe

Source: Otzen. U. (1994).

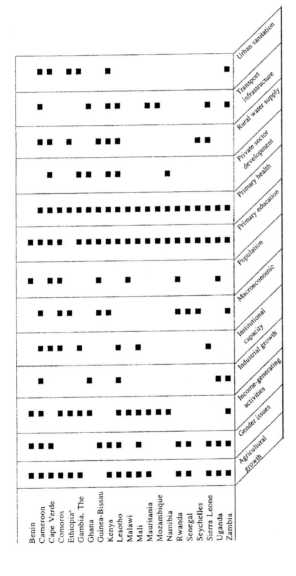

Figure A13 Principal themes of action plans in poverty assessments

Note: Includes all poverty assessments prepared for final publication by March 1996 (indicated by squares), except for Mauritius and Zimbabwe. Poverty assessments for those two countries were prepared as part of a country economic memorandum: they do not contain detailed action plans on poverty reduction.

[a] The poverty assessments for Ethiopia specifically excludes education because of budget constraints on the Bank mission.

Source: World Bank (1997c), p. 68.

Table A1 Effects of structural adjustment in 30 sub-Saharan African Countries,
1982–92

	Three-year average before the programme	Annual average during the programme
GDP growth	(in %)	
A	2.3	4.1
B	2.2	3.5
Inflation	(in %)	
A	27.5	17.5
B	26.9	26.3
Total budget balance	(in % of GDP)[a]	
A	−13.9	−11.4
B	−13.5	−13.5
Current-account balance	(in % of GDP)[b]	
A	−15.6	−16.1
B	−15.0	−17.5
Gross international reserves	(Import months)	
A	2.5	2.8
B	1.8	2.6

A: Countries with continuous programmes
B: All programme countries

[a]　Countries which had concluded the annual programmes or reviews by 31 May 1992.
[b]　Without donations. Effects of trade liberalization on the current account and of effects on the budget of structural reform spending made possible inter alia by foreign financial aid in support of the programmes are included.

Source: World Bank (1994b).

Table A2 Summary of case studies in reviewed volumes

Country	Author(s)	In (volume)	Focus	Growth	Agric.	Manuf.	Social	Comment
Burundi	Engelbert & Hoffman	Husain & Faruquee (1994)	None	?	+/?	?	?	Response to adjustment disappointing because of (a) partial implementation; (b) over-ambitious reform programme (given structural and socio-political constraints).
Cameroon	Blandford et al.	Sahn (1994)	None	?	?	?	?	Extreme external shock suffered by the country has meant that adjustment has initially been expenditure reducing, and expenditure switching has been constrained by membership of the CFA Franc zone.
Cameroon	Ndongko	Adepoju (1993)	Social impact	..	..	..	..	Considered too early to judge programme impact, but severe constraints within which it operates (including Franc zone) are noted.
Côte d'Ivoire	Demery	Husain & Faruquee (1994)	None	x	x	x	x	Initial adjustment efforts in early 1980s had some pay-off but in latter part of decade required policy reform (notably real exchange rate depreciation) not achieved. Negative outcomes (declining real GDP and increasing poverty) are interpreted as showing the costs of inadequate adjustment.

Table A2 (cont.)

Country	Author(s)	In (volume)	Focus	Growth	Agric.	Manuf.	Social	Comment
Gambia	Jabara	Sahn (1994)	None	+	+	+	..	Growth has been restored, but the country will remain dependent on foreign aid to meet debt service obligations for the foreseeable future.
Ghana	Alderman	Sahn (1994)	None	+	+	..	~	The success of the programme to date is only a prologue for sustained growth and poverty alleviation, which will require further investment.
Ghana	Leechor	Husain & Faruquee (1994)	None	+	+	+/~	+	Despite adverse external factors, a far-reaching programme of reforms has been implemented with strong government commitment; however, more could be done to restore business confidence.
Ghana	Mistry	Van der Geest (1994)	Exchange rate	+	+	..	..	Ghana's experience of adjustment has been positive, but one must be cautious in drawing lessons for other countries.
Ghana	Sowa	Adepoju (1993)	Social impact	+	+	+/~	–	Growth has been restored, though this has been modest in agriculture, which is the backbone of the economy: moreover, many groups have suffered from unemployment and lower real wages.

Table A2 (cont.)

Country	Author(s)	In (volume)	Focus	Growth	Agric.	Manuf.	Social	Comment
Guinea	Arulpraga-sam & Sahn	Sahn (1994)	None	~	~	..	–	Agricultural recovery has been held back by non-price factors, illustrating that the reform programme is necessary for sustained recovery but not sufficient.
Kenya	Mwega & Kabubo	Adepoju (1993)	Social impact	..	..	..	–	Budget cuts and cost recovery measures in health and education have fallen most severely on the poor.
Kenya	Swamy	Husain & Faruquee (1994)	None	x/~	x/~	x/~	x/~	Commitment to reform has been intermittent; early success at stabilization later reversed; consequently little observable beneficial impact.
Madagas-car	Dorosh & Bernier	Sahn (1994)	None	+/~	~	..	+/~	Reforms have achieved stabilization but not yet substantial growth, to which impediments remain, notably poor infrastructure.
Malawi	Chipeta	Adepoju (1993)	Social impact	x/~	x/~	..	x/~	Reforms have had little impact on the economy, partly because not implemented as planned; but government expenditure has been squeezed, putting pressure on social services.

Table A2 (cont.)

Country	Author(s)	In (volume)	Focus	Growth	Agric.	Manuf.	Social	Comment
Malawi	Sahn & Arulpragasam	Sahn (1994)	None	~	~	+	..	Reform has not addressed the policy bias toward large estates in agriculture nor redressed the inadequate investment in human capital.
Mozambique	Kyle	Sahn (1994)	None	+	+	+	..	The agricultural supply response has been constrained by goods shortages resulting from poor infrastructure; poor urban residents have been protected by a targeted programme.
Niger	Dorosh	Sahn (1994)	None	x/~	x/~	..	x/~	The reforms to date have been modest and only affected the formal sector, which is only a small part of the economy.
Nigeria	Popoola	Adepoju (1993)	Health	..	..	..	–	Reform programme has adversely affected access to health services and □utriational status through rising prices and the squeeze on the health budget.
Nigeria	Fadayomi	Adepoju (1993)	Education	..	..	..	–	Cuts in education subsidies, resulting from economic crisis and market-oriented philosophy of adjustment, have led to declining quantity and quality of education services.

Table A2 (cont.)

Country	Author(s)	In (volume)	Focus	Growth	Agric.	Manuf.	Social	Comment
Nigeria	Faruquee	Husain & Faruquee (1994)	None	+	+	+	~	Adjustment programme initially implemented with high national commitment had a positive impact, though inadequate protection for social sectors; the reform effort faltered in the late 1980s.
Nigeria	Fashoyin	Adepoju (1993)	Employment	..	..	-	—	Adjustment has resulted in falling real wages and employment which has particularly affected formal sector workers.
Senegal	Kane	Adepoju (1993)	Social impact	..	-	..	—	Although adjustment has been necessary it has been carried out in such a way as to adversely affect agriculture and, hence, the well-being of the majority of the population.
Senegal	Rouis	Husain & Faruquee (1994)	None	x/~	~	+	~	The efforts have been fragile; results achieved are both fragile and modest, and unlikely to provide the basis for sustained growth; the supply response has mostly been from the informal sector.
Sierra Leone	Elliot	Adepoju (1993)	Social impact	x	x	x	x	Reform efforts have been weak, with consequent poor economic performance which has led to inadequate expenditure on health and education.

Table A2 (cont.)

Country	Author(s)	In (volume)	Focus	Growth	Agric.	Manuf.	Social	Comment
Tanzania	Holm	Simon *et al.* (1995)	Urban poverty	..	..	..	−	Adjustment has meant reduced expenditure on social services and planning capacity with adverse consequences for the quality of urban development.
Tanzania	Mans	Husain & Faruquee (1994)	None	+	+	+	+/~	Strong reform programme in place since 1986 with good results, including reduction of poverty; but more attention needs to be paid to the quality of social services and institutional reform.
Tanzania	Mbonile	Simon *et al.* (1995)	Rural development	..	+/−	..	−	Structural adjustment has resulted in return migration; impact of this both positive (educated and skilled returnees who start businesses) and negative (those returning to marginal occupations); education has suffered given a new preference for 'get rich quick' business activities.
Tanzania	Mung'ong'o & Loiske	Simon *et al.* (1995)	Rural development	..	..	..	~/−	Availability of goods and services has increased, but is beyond the purse of the poor, whose access to common property resources has also suffered under adjustment.

Table A2 (cont.)

Country	Author(s)	In (Volume)	Focus	Growth	Agric.	Manuf.	Social	Comment
Tanzania	Sarris & van der Brink	Sahn (1994)	None	+	+	−/−	..	Adjustment has allowed the second economy to come out into the open; given past government failures these private institutions are likely to be the basis for future growth.
Tanzania	Strekenburg & van der Wiel	Simon et al. (1995)	Sugar industry	..	+	+	..	Liberalization, combined with import support, have allowed increases in capacity utilization and profitability of sugar processing plants and increased output from outgrowers.
Tanzania	Van der Geest & Köttering	Van der Geest (1994)	None	..	+	..	..	Government's initial reluctance to reform appears to have been unwarranted in the light of subsequent performance; consumer goods availability has played an important part in agricultural recovery.
Uganda	Henstridge	Van der Geest (1994)	None	+	+	..	..	The success of the programme in reducing inflation was undermined by overestimation of government's institutional capacity.
Zaire	Tshishimbi et al.	Sahn (1994)	None	x	x	x	x	Except for a period in 1983–84, adjustment has not been implemented; this stance has been condoned by the leniency of the World Bank and IMF.

Table A2 (cont.)

Country	Author(s)	In (volume)	Focus	Growth	Agric.	Manuf.	Social	Comment
Zaire	Lututala *et al.*	Adepoju (1993)	Social impact	+	..	..	–	Whilst adjustment has had positive macroeconomic effects, living standards have worsened, in part from cuts in social service budgets.
Zambia	Jones	Van der Geest (1994)	None	~	~	..	..	The reform effort has been undermined by its cyclical nature. A problem compounded by inadequate donor support and problems in programme design.
Zambia	Mwana-wina	Adepoju (1993)	Social impact	..	..	..	–	Pressure on both the capital budget and social spending under adjustment have resulted in adverse consequences for employment and social indicators.
Zambia	Pearse	Van der Geest (1994)	Food security	..	..	..	–	Food security has declined as many poor households will not be able to take advantage of coupon scheme that has replaced more general (and admittedly inefficent) subsidy.
Zimbabwe	Tevera	Simon *et al.* (1995)	Urban poverty	~	..	..	–	Adjustment has failed to revive the economy and at the same time social services have been cut, with adverse consequences for the poor.

Key: + positive effect; ~ negligible effect; – negative effect; x policy not implemented; .. not discussed

Source: White (1996).

Table A3 Marginal returns to infrastructure and technology investments in rural India

Investment	Irrigated areas	High-potential rainfed areas	Low-potential rainfed areas
	(production return in rupees per unit of investment)		
High-yielding varieties[a]	63	243	688
Roads[b]	100598	6451	136173
Canal irrigation[a]	938	3310	1434
Private irrigation[a]	1	2213	4559
Electrification[a]	546	96	1274
Education[c]	360	571	102
	(number of people lifted out of poverty per unit of investment)		
High-yielding varieties[d]	0.00	0.02	0.05
Roads[e]	1.57	3.50	9.51
Canal irrigation[d]	0.01	0.23	0.09
Private irrigation[d]	0.01	0.15	0.30
Eletrification[d]	0.01	0.07	0.10
Education[f]	0.01	0.23	0.01

[a] Return is in rupees per hectare affected by investment;

[b] Return is in rupees per kilometre of road built;

[c] Return is in rupees per worker made literate;

[d] Return is in number of persons lifted out of poverty per hectare affected by investment;

[e]:Return is in number of persons lifted out of poverty per kilometre of road built;

[f] Return is in number of persons lifted out of poverty per worker made literate.

Source: Fan and Hazell (2000).

Table A4 Marginal returns to infrastructure and technology investments in rural China

Investment	High-potential Coastal Region	Mid-potential Central Region	Low-potential Western Region
	(production return in yuan per yuan invested)		
Reconstruction & Development	7.33	8.53	9.23
Irrigation	1.40	0.98	0.93
Roads	3.69	6.90	6.71
Education	6.06	8.45	6.20
Electricity	3.67	4.89	3.33
Rural telephone	4.14	8.05	6.57
	(number of people lifted out of poverty per 10,000 yuan invested)		
Reconstruction & Development	0.97	2.42	14.03
Irrigation	0.15	0.23	1.14
Roads	0.70	2.80	14.60
Education	1.79	5.35	21.09
Electricity	0.92	2.64	9.62
Rural telephone	0.98	4.11	17.99

Source: Fan and Hazell (2000).

Table A5 Fiscal and political decentralization in federal, semi- and non-federal states

	Fiscal decentralization				Electoral decentralization				
	Share of subnational government (%)				**Subnational elections**[a]		**No. of elected subnational tiers**	**No. of jurisdictions**	
	In total public expenditure		In total tax revenue		Inter-mediate[b]	Local[c]		Inter-mediate[b]	Local[c]
Federal	1990	1997	1990	1997	1999	1999	1999	1999	1999
Australia	50.9	47.9	20.0	22.7	Yes	Yes	2	8	900
Brazil	35.3	36.5	30.9	31.3	Yes	Yes	2	28	5581
Germany	40.2	37.8	28.9	28.8	Yes	Yes	3	16	16121
India	51.1	53.3	33.8	36.1	Yes	Yes	2	32	237687[d]
Indonesia	13.1	14.8	2.9	2.9	No	No	0	–	–
Mexico	17.8	26.1	19.0	20.6	Yes	Yes	2	32	2418
United States	42.0	46.4	33.8	32.9	Yes	Yes	3	51	70500
Semi- and Non-Federal									
Botswana	7.9	3.8	0.1	0.6	No	Yes	1	–	17
Ethiopia	1.5	–	1.6	–	Yes	Yes	2	11	910
Ghana	–	–	–	–	No	Yes	1	–	110
Kenya	4.4	3.5	2.2	1.9	No	Yes	1	–	168
Nigeria	–	–	–	–	Yes	Yes	2	31	589
Philippines	6.5	–	4.0	–	Yes	Yes	2	76	1541
South Africa	20.7	49.8	5.5	5.3	Yes	Yes	2	9	840
Uganda	–	–	–	–	Yes	Yes	2	58	1040
Zimbabwe	13.5	–	3.4	–	No	Yes	1	–	80

[a] 'No' indicates that, although the legislature is elected, a nominated executive head (for example, a mayor or governor) holds significant powers.

[b] State, province, region, department, or other elected entity between the local and the national government.

[c] Municipality or equivalent.

[d] Local government consists of 3,609 urban local bodies and, in rural areas 474 *zila parishads*, which wield some authority over the 5,906 *panchayats samithis*, which in turn have some authority over the 227,698 *gram panchayats*. It is therefore not strictly correct to aggregate these into one level of local authority.

Source: World Bank (1999), p. 216 ff.

Table A6 Percentage distribution of actual council revenues by source, Uganda 1993–94

Council	Graduated tax	Market fees	Taxi, bus, parks licences	Trade, other licences and fees	Property tax	Housing rent	Other[a]
Municipalities							
Kampala	40.2	11.3	6.9	11.9	16.4	7.2	6.1
Junja	14.0	13.1	7.8	4.7	28.0	11.4	21.0
Mbale[b]	21.5	52.3		5.5	20.0	–	0.7
Fort Portal[b]	27.1	34.8	–	18.4	15.5	–	4.3
Gulu	19.0	36.5	6.4	3.6	2.1	18.8	13.6
Bushenyi	40.7	13.3	20.4	5.3	–	2.7	17.7
Mukono	36.0	18.0	14.9	11.2	8.1	–	11.8
Tororo	22.1	40.7	14.7	8.8	13.2	–	0.5
Njeru	32.1	8.8	–	5.0	5.0	15.7	33.3
Kitgum	18.3	29.0	–	4.3	–	14.0	34.4
Districts							
Mbale	61.7	13.4	–	14.6	–	0.1	10.3[c]
Kabarole	57.6	13.6	–	8.4	–	0.2	20.2[c,d]
Gulu	73.6	22.4	–	3.0	–	0.3	0.7
Bushenyi	73.5	–	–	13.0	–	0.3	13.3
Luwero	71.0	26.2	–	2.6	–	–	0.2
Mukono	73.1	–	–	–	–	–	4.2
Mubende	66.2	8.5	–	–	–	0.3	25.0
Tororo	88.9	4.9	–	–	–	–	6.3
Iganga	74.4	6.4	–	–	–	–	19.2
Masaka	84.9	11.3	–	–	–	0.1	3.7
Average	49.7	20.2	–	8.0	–	–	–

[a]   Excludes transfers from central government;
[b]   Percentages based on estimates, not actual values;
[c]   Includes education tax;
[d]   Includes *kibanja* fees.

Source: Livingstone and Charlton (2001), p. 86.

Table A7 Distribution of tax revenue among different levels of government

	Year	Total general government revenue[1]			
		As a percentage of GDP	As a percentage of the total		
			Central government	State government	Local government
Industrial countries **Federal systems**					
Australia	1995	28.9	76.7	19.9	3.5
Canada	1993	38.7	53.5	36.5	10.0
Germany	1995	41.1	73.0	21.0	6.0
Spain	1993	33.2	86.6	4.6	8.8
United States	1994	27.0	65.7	20.6	13.7
Unitary systems					
Belgium	1994	45.7	94.8	n.a.	5.2
France	1995	42.4	89.8	n.a.	10.2
Netherlands	1995	44.7	96.3	n.a.	3.7
Norway	1994	40.3	78.6	n.a.	21.4
United Kingdom	1995	34.8	96.4	n.a.	3.6
Developing and transition countries **Federal systems**					
India	1993	14.9	61.8	38.2	u
Argentina	1992	19.8	57.2	42.8	u
Brazil	1993	25.7	71.4	26.0	2.6
Mexico	1993	16.3	84.6	15.4	u
Russian Federation	1995	29.0	60.0	u	40.0

Table A7 (cont.)

	Year	Total general government revenue[1]			
		As a per-centage of GDP	As a percentage of the total		
			Central government	State government	Local government
Unitary systems					
Kenya	1994	21.1	97.8	n.a.	2.2
Poland	1995	40.0	92.1	n.a.	7.9
South Africa	1994	27.6	91.4	3.1	5.5
Thailand	1995	18.2	94.9	n.a.	5.1

[1] General government is defined to include the central government; social security system; and state, provincial, and local governments.

Note: n.a. means not applicable; u means data unavailable

Sources: IMF (1996): *Government Finance Statistics Yearbook*;
IMF (1997): International Financial Statistics (June).

Table A8 Distribution of central government expenditure to sub-national governments varies widely

	Year	Total general government expenditure[1]			
		As a percentage of GDP	As a percentage of the total		
			Central government	State government	Local government
Industrial countries **Federal systems**					
Australia	1995	46.5	59.0	36.0	5.0
Canada	1993	60.1	41.7	41.2	17.1
Germany	1995	57.2	59.2	24.1	16.7
Spain	1993	55.9	70.4	18.2	11.3
United States	1994	41.3	53.4	25.6	21.0
Unitary systems					
Belgium	1994	56.5	88.5	n.a.	11.5
France	1995	56.5	82.3	n.a.	17.7
Netherlands	1995	66.5	76.4	n.a.	23.6
Norway	1994	60.2	68.4	n.a.	31.6
United Kingdom	1995	54.1	77.3	n.a.	22.7
Developing and transition countries **Federal systems**					
India	1993	30.8	54.7	45.3	u
Argentina	1992	21.8	55.1	44.9	u
Brazil	1993	56.6	65.7	24.8	9.5
Mexico	1993	19.1	78.3	21.7	u
Russian Federation	1995	38.5	62.4	u	37.6

Table A8 (cont.)

	Year	Total general government expenditure[1]			
		As a percentage of GDP	As a percentage of the total		
			Central government	State government	Local government
Unitary systems					
Kenya	1994	30.0	96.1	n.a.	3.9
Poland	1995	51.8	83.8	n.a.	16.2
South Africa	1994	50.1	66.3	25.4	8.3
Thailand	1995	17.3	92.6	n.a.	7.4

[1] General government is defined to include the central government; social security system; and state, provincial, and local governments.

Note: n.a. means not applicable; u means data unavailable.

Sources: IMF (1996): *Government Finance Statistics Yearbook*;
         IMF (1997): International Financial Statistics (June).

Table A9 Central and local contributions to projected district revenues in Uganda (%), 1995–96

	Local revenue	Central govt. transfers	Block grants[a]	Donor funds
Arua	19	80	14	1
Gulu	15	73	13	12
Mbale	36	64	10	–
Junja	22	74	6	3
Mukono	27	49	10	24
Mpigi	40	57	9	3
Masaka	39	60	13	2
Mbarara	34	60	11	6
Kabarole	30	53	12	17
Kabale	23	67	11	10
Rakai	29	51	13	20
Bushenyi	37	60	13	3
Iganga	29	63	15	8
Kampala	50	13	2	37[b]
Kasese	35	65	14	–
Kisoro	23	77	35	–
Luwero	37	52	12	11
Moyo	17	77	18	6
Mubende	43	53	12	4
Rukungiri	31	69	14	–
Average	31	69	13	10

[a]   As part of Central Government Transfers;
[b]   Includes loans to municipality.

Source: Livingstone and Charlton (2001), p. 83.

Index

Note: Page numbers in *Italics* represent Tables and page numbers in **Bold** represent Figures.

DATE DUE
